# SOMETHING ABOUT THE AUTHOR®

Something about
the Author *was named
an* **"Outstanding
Reference Source,"**
*the highest honor given
by the American
Library Association
Reference and Adult
Services Division.*

ISSN 0276-816X

# SOMETHING ABOUT THE AUTHOR®

Facts and Pictures about Authors
and Illustrators of Books for Young People

# volume 228

GALE
CENGAGE Learning

Detroit • New York • San Francisco • New Haven, Conn • Waterville, Maine • London

## GALE
CENGAGE Learning·

**Something about the Author, Volume 228**

Project Editor: Lisa Kumar

Permissions: Leitha Etheridge-Sims

Imaging and Multimedia: Leitha Etheridge-Sims, John Watkins

Composition and Electronic Capture: Amy Darga

Manufacturing: Rhonda Dover

Product Manager: Mary Onorato

For product information and technology assistance, contact us at
**Gale Customer Support, 1-800-877-4253.**
For permission to use material from this text or product,
submit all requests online at **www.cengage.com/permissions.**
Further permissions questions can be emailed to
**permissionrequest@cengage.com**

*Gale, Cengage Learning*
27500 Drake Rd.
Farmington Hills, MI, 48331-3535

LIBRARY OF CONGRESS CATALOG CARD NUMBER 62-52046

ISBN-13: 978-1-4144-6131-1
ISBN-10: 1-4144-6131-3

ISSN 0276-816X

This title is also available as an e-book.
ISBN-13: 978-1-4144-6460-2
ISBN-10: 1-4144-6460-6
Contact your Gale, Cengage Learning sales representative for ordering information.

Printed in Mexico
1 2 3 4 5 6 7 15 14 13 12 11

# Contents

# Authors in Forthcoming Volumes

Below are some of the authors and illustrators that will be featured in upcoming volumes of *SATA*. These include new entries on the swiftly rising stars of the field, as well as completely revised and updated entries (indicated with *) on some of the most notable and best-loved creators of books for children.

**Dennis Brian** ▌ An F/A-18 fighter pilot with the United States Marines, Brian was working as a member of Special Forces when he was assigned to a tour of duty in war-torn Iraq. Apart from the danger of the assignment, he also discovered a special friend in a desert dog he named Nubs. The heartwarming story of Brian and Nubs attracted media attention and also earned the affection of children through Brian's picture-book chronicle in *Nubs: A Mutt, a Marine, and a Miracle.*

**\*Margery Cuyler** ▌ Cuyler was already an experienced editor of children's books for New York City-based publisher Holiday House when she decided to try her hand at writing. In addition to authoring a wide range of both nonfiction and fiction picture books, including *Fat Santa, Skeleton Hiccups, Guinea Pigs Add Up,* and *I Repeat, Don't Cheat!,* Cuyler has also written chapter books for more talented readers.

**L. Divine** ▌ Raised in California and now living in Georgia, Divine sets her stories in Los Angeles, where she once taught high-school English. Her experiences as an African American, a mother, and an educator with a front-row seat to contemporary teen culture inspired her to begin her "Drama High" novels, which feature a bright and likeable young woman who, with common sense and the wise counsel of her grandmother, models self-respect as she embraces challenges, gravitates toward healthy relationships, and exhibits a super fashion sense.

**\*Sally Gardner** ▌ A British writer and illustrator, Gardner has a whimsical imagination that enriches her self-illustrated picture books, which include *The Little Nut Tree* and *Mama, Don't Go out Tonight,* as well as chapter books like *The Countess's Calamity* and the multi-volume "Magical Children" series. Written for older readers, her young-adult novels include *The Red Necklace: A Story of the French Revolution, The Silver Blade,* and *I, Coriander,* the last of which earned its author critical acclaim and the coveted 2006 Nestlé Children's Book Prize.

**\*Kathleen Krull** ▌ The recipient of the 2011 Children's Book Guild Nonfiction Award for her body of work, Krull has made a career of educating and entertaining children and young adults. Her critically acclaimed books include *Lives of the Musicians: Good Times, Bad Times (and What the Neighbors Thought), Harvesting Hope: The Story of Cesar Chavez,* and *The Boy Who Invented TV: The Story of Philo Farnsworth,* and she has also teamed up with her husband, Paul Brewer, to create *Fartiste* and *Lincoln Tells a Joke: How Laughter Saved the President (and the Country).* Prior to beginning her writing career, Krull edited books for publishers and had the chance to work with writers such as Tomie dePaola, Eve Bunting, Jane Yolen, Arnold Adoff, and Judy Delton.

**\*Patricia MacLachlan** ▌ Children's author MacLachlan has received the Golden Kite Award from the Society of Children's Book Writers and Illustrators, a National Humanities medal, a Christopher medal, and the prestigious Newbery Medal. Her best-known novel, *Sarah, Plain and Tall,* was adapted for television's Hallmark Hall of Fame and also sparked an engaging series of historical fiction. Other titles by MacLachlan include *For the Very First Time, Cassie Binegar, The True Gift,* and *Waiting for the Magic;* as well as *Painting the Wind* and *Bittle,* two of several titles she has co-authored with her daughter, Emily MacLachlan.

**Holly Robinson Peete** ▌ An actress and vocalist working in both television and radio, as well as the wife of a football star and the co-author of the humorous *Get Your Own Damn Beer, I'm Watching the Game!: A Woman's Guide to Loving Pro Football,* Peete also has a busy life outside the celebrity limelight: she is the mother of four children as well as a dedicated philanthropist who advocates on behalf of several charities. In 2010 she teamed up with her oldest daughter, Ryan Elizabeth Peete, to express Ryan's affection for her twin brother Rodney Peete, Junior, in the picture book *My Brother Charlie: A Sister's Story of Autism.*

**\*Adam Selzer** ▌ Selzer is a Chicago-based writer, historian, and musician. He is also the author of off-beat books for middle graders that include *How to Get Suspended and Influence People, Pirates of the Retail Wasteland,* and *I Kissed a Zombie and I Liked It.* In addition to fiction, Selzer deals with real life (and death) in his book *Your Neighborhood Gives Me the Creeps: True Tales of an Accidental Ghost Hunter,* which was inspired by his interest in ferreting out odd aspects of Chicago history. Another nonfiction work, *The Smart Aleck's Guide to American History* provides fellow history buffs with a humorous and enlightened antidote to politically correct textbooks.

**\*Gloria Velásquez** ▌ Born to migrant farm workers, Chicana/Latina poet and novelist Velásquez grew up in poverty, and her writing reflects her deep yearning to change an environment that allows such widespread disparity. It also reflects her strong feminist viewpoint and her unique perspective as a Chicana (female Mexican American) in modern America. Although much of her work is geared for adults, Velásquez shifts her focus to teen readers in her "Roosevelt High School" series. Beginning with *Juanita Fights the School Board,* these novels incorporate the themes and topics about which their author is passionate, and their emphasis on teen Chicano/Latino culture has been cited as something rare in the young-adult genre.

**Rachel Ward** ▌ Ward began writing as a hobby, beginning with short stories and moving to longer fiction as her fiction gained complexity. Her first novel, *Numbers,* was released in 2009 and attracted the attention of awards committees and readers alike. The first novel in a trilogy, *Numbers* has been followed by *The Chaos* and *Infinity.*

# Introduction

*Something about the Author* (*SATA*) is an ongoing reference series that examines the lives and works of authors and illustrators of books for children. *SATA* includes not only well-known writers and artists but also less prominent individuals whose works are just coming to be recognized. This series is often the only readily available information source on emerging authors and illustrators. You'll find *SATA* informative and entertaining, whether you are a student, a librarian, an English teacher, a parent, or simply an adult who enjoys children's literature.

## What's Inside *SATA*

*SATA* provides detailed information about authors and illustrators who span the full time range of children's literature, from early figures like John Newbery and L. Frank Baum to contemporary figures like Judy Blume and Richard Peck. Authors in the series represent primarily English-speaking countries, particularly the United States, Canada, and the United Kingdom. Also included, however, are authors from around the world whose works are available in English translation. The writings represented in *SATA* include those created intentionally for children and young adults as well as those written for a general audience and known to interest younger readers. These writings cover the entire spectrum of children's literature, including picture books, humor, folk and fairy tales, animal stories, mystery and adventure, science fiction and fantasy, historical fiction, poetry and nonsense verse, drama, biography, and nonfiction. Obituaries are also included in many volumes of *SATA* and are intended not only as death notices but also as concise overviews of people's lives and work. Additionally, each edition features newly revised and updated entries for a selection of *SATA* listees who remain of interest to today's readers and who have been active enough to require extensive revisions of their earlier biographies.

## Autobiography Feature

Beginning with Volume 103, many volumes of *SATA* feature one or more specially commissioned autobiographical essays. These unique essays, averaging about ten thousand words in length and illustrated with an abundance of personal photos, present an entertaining and informative first-person perspective on the lives and careers of prominent authors and illustrators profiled in *SATA*.

## Two Convenient Indexes

In response to suggestions from librarians, *SATA* indexes no longer appear in every volume but are included in alternate (odd-numbered) volumes of the series, beginning with Volume 57.

*SATA* continues to include two indexes that cumulate with each alternate volume: the Illustrations Index, arranged by the name of the illustrator, gives the number of the volume and page where the illustrator's work appears in the current volume as well as all preceding volumes in the series; the Author Index gives the number of the volume in which a person's biographical sketch, autobiographical essay, or obituary appears in the current volume as well as all preceding volumes in the series.

These indexes also include references to authors and illustrators who appear in *Gale's Yesterday's Authors of Books for Children, Children's Literature Review,* and *Something about the Author Autobiography Series.*

## Easy-to-Use Entry Format

Whether you're already familiar with the *SATA* series or just getting acquainted, you will want to be aware of the kind of information that an entry provides. In every *SATA* entry the editors attempt to give as complete a picture of the person's life and work as possible. A typical entry in *SATA* includes the following clearly labeled information sections:

*PERSONAL:* date and place of birth and death, parents' names and occupations, name of spouse, date of marriage, names of children, educational institutions attended, degrees received, religious and political affiliations, hobbies and other interests.

*ADDRESSES:* complete home, office, electronic mail, and agent addresses, whenever available.

*CAREER:* name of employer, position, and dates for each career post; art exhibitions; military service; memberships and offices held in professional and civic organizations.

*MEMBER:* professional, civic, and other association memberships and any official posts held.

*AWARDS, HONORS:* literary and professional awards received.

***WRITINGS:*** title-by-title chronological bibliography of books written and/or illustrated, listed by genre when known; lists of other notable publications, such as plays, screenplays, and periodical contributions.

***ADAPTATIONS:*** a list of films, television programs, plays, CD-ROMs, recordings, and other media presentations that have been adapted from the author's work.

***WORK IN PROGRESS:*** description of projects in progress.

***SIDELIGHTS:*** a biographical portrait of the author or illustrator's development, either directly from the biographee—and often written specifically for the *SATA* entry—or gathered from diaries, letters, interviews, or other published sources.

***BIOGRAPHICAL AND CRITICAL SOURCES:*** cites sources quoted in "Sidelights" along with references for further reading.

***EXTENSIVE ILLUSTRATIONS:*** photographs, movie stills, book illustrations, and other interesting visual materials supplement the text.

## How a *SATA* Entry Is Compiled

*SATA* editors examine a wide variety of published sources to gather information for an entry. Biographical and bibliographic sources are consulted, as are book reviews, feature articles, published interviews, and material sometimes obtained from the biographee's family, publishers, agent, or other associates. Whenever possible, the author or illustrator is sent a copy of the entry to check for accuracy and completeness.

Entries that have not been verified by the biographees or their representatives are marked with an asterisk (*).

## Contact the Editor

We encourage our readers to examine the entire *SATA* series. Please write and tell us if we can make *SATA* even more helpful to you. Give your comments and suggestions to the editor:

Editor
Something about the Author
Gale, Cengage Learning
27500 Drake Rd.
Farmington Hills MI 48331-3535

Toll-free: 800-877-GALE
Fax: 248-699-8070

# *Something about the Author* Product Advisory Board

The editors of *Something about the Author* are dedicated to maintaining a high standard of excellence by publishing comprehensive, accurate, and highly readable entries on a wide array of writers for children and young adults. In addition to the quality of the content, the editors take pride in the graphic design of the series, which is intended to be orderly yet inviting, allowing readers to utilize the pages of *SATA* easily and with efficiency. Despite the longevity of the *SATA* print series, and the success of its format, we are mindful that the vitality of a literary reference product is dependent on its ability to serve its users over time. As literature, and attitudes about literature, constantly evolve, so do the reference needs of students, teachers, scholars, journalists, researchers, and book club members. To be certain that we continue to keep pace with the expectations of our customers, the editors of *SATA* listen carefully to their comments regarding the value, utility, and quality of the series. Librarians, who have firsthand knowledge of the needs of library users, are a valuable resource for us. The *Something about the Author* Product Advisory Board, made up of school, public, and academic librarians, is a forum to promote focused feedback about *SATA* on a regular basis. The nine-member advisory board includes the following individuals, whom the editors wish to thank for sharing their expertise:

**Eva M. Davis**
*Director,*
*Canton Public Library,*
*Canton, Michigan*

**Joan B. Eisenberg**
*Lower School Librarian,*
*Milton Academy,*
*Milton, Massachusetts*

**Francisca Goldsmith**
*Teen Services Librarian,*
*Berkeley Public Library,*
*Berkeley, California*

**Susan Dove Lempke**
*Children's Services Supervisor,*
*Niles Public Library District,*
*Niles, Illinois*

**Robyn Lupa**
*Head of Children's Services,*
*Jefferson County Public Library,*
*Lakewood, Colorado*

**Victor L. Schill**
*Assistant Branch Librarian/Children's Librarian,*
*Harris County Public Library/Fairbanks Branch,*
*Houston, Texas*

**Caryn Sipos**
*Community Librarian,*
*Three Creeks Community Library,*
*Vancouver, Washington*

**Steven Weiner**
*Director,*
*Maynard Public Library,*
*Maynard, Massachusetts*

# SOMETHING ABOUT THE AUTHOR

## ALEXANDER, Claire

### Personal

Born in England. *Education:* Kent Institute of Art and Design, B.A. (painting; with honours), 1995.

### Addresses

*Home*—London, England. *E-mail*—claire@clairealex ander.com.

### Career

Portrait painter and author/illustrator of children's books. Teacher of art and picture-book creation; presenter at schools and festivals. *Exhibitions:* Work included in private collections in the United Kingdom, United States, Australia, Italy, and Germany.

### Member

Association of Illustrators.

### Awards, Honors

Patterson Prize for Books for Young People, 2009, for *Lucy and the Bully;* Mad about Books Stockport Schools Book Award shortlist, 2010, for *Small Florence, a Piggy Pop Star!*

### Writings

*SELF-ILLUSTRATED*

*Lucy and the Bully,* Albert Whitman (Morton Grove, IL), 2008.
*Small Florence, a Piggy Pop Star!,* Gullane Children's Books (London, England), 2009, Albert Whitman (Chicago, IL), 2010.
*Lost in the Snow,* Gullane Children's Books (London, England), 2010.

### Sidelights

A respected portrait artist in her native England, Claire Alexander branched out into book illustration in the late 2000s with her original, self-illustrated *Lucy and the Bully.* With the success of her first book, and excited by the many possibilities that exist within the picture-book medium, Alexander has continued to pursue both creative areas, as well as teaching and appearing at book festivals and schools in and around her home in London. Other self-illustrated stories she has created include the whimsically titled *Small Florence, a Piggy Pop Star!* and *Lost in the Snow,* the latter which follows the adventures of two kits (young foxes) as they stray from their cozy den on a winter day.

Focusing on a timely subject, *Lucy and the Bully* uses animal characters to explore a complex school-time relationship. Lucy is a little lamb who is excited about going to nursery school and doing art. When fellow student Tommy (a young bull) makes things difficult by destroying her artwork, the lamb decides to confide in her mother. With the help of both youngsters' parents—and Lucy's ability to forgive—the two children eventually become friends. The lamb's "willingness to go the extra mile . . . might inspire readers to do the same," noted Ilene Cooper in her *Booklist* review of *Lucy and the Bully,* the critic also praising the emotional depth of Alexander's "child-friendly" water-color art. In *School Library Journal* Kathleen Kelly MacMillan dubbed the story "appealing" and noted that it depicts bullying from a child's point of view, "showing a positive world in which the adults are in control." A *Kirkus Reviews* writer also enjoyed Alexander's debut picture book, citing as a high point illustrations that "are both bright and textured and have a lovely transparent quality."

A little pig with big dreams is the focus of *Small Florence, a Piggy Pop Star!* Little Florence has always wanted to be a musical star, but when she gets the chance to sing at a local contest her two older sisters decide to hog the stage. Fortunately the two piggy singers are so frightened on stage that they barely utter an oink, leaving Florence to perform their parts to perfection from her seat in the audience. For a *Kirkus Reviews* writer, Alexander's illustrations are the stand out in *Small Florence, a Piggy Pop Star!:* "The artwork is sumptuous, like great dollops of ice cream," with shades of blue, pink and yellow "commingling with an eye for harmony," the reviewer wrote. A *Publishers Weekly* critic was impressed by the humor in Alexander's work, predicting that the book's "many laughs will find Florence lots of fans," while in *Booklist* Cooper dubbed

*Claire Alexander shares her whimsical, high-fashion humor in her self-illustrated picture book* Small Florence, a Piggy Pop Star! (Albert Whitman & Company, 2010. Illustration copyright © 2009 by Claire Alexander. Reproduced with permission.)

*Small Florence, a Piggy Pop Star!* a "charming little tale" that is brought to life with "verve and humor." In her *Bulletin of the Center for Children's Books* appraisal, Jeannette Hulick wrote that Alexander's "satisfyingly simple and succinct" text pairs well with "vibrant" illustrations that use "clever perspectives to capture the emotions . . . of a small child."

## Biographical and Critical Sources

*PERIODICALS*

*Booklist,* October 15, 2008, Ilene Cooper, review of *Lucy and the Bully,* p. 40; April 15, 2010, Ilene Cooper, review of *Small Florence, a Piggy Pop Star!,* p. 53.
*Bulletin of the Center for Children's Books,* April, 2010, Jeannette Hulick, review of *Small Florence, a Piggy Pop Star!,* p. 322.
*Kirkus Reviews,* September 1, 2008, review of *Lucy and the Bully;* February 15, 2010, review of *Small Florence, a Piggy Pop Star!*
*Publishers Weekly,* January 18, 2010, review of *Small Florence, a Piggy Pop Star!,* p. 47.
*School Library Journal,* November, 2008, Kathleen Kelly MacMillan, review of *Lucy and the Bully,* p. 84; February, 2010, Kris Hickey, review of *Small Florence, a Piggy Pop Star!,* p. 73.

*ONLINE*

*Claire Alexander Home Page,* http://www.clairealexander.com (February 16, 2011).

\*     \*     \*

# ANINNO, J.G.
## See ANNINO, Jan Godown

\*     \*     \*

# ANNINO, Jan Godown 1952-
## (J.G. Aninno, Jan Godown)

## Personal

Born 1952, in NJ; daughter of a farmer-turned state vehicle inspector and a newspaper editor; married; husband a public interest lawyer; children: one daughter. *Education:* University of Florida, B.S. (journalism); graduate study at Hollins Collins (now Hollins University). *Hobbies and other interests:* Walking, hiking.

## Addresses

*Home and office*—P.O. Box 14143, Tallahassee, FL 32317-4143. *E-mail*—jgaoffice@gmail.com.

*Jan Godown Annino* (Photograph by Priyanka Lamichhane. Reproduced by permission.)

## Career

Writer and journalist. Features writer for Gannett and Knight-Ridder newspapers in FL. Has also taught memoir writing with an adult outreach program.

## Member

Authors Guild, Society of Children's Book Writers and Illustrators.

## Awards, Honors

Elmer Emig Award, University of Florida; Florida Humanities Council grant; Atlantic Center for the Arts residency; Notable Social Studies Trade Book for Young People selection, National Council for the Social Studies/Children's Book Council, and Gold Medal for Children's Literature, Florida Book Awards, 2010, and Amelia Bloomer Project listee, American Library Association, 2011, all for *She Sang Promise.*

## Writings

(As Jan Godown) *Scenic Driving Florida,* Falcon Press (Helena, MT), 1998, third edition, published under name Jan Godown Annino, Globe Pequot Press (Guildford, CT), 2010.
(As Jan Godown; with Anna Annino) *Family Fun in Florida,* Falcon Press (Helena, MT), 2000.
(As J.G. Annino) *Florida's Famous Animals: True Stories of Sunset Sam the Dolphin, Snooty the Manatee, Big Guy the Panther, and Others,* Globe Pequot Press (Guildford, CT), 2008.
*She Sang Promise: The Story of Betty Mae Jumper, Seminole Tribal Leader,* illustrated by Lisa Desimini, afterword by Moses Jumper, Jr., National Geographic (Washington, DC), 2010.

Also coauthor and producer of one-act play. Contributor to books, including *The Book of the Everglades,* Milkweed Editions (Minneapolis, MN), 2002, *The South Atlantic Coast and Piedmont: A Literary Field Guide,* Milkweed Editions, 2006, and *The Florida Handbook.* Contributor to periodicals, including *Atlanta Constitution, Orlando Sentinel, Storytelling,* and *Publishers Weekly.*

## Sidelights

Jan Godown Annino, a freelance writer based in Florida, presents the little-known tale of a remarkable woman in her picture-book biography *She Sang Promise: The Story of Betty Mae Jumper, Seminole Tribal Leader,* which received a Florida Book Award for children's literature. Jumper, the daughter of a white trapper and a Seminole medicine woman, was the first in her tribe to graduate from high school. Later in life she served as a health-care worker and journalist and became the first female elected to head the Seminole Tribal Council. As Annino told *School Library Journal* blogger Amy Bowllan, Jumper "is an exemplar because she never gave up on her dreams of a good education and improvements for the people she loves—the unconquered Seminole Tribe of Florida."

Annino first became acquainted with Jumper in 1967, after reading an account of the woman's election to the Seminole Tribal Council in a local newspaper. Years later, she spotted Jumper while attending a Native American festival. "She sat by herself on a folding chair behind a pile of patchwork clothing for sale," Annino recalled on her Web log. "People passed by without giving a glance. They knew nothing of the exciting stories of her days growing up outdoors, or her historic election in 1967." The two women struck up a friendship, and Jumper eventually authorized Annino to write her biography.

Beginning with Jumper's birth in the Florida Everglades in 1923, *She Sang Promise* focuses on the woman's commitment to education, her training as a nurse, and her desire to serve the Seminoles. Annino also includes information regarding some of the more unusual facets of her subject's life, such as Jumper's days as an alligator wrestler. According to *Booklist* critic Hazel Rochman, *She Sang Promise* offers "a dramatic present-tense narrative that blends details of [Jumper's] life with the historical struggle of her people." Maggie Chase, writing in *School Library Journal,* noted that, with its engaging illustrations by Lisa Desimini, Annino's picture book joins "the growing number of biographies of women whose strong leadership has made a difference in the lives of many people."

## Biographical and Critical Sources

*PERIODICALS*

*Booklist,* April 1, 2010, Hazel Rochman, review of *She Sang Promise: The Story of Betty Mae Jumper, Seminole Tribal Leader,* p. 37.

*Kirkus Reviews,* February 15, 2010, review of *She Sang Promise.*
*Library Media Connection,* March-April, 2010, Barbara S. Zinkovich, review of *She Sang Promise,* p. 60.
*School Library Journal,* April, 2010, Maggie Chase, review of *She Sang Promise,* p. 143.
*Yellow Brick Road* (Cortland, NY), March-April, 2011, Joy Mosher, interview with Annino.

*ONLINE*

*Amy Bowllan's Web log,* http://blog.schoollibraryjournal.com/bowllansblog/ (May 25, 2010), Amy Bowllan, "Writers against Racism: Jan Godown Annino."
*Fuse 8 Production Web log,* http://blog.schoollibraryjournal.com/afuse8production/ (November 8, 2010), Elizabeth Bird, review of *She Sang Promise.*
*Jan Godown Annino Web log,* http://bookseedstudio.wordpress.com (April 1, 2011).
*Sarasota Herald-Tribune Online,* http://www.ticketsarasota.com/ (March 11, 2011), Susan Rife, "Picture Book about Seminole Leader Betty Mae Jumper Wins Florida Book Award."
*Tallahassee Magazine Online,* http://tallahasseemagazine.com/ (March-April, 2010), Jennifer Ewing, "Seminole History Shines in Local Author's Picture Book."

\* \* \*

# ARNOLD, Caroline 1944-

## Personal

Born May 16, 1944, in Pittsburgh, PA; daughter of Lester L. (a social worker) and Catherine Young (a social worker) Scheaffer; married Arthur Arnold (a neuroscientist), June 24, 1967; children: Jennifer Elizabeth, Matthew William. *Education:* Grinnell College, B.A., 1966; University of Iowa, M.A., 1968. *Hobbies and other interests:* Playing tennis, gardening, traveling, watching movies, spending time with friends and family.

## Addresses

*Home and office*—Los Angeles, CA. *E-mail*—caroline@carolinearnoldbooks.com.

## Career

Freelance writer and artist. Art teacher and substitute teacher in Yellow Springs and Xenia, OH, 1968-69; New York Hospital, New York, NY, secretary, 1969-70; Rockefeller University, New York, NY, laboratory assistant, 1971-72, 1972-76; University of California—Los Angeles, laboratory assistant, 1976-79; University of California—Los Angeles Extension, instructor in writers' program, 1982—.

## Member

Society of Children's Book Writers and Illustrators, PEN, Southern California Council on Literature for Children and Young People, Children's Literature Council of Southern California.

*Caroline Arnold* (Photograph by Arthur P. Arnold. Reproduced by permission.)

## Awards, Honors

Outstanding Science Trade Book citations, National Science Teachers Association/Children's Book Council (CBC), 1980, for *Five Nests* and *Electric Fish,* 1982, for *Animals That Migrate,* 1983, for *The Biggest Living Thing* and *Pets without Homes,* 1985, for *Saving the Peregrine Falcon,* 1987, for *Genetics, Trapped in Tar, Koala, Kangaroo, Giraffe,* and *Zebra,* 1988, for *Llama, Penguin,* and *A Walk of the Great Barrier Reef,* 1989, for *Tule Elk, Hippo,* and *Cheetah,* 1991, for *Flamingo* and *Snake,* 1992, for *House Sparrows Everywhere,* 1995, for *Rhino* and *Lion,* 1997, for *Bat* and *Fox,* 1998, for *Hawk Highway in the Sky,* 2004, for *Uluru,* 2005, for *Pterosaurs, Rulers of the Sky in the Dinosaur Age,* 2008, for *Giant Sea Reptiles of the Dinosaur Age,* 2009, for *A Platypus' World,* 2010, for *Global Warming and the Dinosaurs;* Children's Science Book Award honorable mention, 1983, for *Animals That Migrate;* Golden Kite Honor Book designation, Society of Children's Book Writers, 1984, for *Pets without Homes;* nonfiction award, Southern California Council on Literature for Children and Young People, 1985, for *Too Fat? Too Thin?; Booklist* Children's Editors' Choice selection, 1985, *School Library Journal* Best Book designation, and American Library Association Notable Book designation, all 1985, and special achievement award, PEN Los Angeles Center, 1986, all for *Saving the Peregrine Falcon;* Best Children's Books and Films selection, American Association for the Advancement of Science, 1987, for *Trapped in Tar* and *Koala,* 1988, for *A Walk on the Great Barrier Reef,* 1990, for *Orangutan* and *Wild Goat,* 1999, for *Bobcats;* John Burroughs Nature

Award, 1988, for *A Walk on the Great Barrier Reef;* Orbis Pictus Award for Outstanding Nonfiction, National Council of Teachers of English, 1989, for *Cheetah* and *Hippo; School Library Journal* Best Books designation, 1992, for *The Ancient Cliff Dwellers of Mesa Verde,* 2001, for *Easter Island;* Best Children's Books of the Year designation, Bank Street College of Education, 1999, for *Bobcats,* 2004, for *Birds,* 2008, for *Wiggle and Waggle;* Notable Children's Book in the Field of Social Studies designation, National Council for the Social Studies/CBC, 1999, for *Children of the Settlement Houses,* 2001, for *Easter Island,* 2004, for *Uluru,* 2008, for *Taj Mahal;* CCBC Choices selection, Cooperative Children's Book Center, 2004, for *Birds,* 2007, for *A Killer Whale's World; Washington Post* Children's Book Guild Nonfiction Award, 2005, for body of work; Parent's Choice Gold Award, 2006, for *The Terrible Hodag and the Animal Catchers;* Honor Book selection, Society of School Librarians International, 2007, for *Taj Mahal;* Leo Politi Golden Author Award, 2008; Best of the Best designation, Chicago Public Library, 2008, for *Wiggle and Waggle;* Eureka! Nonfiction Children's Book Award, California Reading Association, 2010, for *A Polar Bear's World.*

## Writings

*JUVENILE NONFICTION*

*Five Nests,* illustrated by Ruth Sanderson, Dutton (New York, NY), 1980.

*Electric Fish,* illustrated by George Gershinowitz, Morrow (New York, NY), 1980.

(Self-illustrated) *Sun Fun,* Franklin Watts (New York, NY), 1981.

*Sex Hormones: Why Males and Females Are Different,* illustrated by Jean Zallinger, Morrow (New York, NY), 1981.

*Animals That Migrate,* illustrated by Michele Zylman, Carolrhoda (Minneapolis, MN), 1982.

*What Is a Community?,* illustrated by Carole Bertol, Franklin Watts (New York, NY), 1982.

*Where Do You Go to School?,* illustrated by Carole Bertol, Franklin Watts (New York, NY), 1982.

*Who Works Here?,* illustrated by Carole Bertol, Franklin Watts (New York, NY), 1982.

*Who Keeps Us Healthy?,* illustrated by Carole Bertol, Franklin Watts (New York, NY), 1982.

*Who Keeps Us Safe?,* illustrated by Carole Bertol, Franklin Watts (New York, NY), 1982.

*Why Do We Have Rules?,* illustrated by Ginger Giles, Franklin Watts (New York, NY), 1983.

*What Will We Buy?,* illustrated by Ginger Giles, Franklin Watts (New York, NY), 1983.

*How Do We Have Fun?,* illustrated by Ginger Giles, Franklin Watts (New York, NY), 1983.

*How Do We Travel?,* illustrated by Ginger Giles, Franklin Watts (New York, NY), 1983.

*How Do We Communicate?,* illustrated by Ginger Giles, Franklin Watts (New York, NY), 1983.

(Self-illustrated) *The Biggest Living Thing,* Carolrhoda (Minneapolis, MN), 1983.

*Pets without Homes,* illustrated by Richard Hewett, Houghton Mifflin (Boston, MA), 1983.

*Summer Olympics,* Franklin Watts (New York, NY), 1983, 2nd updated edition, 1988.

*Winter Olympics,* Franklin Watts (New York, NY), 1983.

*Measurements: Fun, Facts, and Activities,* Franklin Watts (New York, NY), 1984.

*Maps and Globes,* Franklin Watts (New York, NY), 1984.

*Charts and Graphs,* Franklin Watts (New York, NY), 1984.

*Too Fat? Too Thin?: Do You Have a Choice?,* Morrow (New York, NY), 1984.

*Land Masses,* Franklin Watts (New York, NY), 1985.

*Natural Resources: Fun, Facts, and Activities,* Franklin Watts (New York, NY), 1985.

*Saving the Peregrine Falcon,* Carolrhoda (Minneapolis, MN), 1985.

*Music Lessons for Alex,* photographs by Richard Hewett, Houghton Mifflin (Boston, MA), 1985.

(With Herma Silverstein) *Anti-Semitism: A Modern Perspective,* Messner (New York, NY), 1985.

(With Herma Silverstein) *Hoaxes That Made Headlines,* Messner (New York, NY), 1985.

*Bodies of Water: Fun, Facts, and Activities,* illustrated by Lynn Sweat, Franklin Watts (New York, NY), 1985.

*Pain: What Is It? How Do We Deal with It?,* illustrated by Frank Schwarz, Morrow (New York, NY), 1986.

*Genetics: From Mendel to Gene Splicing,* Franklin Watts (New York, NY), 1986.

*The Golden Gate Bridge,* Franklin Watts (New York, NY), 1986.

*Everybody Has a Birthday,* Franklin Watts (New York, NY), 1987.

*How People Get Married,* Franklin Watts (New York, NY), 1987.

*What We Do When Someone Dies,* Franklin Watts (New York, NY), 1987.

*Australia Today,* Franklin Watts (New York, NY), 1987.

*Coping with Natural Disasters,* Walker (New York, NY), 1987.

*Kangaroo,* Morrow (New York, NY), 1987.

*Giraffe,* Morrow (New York, NY), 1987.

*Zebra,* Morrow (New York, NY), 1987.

*A Walk on the Great Barrier Reef,* Carolrhoda (Minneapolis, MN), 1987.

*Trapped in Tar: Fossils from the Ice Age,* Houghton Mifflin (Boston, MA), 1987.

*Koala,* photographs by Richard Hewett, Morrow (New York, NY), 1987.

*Llama,* Morrow (New York, NY), 1988.

*Penguin,* Morrow (New York, NY), 1988.

*Saving the Tule Elk,* Carolrhoda (Minneapolis, MN), 1988.

*Juggler,* Houghton Mifflin (Boston, MA), 1988.

*Ole Swenson and the Hodag,* Harcourt (New York, NY), 1988.

*Dinosaur Mountain: Graveyard of the Past,* Clarion (New York, NY), 1989.

*Hippo,* photographs by Richard Hewett, Morrow (New York, NY), 1989.

*Cheetah,* photographs by Richard Hewett, Morrow (New York, NY), 1989.

*Dinosaurs Down Under, and Other Fossils from Australia,* photographs by Richard Hewett, Clarion (New York, NY), 1990.

*Ostriches and Other Flightless Birds,* photographs by Richard Hewett, Carolrhoda (Minneapolis, MN), 1990.

*A Walk in the Woods,* illustrated by Freya Tanz, Silver Press (Parsippany, NJ), 1990.

*Orangutan,* photographs by Richard Hewett, Morrow (New York, NY), 1990.

*Wild Goat,* photographs by Richard Hewett, Morrow (New York, NY), 1990.

*A Walk up the Mountain,* illustrated by Freya Tanz, Silver Press (Parsippany, NJ), 1990.

*A Walk by the Seashore,* illustrated by Freya Tanz, Silver Press (Parsippany, NJ), 1990.

*Heart Disease,* Franklin Watts (New York, NY), 1990.

*A Walk in the Desert,* illustrated by Freya Tanz, Silver Press (Parsippany, NJ), 1990.

*Watch out for Sharks!,* photographs by Richard Hewett, Clarion (New York, NY), 1991.

*A Guide Dog Puppy Grows Up,* photographs by Richard Hewett, Harcourt (New York, NY), 1991.

*Flamingo,* photographs by Richard Hewett, Morrow (New York, NY), 1991.

*Snake,* photographs by Richard Hewett, Morrow (New York, NY), 1991.

*The Olympic Summer Games,* Franklin Watts (New York, NY), 1991.

*The Olympic Winter Games,* Franklin Watts (New York, NY), 1991.

*Soccer: From Neighborhood Play to the World Cup,* Franklin Watts (New York, NY), 1991.

*The Ancient Cliff Dwellers of Mesa Verde,* photographs by Richard Hewett, Clarion (New York, NY), 1992.

*Camel,* photographs by Richard Hewett, Morrow (New York, NY), 1992.

*Panda,* photographs by Richard Hewett, Morrow (New York, NY), 1992.

*House Sparrows Everywhere,* photographs by Richard Hewett, Carolrhoda (Minneapolis, MN), 1992.

*Pele: The King of Soccer,* Franklin Watts (New York, NY), 1992.

*On the Brink of Extinction: The California Condor,* photographs by Michael Wallace, Harcourt (San Diego, CA), 1993.

*Dinosaurs All Around: An Artist's View of the Prehistoric World,* photographs by Richard Hewett, Clarion (New York, NY), 1993.

*Elephant,* photographs by Richard Hewett, Morrow (New York, NY), 1993.

*Monkey,* photographs by Richard Hewett, Morrow (New York, NY), 1993.

*Prairie Dogs,* illustrations by Jean Cassels, Scholastic (New York, NY), 1993.

*Reindeer,* illustrated by Pamela Johnson, Scholastic (New York, NY), 1993.

*Cats: In from the Wild,* photographs by Richard Hewett, Carolrhoda (Minneapolis, MN), 1993.

*Sea Turtles,* illustrated by Marshall Peck III, Scholastic (New York, NY), 1994.

*Fireflies,* illustrated by Pamela Johnson, Scholastic (New York, NY), 1994.

*Killer Whale,* photographs by Richard Hewett, Morrow (New York, NY), 1994.

*Sea Lion,* photographs by Richard Hewett, Morrow (New York, NY), 1994.

*Watching Desert Wildlife,* photographs by Arthur Arnold, Carolrhoda (Minneapolis, MN), 1994.

*City of the Gods: Mexico's Ancient City of Teotihuacan,* photographs by Richard Hewett, Clarion (New York, NY), 1994.

*Rhino,* photographs by Richard Hewett and Arthur P. Arnold, Morrow (New York, NY), 1995.

*Lion,* photographs by Richard Hewett, Morrow (New York, NY), 1995.

*Bat,* photographs by Richard Hewett, Morrow (New York, NY), 1996.

*Fox,* photographs by Richard Hewett, Morrow (New York, NY), 1996.

(And photographer) *El Niño: Stormy Weather for People and Wildlife,* Clarion (New York, NY), 1996.

*Stories in Stone: Rock Art Pictures by Early Americans,* photographs by Richard Hewett, Clarion (New York, NY), 1996.

(And photographer) *African Animals,* Morrow (New York, NY), 1997.

*Stone Age Farmers beside the Sea: Scotland's Prehistoric Village of Skara Brae,* photographs by Arthur P. Arnold, Clarion (New York, NY), 1997.

*Hawk Highway in the Sky: Watching Raptor Migration,* photographs by Robert Kruidenier, Harcourt (San Diego, CA), 1997.

*Bobcats,* photographs by Richard Hewett, Lerner (Minneapolis, MN), 1997.

*Children of the Settlement Houses,* Carolrhoda (Minneapolis, MN), 1998.

*Baby Whale Rescue: The True Story of J.J.,* photographs by Richard Hewett, Bridgewater, 1999.

*Cats,* Lerner Publications (Minneapolis, MN), 1999.

*Splashtime for Zoo Animals,* photographs by Richard Hewett, Carolrhoda (Minneapolis, MN), 1999.

*Sleepytime for Zoo Animals,* photographs by Richard Hewett, Carolrhoda (Minneapolis, MN), 1999.

*Noisytime for Zoo Animals,* photographs by Richard Hewett, Carolrhoda (Minneapolis, MN), 1999.

*Playtime for Zoo Animals,* photographs by Richard Hewett, Carolrhoda (Minneapolis, MN), 1999.

*Mother and Baby Zoo Animals,* photographs by Richard Hewett, Carolrhoda (Minneapolis, MN), 1999.

*Mealtime for Zoo Animals,* photographs by Richard Hewett, Carolrhoda (Minneapolis, MN), 1999.

(And photographer) *South American Animals,* Morrow (New York, NY), 1999.

*Shockers of the Sea, and Other Electric Animals,* illustrated by Crista Forest, Charlesbridge (Watertown, MA), 1999.

(And photographer) *Easter Island: Giant Stone Statues Tell of a Rich and Tragic Past,* Clarion (New York, NY), 2000.

(And photographer) *Australian Animals,* Morrow (New York, NY), 2000.

*Giant Shark: Megalodon, Prehistoric Super Predator,* illustrated by Laurie Caple, Clarion (New York, NY), 2000.

*Ostriches,* photographs by Richard Hewett, Lerner (Minneapolis, MN), 2000.

*Did You Hear That?: Animals with Super Hearing,* illustrations by Cathy Trachok, Charlesbridge (Watertown, MA), 2001.

*Dinosaurs with Feathers: The Ancestors of Modern Birds,* Clarion (New York, NY), 2001.

*The Geography Book: Activities for Exploring, Mapping, and Enjoying Your World,* Wiley (New York, NY), 2002.

*When Mammoths Walked the Earth,* Clarion (New York, NY), 2002.

*Birds: Nature's Magnificent Flying Machines,* Charlesbridge (Watertown, MA), 2003.

(And photographer) *Uluru: Australia's Aboriginal Heart,* Clarion (New York, NY), 2003.

*Who Has More? Who Has Fewer?,* Charlesbridge (Watertown, MA), 2004.

(Self-illustrated) *Who Is Bigger? Who Is Smaller?,* Charlesbridge (Watertown, MA), 2004.

*Pterosaurs: Rulers of the Skies in the Dinosaur Age,* illustrated by Laurie Caple, Clarion (New York, NY), 2004.

*The Skeletal System,* Lerner (Minneapolis, MN), 2005.

(Self-illustrated) *A Zebra's World,* Picture Window Books (Minneapolis, MN), 2006.

(Self-illustrated) *A Penguin's World,* Picture Window Books (Minneapolis, MN), 2006.

(Self-illustrated) *A Panda's World,* Picture Window Books (Minneapolis, MN), 2006.

(Self-illustrated) *A Killer Whale's World,* Picture Window Books (Minneapolis, MN), 2006.

*Super Swimmers: Whales, Dolphins, and Other Mammals of the Sea,* illustrated by Patricia J. Wynne, Charlesbridge (Watertown, MA), 2007.

*Giant Sea Reptiles of the Dinosaur Age,* illustrated by Laurie Caple, Clarion (New York, NY), 2007.

(With Madeleine Comora) *Taj Mahal,* illustrated by Rahul Bushan, Carolrhoda Books (Minneapolis, MN), 2007.

(Self-illustrated) *A Kangaroo's World,* Picture Window Books (Minneapolis, MN), 2008.

(Self-illustrated) *A Koala's World,* Picture Window Books (Minneapolis, MN), 2008.

(Self-illustrated) *A Platypus' World,* Picture Window Books (Minneapolis, MN), 2008.

(Self-illustrated) *A Wombat's World,* Picture Window Books (Minneapolis, MN), 2008.

*Global Warming and the Dinosaurs: Fossil Discoveries at the Poles,* illustrated by Laurie Caple, Houghton Mifflin Harcourt (Boston, MA), 2009.

(Self-illustrated) *A Bald Eagle's World,* Picture Window Books (Minneapolis, MN), 2010.

(Self-illustrated) *A Moose's World,* Picture Window Books (Minneapolis, MN), 2010.

(Self-illustrated) *A Polar Bear's World,* Picture Window Books (Minneapolis, MN), 2010.

(Self-illustrated) *A Walrus' World,* Picture Window Books (Minneapolis, MN), 2010.

Author's works have been translated into Spanish.

*JUVENILE FICTION*

*My Friend from Outer Space* (picture book), illustrated by Carol Nicklaus, Franklin Watts (New York, NY), 1981.

*The Terrible Hodag,* illustrated by Lambert Davis, Harcourt Brace (San Francisco, CA), 1989.

*An Apple a Day,* Metropolitan Museum of Art (New York, NY), 2003.

*The Terrible Hodag and the Animal Catchers,* illustrated by John Sandford, Boyds Mills Press (Honesdale, PA), 2006.

*Wiggle and Waggle,* illustrated by Mary Peterson, Charlesbridge (Watertown, MA), 2007.

*OTHER*

(Illustrator) Elizabeth Bremner and John Pusey, *Children's Gardens: A Field Guide for Teachers, Parents, and Volunteers,* Cooperative Extension, University of California, Los Angeles (Los Angeles, CA), 1982.

Also author of episode "Fire for Hire," *K-I-D-S* (television series), broadcast 1984. Contributor to books, including *The ABC's of Writing for Children* by Lisa Koehler-Pentakoff, Quill Driver Books, 2003; and *Authors in the Kitchen: Recipes, Stories, and More,* Libraries Unlimited, 2005. Contributor of articles and stories to magazines, including *Highlights for Children, Friend, Humpty Dumpty,* and *Cricket.*

Some of Arnold's manuscripts and papers are included in the Kerlan Collection, University of Minnesota, Minneapolis.

## Adaptations

*My Friend from Outer Space* was adapted as a filmstrip, Westport Community Group, 1981.

## Sidelights

Caroline Arnold is the author of more than one hundred nonfiction books for children, including such critically acclaimed titles as *Saving the Peregrine Falcon, Taj Mahal,* and *Global Warming and the Dinosaurs: Fossil Discoveries at the Poles.* The recipient of a *Washington Post* Children's Book Guild nonfiction award, among her numerous other honors, Arnold covers a wide range of subjects in her books, from monkeys, bats, and foxes to prehistoric natural history, the giant statues of Easter Island, and weather patterns. As she once commented to *SATA:* I have found that I enjoy the challenge of writing about complicated subjects in language that even a very young child can understand. My fascination with scientific subjects is reinforced by my own and other children's eagerness to know more about the world around them."

Born in 1944, Arnold lived in Pennsylvania and New York before her family settled in Minneapolis, Minnesota. "I cannot remember a time when books

were not part of my life," she recalled in an essay for the *Something about the Author Autobiography Series* (*SAAS*). "Both of my parents were avid readers, and they read to me from the time I was very young." In addition to her love of reading, Arnold developed an interest in drawing and painting as a child, taking lessons at the Minneapolis Art Institute on weekends. After graduating from high school, she attended Grinnell College in Iowa, where she majored in art. "In retrospect I realize that the most important part of my Grinnell education was learning how to write and how to be a critical thinker," she remarked in *SAAS.* The particular facts I learned were less important than knowing how to find information, select the elements necessary to support an idea, and then organize the material into a cohesive whole. I also learned that, whether the subject was art, science, or literature, it was important to develop a keen sense of observation."

Arnold earned her master's degree at the University of Iowa and then worked as a teacher, a secretary, and a lab assistant before entering the world of literature at the urging of several friends and family members. "After I got married and had my own children, I read stories to them," she once recalled to *SATA.* "I realized that perhaps I could use my training in art to be a chil-

*One of the most fascinating civilizations of the ancient world is brought to life in Arnold's* **Easter Island: Giant Stone Statues Tell of a Rich and Tragic Past.** (Copyright © 2000 by Caroline Arnold. Reprinted by permission of Clarion Books, an imprint of Houghton Mifflin Company. All rights reserved.)

dren's book illustrator. I started to write stories so that I could illustrate them and soon discovered that I liked writing very much. I've been writing ever since."

Many of Arnold's nonfiction works, which she sometimes illustrates, focus on animals and other wonders of the natural world. "I've always loved animals," she once noted. "I got my first kitten when I was three—I named her Snoozy after a character in one of my books—and have always had pets. During the summers our family spent in northern Wisconsin, I learned the thrill of spotting birds, deer, porcupines, and other wild animals in the forest. In 1971, I spent four months in East Africa with my husband and young daughter. We lived in a national park, side by side with lions, giraffes, zebras, and all sorts of other animals whose home is the African plain. A few of the photos we took on that trip are in my book *African Animals*.

"Birds have always been a favorite topic in my books. When I was a child, I went on early morning bird walks with my father, who was an amateur birdwatcher, and now my husband, Art, studies birds in his research at the University of California—Los Angeles. For my book *Hawk Highway in the Sky: Watching Raptor Migration*, I spent a week in the Goshutes watching and helping HawkWatch volunteers trap and band migrating hawks, eagles, and falcons. Nothing is more exciting than getting close to these magnificent birds, and my close involvement with the process helped me learn the details that I needed to write my book. My book *Birds: Nature's Magnificent Flying Machines* also focuses on birds and their amazing ability to fly.

"There are so many different kinds of animals in the world that I could spend the rest of my life writing about animals and never run out of ideas. When I choose an animal for a book, I often pick endangered species such as pandas or cheetahs. The more we all know about these animals, the more we will care about saving them from extinction."

*Bat* is typical of Arnold's books on animals. Reviewing both *Bat* and *Fox* for *Booklist*, Carolyn Phelan called the volumes "succinct" and "readable." Although both books are short, they cover a great deal of material, including the respective creature's anatomy, habitat, behavior; its food and the other animals that may prey upon it; myths and history surrounding it; and threats to its continued survival as a species. Discussing the author's books *Lion* and *Rhino* in another review, Phelan noted that Arnold offers interesting comments on the differences in the animals' behavior based on whether the creature is living in the wild or in captivity.

*Lion* and *Rhino,* like many of Arnold's books, are illustrated with photographs. "The advantage of a photo is that it shows what the subject really looks like," the author explained. "In today's world, where children are exposed to amazing nature films on video and television, they want to see pictures of real animals in books.

*A link between the fate of Earth's dinosaurs and theories of climate change are the focus of Arnold's* **Global Warming and the Dinosaurs,** *featuring artwork by Laurie Caple.* (Illustration copyright © 2009 by Laurie Capie. Reproduced with permission of Houghton Mifflin Harcourt Publishing Company.)

But photography isn't always the best way to illustrate a book. It doesn't work well for animals such as pandas, which have elusive life styles, or animals such as sharks and whales, which live under water, or nocturnal animals. It also doesn't work for events that do not have a photographic record or which occurred before the invention of photography."

While Arnold illustrated several of her early works, as the list of her titles grew, she passed illustration duties on to others. However, as she more recently explained to *SATA,* "after nearly twenty years away from my art, I have begun doing some of my own illustrating again. I am using cut-paper collage, a technique that lends itself to books for younger children. I first used this method in the baby board books *Who Is Bigger? Who Is Smaller?* and *Who Has More? Who Has Fewer?* In 2006 I expanded the technique in four large-format books about black-and-white animals: pandas, penguins, killer whales, and zebras. I wanted to give a bright, contemporary look to these books. I also felt that the black-and-white animals, which are already rather abstract in their appearance, lend themselves to this bold treatment. The challenge in doing a series such as this is making each book stand on its own, while making sure that all of the titles have a similar approach."

Detailing an Adelie penguin family as they build a nest and harbor their eggs, *A Penguin's World* concludes by revealing a four-month old chick moving toward independence. In her review for *Booklist,* Gillian Engberg described *A Penguin's World* as featuring a "simple, well-paced text [that] weaves basic concepts into the captivating narrative." Arnold adds to the wealth of information by including a map of Antarctica giving young readers insight to where Adelie penguins live.

Additional self-illustrated titles include _A Killer Whale's World, A Panda's World,_ and _A Zebra's World._ Suzanne Myers Harold, writing in _School Library Journal_ about these titles, noted that "each book reads like a story with scientific details woven into the narrative" and concluded that the books "work well as read-alouds and provide enough factual information for simple reports." Each animal-based book introduces the topic animal by listing various facts about the species and includes related maps and Web sites. Text boxes are also utilized to add interesting side notes without interrupting the narrative flow of the story.

In _A Wombat's World_ Arnold introduces young readers to the burrowing Australian marsupial, following a year in the life of a female wombat. In _Booklist,_ Engberg applauded the "clear, compelling" narrative, citing Arnold's "uncluttered cut-paper collages and simple,

straightforward text" as highlights of the work. Reviewing that story, as well as _A Platypus's World,_ which examines another unusual Australian mammal, Gay Lynn Van Vleck found Arnold's work to be "visually engaging and brimming with data" in her review for _School Library Journal._ Miriam Aronin, in her _Booklist_ critique of _A Bald Eagle's World, A Polar Bear's World,_ and _A Walrus' World,_ applauded the "perfectly balanced mix of facts, story, and pictures" in each, citing especially "Arnold's beautiful but simple artwork, which cleanly captures the essence of each animal."

Exploring another area of interest, Arnold introduces Aztec culture and its surviving artifacts in _City of the Gods: Mexico's Ancient City of Teotihuacan._ Aerial photographs provide insight into the city that was one of the most important in the Aztec world, and Arnold's text explains Teotihuacan's importance to Aztec culture. Another mysterious ancient site is explored in _Easter Island: Giant Stone Statues Tell of a Rich and Tragic Past._ Located in the South Pacific, Easter Island is home to a number of huge stone icons. For decades, no one was able to definitely answer the many questions sur-

_Arnold's_ **Did You Hear That?: Animals with Super Hearing** _features detailed paintings by artist Cathy Trachok._ (Illustration © 2001 by Cathy Trachok. Reproduced by permission of Charlesbridge Publishing, Inc. All rights reserved.)

rounding these figures, such as how the primitive inhabitants of the island, the Rapanui, managed to carve and erect them. As a reviewer for *Horn Book* noted, "Arnold avoids theatrical speculation in this straightforward account." She also provides information about the Rapanui and their modern descendants, and discusses the island's decline due to overpopulation and residents' disregard for their fragile environment.

Arnold explores the history of one of the world's true architectural treasures in *Taj Mahal,* a picture book co-authored by Madeleine Comora and illustrated by Rahul Bushan. Arnold was inspired to begin thisthe autho work after visiting the celebrated landmark while traveling in India, noting on her home page: "I knew that the Taj Mahal would be the perfect subject for a book because of the love story that inspired it, the artistic and technical achievement of its architecture, and for what it tells us about Mughal culture in India." The coauthors focus on the legendary romance of Shah Jahan and his beloved wife, Mumtaz Mahal, for whom he constructed the monument. According to a critic in *Kirkus Reviews,* the book's "lyrical account frames a touching tale of love and loss in magnificent visuals," and Margaret Bush maintained in *School Library Journal* that *Taj Mahal* "is sumptuous in appearance and presents a bit of history not often told for children."

*Pterosaurs: Rulers of the Skies in the Dinosaur Age* provides young dino fans with a factual look at the ancient pterosaurs, detailing their daily living habits and characteristic features as well as noting fossil discoveries related to the species. As Arnold notes in her book, pterosaurs are the only reptiles known to have the ability to remain airborne through their own power. In addition to including descriptions of twenty pterosaur species, the author also incorporates a list of museums that house pterosaur fossils. Acknowledged as a "solid overview" by *Booklist* reviewer Jennifer Mattson, *Pterosaurs* presents scientific information to children in a fun and easy-to-understand manner by making comparisons between the dinosaurs and objects that children can relate to. Arnold, for instance, makes a comparison between the length of a pterosaur's wings and the length of a human child's little finger. A contributor to *Kirkus Reviews* noted that the results of *Pterosaurs* "will please dino-fans at any level of expertise."

In *Giant Sea Reptiles of the Dinosaur Age* Arnold looks at creatures from the three major groups of marine reptiles that existed during the Mesozoic Era: ichthyosaurs, plesiosaurs, and mosasaurs. In addition to describing the dinosaur's physical characteristics and diet, Arnold also presents accounts of fossil finds, including the work of nineteenth-century British paleontologist Mary Anning. According to *School Library Journal* contributor Sandra Welzenbach, the author "has taken an immense amount of data and organized it in an appealing format."

The idea for *Global Warming and the Dinosaurs* developed over a twenty-year period as Arnold learned about fossil records near the North and South poles. In this work she examines the creatures' ability to adapt to colder, harsher conditions than previously imagined, outlining the species that existed in such polar climates. A critic in *Kirkus Reviews* reported that "Arnold has found a topic that hasn't been treated in such detail elsewhere," and Phelan, writing in *Booklist,* also complimented the "clearly written, informative, and handsome book."

Arnold has also written a number of fictional works for young readers. In *The Terrible Hodag and the Animal Catchers* she provides a fictional account of a legendary creature known as the Hodag. Originating in a Wisconsin logging-camp myth, the Hodag has the "head of an ox, feet of a bear, back of dinosaur, and tail of an alligator." The main character in Arnold's tale—a logger by the name of Ole Swenson—is intent on saving the gentle and friendly creature from a group of city slickers who hope to capture it and place it in a zoo. In *Kirkus Reviews* a critic regarded Arnold's tale of the Hodag as "a bit stiff" but also noted that the Hodag "seems more friendly than fearsome, and tales about it are rare enough that it may be new to young readers." Carolyn Janssen, reviewing the book for *School Library Journal,* predicted that *The Terrible Hodag and the Animal Catchers* "will be enjoyed both as a read-aloud and a read-alone." The book is a sequel to Arnold's earlier book, *The Terrible Hodag,* in which the Hodag befriends the loggers and helps them get rid of a mean bossman.

*Wiggle and Waggle,* a picture book, had its origins when Arnold's children were preschoolers and her family moved to a farmhouse in the countryside. The story concerns a pair of earthworms who join forces to remove a rock from their garden, enjoy a picnic outing, and learn to appreciate the joys of a rainy day. "Arnold's writing has an easygoing cadence and just the right amount of repetition," a reviewer stated in *Publishers Weekly.* "The writing of *Wiggle and Waggle* may illustrate the value of perseverance—or perhaps it was just one of those garden plants that didn't mature in the first year, but required more time to reach its peak," Arnold stated on her home page.

Discussing her decades-long efforts as an author, Arnold noted on her home page: "Like the seasons, my writing career has also come full cycle. I started writing when my own children were small and mainly focused on books for young readers. As my children grew up, I shifted to writing more for older readers. My son and daughter are now grown and have their own children, who have inspired me to go back to writing for younger readers." Her passion for nonfiction is as strong as ever, she once told *SATA.* "Truth is often stranger than fiction and certainly just as much fun to write. With every book I've written, I have learned something that I never knew before. If the children who read my books are as excited about reading them as I am about writing them, then I feel that I have accomplished a great deal."

## Biographical and Critical Sources

*BOOKS*

Arnold, Caroline, *The Terrible Hodag and the Animal Catchers,* illustrated by John Sandford, Boyds Mills Press (Honesdale, PA), 2006.

Roginski, Jim, *Behind the Covers: Interviews with Authors and Illustrators of Children's Books,* Libraries Unlimited, 1989.

*Something about the Author Autobiography Series,* Volume 23, Gale (Detroit, MI), 1996.

*PERIODICALS*

*Booklist,* October 15, 1992, Stephanie Zvirin, review of *Camel,* p. 419; April 15, 1993, Stephanie Zvirin, review of *Dinosaurs All Around: An Artist's View of the Prehistoric World,* p. 1507, and Chris Sherman, review of *On the Brink of Extinction: The California Condor,* p. 1512; August, 1993, Stephanie Zvirin, review of *Cats: In from the Wild,* p. 2051; November 1, 1993, Kay Weisman, review of *Elephant* and *Monkey,* p. 516; September 15, 1994, Carolyn Phelan, reviews of *Sea Lion* and *Killer Whale,* both p. 128; December 1, 1994, Mary Harris Veeder, review of *Watching Desert Wildlife,* p. 670; December 15, 1994, Ilene Cooper, review of *City of the Gods: Mexico's Ancient City of Teotihuacan,* p. 747; September 15, 1995, Carolyn Phelan, reviews of *Rhino* and *Lion,* both p. 154; December 15, 1996, Sally Estes, review of *Stories in Stone: Rock Art Pictures by Early Americans,* p. 722; October 15, 1999, Shelley Townsend-Hudson, review of *Shockers of the Sea, and Other Electric Animals,* p. 448; August, 1996, Carolyn Phelan, reviews of *Fox* and *Bat,* both p. 1897; March 15, 1997, Julie Corsaro, review of *African Animals,* p. 1236; April 15, 1997, Ilene Cooper, review of *Stone Age Farmers beside the Sea: Scotland's Prehistoric Village of Skara Brae,* p. 1424; June 1, 1997, Candace Smith, review of *Hawk Highway in the Sky: Watching Raptor Migration,* p. 1687; September 15, 1998, Shelle Rosenfeld, review of *Children of the Settlement Houses,* p. 221; October 1, 1998, Chris Sherman, review of *El Niño: Stormy Weather for People and Wildlife,* p. 326; March 1, 1999, Lauren Peterson, review of *Baby Whale Rescue: The True Story of J.J.,* p. 1204; June 1, 1999, Susan Dove Lempke, reviews of *Noisytime for Zoo Animals* and *Mealtime for Zoo Animals,* both p. 1832; July, 1999, Lauren Peterson, review of *South American Animals,* p. 1939; March 15, 2000, Ilene Cooper, review of *Easter Island: Giant Stone Statues Tell of a Rich and Tragic Past,* p. 1371; November 1, 2000, Todd Morning, review of *Giant Shark: Megalodon, Prehistoric Super Predator,* p. 528; December 1, 2001, Carolyn Phelan, review of *Did You Hear That? Animals with Super Hearing,* p. 654; February 15, 2002, Carolyn Phelan, review of *The Geography Book: Activities for Exploring, Mapping, and Enjoying Your World,* p. 1001; August, 2002, Julie Cummins, review of *When Mammoths Walked the Earth,* p. 1952; June 1, 2003, John Peters, review of *Birds: Nature's Magnificent Flying Machines,* p. 1762; December 15, 2003, Carolyn Phelan, review of *Uluru: Australia's Aboriginal Heart,* p. 1220; December 1, 2004, Jennifer Mattson, review of *Pterosaurs,* p. 665l; April 1, 2006, Julie Cummins, review of *The Terrible Hodag and the Animal Catchers,* p. 47, and Gillian Engberg, review of *A Penguin's World,* p. 65; February 1, 2007, Carolyn Phelan, review of *Super Swimmers: Whales, Dolphins, and Other Mammals of the Sea,* p. 48; June 1, 2007, Jennifer Mattson, review of *Taj Mahal,* p. 66; July 1, 2007, Ilene Cooper, review of *Wiggle and Waggle,* p. 67; August, 2007, Ilene Cooper, review of *Giant Sea Reptiles of the Dinosaur Age,* p. 67; March 15, 2008, Gillian Engberg, review of *A Wombat's World,* p. 55; December 1, 2009, Carolyn Phelan, review of *Global Warming and the Dinosaurs: Fossil Discoveries at the Poles,* p. 56; September 15, 2010, Miriam Aronin, reviews of *A Bald Eagle's World, A Polar Bear's World,* and *A Walrus' World,* all p. 60.

*Fresno Bee,* December 15, 2002, Lisa Liberman, "Author Taps Children's Interest to Teach Writing."

*Horn Book,* November-December, 1992, Margaret A. Bush, reviews of *Camel* and *Panda,* both p. 735; June-May, 1993, Margaret A. Bush, review of *On the Brink of Extinction,* p. 343; July-August, 1993, Elizabeth S. Watson, review of *Dinosaurs All Around,* p. 474; November-December, 1994, Margaret A. Bush, reviews of *Sea Lion* and *Killer Whale,* both p. 742; March-April, 1995, Elizabeth S. Watson, review of *City of the Gods,* p. 218; May, 2000, review of *Easter Island,* p. 329; October 1, 2001, John Peters, review of *Dinosaurs with Feathers: The Ancestors of the Modern Birds,* p. 313; November-December, 2002, Danielle J. Ford, review of *When Mammoths Walked the Earth,* p. 772; November-December, 2003, Barbara Bader, review of *Uluru,* p. 760; January-February, 2008, Danielle J. Ford, review of *Giant Sea Reptiles of the Dinosaur Age,* p. 105; January-February, 2010, Danielle J. Ford, review of *Global Warming and the Dinosaurs,* p. 99.

*Kirkus Reviews,* June 15, 2003, review of *Birds,* p. 855; October 1, 2003, review of *Uluru,* p. 1220; November 15, 2004, review of *Pterosaurs,* p. 1087; December 15, 2005, review of *The Terrible Hodag and the Animal Catchers,* p. 1317; April 15, 2007, review of *Taj Mahal*; June 1, 2007, review of *Wiggle and Waggle*; November 1, 2009, review of *Global Warming and the Dinosaurs.*

*Los Angeles Times,* November 8, 1996, "Author Gets a Read on What Students Want," p. 2.

*Publishers Weekly,* February 6, 2006, review of *The Terrible Hodag and the Animal Catchers,* p. 69; May 28, 2007, review of *Taj Mahal,* p. 65; July 9, 2007, review of *Wiggle and Waggle,* p. 53.

*Reading Teacher,* September, 1998, review of *African Animals,* p. 58.

*School Library Journal,* November, 1992, Myra R. Oleynik, review of *Camel,* p. 100; January, 1993, Barbara B. Murphy, review of *Panda,* p. 106; May, 1993, Cathryn A. Campter, review of *Dinosaurs All Around,* p.

112; June, 1993, Amy Nunley, review of *On the Brink of Extinction,* p. 113; December, 1993, Barbara B. Murphy, reviews of *Monkey* and *Elephant,* both p. 118; October, 1994, Frances E. Millhouser, review of *Killer Whale,* p. 130; December, 1994, Cynthia M. Sturgis, review of *City of the Gods,* p. 117; January, 1995, George Gleason, review of *Watching Desert Wildlife,* p. 110; December, 1995, Barbara B. Murphy, reviews of *Lion* and *Rhino,* both p. 111; September, 1996, Lisa Wu Stowe, reviews of *Fox* and *Bat,* both p. 210; December, 1996, Pam Gosner, review of *Stories in Stone,* p. 126; March, 1997, Susan Oliver, review of *African Animals,* p. 170; June, 1997, Susan Scheps, review of *Hawk Highway in the Sky,* p. 130; July, 1997, Pam Gosner, review of *Stone Age Farmers beside the Sea,* p. 99; March, 1998, Susan Oliver, review of *Bobcats,* p. 191; December, 1998, Patricia Manning, review of *El Niño,* p. 132; January, 1999, Anne Chapman Callaghan, review of *Children of the Settlement Houses,* p. 109; March, 1999, Patricia Manning, review of *Baby Whale Rescue,* p. 216; August, 1999, Dawn Amsberry, reviews of *Splashtime for Zoo Animals* and *Sleepytime for Zoo Animals,* both p. 143; September, 1999, Frances E. Millhouser, review of *South American Animals,* p. 210; January, 2000, Patricia Manning, review of *Shockers of the Sea, and Other Electric Animals,* p. 115; April, 2000, Jeanette Larson, review of *Easter Island,* p. 144; October, 2000, Krista Grosick, review of *Australian Animals,* p. 144; November, 2000, Patricia Manning, review of *Giant Shark,* p. 167; August, 2001, Margaret Bush, review of *Did You Hear That?,* p. 166; November, 2001, Steven Engelfried, review of *Dinosaurs with Feath-* ers, p. 140; March, 2002, Robyn Ryan Vandenbroek, review of *The Geography Book,* p. 206; October, 2002, Ellen Heath, review of *When Mammoths Walked the Earth,* p. 136; March, 2006, Carolyn Janssen, review of *The Terrible Hodag and the Animal Catchers,* p. 174; June, 2006, Suzanne Myers Harold, review of *A Killer Whale's World, A Panda's World, A Penguin's World,* and *A Zebra's World,* p. 132; April, 2007, Patricia Manning, review of *Super Swimmers,* p. 154; July, 2007, Margaret Bush, review of *Taj Mahal,* p. 112; September, 2007, Sandra Welzenbach, review of *Giant Sea Reptiles of the Dinosaur Age,* p. 213; November, 2007, Elaine Lesh Morgan, review of *Wiggle and Waggle,* p. 86; August, 2008, Gay Lynn Van Vleck, reviews of *A Platypus' World* and *A Wombat's World,* both p. 108; February, 2010, Denise Schmidt, review of *Global Warming and the Dinosaurs,* p. 99.

*Wilson Library Bulletin,* February, 1994, Frances Bradburn, review of *Elephant,* p. A89.

*ONLINE*

*California Readers Web site,* http://www.californiareaders. org/ (April 1, 2011), Ann Stalcup, "Meet Caroline Arnold."

*Caroline Arnold Home Page,* http://www.carolinearnold books.com (April 1, 2011).

*Caroline Arnold Web log,* http://carolinearnoldart.blogspot. com (April 1, 2011).

*Celebrity Parents Magazine Online,* http://www.celebrity parentsmag.com/ (October 22, 2010), "Caroline Arnold."

# B

## BEHRENS, Andy

### Personal
Married; children: one daughter. *Education:* University of Iowa, degree, 1993.

### Addresses
*Home*—Chicago, IL. *E-mail*—rotoarcade@yahoo.com.

### Career
Writer and editor. McMaster Carr, operations manager, 1994-2002; freelance writer, beginning 2002; *Yahoo! Sports,* writer and editor of *Roto Arcade* Web log, 2007—.

### Awards, Honors
Fantasy Sports Writers Association award for Best Print Article (baseball), 2008.

### Writings

*NOVELS*

*All the Way,* Dutton Books (New York, NY), 2006.
*Beauty and the Bully,* Dutton Books (New York, NY), 2008.
*The Fast and the Furriest,* Knopf (New York, NY), 2010.

*OTHER*

Contributor to periodicals, including *Chicago Reader* and *Flak,* and to Web sites, including *ESPN.com* and *NBA.com.*

### Adaptations
*All the Way* was adapted as the motion picture *Sex Drive,* Summit Entertainment, 2008. *The Fast and the Furriest* was adapted as an audiobook, Listening Library, 2010.

### Sidelights
Andy Behrens, a well-known fantasy sports columnist, has also written novels for children and young adults, among them *All the Way* and *The Fast and the Furriest.* The former centers on Ian Lafferty, a soon-to-be high school senior forced to spend his summer working at a suburban Chicago shopping mall while best friend, Lance, enjoys a cushy job in a resort town and gal pal, Felicia, vacations along the Mediterranean. After posing as a college football player to impress Danielle Morrison, a sexy South Carolina coed whom he met in a chat room, the virginal Ian accepts her invitation to visit Charleston for a weekend of passion. Lance and Felicia stumble onto his plan, however, and decide to come along for the ride, piling into Ian's yellow Oldsmobile (affectionately nicknamed "the Creature") for a raucous adventure. "The characterizations of the three friends and the dynamics between them keep this road show rolling," noted a critic in *Publishers Weekly.* Susan Riley in *School Library Journal* called *All the Way* a "laugh-out-loud funny novel with hilarious near disasters," and a *Kirkus Reviews* contributor applauded Behrens's portrayal of Ian, stating that male readers "will laugh at how well he's inside their heads, and their shorts."

A shy teen devises an elaborate plan to capture the attention of a gorgeous, ambitious classmate in *Beauty and the Bully,* Behrens's second novel. Although he pines for Carly Garfield, his school's resident do-gooder, Duncan Boone finds her completely unapproachable and expresses his angst in the cheesy love songs he pens for his garage band. When an accident leaves Duncan with a bruised face and his band mates claim that he was mugged, Carly suddenly takes an interest in the downtrodden teen, believing him to be an underdog in need of her care. Realizing that Carly's concern for him will fade as soon as his injuries heal, Duncan decides to make himself a permanent victim, hiring the school bully, Freddy, to terrorize him. In exchange, Duncan allows Freddy's sister, Syd, to join his band, but she quickly develops a crush on him, forcing Duncan to choose between the two girls.

In *The Fast and the Furriest* a twelve-year-old couch potato discovers a love of competition and, in the process, finds common ground with his sports-minded father. The son of Howie Pugh, a beloved former player for the Chicago Bears, Kevin hopes to spend his summer fine-tuning his video-game skills. After viewing a dog-agility competition on television, he decides to enroll his pet, Cromwell, in training classes. Even though Kevin's father has doubts about the legitimacy of the sport, he soon sees the normally lazy family mutt leaping over hurdles, weaving through poles, and scrambling through tunnels. "Behrens's engaging style will appeal to children," predicted Kim Dare in her *School Library Journal* review of *The Fast and the Furriest*, and a contributor in *Kirkus Reviews* wrote that "readers will appreciate [Behrens'] . . . gentle humor and root for Kevin."

**Cover of Andy Behrens' engaging pet-centered picture book** The Fast and the Furriest. (Cover photograph by Superstock and Brian Sheridan. Alfred A. Knopf, 2010. Copyright © 2010 by Alloy Entertainment and Andy Behrens. Reproduced with permission of Alfred A. Knopf, an imprint of Random House Children's Books, a division of Random House, Inc.)

## Biographical and Critical Sources

*PERIODICALS*

*Booklist,* February 1, 2010, Kara Dean, review of *The Fast and the Furriest,* p. 42.
*Kirkus Reviews,* April 15, 2006, review of *All the Way,* p. 401; January 15, 2010, review of *The Fast and the Furriest.*
*Publishers Weekly,* May 8, 2006, review of *All the Way,* p. 68.
*School Library Journal,* May, 2006, Susan Riley, review of *All the Way,* p. 120; October, 2008, Jessie Spalding, review of *Beauty and the Bully,* p. 138; March, 2010, Kim Dare, review of *The Fast and the Furriest,* p. 152.
*Voice of Youth Advocates,* August, 2008, Ed Goldberg, review of *Beauty and the Bully,* p. 236.*

\*     \*     \*

## BEREAL, JaeMe 1959(?)-

### Personal

Born c. 1959, in CA; daughter of painters. *Education:* University of California, Berkeley, B.A. (sculpture), 1981; earned teaching credentials, 1995; Academy of Art College (San Francisco, CA), B.F.A. (illustration), 2002. *Hobbies and other interests:* Yoga, dance.

### Addresses

*Home*—Berkeley, CA. *Office*—Studio Girl, 456 Santa Clara Ave., Oakland, CA 94610. *E-mail*—jaemegrrl@ earthlink.net.

### Career

Illustrator, painter, and beautician. JaeMae's Studio Hair, Grand Lake, CA, owner and master stylist, beginning c. 1980s. *Exhibitions:* Work exhibited in group shows at Studio One, Berkeley, CA, 1992; San Francisco African-American Historical and Cultural Society Museum, 2004, 2007; Richmond Art Center, Richmond, CA, beginning 2004; John Muir Medical Center, 2009.

### Member

San Francisco Illustrators Society, Oakland Art Association.

### Illustrator

Alan Schroeder, *In Her Hands: The Story of Sculptor Augusta Savage,* Lee & Low Books (New York, NY), 2009.

### Sidelights

JaeMe Bereal is a painter and sculptor whose artwork is a feature of Alan Schroeder's fictionalized biography *In Her Hands: The Story of Sculptor Augusta Savage,* which discusses the childhood of a well-known artist of the early-twentieth-century Harlem Renaissance. An artist whose work expresses her unique perspectives as an African-American woman raised in a multiracial family, Bereal also finds creative fulfillment through her work as a master stylist at the salon she owns near her home in northern California.

Bereal grew up in a creative family where both parents were artistic. Single-minded in her interest in art, she earned a scholarship to the University of California at Berkeley, where she studied sculpture and graduated in 1981. After college a career as a sculptor took a back seat to more practical concerns, although Bereal was able to draw on her creative talents while working as a textile artist and patternmaker as well as through her work as a hair stylist and makeup artist for both private clients as well as Hollywood actors. In her forties she returned to school and earned her B.F.A. in illustration. Awarded her first book-cover assignment in 2004, Bereal then took on the project of creating art for Schroeder's biography of Savage.

*In Her Hands* follows the life of Augusta Savage, who was born in 1892 and grew up in Florida, the daughter of a preacher. Although her father disapproved of Au-

gusta's ability to sculpt things out of clay, her mother's encouragement fueled the girl's desire to become an artist and gave her the courage to eventually move north to New York City, there to attend art school and establish herself as a teacher and sculptor. As Lisa Glasscock noted in her review of *In Her Hands,* Bereal's "illustrations glow with the sunset hue of the red clay Savage first discovered as a child" and reflecting the shared passion of both illustrator and subject. Praising Schroeder's "gentle recounting" of Savage's informative years, a *Kirkus Reviews* critic also cited Bereal's contribution, describing her acrylic paintings as "warm and inviting."

## Biographical and Critical Sources

*PERIODICALS*

*Kirkus Reviews,* October 15, 2009, review of *In Her Hands: The Story of Sculptor Augusta Savage.*
*School Library Journal,* December, 2010, Lisa Glasscock, review of *In Her Hands,* p. 100.

*ONLINE*

*California Readers Web site,* http://www.californiareaders. org/ (March 20, 2011), Bonnie O'Brian, interview with Bereal.
*JaeMe Bereal Home Page,* http://jaemebereal.com (February 16, 2011).*

*            *            *

## BILL, Tannis

### Personal

Born in Canada; married Duane Bill. *Education:* College degree.

### Addresses

*Home*—Calgary, Alberta, Canada.

### Career

Author and educator. Elementary-school teacher for nineteen years.

### Writings

*Pika: Life in the Rocks,* photographs by Jim Jacobson, Boyds Mills Press (Honesdale, PA), 2010.

### Biographical and Critical Sources

*PERIODICALS*

*Booklist,* March 1, 2010, Daniel Kraus, review of *Pika: Life in the Rocks,* p. 75.
*Kirkus Reviews,* January 15, 2010, review of *Pika.*

*JaeMe Bereal's illustration projects include creating the art for Alan Schroeder's picture-book biography* **In Her Hands: The Story of Sculptor Augusta Savage.** (Illustration copyright © 2009 by JaeMe Bereal. Reproduced with permission of Lee & Low Books.)

*School Library Journal,* April, 2010, Nancy Call, review of *Pika,* p. 144.

ONLINE

*Tannis Bill Web log,* http://tannisbill.wordpress.com (April 1, 2011).*

*       *       *

## BRAMSEN, Kirsten

### Personal
Female. *Hobbies and other interests:* Gardening.

### Addresses
*Home*—Brooklyn, NY.

### Career
Singer, actor, and author.

### Writings

*The Yellow Tutu,* illustrated by Carin Bramsen, Random House (New York, NY), 2009.

### Biographical and Critical Sources

PERIODICALS

*Kirkus Reviews,* August 1, 2009, review of *The Yellow Tutu.*
*School Library Journal,* September, 2009, Donna Cardon, review of *The Yellow Tutu,* p. 116.*

*       *       *

## BRUCHAC, Joseph 1942-
## (Joseph Bruchac, III)

### Personal
Surname pronounced "*brew*-shack"; born October 16, 1942, in Saratoga Springs, NY; son of Joseph E., Jr. (a taxidermist and publisher) and Marion (a homemaker and publisher) Bruchac; married Carol Worthen (director of a nonprofit organization), June 13, 1964; children: James Edward, Jesse Bowman. *Ethnicity:* "Native American (Abenaki)/Slovak/English." *Education:* Cornell University, A.B., 1965; Syracuse University, M.A., 1966; graduate study at State University of New York—Albany, 1971-73; Union Institute of Ohio Graduate

*Joseph Bruchac* (Photograph by Benjamin Martin. Reproduced by permission.)

School, Ph.D., 1975. *Politics:* "Liberal Democrat." *Religion:* "Methodist and Native-American spiritual traditions." *Hobbies and other interests:* Gardening, music, martial arts.

### Addresses
*Home and office*—Greenfield Review Press, P.O. Box 308, Greenfield Center, NY 12833. *Agent*—Barbara Kouts Agency, P.O. Box 560, Bellport, NY 11713. *E-mail*—nudatlog@earthlink.net.

### Career
Writer, editor, publisher, educator, and musician. Keta Secondary School, Ghana, West Africa, teacher of English and literature, 1966-69; Skidmore College, Saratoga Springs, NY, instructor in creative writing and African and black literatures, 1969-73; University without Walls, coordinator of college program at Great Meadow Correctional Facility, 1974-81; writer and storyteller, 1981—. Greenfield Review Press, Greenfield Center, NY, publisher and editor of *Greenfield Review,* 1969-87; Greenfield Review Literary Center, director, 1981—; editor of periodicals, including *Trojan Horse,* 1964, *Prison Writing Review,* 1976-85, and *Studies in American Indian Literature,* 1989—. Musician with

Dawn Land Singers, recording stories and music on *Abenaki Cultural Heritage* and *Alnobak.* Member of adjunct faculty at Hamilton College, 1983, 1985, 1987, and State University of New York—Albany, 1987-88; storyteller-in-residence at CRC Institute for Arts in Education, 1989-90, and at other institutions, including Oklahoma Summer Arts Institute, St. Regis Mohawk Indian School, Seneca Nation School, Onondaga Indian School, Institute of Alaska Native Arts, and Annsville Youth Facility. Featured storyteller at festivals and conferences; presents workshops, poetry readings, and storytelling programs. Print Center, member of board of directors, 1975-78; Returning the Gift, national chairperson, 1992; judge of competitions, including PEN Prison Writing Awards, 1977, National Book Award for Translation, 1983, and National Book Award for Poetry, 1995; past member of literature panels, Massachusetts Arts Council, Vermont State Arts Council, Illinois Arts Council, and Ohio Arts Council.

## Member

Poetry Society of America, PEN, National Storytelling Association (member of board of directors, 1992-94), Native Writers Circle of the Americas (chairperson, 1992-95), Wordcraft Circle of Native Writers and Storytellers, Hudson Valley Writers Guild, Black Crow Network.

## Awards, Honors

Poetry fellow, Creative Artists Public Service, 1973, 1982; fellow, National Endowment for the Arts, 1974; editors' fellow, Coordinating Council of Literary Magazines, 1980; Rockefeller fellow, 1982; PEN Syndicated Fiction Award, 1983; American Book Award, 1984, for *Breaking Silence;* Yaddo residency, 1984, 1985; Cherokee Nation Prose Award, 1986; fellow, New York State Council on the Arts, 1986; Benjamin Franklin Audio Award, Publishers Marketing Association, 1992, for *The Boy Who Lived with the Bears,* and Person of the Year award, 1993; Hope S. Dean Memorial Award, 1993, for notable achievement in children's literature; Mountains and Plains Award, 1995, for *A Boy Called Slow;* Knickerbocker Award, 1995; *Scientific American* Young Readers Book Award, for *The Story of the Milky Way;* Paterson Prize for Books for Young People, 1996, for *Dog People; Boston Globe/Horn Book* Honor Book selection, 1996, for *The Boy Who Lived with the Bears;* Notable Book in the Field of Social Studies selection, National Council for the Social Studies/International Reading Association (IRA), for *Bowman's Store;* Writer of the Year Award, and Storyteller of the Year Award, Wordcraft Circle of Native Writers and Storytellers, both 1998; Lifetime Achievement Award, Native Writers Circle of the Americas, 1999; Notable Children's Book selection, American Library Association, Best Children's Books of the Year designation, Bank Street College of Education, Parent's Choice Gold Award, and Teachers' Choices designation, IRA, all 2000, all for *Crazy Horse's Vision;* Independent Publishers Outstanding Book of the Year designation, 2003, for *Our Stories Remember;* Sequoyah Book Award, Oklahoma Library Association, 2004, for *Skeleton Man; Storytelling World* Award, 2004, Spur Awards finalist, Western Writers of America, and Teachers' Choices designation, IRA, all 2004, all for *Jim Thorpe's Bright Path; Skipping Stones* Honor Award for Multicultural Children's Literature; Virginia Hamilton Literary Award, 2005; American Indian Youth Literature Award, American Indian Library Association, 2006, for *Hidden Roots;* Paterson Prize for Books for Young People Honor Book selection, 2008, for *Buffalo Song;* numerous state reading association awards.

## Writings

*RETELLER; FOLK-TALE COLLECTIONS*

*Turkey Brother and Other Iroquois Folk Tales,* Crossing Press (Trumansburg, NY), 1975.

*Stone Giants and Flying Heads: Adventure Stories of the Iroquois,* Crossing Press (Trumansburg, NY), 1978.

*Iroquois Stories: Heroes and Heroines, Monsters and Magic,* Crossing Press (Trumansburg, NY), 1985.

*The Wind Eagle,* Bowman Books, 1985.

*The Faithful Hunter, and Other Abenaki Stories,* Bowman Books, 1988.

*Return of the Sun: Native American Tales from the Eastern Woodlands,* Crossing Press (Trumansburg, NY), 1990.

*Native American Stories,* Fulcrum Publishing (Golden, CO), 1991.

*Hoop Snakes, Hide-behinds, and Sidehill Winders,* Crossing Press (Trumansburg, NY), 1991.

(With Jonathan London) *Thirteen Moons on Turtle's Back: A Native American Year of Moons,* Philomel (New York, NY), 1992.

*Flying with the Eagle, Racing the Great Bear: Stories from Native North America,* Bridgewater (New York, NY), 1993, reprinted, Fulcrum Publishing (Golden, CO), 2011.

*Native American Animal Stories,* Fulcrum Publishing (Golden, CO), 1993.

*The Native American Sweat Lodge,* Crossing Press (Trumansburg, NY), 1993.

(With Gayle Ross) *The Girl Who Married the Moon: Tales from Native North America,* BridgeWater (New York, NY), 1994.

*Dog People: Native Dog Stories,* Fulcrum Publishing (Golden, CO), 1995.

*Native Plant Stories,* Fulcrum Publishing (Golden, CO), 1995.

*The Boy Who Lived with the Bears, and Other Iroquois Stories,* HarperCollins (New York, NY), 1995.

*Between Earth and Sky: Legends of Native-American Sacred Places,* illustrated by Thomas Locker, Harcourt (San Diego, CA), 1996.

*The Circle of Thanks,* BridgeWater (New York, NY), 1996.

*Four Ancestors: Stories, Songs, and Poems,* BridgeWater (New York, NY), 1996.

(With son, James Bruchac) *When the Chenoo Howls: Native-American Tales of Terror*, illustrated by William Sauts Netamu'xwe Bock, Walker (New York, NY), 1998.

(With James Bruchac) *Native American Games and Stories*, illustrated by Kayeri Akwek, Fulcrum Publishing (Golden, CO), 2000.

*Foot of the Mountain, and Other Stories*, Holy Cow! Press (Duluth, MN), 2002.

(With James Bruchac) *The Girl Who Helped Thunder and Other Native American Folktales*, illustrated by Stefano Vitale, Sterling Publishing (New York, NY), 2008.

*PICTURE BOOKS*

(Reteller) *The First Strawberries*, illustrated by Anna Vojtech, Dial (New York, NY), 1993.

*Fox Song*, illustrated by Paul Morin, Philomel (New York, NY), 1993.

(Reteller) *The Great Ball Game*, illustrated by Susan L. Roth, Dial (New York, NY), 1994.

*A Boy Called Slow: The True Story of Sitting Bull*, illustrated by Rocco Baviera, Philomel (New York, NY), 1995.

*Gluskabe and the Four Wishes*, illustrated by Christine Shrader, Cobblehill Books (Boston, MA), 1995.

(With Gayle Ross) *The Story of the Milky Way*, illustrated by Virginia A. Stroud, Dial (New York, NY), 1995.

*The Maple Thanksgiving*, illustrated by Anna Vojtech, Celebration (Nobleboro, ME), 1996.

(With Melissa Fawcett) *Makiawisug: Gift of the Little People*, Little People (Warsaw, IN), 1997.

*Many Nations: An Alphabet of Native America*, Troll Publications (Mahwah, NJ), 1997.

*Crazy Horse's Vision*, illustrated by S.D. Nelson, Lee & Low Books (New York, NY), 2000.

*Squanto's Journey: The Story of the First Thanksgiving*, illustrated by Greg Shed, Silver Whistle (San Diego, CA), 2000.

(Reteller, with James Bruchac) *How Chipmunk Got His Stripes*, illustrated by José Aruego and Ariane Dewey, Dial (New York, NY), 2001.

*Seasons of the Circle: A Native-American Year*, illustrated by Robert F. Goetzel, BridgeWater (New York, NY), 2002.

(Reteller, with James Bruchac) *Turtle's Race with Beaver: A Traditional Seneca Story*, illustrated by José Aruego and Ariane Dewey, Dial Books for Young Readers (New York, NY), 2003.

(Reteller, with James Bruchac) *Raccoon's Last Race: A Traditional Abenaki Story*, illustrated by José Aruego and Ariane Dewey, Dial Books for Young Readers (New York, NY), 2004.

*Buffalo Song*, illustrated by Bill Farnsworth, Lee & Low Books (New York, NY), 2008.

*My Father Is Taller than a Tree*, illustrated by Wendy Anderson Halperin, Dial Books for Young Readers (New York, NY), 2010.

*JUVENILE FICTION*

*Children of the Longhouse*, Dial (New York, NY), 1996.

*Eagle Song* (chapter book), Dial (New York, NY), 1997.

*The Arrow over the Door* (chapter book), illustrated by James Watling, Dial (New York, NY), 1998.

*The Heart of a Chief*, Dial (New York, NY), 1998.

*Sacajawea: The Story of Bird Woman and the Lewis and Clark Expedition*, Silver Whistle (San Diego, CA), 2000.

*Skeleton Man*, HarperCollins (New York, NY), 2001.

*The Journal of Jesse Smoke: A Cherokee Boy* ("My Name Is America" series), Scholastic (New York, NY), 2001.

*The Winter People*, Dial (New York, NY), 2002.

*Pocahontas* (young-adult novel), Silver Whistle (Orlando, FL), 2003.

*The Warriors*, Darby Creek (Plain City, OH), 2003.

*Hidden Roots* (novel), Scholastic (New York, NY), 2004.

*Dark Pond*, illustrated by Sally Wern Comport, HarperCollins (New York, NY), 2004.

*Whisper in the Dark*, illustrated by Sally Wern Comport, HarperCollins (New York, NY), 2005.

*Code Talker: A Novel about the Navajo Marines of World War II* (young-adult novel), Dial Books for Young Readers (New York, NY), 2005.

*The Return of Skeleton Man*, illustrated by by Sally Wern Comport, HarperCollins (New York, NY), 2006.

*Wabi: A Hero's Tale* (young-adult novel), Dial (New York, NY), 2006.

*Geronimo* (young-adult novel), Scholastic (New York, NY), 2006.

*Bearwalker*, illustrated by Sally Wern Comport, HarperCollins (New York, NY), 2007.

*The Way*, Darby Creek (Plain City, OH), 2007.

*March toward the Thunder* (young-adult novel), Dial Books for Young Readers (New York, NY), 2008.

*Night Wings* (young-adult novel), illustrated by Sally Wern Comport, HarperCollins (New York, NY), 2009.

*Dragon Castle* (fantasy novel), Dial Books for Young Readers (New York, NY), 2011.

*FICTION; FOR ADULTS*

*The Road to Black Mountain* (short stories), Thorp Springs Press (Austin, TX), 1976.

*The Dreams of Jesse Brown* (short stories), Cold Mountain Press, 1978.

*The White Moose* (short stories), Blue Cloud Quarterly, 1988.

*Turtle Meat, and Other Stories* (short stories), Holy Cow! Press (Minneapolis, MN), 1992.

*Dawn Land* (novel), Fulcrum Publishing (Golden, CO), 1993.

*Long River* (sequel to *Dawn Land*), Fulcrum Publishing (Golden, CO), 1995.

*The Waters Between: A Novel of the Dawn Land*, University Press of New England (Hanover, NH), 1998.

*POETRY*

*Indian Mountain*, Ithaca House (Ithaca, NY), 1971.

*The Buffalo in the Syracuse Zoo,* Greenfield Review Press (Greenfield Center, NY), 1972.

*Great Meadow,* Dustbooks (Paradise, CA), 1973.

*The Manabozho,* Blue Cloud Quarterly, 1973.

*Flow,* Cold Mountain Press, 1975.

*This Earth Is a Drum,* Cold Mountain Press, 1976.

*There Are No Trees inside the Prison,* Blackberry Press, 1978.

*Mu'ndu Wi Go,* Blue Cloud Quarterly, 1978.

*Entering Onondaga,* Cold Mountain Press, 1978.

*The Good Message of Handsome Lake,* Unicorn Press (Greensboro, NC), 1979.

*Translators' Son,* Cross-Cultural Communications (Merrick, NY), 1980.

*Ancestry,* Great Raven (Fort Kent, ME), 1981.

*Remembering the Dawn,* Blue Cloud Quarterly, 1983.

*Walking with My Sons,* Landlocked Press, 1985.

*Tracking,* Ion Books, 1985.

*Near the Mountains,* White Pine (Buffalo, NY), 1986.

*Langes Gedachtnis/Long Memory,* OBEMA (Osnabruck, Germany), 1988.

*The Earth under Sky Bear's Feet,* illustrated by Thomas Locker, Philomel (New York, NY), 1995.

*No Borders,* Holy Cow! Press (Duluth, MN), 1999.

*Above the Line,* West End Press (Albuquerque, NM), 2003.

*NONFICTION*

*The Poetry of Pop,* Dustbooks (Paradise, CA), 1973.

*How to Start and Sustain a Literary Magazine,* Provision (Austin, TX), 1980.

*Survival This Way: Interviews with American Indian Poets,* University of Arizona (Tucson, AZ), 1987.

(With Michael Caduto) *Keepers of the Earth: Native American Stories and Environmental Activities for Children,* Fulcrum Publishing (Golden, CO), 1989.

(With Michael Caduto) *Keepers of the Animals: Native American Stories and Wildlife Activities for Children,* Fulcrum Publishing (Golden, CO), 1990.

(With Michael Caduto) *Keepers of the Night: Native American Stories and Nocturnal Activities for Children,* Fulcrum Publishing (Golden, CO), 1994.

(With Michael Caduto) *Keepers of Life: Discovering Plants through Native American Stories and Earth Activities for Children,* Fulcrum Publishing (Golden, CO), 1994.

*Native Wisdom,* HarperSanFrancisco (San Francisco, CA), 1995.

*Roots of Survival: Native American Storytelling and the Sacred,* Fulcrum Publishing (Golden, CO), 1996.

(With Michael Caduto) *Native American Gardening,* Fulcrum Publishing (Golden, CO), 1996.

*Bowman's Store* (autobiography), Dial (New York, NY), 1997.

*Lasting Echoes: An Oral History of Native American People,* Harcourt (New York, NY), 1997.

*Tell Me a Tale: A Book about Storytelling,* Harcourt (New York, NY), 1997.

*Buffalo Boy* (biography), illustrated by Rocco Baviera, Silver Whistle Books (San Diego, CA), 1998.

*Seeing the Circle* (autobiography), photographs by John Christian Fine, R.C. Owen (Katonah, NY), 1999.

*The Trail of Tears* (chapter book), illustrated by Diana Magnuson, Random House (New York, NY), 1999.

*Trails of Tears, Paths of Beauty,* National Geographic Society (Washington, DC), 2000.

*Navajo Long Walk: The Tragic Story of a Proud People's Forced March from Their Homeland,* illustrated by Shonto Begay, National Geographic Society (Washington, DC), 2002.

*Our Stories Remember: American Indian History, Culture, and Values through Storytelling,* Fulcrum Publishing (Golden, CO), 2003.

*Jim Thorpe's Bright Path* (biography; for children), illustrated by S.D. Nelson, Lee & Low Books (New York, NY), 2004.

(With James Bruchac) *Rachel Carson: Preserving a Sense of Wonder* (biography; for children), Fulcrum Publishing (Golden, CO), 2004.

*At the Edge of Ridge Road* (memoir), Milkweed Editions (Minneapolis, MN), 2005.

*Jim Thorpe: Original All-American* (biography; for children), Dial (New York, NY), 2006.

*OTHER*

*Pushing up the Sky: Seven Native American Plays for Children,* illustrated by Teresa Flavin, Dial (New York, NY), 2000.

(Editor) *Lay-ups and Long Shots: An Anthology of Short Stories,* Darby Creek Publishing (Plain City, OH), 2008.

Also editor of anthologies, including *The Last Stop: Prison Writings from Comstock Prison,* 1973; *Words from the House of the Dead: Prison Writing from Soledad,* 1974; *Aftermath: Poetry in English from Africa, Asia, and the Caribbean,* 1977; *The Next World: Thirty-two Third World American Poets,* 1978; *Songs from Turtle Island: Thirty-two American Indian Poets,* [Yugoslavia], 1982; *Songs from This Earth on Turtle's Back: Contemporary American Indian Poetry,* 1983; *Breaking Silence: Contemporary Asian-American Poets,* 1983; *The Light from Another Country: Poetry from American Prisons,* 1984; *North Country: An Anthology of Contemporary Writing from the Adirondacks and the Upper Hudson Valley,* 1986; *New Voices from the Longhouse: Contemporary Iroquois Writing,* 1989; *Raven Tells Stories: Contemporary Alaskan Native Writing,* 1990; *Singing of Earth,* 1993; *Returning the Gift,* 1994; *Smoke Rising,* 1995; and *Native Wisdom,* 1995.

Work recorded on audiotape includes *Iroquois Stories, Alnobak, Adirondack Tall Tales,* and *Abenaki Cultural Heritage,* all Good Mind Records; and *Gluskabe Stories,* Yellow Moon Press. Work represented in numerous anthologies, including *Carriers of the Dream Wheel; Come to Power; For Neruda, for Chile; New Worlds of Literature; Paris Review Anthology, Sports Shorts: An Anthology of Short Stories,* 2005; and *Amazing Faces,* edited by Lee Bennett Hopkins, Lee & Low Books (New York, NY), 2010. Contributor of numerous stories, poems, articles, and reviews to magazines, including *American Poetry Review, Akwesasne Notes, Beloit Poetry Journal, Chariton Review, Kalliope, Mid-American Review, Nation, Poetry Northwest, River Styx,* and *Virginia Quarterly Review.* Member of editorial board, Cross-Cultural Communications, *Parabola, Storytelling Journal, MELUS,* and *Obsidian.* Translator from Abenaki, Ewe, Iroquois, and Spanish.

## Adaptations

Several of Bruchac's books have been recorded on audiocassette, including *Keepers of the Earth, Keepers of the Animals, Keepers of Life,* and *Dawn Land,* all released by Fulcrum Publishing; and *The Boy Who Lived with the Bears,* released by Caedmon/Parabola. *Dawn Land* was adapted as a graphic novel by Will Davis, First Second (New York, NY), 2010.

## Sidelights

A novelist, poet, editor, storyteller, and scholar, Joseph Bruchac draws on his ethnic heritage in producing his critically acclaimed works, such as *The Girl Who Married the Moon: Tales from Native North America, Dawn Land, Buffalo Song,* and *March toward the Thunder.* A member of the Abenaki tribe, Bruchac "has devoted his life to translating one culture to another through his

*Bruchac's retelling of a story from the Cherokee tribe in* **The First Strawberries** *is brought to life in colorful illustrations by Anna Vojtech.*
(Illustration copyright © 1993 by Anna Vojtech. Reproduced by permission of Dial Books for Young Readers, a division of Penguin Young Readers Group, a member of Penguin Group (USA) Inc.)

writing and teaching," according to *MELUS* contributor Meredith Ricker. "My interest in Native American stories comes from a number of what I consider to be logical sources," Bruchac remarked in an interview on the Scholastic Web site. "First of all, it is part of my own cultural heritage—my family is Abenaki on my mother's side. Second, I've always been fascinated by the natural world. Many American Indian stories and traditions help us understand and relate to nature. And third, the lessons found in our traditional stories seem to be even more meaningful today."

Bruchac grew up in New York's Adirondack Mountain region, raised by his maternal grandparents. Of Slovak heritage on his father's side, he also gained, on his mother's, a mixture of English and Native American. "Everybody in the county knew he was Indian," Bruchac recalled of his grandfather in an interview with Susan Stan for *Five Owls.* "It was taken for granted—but he would not talk about it because there was a lot of shame connected with being dark-skinned, being native." That feeling of shame is one of the reasons Bruchac has devoted a large portion of his life to writing, story telling, and working with children in order to make different cultures understood and respected.

Despite his neglected heritage, Bruchac felt drawn to his Native American roots. As a teenager he began to meet other Native Americans and to take interest in Abenaki culture and language. His first poems while a student at Cornell University were about "American Indian themes," he recalled in an interview with Kit Alderdice for *Publishers Weekly.* A deep immersion into such themes did not happen until after he completed his master's degree at Syracuse State University and spent three years teaching in Africa with his wife. Returning to the United States, Bruchac settled in the home where he had grown up, and he eventually had two sons of his own. He ultimately converted the former house and gas station/general store of his grandparents into a home and an office that would house the Greenfield Review Press, an independent publishing house he founded with his wife. "Our aim was to publish people who wouldn't normally be published," Bruchac explained in an interview with Becky Rodia for *Teaching K-8.* "At the time, that meant people in prison, women writers, African writers, Native American writers, Asian American writers and other ethnic minorities." Their literary magazine, *Greenfield Review,* published multicultural poetry and stories for over twenty years while its publishing arm released dozens of titles by Bruchac and many others.

With the 1975 publication of *Turkey Brother and Other Tales,* Bruchac's work took a new turn. Recalling several Iroquois legends and stories from his childhood, he had started to collect them in earnest to tell to his own sons, with whom he has a close relationship. He searched out such stories from books and from tribal elders, and many of these found a retelling in *Turkey Brother, and Other Tales.* The first three stories feature

Turtle, a trickster character similar to the Anansi figure of Ashanti folklore, and in these stories he is both a crafty winner and is himself undone. "All the legends are fascinating and well told," commented a reviewer in *Publishers Weekly,* and a *Booklist* critic wrote that "the prose is smooth, simple and written to be read aloud." Bruchac did exactly that at one bookstore signing, but halfway through reading the first tale, he stopped and began telling the tales from memory, enchanting his audience and also starting his work as a storyteller.

Further Iroquois legends and adventure stories are collected in *Stone Giants and Flying Heads: Adventure Stories of the Iroquois,* which introduces readers to characters such as the trickster Skunny-Wundy and highlights virtues such as "bravery, obedience or goodness rewarded," according to a critic in *Booklist.* Gale Eaton noted in *School Library Journal* that the stories "should be quite accessible to reluctant readers." Bruchac's interest in his heritage paid off close to home. "My own sons have grown up taking such things as sweat lodges and powwows and pride in Indian ancestry for granted. The small amount I have learned I've tried, when right to do so, to share with others," he once wrote in *Native North American Literature.*

Bruchac has continued his exploration of Native American history, culture, and literature, as well as his fascination with the themes of spirituality and the sacredness of the natural world, in his picture books, novels, and story collections for both young and old. In *Thirteen Moons on Turtle's Back: A Native American Year of Moons* he employs poetry and oil paintings to tell thirteen different moon legends from various tribes from Cree to Huron. In *Turtle Meat and Other Stories* Bruchac again draws on Abenaki heritage to tell seventeen stories about Native and white relations in the Adirondacks from Viking times to World War II. He also incorporates ideas from the Native Americans' ever-present eco-consciousness. "Style, humor and grace enliven familiar themes; atypical for folklore writing, most characters emerge three-dimensional and real," stated a contributor in reviewing *Turtle Meat and Other Stories* for *Kirkus Reviews.*

*Dawn Land,* Bruchac's first novel, introduces readers to Young Hunter, a character who returns in *Long River,* as he battles both a wooly mammoth and an evil giant. In *Dawn Land* and *Long River,* as well as the concluding novel of the sequence, *The Waters Between,* Bruchac incorporates actual myths from his own Abenaki heritage. His children's stories, like his novels, entertain and educate young readers by interweaving Native American history and myth. The biography *A Boy Called Slow,* for example, recounts the story of the Lakota boy who would grow up to become Sitting Bull. Bruchac's ability to "gently correct" stereotypes of Native-American culture was noted by Carolyn Polese in *School Library Journal.* In *The Great Ball Game* he relates the importance of ball games in Native-American tradition as a substitute for war, tying neatly together history and ethics lessons in "an entertaining tale," commented Polese. He also combines several versions of a Native-American tale in *Gluskabe and the Four Wishes.*

Bruchac's nonfiction titles for young people include biographies of Native Americans as well as of pivotal figures in the environmental movement. In *Rachel Carson: Preserving a Sense of Wonder* he presents a biography of the author of *Silent Spring,* a book credited with inspiring the environmental movement in the 1960s. In *Booklist* Carolyn Phelan noted that "Bruchac writes lyrically about [Carson's] . . . love of nature, particularly the ocean, and concludes with an appreciation of her impact on the environment." The picture-book biography *Jim Thorpe's Bright Path* recounts the life of famed Native-American athlete. *School Library Journal* contributor Liza Graybill noted that Bruchac's "theme of overcoming personal and societal obstacles to reach success is strongly expressed." Bruchac returns to Thorpe in *Jim Thorpe: Original All-American,* a fictionalized account of the iconic figure's life. Concentrating on Thorpe's early accomplishments, Bruchac writes in the athlete's own voice, "creating a believably plainspoken, youthfully blinkered narration and an account of Thorpe's life that's both poignant and triumphant," as Deborah Stevenson maintained in *Horn Book.* According to a contributor in *Kirkus Reviews, Jim Thorpe* "is a superb blend of fiction and nonfiction, rooted in the author's usual careful research."

Many of Bruchac's titles for the very young are based on traditional Native-American tales. *The First Strawberries,* his first picture book, is based on a Cherokee tale, while *Raccoon's Last Race* features a story drawn from the Abenaki tradition. The latter tale explains how Raccoon, once tall and fast, became the squat, slow creature he is today. Noting that *Raccoon's Last Race* is one of several collaborations between Bruchac, son James Bruchac, and husband-and-wife illustration team José Aruego and Ariane Dewey, a *Kirkus Reviews* contributor wrote: "Readers will hope this foursome keeps on rolling." *Horn Book* reviewer Kitty Flynn noted that "the Bruchacs' well-paced retelling is alive with sound, . . . making the story well suited for reading aloud."

Another work for beginning readers, *My Father Is Taller than a Tree,* celebrates the joys of the father-son relationship through verse while in Bruchac's picture book *Buffalo Song* Walking Coyote, a Native American, helps save the buffalo from extinction. "The gentle narrative eloquently conveys the beauty and importance of this animal," commented *School Library Journal* reviewer Steven Engelfried in his review of *Buffalo Song.* In an interview for the Lee & Low Web site, Bruchac noted that "*Buffalo Song* is a sort of hybrid of fiction and nonfiction in that it is a story that exists within a well-researched historical framework, telling the story of real events and real people (without changing them), but adding details within that framework—such as conversations between characters or imagining the thoughts or motivations of the principal actors."

Demonstrating his ability to write stories in a wide-range of genres, Bruchac crafts a Native-American mystery in *Skeleton Man. School Library Journal* contributor Carol A. Edwards remarked favorably on his skills as a writer of suspense, noting that, "better than many mystery writers . . . Bruchac makes every word add to the tension right up to the final few pages." Strangely, the parents of a sixth-grade student named Molly have disappeared. An old, bony stranger then shows up, claiming he is Molly's only remaining kin and taking her to his home. Only allowed out of the house to attend school, Molly uses her time locked in her bedroom to decipher her dreams, a talent taught to her by her Mohawk relatives. With the aid of a teacher and other resources, Molly uses her skills and courage to solve the mystery of what actually happened to her parents. Finding the book's blend of "traditional and contemporary cultural references" appealing, a critic in *Publishers Weekly* predicted that "the quick pace and suspense" of *Skeleton Man* "will likely hold the interest of young readers." *The Return of Skeleton Man*, a sequel, "blends Mohawk tradition and legend with contemporary details," according to *Booklist* contributor Hazel Rochman.

In *The Dark Pond* Bruchac revisits a genre he previously explored in *Skeleton Man*: the young-adult thriller. In *The Dark Pond* Arnie, a half-Shawnee student at an all-white prep school, is drawn to a mysterious dark pool in the woods. He senses that something is lurking there, and his fears are confirmed when he discovers that Native-American groundskeeper Mitch Sabattis believes that a gigantic worm lives in the pond. Mitch is determined to kill the creature, and Arnie, remembering the traditional tales of his family, decides to do what he can to help slay this monster. *The Dark Pond* "is a creepy, fast-moving tale that will appeal to fans of horror stories, with a message about self-discovery neatly tucked in as well," wrote Paula Rohrlick in *Kliatt*. B. Allison Gray noted in *School Library Journal* that Bruchac's "eerie story skillfully entwines Native American lore, suspense, and the realization that people are not always what they seem."

Another teen thriller, *Whisper in the Dark*, wraps Narragansett legend around an all-too-real modern danger as Maddie confronts the mystery of a seemingly supernatural stalker. "Bruchac interweaves suspense with Indian folklore endlessly," commented Claire Rosser in *Kliatt*, while Wendi Hoffenberg wrote in *School Library Journal* that "Maddie's narration is swirl and spare, creating a mood of terror tempered by Narragansett words and chants of courage."

Bruchac draws on history for many of his novels for teens. *Code Talker: A Novel about the Navajo Marines of World War II*, for example, gives readers an inside perspective on the role Navajo Marines played in sending vital encoded messages during World War II. Told from the perspective of sixteen-year-old Ned Begay, who is technically too young to be in the military, the story reveals how the Navajo language, once a tongue

*In his artwork for Bruchac's* Crazy Horse's Vision *S.D. Nelson captures the majesty of the well-known Native-American leader.* (Illustration copyright © 2000 by S.D. Nelson. Reproduced with permission of Lee & Low Books, Inc.)

the U.S. government attempted to eliminate, became valued highly by the U.S. military during wartime. "The narrative pulls no punches about war's brutality and never adopts an avuncular tone," noted Phelan in *Booklist*. As *Kliatt* reviewer Paula Rohrlick commented, "readers unfamiliar with the fascinating story of the code talkers will come away impressed by their achievements."

In *Geronimo* Bruchac relates the story of the famous Native-American leader through the eyes of the man's adopted grandson. "Fans of history, or of themes of survival and freedom, will find it fascinating—certainly different from other fare about the man," wrote Nina Lindsay in her *School Library Journal* review of the novel, while he weaves fact and fiction together in *Geronimo* Other novels draw solely on legend. In *Wabi: A Hero's Tale* an owl learns a secret about its people: it can shape shift and take human form. Wabi falls in love with a local tribal woman, but her people banish him when they discover his true identity. In order to save his love's people the shapeshifting owl must go on a dangerous quest. "Bruchac's storytelling skills are on full display in this tale," wrote a *Publishers Weekly* contributor, and a critic for *Kirkus Reviews* maintained of *Wabi* that "readers won't be able to turn the pages fast enough."

A Native-American teen calls upon his Mohawk ancestors to help him defeat a legendary creature in *Bear-*

*walker,* an "exciting horror story," according to Rohrlick in *Kliatt.* While on a class trip in the Adirondacks, eighth-grader Baron Braun senses an evil presence stalking his classmates: a vicious bear that masquerades as a human. When the only road to the isolated camp is blocked by greedy land-developers, Baron springs into action to rescue the group. "Part wilderness adventure, part grisly monster tale, this is also an exciting coming-of-age story," Rochman noted of *Bearwalker.* In *Night Wings* a thirteen year old teams with his grandfather, an Abenaki wilderness guide, to lead a film crew searching for the Pmola, a mythical winged beast. The Native American lore "injects this otherwise straightforward thriller with a sense of meaning and even spirituality," Daniel Kraus remarked in his review of *Night Wings* for *Booklist.*

A contemporary young-adult novel, *The Way* centers on Cody LeBeau, a fatherless and oftenpicked-upon high-school freshman who dreams of becoming an heroic ninja. When Cody's uncle John arrives in town for a mixed martial arts competition, he takes the teen under his wing, teaching him a philosophy known as "The Way," based on Native American principles. Cody's newfound skills are put to the test when a crisis arises at his school. According to a *Kirkus Reviews* contributor, "Bruchac successfully pulls together a winning mix of elements" in the tale.

A member of the Abenaki tribe enlists with the Union Army in *March toward the Thunder* a work of historical fiction set during the U.S. Civil War. Assigned to the Irish Brigade, a unit famed for its courage and daring, fifteen-year-old Louis Nolette (a character based on the author's great-grandfather) is regarded with suspicion by his white comrades although he quickly earns their respect with his exploits on the battlefield. "The fact that so many Native Americans fought in the American Civil War helps to underscore that many men of various heritages, who had no political or financial gain from the outcome of the war, gave their lives to it," James Blasingame observed in the *Journal of Adolescent & Adult Literacy.* "*March toward the Thunder* is a powerful book that centers on the senseless nature of

***Wendy Anderson Halperin created the family-centered artwork in Bruchac's story for* My Father Is Taller than a Tree.** (Illustration copyright © 2010 by Wendy Halperin. Reproduced with permission of Dial Books for Young Readers, a division of Penguin Young Readers Group, a member of Penguin Group (USA), Inc.)

war and the irony that it can actually draw people of different heritages together rather than drive them apart."

Bruchac believes that storytellers have a responsibility to improving society. As he commented on the Scholastic Web site, "The central themes in my work are simple ones—that we have to listen to each other and to the earth, that we have to respect each other and the earth, that we never know anyone until we know what they have in their heart."

## Biographical and Critical Sources

*BOOKS*

*Children's Literature Review,* Volume 46, Gale (Detroit, MI), 1998.
*Dictionary of Literary Biography,* Volume 342, *Twentieth-Century American Nature Poets,* Gale (Detroit, MI), 2008.
*Native North American Literature,* Gale (Detroit, MI), 1994.
*Notable Native Americans,* Gale (Detroit, MI), 1995.
*St. James Guide to Children's Writers,* 5th edition, St. James Press (Detroit, MI), 1999.

*PERIODICALS*

*Booklist,* March 1, 1976, review of *Turkey Brother and Other Iroquois Folk Tales,* p. 974; April 1, 1979, review of *Stone Giants and Flying Heads: Adventure Stories of the Iroquois,* p. 1217; July, 1993, Carolyn Phelan, review of *The First Strawberries: A Cherokee Story,* p. 1969; October 15, 1998, Randy Meyer, review of *The Heart of a Chief,* p. 420; April 1, 2000, Gillian Engberg, review of *Sacajawea: The Story of Bird Woman and the Lewis and Clark Expedition,* p. 1473; July, 2001, Karen Hutt, review of *The Journal of Jesse Smoke: A Cherokee Boy,* p. 2005; October 1, 2002, Heather Hepler, review of *Seasons of the Circle: A Native-American Year,* p. 316, and GraceAnne A. DeCandido, review of *The Winter People,* p. 322; April 15, 2003, Deborah Donovan, review of *Our Stories Remember: American Indian History, Culture, and Values through Storytelling,* p. 1444; September 15, 2003, Ed Sullivan, review of *Pocahontas,* p. 229, and John Peters, review of *Turtle's Race with Beaver,* p. 244; July, 2004, Carolyn Phelan, review of *Rachel Carson: Preserving a Sense of Wonder,* p. 1838; August, 2004, Todd Morning, review of *The Dark Pond,* p. 1932, and Stephanie Zvirin, review of *Jim Thorpe's Bright Path,* p. 1938; February 15, 2005, Carolyn Phelan, review of *Code Talker: A Novel about the Navajo Marines of World War II,* p. 1078; September 1, 2005, Holly Koelling, review of *Whisper in the Dark,* p. 131; March 15, 2006, GraceAnne A. DeCandido, review of *Geronimo,* p. 43; September 15, 2006, Hazel Rochman, review of *The Return of Skeleton Man,*

p. 62; September 15, 2007, Hazel Rochman, review of *Bearwalker,* p. 65; October 1, 2007, Heather Booth, review of *The Way,* p. 48; April 15, 2008, Carolyn Phelan, review of *March toward the Thunder,* p. 53; June 1, 2009, Daniel Kraus, review of *Night Wings,* p. 56; January 1, 2010, Julie Cummins, review of *My Father Is Taller than a Tree,* p. 98.
*Five Owls,* February, 1993, Susan Stan, "Joseph Bruchac: Poet, Storyteller, Publisher, Activist," pp. 57-58.
*Horn Book,* January-February, 2005, Kitty Flynn, review of *Raccoon's Last Race,* p. 102; January-February, 2009, Deborah Stevenson, review of *Jim Thorpe: Original All-American,* p. 51, and Barbara Bader, review of *The Girl Who Helped Thunder and Other Native American Folktales,* p. 106.
*Journal of Adolescent & Adult Literacy,* February, 2009, James Blasingame, review of *March toward the Thunder,* p. 443, and interview with Bruchac, p. 445.
*Kirkus Reviews,* October 1, 1992, review of *Turtle Meat, and Other Stories,* p. 1201; January 1, 2004, review of *Hidden Roots,* p. 34; October 15, 2004, review of *Raccoon's Last Race,* p. 1002; January 15, 2005, review of *Code Talker,* p. 117; July 1, 2005, review of *Whisper in the Dark,* p. 732; February 1, 2006, review of *Wabi: A Hero's Tale,* p. 128; June 1, 2006, review of *Jim Thorpe,* p. 569; June 1, 2007, review of *Bearwalker;* September 15, 2007, review of *The Way;* April 15, 2008, review of *March toward the Thunder;* May 15, 2008, review of *Buffalo Song;* June 1, 2009, review of *Night Wings.*
*Kliatt,* July, 2004, Paula Rohrlick, review of *The Dark Pond,* p. 7; March, 2005, Paula Rohrlick, review of *Code Talker,* p. 8; July, 2005, Claire Rosser, review of *Whisper in the Dark,* p. 8; January, 2006, Edna Boardman, review of *Foot of the Mountain, and Other Stories,* p. 26; March, 2006, Paula Rohrlick, review of *Geronimo,* p. 6; March, 2007, Janet Julian, review of *The Girl Who Married the Moon: Tales from Native North America,* p. 30; July, 2007, Paula Rohrlick, review of *Bearwalker,* p. 10; September, 2007, Paula Rohrlick, review of *The Way,* p. 8; May, 2008, Paula Rohrlick, review of *March toward the Thunder,* p. 7.
*MELUS,* fall, 1996, Meredith Ricker, interview with Bruchac, pp. 159-178.
*Publishers Weekly,* April 26, 1976, review of *Turkey Brother and Other Iroquois Folk Tales,* p. 60; October 19, 1992, review of *Turtle Meat, and Other Stories,* p. 73; March 15, 1993, review of *Dawn Land,* p. 68; January 9, 1995, review of *A Boy Called Slow,* p. 64; October 2, 1995, review of *The Story of the Milky Way,* p. 74; February 19, 1996, Kit Alderdice, "Joseph Bruchac: Sharing a Native-American Heritage," pp. 191-192; November 16, 1998, review of *The Heart of a Chief,* p. 75; February 14, 2000, review of *Sacajawea,* p. 201; August 13, 2001, review of *Skeleton Man,* p. 313; May 31, 2004, review of *Jim Thorpe's Bright Path,* p. 76; May 1, 2006, review of *Wabi,* p. 64; July 24, 2006, review of *Jim Thorpe,* p. 60.
*School Library Journal,* April, 1979, Gale Eaton, review of *Stone Giants and Flying Heads,* p. 53; December, 1992, Yvonne Frey, review of *Turtle Meat, and Other Stories,* p. 137; August, 1993, Judy Sokoll, review of

*Dawn Land,* p. 205; September, 1993, Yvonne Frey, review of *Flying with the Eagle, Racing the Great Bear: Stories from Native North America,* p. 238; September, 1995, Donna L. Scanlon, review of *The Story of the Milky Way,* p. 192; October, 1995, Carolyn Polese, review of *A Boy Called Slow,* p. 145; January, 1996, Kathleen McCabe, review of *Dog People: Native Dog Stories,* pp. 114-115; August, 2001, Carol A. Edwards, review of *Skeleton Man,* p. 176; July, 2002, Anne Chapman Callaghan, review of *Navajo Long Walk: The Tragic Story of a Proud People's Forced March from Their Homeland,* p. 131; November, 2002, Rita Soltan, review of *The Winter People,* p. 154; July, 2003, S.K. Joiner, review of *Our Stories Remember,* p. 155; February, 2004, Alison Follos, review of *Hidden Roots,* p. 141; May, 2004, Sean George, review of *Pocahontas,* p. 140; June, 2004, Liza Graybill, review of *Jim Thorpe's Bright Path,* p. 124; August, 2004, B. Allison Gray, review of *The Dark Pond,* p. 115; December, 2004, Catherine Threadgill, review of *Raccoon's Last Race,* p. 127; May, 2005, Patricia Manning, review of *Code Talker,* p. 24; August, 2005, Wendi Hoffenberg, review of *Whisper in the Dark,* p. 121; November, 2005, Alison Follos, review of *Sports Shorts: An Anthology of Short Stories,* p. 128; April, 2006, Lisa Prolman, review of *Wabi,* and Nina Lindsay, review of *Geronimo,* both p. 134; August, 2006, Adrienne Furness, review of *The Return of Skeleton Man,* p. 116, and Janice Hayes, review of *Jim Thorpe,* p. 134; August, 2007, Sheila Fiscus, review of *Bearwalker,* p. 111; June, 2008, Steven Engelfried, review

of *Buffalo Song,* p. 119; March, 2010, Maryann H. Owen, review of *My Father Is Taller than a Tree,* p. 116.

*Teacher Librarian,* February, 2005, Betty Winslow, review of *The Journal of Jesse Smoke,* p. 14.

*Teaching K-8,* January, 2002, Becky Rodia, "The Good Mind of Joseph Bruchac," pp. 56-58.

*Voice of Youth Advocates,* February, 2006, Tracy Piombo, review of *At the End of Ridge Road,* p. 508.

*ONLINE*

*Cooperative Children's Book Center Web site,* http://www. education.wisc.edu/ccbc/ (October 22, 1999), Eliza T. Dresang, interview with Bruchac.

*Lee & Low Books Web site,* http://www.leeandlow.com/ (April 1, 2011), "Booktalk with Joseph Bruchac."

*Joseph Bruchac Home Page,* http://www.josephbruchac. com (April 1, 2011).

*Scholastic Web site,* http://www2.scholastic.com/ (April 1, 2011), autobiographical essay and interview transcript.*

\*     \*     \*

# BRUCHAC, Joseph, III
## See BRUCHAC, Joseph

# C-D

## CARTER, David A. 1957-

### Personal

Born March 4, 1957, in Salt Lake City, UT; son of H. Craig (a draftsperson) and Lavon (a homemaker) Carter; married Noelle Lokvig (an illustrator and author), August 10, 1985; children: Molly, Emma. *Education:* Attended Utah State University. *Hobbies and other interests:* Skiing, travel, gardening, fishing, tennis.

### Addresses

*Home and office*—14009 Sheridan Ct., Auburn, CA 95603. *E-mail*—PopArt123@aol.com.

### Career

Author, illustrator, and paper engineer. Graphic designer and advertising illustrator, c. late 1970s; Intervisual Communications, Inc., Los Angeles, CA, artist, paper engineer, and book designer, c. 1980-87; freelance author and illustrator of children's books, 1987—. Presenter at schools.

### Writings

SELF-ILLUSTRATED

*What's in My Pocket?,* Putnam (New York, NY), 1989.
*Surprise Party,* Grosset & Dunlap (New York, NY), 1990.
(With Lynette Ruschak) *Snack Attack: A Tasty Pop-up Book,* Simon & Schuster (New York, NY), 1990.
*Playful Pandas,* National Geographic Society (Washington, DC), 1991.
*In a Dark, Dark Wood,* Simon & Schuster (New York, NY), 1991, published as *In a Dark, Dark Wood: An Old Tale with a New Twist,* Simon & Schuster (New York, NY), 2002.
*Opposites,* Simon & Schuster (New York, NY), 1993.

*David A. Carter* (Photograph by Keith Sutter. Reproduced by permission.)

*Colors,* Simon & Schuster (New York, NY), 1993.
*Counting,* Simon & Schuster (New York, NY), 1993.
*I'm Shy,* Simon & Schuster (New York, NY), 1993.
(With Roger Smith) *In and Out,* Simon & Schuster (New York, NY), 1993.
*Says Who?,* Simon & Schuster (New York, NY), 1993.

(With James Diaz) *The Elements of Pop-up: A Pop-up Book for Aspiring Paper Engineers,* Simon & Schuster (New York, NY), 1999.

*Flapdoodle Dinosaurs: A Colorful Pop-up Book,* Simon & Schuster (New York, NY), 2001.

*Who Took the Cookie from the Cookie Jar?: Fun Flaps and Pop-up Surprises,* Scholastic (New York, NY), 2002.

*Glitter Critters,* Piggy Toes Press (Los Angeles, CA), 2003.

(With James Diaz) *Let's Make It Pop-up,* Simon & Schuster (New York, NY), 2004.

*One Red Dot,* Simon & Schuster (New York, NY), 2005.

*Woof! Woof!,* Simon & Schuster (New York, NY), 2006.

*Blue 2,* Simon & Schuster (New York, NY), 2006.

*600 Black Spots: A Pop-up Book for Children of All Ages,* Little Simon (New York, NY), 2007.

*The Glittery Crittery Pop-up Counting Book,* Intervisual Books (Atlanta, GA), 2007.

*Whoo? Whoo?,* Little Simon (New York, NY), 2007.

*Yellow Square: A Pop-up Book for Children of All Ages,* Little Simon (New York, NY), 2008.

*White Noise: A Pop-up Book for Children of All Ages,* Little Simon (New York, NY), 2009.

### SELF-ILLUSTRATED; "BUGS" SERIES

*How Many Bugs in a Box?,* Simon & Schuster (New York, NY), 1988.

*More Bugs in Boxes,* Simon & Schuster (New York, NY), 1990.

*Jingle Bugs,* Simon & Schuster (New York, NY), 1992.

*Alpha Bugs,* Simon & Schuster (New York, NY), 1994.

*Love Bugs,* Simon & Schuster (New York, NY), 1995.

*Feely Bugs,* Simon & Schuster (New York, NY), 1995, board-book edition, 2005.

*Bugs in Space,* Simon & Schuster (New York, NY), 1997.

*Finger Bugs Love Bug,* Simon & Schuster (New York, NY), 1997.

*Bugs at Play,* Simon & Schuster (New York, NY), 1997.

*Bugs at Work,* Simon & Schuster (New York, NY), 1997.

*Busy Bugs, Lazy Bugs,* Simon & Schuster (New York, NY), 1997.

*Bugs on the Go,* Simon & Schuster (New York, NY), 1997.

*Stinky Bugs,* Simon & Schuster (New York, NY), 1998.

*Bed Bugs: A Pop-up Bedtime Book,* Simon & Schuster (New York, NY), 1998.

*The Twelve Bugs of Christmas: A Pop-up Christmas Counting Book,* Simon & Schuster (New York, NY), 1999.

*Giggle Bugs: A Lift-and-Laugh Book,* Simon & Schuster (New York, NY), 1999.

*Easter Bugs: A Springtime Pop-up,* Simon & Schuster (New York, NY), 2001.

*Chanukah Bugs: A Pop-up Celebration,* Simon & Schuster (New York, NY), 2002.

*Peekaboo Bugs: A Hide-and-Seek Book,* Simon & Schuster (New York, NY), 2002.

*Halloween Bugs: A Trick-or-Treat Pop-up,* Simon & Schuster (New York, NY), 2003.

*Beach Bugs: A Sunny Pop-up Book,* Little Simon (New York, NY), 2008.

*The Big Bug Book: A Pop-up Celebration,* Little Simon (New York, NY), 2008.

*School Bugs: An Elementary Pop-up Book,* Little Simon (New York, NY), 2009.

*Snow Bugs: A Wintery Pop-up Book,* Little Simon (New York, NY), 2009.

*Bedtime Bugs: A Pop-up Bedtime Book,* Little Simon (New York, NY), 2010.

### AND ILLUSTRATOR, WITH WIFE, NOELLE CARTER

*I'm a Little Mouse,* Holt (New York, NY), 1990.

*Merry Christmas, Little Mouse: A Scratch-the-Scent and Lift-the-Flap Book,* Holt (New York, NY), 1993.

*Peek-a-Boo Little Mouse: A Pat and Play Lift-the-Flap Book,* Holt (New York, NY), 1993.

*The Nutcracker: A Pop-up Adaptation of E.T.A. Hoffman's Original Tale,* Simon & Schuster (New York, NY), 2000.

*Little Mouse's Christmas,* Piggy Toes Press (Los Angeles, CA), 2003.

### ILLUSTRATOR, DESIGNER, AND/OR PAPER ENGINEER

(With Dick Dudley) Joan Knight, *Journey to Egypt,* illustrated by Piero Ventura, Viking Kestrel (New York, NY), 1986.

Peter Seymour, *Sleeping Beauty,* illustrated by John Wallner, Viking Penguin (New York, NY), 1987.

Peter Seymour, *The Three Little Pigs,* illustrated by John Wallner, Viking Penguin (New York, NY), 1987.

Jannat Messenger, *Lullaby and Goodnight: A Bedtime Book with Music,* Aladdin Books (New York, NY), 1988.

Peter Seymour, *How Things Are Made,* illustrated by Linda Griffith, E.P. Dutton (New York, NY), 1988.

Seymour Simon, *How to Be an Ocean Scientist in Your Own Home,* Lippincott (Philadelphia, PA), 1988.

Peter Seymour, *What's in the Jungle?,* Holt (New York, NY), 1988.

Peter Seymour, *If Pigs Could Fly,* Child's Play, 1988.

Tony Ross, *The Pop-up Book of Nonsense Verse,* Random House (New York, NY), 1989.

Karen E. Lotz, *The First Christmas: With Four Classic Nativity Ornaments,* illustrated by Joyce Patti, Dutton Children's Books (New York, NY), 1990.

Peter Seymour, *What's in the Prehistoric Forest?,* Holt (New York, NY), 1990.

Peter Seymour, *What's in the Deep Blue Sea?,* Holt (New York, NY), 1990.

Olive A. Wadsworth, *Over in the Meadow: An Old Counting Rhyme,* Scholastic (New York, NY), 1992.

Peter Seymour, *What's in the Cave?,* Holt (New York, NY), 1995.

Grace Maccarone, *Cars, Cars, Cars,* Scholastic (New York, NY), 1995.

Peter Seymour, *What's at the Beach?,* Holt (New York, NY), 1995.

Sarah Weeks, *Noodles: A Pop-up Book,* HarperCollins (New York, NY), 1996.

Mary Serfozo, *There's a Square: A Book about Shapes,* Scholastic (New York, NY), 1996.

(With David Pelham) Michael Foreman, *Ben's Box: A Pop-up Fantasy,* Piggy Toes Press (Kansas City, MO), 1997.

Deborah Nourse Lattimore, *I Wonder What's under There?: A Brief History of Underwear,* Browndeer Press (San Diego, CA), 1998.

Alan Benjamin, *Curious Critters: A Pop-up Menagerie,* Simon & Schuster (New York, NY), 1998.

Sarah Weeks, *Ruff! Ruff! Where's Scruff?,* Harcourt (New York, NY), 2006.

Sarah Weeks, *Ruff! Ruff! Where's Scruff?: A Lift-the-Flap Adventure,* Harcourt (New York, NY), 2006.

Dr. Seuss, *Horton Hears a Who!,* pop-up edition, Robin Corey Books (New York, NY), 2008.

## Sidelights

David A. Carter is the author or illustrator of dozens of pop-up books for young children, several of which are written with his wife, author and illustrator Noelle Carter. Carter's work has earned praise for its clever tactile quality and incorporation of appealing shapes and colors. As the artist once told *SATA:* "I am often asked by children where I get my ideas for books. I have spent many hours contemplating this question and I still do not have the answer." Carter's many self-illustrated books include *Flapdoodle Dinosaurs: A Colorful Pop-up Book, Woof! Woof!,* and *600 Black Spots: A Pop-up Book for Children of All Ages,* as well as his "Bugs" series. In addition, he has created pop-up collaborations with his wife that include *Little Mouse's Christmas* as well as tackling illustration/engineering projects for other writers. Reviewing Carter's pop-up adaptation of Dr. Seuss's popular easy reader *Horton Hears a Who!,* a *Publishers Weekly* critic concluded that "Carter's pop-ups capably amplify the message about finding balance when life overwhelms."

Describing his childhood growing up in Utah, Carter recalled: "I would play outside all day, spending hours on end in the fields around my home, lifting up rocks and boards in search of bugs. It was always very exciting to lift up the rocks because I never knew what I would find." "Lifting something to find a bug was one of my greatest thrills as a child," he added, "and that is exactly what I had created, unconsciously, in *How Many Bugs in a Box?*" Carter's first book, *How Many Bugs in a Box?* is also the first of his books to use insects as a theme to enchant preschoolers. The book serves as a counting lesson, with each page depicting a different type and quantity of insect, numbering from one insect to ten. A *Publishers Weekly* reviewer wrote of *How Many Bugs in a Box?* that Carter's use of "startlingly bright illustrations" will likely entice young readers.

Carter's "Bugs" books have been among his most popular titles, and they range in theme from concept books to holiday and activities books to collections of games to jokes. The questions in *More Bugs in Boxes* lead

*Cover of Carter's imaginative and interactive debut picture book* **How Many Bugs in a Box?**, *which mixes a counting exercise with fun.* (Copyright © 1988 by Intervisual Books, Inc. Reproduced by permission of Little Simon, an imprint of Simon & Schuster Macmillan.)

young readers into guessing the contents of each box. The bugs revealed are, like the pages themselves, drawn in vivid colors and also boast interesting textures: spitfire flies are silvery, for instance, while basketball bugs possess a rubbery texture. Anne Connor, reviewing the book for *School Library Journal,* called *More Bugs in Boxes* an "engineering feat" with "sometimes amazing effects." In *Giggle Bugs: A Lift-and-Laugh Book* a pull of the flap reveals "punchlines to fifty-eight bug-related jokes," according to a reviewer for *Publishers Weekly. The Twelve Bugs of Christmas: A Pop-up Christmas Counting Book* parodies the traditional holiday carol; there are boxes to unwrap on each spread and "inside each box is a new bug surprise," wrote a *Publishers Weekly* reviewer. *Chanukah Bugs: A Pop-up Celebration* features creatures hiding in dreidels and among the latke, "combining humor with handsome graphics" according to Susan Patron in *School Library Journal.*

Carter has also won praise for other works that play upon children's fascination with the animal kingdom. Geared for preschoolers, *What's in My Pocket?* employs five animals whose heads pop up as the pages are turned. His text poses questions that lead the reader to open another flap on each page, a pocket for the creature that, when lifted, shows what the animal's favorite food is: the rabbit has a carrot, the mouse hides cheese, and so forth. A reviewer for *Junior Bookshelf* found that "the animals have distinctive characters" and, "altogether, there are many things to notice and plenty of movement" in *What's in My Pocket?* Reviewing the same work in the *Bulletin of the Center for Children's Books,* Zena Sutherland cited Carter's talent for "nice composition and bright color in pictures with no clutter."

*Flapdoodle Dinosaurs* finds members of the early animal kingdom popping up in a modern setting. Shrunk small enough so that they fit into pickle jars or loaves of bread, each of the dinosaurs is hidden behind flaps to pop out at young readers. A *Publishers Weekly* critic found *Flapdoodle Dinosaurs* to be "just plain fun." *Who Put the Cookie in the Cookie Jar?* uses the same technique although this tune Carter hides miniature thieves in large cookie jars, giving the traditional rhyme "a new twist" according to a *Publishers Weekly* critic.

Working to create new and different "kinetic sculpture," Carter designed and created *One Red Dot,* the first book in a series that includes *Yellow Square, Blue 2, 600 Black Spots,* and *White Noise.* A combination counting book and seek-and-find game, *One Red Dot* reveals paper sculptures with a different number of features on each page, but with one red dot hidden somewhere on each sculpture. The "graphically bold pop-up book . . . entices readers" to hunt for the single red dot, according to Lisa Gangemi Kropp in *School Library Journal.* Bao Ong, writing in *Newsweek,* recommended the book for "children of all ages," and Lolly Robinson wrote in *Horn Book* that many adult "pop-up aficionados" will appreciate the abstract designs. Robinson also felt that with *One Red Dot,* "Carter pulls out all the stops in a veritable catalog of paper-engineering effects."

In *Blue 2* Carter hides a blue numeral 2 within a sequence of nine brightly colored sculptural images, each containing a three-word portion of a text that, when read from start to finish, represent each letter from A to Z. *600 Black Spots* and *Yellow Square* continue what a *Kirkus Reviews* writer described as Carter's colorful "three-dimensional homages to modern art," while in *White Noise* the pop-up images are capable of producing sound when strummed or otherwise manipulated. In *Booklist* Ilene Cooper dubbed *600 Black Spots* "simple and stunning" in its evocation of modernist art, while in *School Library Journal* critic Joy Fleishhacker wrote that "each of the nine "intricately designed abstract paper sculptures is a surprise and a delight." Appraising *White Noise,* Fleishhacker deemed Carter's intricately engineered sculptures "as breathtaking as ever," while a *Kirkus Reviews* critic predicted of the same book that "children will simply be enthralled" by the artist's moveable, musical, modernistic creations.

Along with pop-up sculptures and lift-the-flap puzzles, Carter has created *Woof! Woof!* and *Whoo? Whoo?,* two tactile guessing-game books featuring die-cut holes for readers to feel as well as look through. At the beginning of *Woof! Woof!* the shapes have little meaning, but by the end the geometric patterns have become dogs. In *Whoo? Whoo?* Carter's jumbled assemblage of shapes is reordered with a turn of the page, revealing a frog, mice, a cat, a goose, and an owl. "The graphical simplicity combines with the touch-and-feel feature to create a perfectly delightful interactive mystery," wrote a contributor in reviewing *Woof! Woof!* for *Kirkus Reviews,* and in *School Library Journal* Martha Simpson recommended *Whoo? Whoo?* as "an excellent starting point for an art lesson."

One of several collaborations with wife Noelle, Carter's *I'm a Little Mouse* centers on a young rodent that has become lost and goes about introducing itself to other animals by explaining that it has fuzzy gray fur and a long tail. In response, the other creatures describe their unique characteristics to the mouse, whether they be shiny, scaly skin or scruffy fur. Carter creates unusual simulations of such textured surfaces, thus reinforcing his story's text. "Preschoolers will want to touch the mouse and his perky pals again and again," wrote a reviewer in appraising *I'm a Little Mouse* for *Publishers Weekly.*

In addition to his solo works, Carter has also collaborated with other authors, such as Mary Serfozo, with whom he created *There's a Square: A Book about Shapes,* and Peter Seymour, with whom Carter has worked for several years. One of Seymour and Carter's joint efforts, *What's in the Deep Blue Sea?,* offers an unusual strategy: a young tiger stalks through the jungle on his way to the water, where he looks down to see a pair of whiskers, much like his own, appraising him. Throughout the pages, animals hide behind lift-up flaps, and like many books in the pop-up genre, the story's grand finale is designed to electrify young imaginations. In a review of *What's in the Deep Blue Sea?* a *Publishers Weekly* contributor called Carter's images "luxuriant" and commended his "use of dark, saturant color and dry over dry painting to create stunning spreads."

James Diaz and Carter collaborated on a nonfiction instructional book for young artists interested in designing pop-up art. *The Elements of Pop-up: A Pop-up Book for Aspiring Paper Engineers* "is more than a how-to manual on pop-ups," according to Lolly Robinson in a review of the work for *Horn Book.* Robinson noted that the authors describe "the geometry and physics of paper engineering" and the math concepts used in their creation, "explaining the usefulness of kinetic energy." Featuring the art of both creators, *The Elements of Pop-up* is as much about science as it is about art, and also provides a section on the history of pop-up books. The pair have continued their educational series with *Let's Make It Pop-up.*

As Carter once told *SATA,* while he "cannot explain the creative process" that produces his books, "link between my childhood curiosities and thrills and my books has something to do with where my ideas come from. My goal in creating a book is to engage this natural curiosity, to entertain with surprise and silliness and whenever possible to educate, because for me the end result of curiosity is learning.

"The term interactive has become popular in reference to computer software. Pop-up books are also interactive; of course to a big kid like myself the term interactive is nothing more than a big word for play. I believe children learn by playing. One of the things that I like most about pop-up books is that a child who may not be reading yet can interact, or play, with the book. My hope is that this will draw the young reader into the book and hopefully into reading in general.

"If my books can entertain and excite a child who is not a reader, and draw him or her into books and reading, then I have accomplished my goal."

## Biographical and Critical Sources

*PERIODICALS*

*Booklist,* December 15, 1999, Ilene Cooper, review of *The Elements of Pop-up: A Pop-up Book for Aspiring Paper Engineers,* p. 786; December 1, 2000, review of *The Nutcracker: A Pop-up Adaptation of E.T.A. Hoffman's Original Tale,* p. 728; November 1, 2007, Ilene Cooper, review of *600 Black Spots: A Pop-up Book for Children of All Ages,* p. 58; December 15, 2009, Ilene Cooper, review of *White Noise: A Pop-up Book for Children of All Ages,* p. 42.
*Bulletin of the Center for Children's Books,* October, 1989, Zena Sutherland, review of *What's in My Pocket?,* p. 30.
*Horn Book,* January, 2000, Lolly Robinson, review of *The Elements of Pop-up,* p. 94; November-December, 2005, Lolly Robinson, review of *One Red Dot,* p. 703.
*Junior Bookshelf,* February, 1990, review of *What's in My Pocket?,* p. 23.
*Kirkus Reviews,* September 15, 2005, review of *One Red Dot,* p. 1023; February 1, 2006, review of *Woof! Woof!,* p. 129; September 1, 2007, review of *600 Black Spots*; October 15, 2008, review of *Yellow Square: A Pop-up Book for Children of All Ages*; November 15, 2009, review of *White Noise.*
*Newsweek,* September 26, 2005, Bao Ong, "Pop Culture Phenomenon," p. 9.
*New York Times Book Review,* November 12, 2006, Dwight Garner, review of *Blue 2: A Pop-up Book for Children of All Ages,* p. 48; November 11, 2007, Joanna Rudge Long, review of *600 Black Spots,* p. 44; November 8, 2009, Steven Heller, review of *White Noise,* p. 16.
*Publishers Weekly,* December 11, 1987, review of *How Many Bugs in a Box?,* p. 62; October 12, 1990, review of *What's in the Deep Blue Sea?,* p. 62; January 11, 1991, review of *I'm a Little Mouse,* p. 100; December 21, 1998, review of *Stinky Bugs,* p. 69; September 27, 1999, review of *The Twelve Bugs of Christmas,* p. 54; September 25, 2000, review of *The Nutcracker,* p. 76; February 19, 2001, review of *Easter Bugs,* p. 63; December 17, 2001, review of *Flapdoodle Dinosaurs,* p. 93; March 1, 2004, "Pop (up) Culture," p. 71; January 14, 2008, review of *Horton Hears a Who,* p. 58; November 16, 2009, review of *White Noise,* p. 52; February 15, 2010, review of *Oh, the Places You'll Go!,* p. 128.
*School Library Journal,* August, 1990, Anne Connor, review of *More Bugs in a Box,* p. 126; October, 2002, review of *Chanukah Bugs,* p. 58; November, 2005, Lisa Gangemi Kropp, review of *One Red Dot,* p. 89; January, 2007, Joy Fleishhacker, review of *Blue 2,* p. 90; August, 2007, Martha Simpson, "Whoo? Whoo?," p. 78; January, 2008, Joy Fleishhacker, review of *600 Black Spots,* p. 83; October, 2008, Joy Fleishhacker, review of *Yellow Square;* January, 2010, Joy Fleishhacker, review of *White Noise,* p. 70.
*Tribune Books* (Chicago, IL), February 26, 2006, Mary Harris Russell, review of *Woof! Woof!,* p. 7.

*ONLINE*

*David and Noelle Carter Home Page,* http://www.popupbooks.com (March 20, 2011).
*Harcourt Trade Publishers Web site,* http://www.harcourtbooks.com/ (March 20, 2011), "David A. Carter."

\*      \*      \*

# CASSINO, Mark

## Personal

Born in MI; married; wife's name Pam. *Education:* University of Michigan, B.A. (English literature).

## Addresses

*Home*—Kalamazoo, MI. *Office*—Mark Cassino Photography, 5047 W. Main St., No. 393, Kalamazoo, MI 49009-1001. *E-mail*—cassino@markcassino.com.

## Career

Photographer and author. *Exhibitions:* Work included in exhibitions at National Botanical Gardens, Washington, DC; Center for Fine Art Photography, Fort Collins, CO; Soho Photo Gallery, New York, NY; and Rakin Art Gallery at Ferris State University; and juried shows sponsored by Kalamazoo Institute of Art and Maryland Federation of Art.

## Awards, Honors

Outstanding Science Trade Book selection, National Science Teachers Association, and One Hundred Titles for Reading and Sharing selection, New York Public Library, both 2009, both for *The Story of Snow;* numerous awards from juried photography shows.

## Writings

(With Jon Nelson; and photographer) *The Story of Snow: The Science of Winter's Wonder,* illustrated by Nora Aoyagi, Chronicle Books (San Francisco, CA), 2009.

Contributor to periodicals, including *American Entomologist* and *Science World.*

## Sidelights

Michigan-based photographer Mark Cassino uses a range of technology—including macro-and close-up lenses, varied films and darkroom techniques, digital systems, medium-format film, infrared, standard SLR, and antique and toy cameras—in creating his nature-themed images. While his landscapes reflect the Midwestern region where he lives and works, Cassino's close-up images range from plants and animals to insects and the snow crystals that have become his special passion. His artistic images have appeared in numerous exhibits, while his detailed, scientific photos can be found in periodicals and textbooks as well as on Web sites with a scientific focus. Cassino's photographs of snow crystals also inject an element of magic into *The Story of Snow: The Science of Winter's Wonder,* a book coauthored by Japanese-based teacher and physicist Jon Nelson and illustrated in watercolor-and-ink art by Nora Aoyagi.

In *The Story of Snow* Cassino and Nelson address many of the questions about snowflakes that fascinate children, using what *Horn Book* contributor Danielle J. Ford described as "an inventive combination of text and illustration." From how snow crystals form, grow, and float from the sky to the varied shapes they take, readers also learn how to capture and view these ephemeral works of nature's art through the coauthors' clear directions. Paired with "simple sentences in large type," the book's large-format photographic images "reveal details of common shapes such as stars, plates and columns," observed Kathy Piehl in *School Library Journal.* Cassino's photographs of snow crystals impressed a *Kirkus Reviews* writer as "astonishing," the reviewer going on to praise both Cassino and Nelson for their "clear and direct narrative." John Peters wrote in *Booklist* that *The Story of Snow* reflects the coauthors' "contagious sense of wonder," and *Washington Post* critic Abby McGanney Nolan predicted that the book "will instill appreciation for these tiny, cool objects."

## Biographical and Critical Sources

*PERIODICALS*

*Booklist,* December 1, 2009, John Peters, review of *The Story of Snow: The Science of Winter's Wonder,* p. 57.

*Horn Book,* January-February, 2010, Danielle J. Ford, review of *The Story of Snow,* p. 101.

*Kirkus Reviews,* October 15, 2009, review of *The Story of Snow.*

*School Library Journal,* November, 2009, Kathy Piehl, review of *The Story of Snow,* p. 93.

*Washington Post,* January 6, 2010, Abby McGanney Nolan, review of *The Story of Snow.*

*ONLINE*

*Mark Cassino Home Page,* http://www.markcassino.com (February 16, 2011).

---

## COFFIN, M.T.
### See STANLEY, George Edward

\*    \*    \*

## COHAGAN, Carolyn 1972-

### Personal

Born 1972, in Austin, TX. *Education:* Earned college degree; attended Barnard College, Columbia University; attended École Jacques LeCoq (Paris, France).

### Addresses

*Home*—Los Angeles, CA. *E-mail*—carolyn@ thelostchildrenbook.com.

### Career

Film director, comedian, and author. Stand-up comic performing in comedy clubs in the United States, England, Australia, and the Netherlands; creator and performer in one-woman shows, including *No Spleen* and *If Americans Are So Awful Then Take Your Hand off My Knee;* performer and producer of stage show *Splice,* 2001-02. Director of stage productions, including *Society Blues, Tami Boy,* and *In Search of Tulla Berman,* 2002. Director of films *Rigid: The Birth of the Human Statue* and *Million Dollar Xanadu.* Film Independent (nonprofit agency), Los Angeles, CA, interviewer, Web content editor, and blogger. Volunteer mentor with Reading to Kids and Young Storytellers Foundation.

### Awards, Honors

Umbrella Award nominations for Best Production, Best Female Performer, and Best Use of Space, all for *If Americans Are So Awful Then Take Your Hand off My Knee;* Most Outstanding Production and Most Creative Production awards, Toronto International Fringe Festival, both 2002, both for *Splice.*

### Writings

*The Lost Children,* Aladdin (New York, NY), 2010.

Author of stage productions, including *No Spleen, If Americans Are So Awful Then Take Your Hand off My Knee,* and *Splice;* author of short films *Rigid: The Birth of the Human Statue* and *Million Dollar Xanadu.*

### Sidelights

Since beginning her career, Carolyn Cohagan has focused much of her creative energy on performance, working as a comedian, stage performer, and producer and director of plays and original short films. In 2010

Cohagan also earned a new type of credit—as an author for children—with the publication of her middle-grade fantasy novel *The Lost Children*. Interestingly, the novel started life as the outline for a screenplay; as the author explained to *Writeononline.com* interviewer Debra Eckerling, "Once I got into it, I found I really preferred writing prose and I just kept going. Each time I ended a chapter, I would end with a cliffhanger and I would have no idea how I was going to solve it."

Immediately after completing college, Cohagan spent five years performing in comedy clubs in London, New York City, and several other major cities around the world. Then she moved to Paris to study physical theatre at the École Jacques LeCoq. Her original one-woman shows *No Spleen* and *If Americans Are So Awful Then Take Your Hand off My Knee* gained Cohagan recognition as well as earning several award nominations, while her work as a stage director allowed her to explore the creative possibilities of a larger cast and a more complete narrative. A move to Los Angeles resulted in several short films, as well as her current affiliation with Film Independent, producer of both the Los Angeles Film Festival and the annual Independent Spirit Awards, where she has worked in many capacities.

In *The Lost Children* readers meet twelve-year-old Josephine Russing, who lives with her stern father and has few friends at school. Josephine's lonely life is transformed when she meets Fargus, a mute boy who appears in the backyard of her home, and follows him down a wormhole and into a magical town called Gulm. When she learns that Fargus and his friend and fellow orphan Ida are destined to have their life energy consumed by Gulm's young and greedy ruler, Josephine helps them escape. The Master and his monstrous henchmen feed on the energy of Gulm's children, who are taken from their parents and kept as captives until required. When the Master's spies eventually alert him to the whereabouts of his two planned victims, Ida and Fargus are captured. Now Josephine must risk her own safety to help her new friends, and maybe rid Gulm of its harsh government as well.

"The main characters are well developed," noted *Booklist* critic Kay Weisman in her review of *The Lost Children,* the reviewer adding that Josephine's "journey uncovers hidden strengths" that allow Cohagan's pre-teen heroine to take each challenge in stride. Calling the novel an "ambitious fairy-tale adventure," Riva Pollard added in *School Library Journal* that Cohagan's fiction debut entertains readers with "funny foibles, tragic histories, twists, and family secrets revealed." Also praising the book, a *Publishers Weekly* contributor recommended *The Lost Children* for its "quirky and charming style," a style that "should draw readers in from the outset," according to the critic.

## Biographical and Critical Sources

*PERIODICALS*

*Booklist,* January 1, 2010, Kay Weisman, review of *The Lost Children,* p. 84.
*Kirkus Reviews,* January 15, 2010, review of *The Lost Children.*
*Publishers Weekly,* January 18, 2010, review of *The Lost Children,* p. 48.
*School Library Journal,* March, 2010, Riva Pollard, review of *The Lost Children,* p. 154.

*ONLINE*

*Carolyn Cohagan Home Page,* http://carolyncohagan.com (February 16, 2011).
*Write On Online Web log,* http://writeononline.com/ (March 15, 2010), Debra Eckerling, interview with Cohagan.

\*    \*    \*

# COHN, Rachel 1968-

## Personal

Born December 14, 1968, in Silver Spring, MD. *Education:* Barnard College, B.A. (political science).

## Addresses

*Home*—New York, NY.

## Career

Writer. Formerly worked at a law firm in San Francisco, CA.

## Member

Author's Guild.

## Awards, Honors

American Library Association (ALA) Best Book for Young Adults selection, and New York Public Library Books for the Teen Age selection, both 2003, and International Reading Association (IRA) Young Adults' Choice, 2004, all for *Gingerbread;* ALA Teens' Top Ten Books nomination, 2003, and IRA Children's Choice selection, 2004, both for *The Steps;* New York Public Library Books for the Teen Age selection, 2005, for *Pop Princess,* 2008, for *You Know Where to Find Me.*

## Writings

*YOUNG-ADULT NOVELS*

*Gingerbread,* Simon & Schuster (New York, NY), 2002.
*The Steps,* Simon & Schuster (New York, NY), 2003.
*Pop Princess,* Simon & Schuster (New York, NY), 2004.

*Shrimp* (sequel to *Gingerbread*), Simon & Schuster (New York, NY), 2005.

(With David Levithan) *Nick and Nora's Infinite Playlist,* Knopf (New York, NY), 2006.

*Two Steps Forward,* Simon & Schuster Books for Young Readers (New York, NY), 2006.

*Cupcake,* Simon & Schuster Books for Young Readers (New York, NY), 2007.

(With David Levithan) *Naomi and Ely's No Kiss List,* Alfred A. Knopf (New York, NY), 2007.

*You Know Where to Find Me,* Simon & Schuster Books for Young Readers (New York, NY), 2008.

(With David Levithan) *Dash and Lily's Book of Dares,* Alfred A. Knopf (New York, NY), 2010.

*Very LeFreak,* Alfred A. Knopf (New York, NY), 2010.

## Adaptations

*The Steps, Pop Princess, Gingerbread,* and *Shrimp* were adapted as audiobooks. *Nick and Norah's Infinite Playlist* was adapted for film by Lorene Scafaria and produced by Sony Pictures, 2006. *Dash and Lily's Book of Dares* was also filmed.

## Sidelights

Rachel Cohn is the author of the highly regarded young-adult novels *Gingerbread, Pop Princess, The Steps,* and *You Know Where to Find Me. Nick and Nora's Infinite Playlist,* the first of several collaborative novels Cohn has written with fellow author David Levithan, was adapted as a feature film directed by Peter Sollett that is filmed in New York City, where the novel is set and where both Cohn and Levithan make their homes.

Raised near Washington, DC, in a family of teachers, Cohn knew that she wanted to become an author at an early age. "From the time I learned how to read and write I was always trying to create stories," as she stated on her home page."When I was a kid, I loved books by Judy Blume, Ellen Conford and E.L. Konigsburg. (I loved Judy Blume's books so much that I used to actively wish I would get scoliosis so I could be like Deenie.)" After graduating from Barnard College with a major in political science, Cohn considered a career as a journalist, but realized that she would rather make up stories than report them. To support herself, she worked in a law firm in San Francisco, where she lived for several years while refining her fiction-writing skills and producing several novels. Her first published work, *Gingerbread,* was released in 2002 and its success enabled Cohn to return to her native New York City as a full-time author.

*Gingerbread* concerns Cyd Charisse, a rebellious sixteen year old who is living in San Francisco with her mother and stepfather since being expelled from boarding school. Cyd quickly wears out her welcome at home, however; after she breaks curfew with her boyfriend, Shrimp, she is sent across the country to New York City to live with her estranged biological father,

"Frank real-dad." Although Cyd's relationship with Frank and his two other children is strained, over time she develops a close bond with her half-brother and begins to accept responsibility for her actions. Through her experiences, "Cyd's appreciation of her family back home grows, as does her confidence that she is lovable and valuable," observed a critic in *Kirkus Reviews.* According to *Booklist* contributor Gillian Engberg, "teens will recognize themselves in Cyd's complex, believable mix of the arch and the vulnerable, the self-aware and the self-destructive," and *Kliatt* reviewer Paula Rohrlick called *Gingerbread* "an engaging tale about a girl coming to terms with her family and her relationships."

Cyd Charisse makes a return engagement in both *Shrimp* and *Cupcake,* although she now calls herself "CC." The feisty teen returns to San Francisco in *Shrimp,* and when she reunites with her surfer boyfriend he tries to convince her to move overseas with him. In *Cupcake* CC is busy crafting her adult life, which means finding a job and scouting out the best coffee shop, a good source of cupcakes in her new New York City neighborhood. The search for a new boyfriend is also pressing, but when

*When a teen is "discovered" in classic show-biz fashion, she learns that the pop-star life is not what she thought in Rachel Cohn's* **Pop Princess***, a novel featuring artwork by Russell Gordon.* (Cover photograph © by Brand X Images/Getty Images.)

she breaks her leg, the candidates must come to her. Unfortunately, none of the guy options can keep memories of Shrimp from returning. Then Shrimp suddenly shows up at her doorstep and proclaims that he would rather be with her than go surfing. CC now must re-evaluate the progress she has made toward independence and decide what would be risked if she lets Shrimp back into her life.

CC "is a complete character, likeable as much for her daring outfits and attitude as for her good heart and energy," asserted a *Publishers Weekly* critic in reviewing *Shrimp,* and Rohrlick predicted that the story's "humor, . . . emotionally painful moments, and Cyd's original voice will pull readers in." Describing CC's narrative as "told in a cocky, self-assured voice that tends to ramble in humorous riffs," *Kliatt* contributor Myra Marler dubbed *Cupcake* "both fun and intriguing" as it deals with a young woman confronting life-defining choices. In *School Library Journal* Caryl Soriano deemed the novel a "thoroughly satisfying conclusion" to Cohn's three-volume "saga," and a *Publishers Weekly* enjoyed yet another outing with the author's "irrepressible" and free-spirited heroine.

A high school student is propelled to stardom in the engagingly titled *Pop Princess.* While working at the local Dairy Queen, Wonder Blake is discovered by a talent agent, the same man who helped Wonder's sister land a recording contract before the older teen was killed in a tragic accident. Although at first excited about her glamorous new career, after releasing a hit single Wonder "discovers that the life of a pop star is not a bed of roses," observed *School Library Journal* reviewer Miranda Doyle. "The most alluring scenes here are visions of the pop princess world—all packaging and no content," noted a *Publishers Weekly* contributor, and *Kliatt* reviewer Claire Rosser described the work as "thoughtful and intelligent."

Cohn continues to entertain teen readers with the novels *You Know Where to Find Me* and *Very LeFreak* Although they have been lifelong friends, for Miles, the Goth, overweight, and eighteen-year-old narrator of *You Know Where to Find Me,* life has been lived on the low end of the scale in comparisons to her beautiful and brainy cousin Laura. While Laura has two parents and goes to an expensive prep school, Miles's single artist mom has always struggled to get by. Consequently, when Laura kills herself with a drug overdose, it comes as a shock to Miles, who has few people she can confide in. Shortly afterward, her mother leaves for London to live with her boyfriend, dumping Miles with the alcoholic father she hardly knows. When her best friend, Jamal, who she secretly loves, decides to move to the city with a new girlfriend, Miles searches for solace and finds it with drugs until she is once again surrounded by people who care about her. "Cohn's slick, upbeat, urban prose intensifies the sharply drawn characters that frame Miles's world," noted a *Kirkus Reviews* writer, describing the story's narrator as angry

and "defiantly admirable." "Teens will be riveted by Miles," predicted Gillian Engberg in *Booklist,* as well as by "her harrowing path through grief and addiction." Noting that *You Know Where to Find Me* marks a change of pace for Cohn due to its "darker, more wrenching and poetic narrative" and its "overabundance of social and political themes," Riva Pollard added in *School Library Journal* that the author's ability to craft "evolving relationships" will draw readers to the story's "dramatic conclusion."

As a freshman at New York City's Columbia University, Veronica "Very" LeFreak focuses most of her time on friends, romantic fantasies with an Internet paramour named El Virus, and organizing parties and other campus entertainments through her social-network Web site. Despite her popularity, the teen soon finds herself on the verge of being expelled, prompting her three best friends to team up with the dean and stage an intervention: either Very unplugs from texting, twittering, IMing, and otherwise tapping into social media or she loses her scholarship. Soon Very finds herself at a retreat for computer addicts located in northern New

*Cover of Cohn's teen-centered* Very LeFreak, *which finds a free-spirited college freshman socialite sent to rehab after flunking out of a prestigious New York university.* (Copyright © 2010 by Rachel Cohn. Reproduced with permission of Random House Children's Books, a division of Random House, Inc.)

England where she is totally unplugged and uncomfortable with the quiet that now surrounds her. "Very's unique take on the world brings plenty of humor and a vicarious ride through racy modern college life," wrote Suzanne Gordon in her *School Library Journal* of Cohn's entertaining novel, although a *Kirkus Reviews* writer noted the story's "sometimes preachy themes of addiction and information-overload . . . make for a book that is heavy on the message."

In *Nick and Nora's Infinite Playlist* Cohn presents her first collaboration with fellow author David Levithan. Writing in two voices, the coauthors decided to bypass the plotting stage of novel-writing and trust to serendipity. They passed chapters back and forth via e-mail and let their story's two main characters navigate the plot line forward. "The wattage goes way up as two of the bright lights of contemporary writing for teens come together for an incandescent he said/she said night of storytelling," proclaimed a *Kirkus Reviews* writer after perusing the result of these collaborative efforts. During a performance of his punk rock band at a New York City nightclub, Nick, a musician from Hoboken, New Jersey, asks upscale Norah to pose as his girlfriend in order to avoid a persistent ex who has just made an appearance. However, a passionate kiss catapults both teens into a new relationship and the excitement and angst of this surprising romance plays out against the bustle of New York City. "There are many heart-stopping, insightful moments in this supremely satisfying and sexy romance," asserted *School Library Journal* critic Tracy Karbel, dubbing *Nick and Nora's Infinite Playlist* "a first-rate read." In *Booklist* Engberg recommended Cohn and Levithan's "high-energy romance" to older teens who "will respond to the tough, clever, amped-up narrative."

Cohn and Levithan have also coauthored *Naomi and Ely's No-Kiss List* and *Dash and Lily's Book of Dares,* both which feature dual narrators that shaped the plot through their entertaining and imaginative interactions. In *Naomi and Ely's No-Kiss List* Naomi and Ely are college freshmen who have grown up in the same apartment building. Although they are best friends, romance between the two teens is out of the question because Ely is gay. To prevent other relationships from threatening their affection they make a list of everyone who is off limits as far as romance goes, but feelings cause problems anyway. Citing the coauthor's use of "oh-so-hip music and pop-culture references," Kathleen E. Gruver wrote in *School Library Journal* that *Naomi and Ely's No-Kiss List* will appeal to teens who will "love the main characters" and "empathize with their confusion as they attempt to sort out their relationships and themselves." A *Kirkus Reviews* writer also hailed Cohn and Leviathan's collaborative novel, dubbing it "a brilliant tour-de-force—funny, sweet, sly, and sexy."

The search for adventure motivates sixteen-year-old Lily in *Dash and Lily's Book of Dares.* In a red spiral notebook she lists several literary clues, then places it on a shelf of New York's well-known Strand Bookstore. When loner Dash discovers it, he decides to join the mystery writer in the game and soon the teens are traveling to different city sites to uncover messages. The red notebook remains their only means of connecting with each other, and their writings in it form the basis of a growing friendship. When Dash and Lily come face to face, it remains to be seen whether their real-life selves will hold up well against the "selves" they crafted on paper. "As they did in *Nick and Nora's Infinite Playlist,*" Cohn and Levithan "combine their talents to write an appealing book," concluded *School Library Journal* contributor Suanne Roush, while in *Publishers Weekly* a reviewer wrote that the authors' "familar but fun formula" generates a story featuring "more than enough amusing turns of phrase and zigzag plot twists to keep [readers'] . . . attention."

Cohn examines another blended family in the humorous *The Steps,* a novel that, like its sequel *Two Steps Forward,* is geared for middle-grade readers. In *The Steps* twelve-year-old Annabel lives with her mother and her boyfriend in Manhattan, while Annabel's father, Jack, has settled in Australia with his new family. During a Christmas holiday, Annabel travels to Sydney for a visit, although she is initially hostile toward her step-siblings, Angus and Lucy, for "stealing" her father. "That Annabel and Lucy will eventually become close friends . . . and that Annabel will become reconciled to the Steps is never in doubt," Martha V. Parravano wrote in *Horn Book,* while *School Library Journal* contributor Maria B. Salvadore remarked that Cohn's narrative reflects the author's "insight into families and individuals." *Booklist* reviewer Ilene Cooper praised *The Steps,* writing that "readers will identify with the mixed-up emotions that mixed families engender."

Set two years later, *Two Steps Forward* finds fourteen-year-old Annabel in Los Angeles to spend the summer visiting her dad and stepsiblings Angus and Lucy, who are now living in California. With her comes stepbrother Wheaties, who has a crush on Annabel but who Annabel likes only as a friend. What the teen does not know is that Ben, Lucy's stepbrother, will be traveling from Australia to visit as well, and as the very mixed family converges feelings are bound to be hurt. "The tone of the novel resembles a juicy note scribbled during class," maintained Sarah Couri in her review of *Two Steps Forward* for *School Library Journal,* and "Cohn's four narrators"—Annabel, Lucy, Ben, and Wheaties—"are pitch perfect." A *Kirkus Reviews* contributor wrote that, while the author crafts a "fairly artificial emotional Petri dish" by having all her characters migrate to one central location, her "fully developed characters . . . clash, compromise, and make . . . up with genuinely human imperfection."

## Biographical and Critical Sources

*PERIODICALS*

*Booklist,* April 15, 2002, Gillian Engberg, review of *Gingerbread,* p. 1394; January 1, 2003, Ilene Cooper, review of *The Steps,* pp. 887-888; January 1, 2004, Jennifer Mattson, review of *Pop Princess,* pp. 843-844; April 1, 2006, Gillian Engberg, review of *Nick and Norah's Infinite Playlist,* p. 31; April 1, 2008, Gillian Engberg, review of *You Know Where to Find Me,* p. 42; November 1, 2009, Daniel Kraus, review of *Very LeFreak,* p. 39.

*Bulletin of the Center for Children's Books,* April, 2002, review of *Gingerbread,* p. 274.

*Horn Book,* May-June, 2003, Martha V. Parravano, review of *The Steps,* pp. 341-342; March-April, 2005, Christine M. Heppermann, review of *Shrimp,* p. 198; January-February, 2007, Christine M. Heppermann, review of *Cupcake,* p. 63; January-February, 2010, Tanya D. Auger, review of *Very LeFreak,* p. 84.

*Kirkus Reviews,* January 15, 2002, review of *Gingerbread,* p. 101; February 1, 2003, review of *The Steps,* p. 227; February 1, 2004, review of *Pop Princess,* p. 130; February 15, 2005, review of *Shrimp,* p. 227; February 15, 2006, review of *Two Steps Forward,* p. 180; April 15, 2006, review of *Nick and Norah's Infinite Playlist,* p. 402; December 1, 2006, review of *Cupcake,* p. 1218; August 1, 2007, review of *Naomi and Ely's No Kiss List;* February 15, 2008, review of *You Know Where to Find Me;* November 15, 2009, review of *Very LeFreak.*

*Kliatt,* March, 2002, Paula Rohrlick, review of *Gingerbread,* pp. 7-8; March, 2004, Claire Rosser, review of *Pop Princess,* pp. 8-9; March, 2005, Paula Rohrlick, review of *Shrimp,* p. 9; January, 2007, Myrna Marler, review of *Cupcake,* p. 11; September, 2007, Janis Flint-Ferguson, review of *Naomi and Ely's No Kiss List,* p. 8.

*Publishers Weekly,* June 24, 2002, "Flying Starts," pp. 27-30; March 10, 2003, review of *The Steps,* p. 32; May 12, 2003, Sally Lodge, "Tales from the 'Tween Tour," pp. 27-28; January 5, 2004, review of *Pop Princess,* p. 63; January 24, 2005, review of *Shrimp,* p. 245; May 1, 2006, review of *Nick and Norah's Infinite Playlist,* p. 65; December 4, 2006, review of *Cupcake,* p. 59; August 6, 2007, review of *Naomi and Ely's No-Kiss List,* p. 191; December 24, 2007, review of *You Know Where to Find Me,* p. 57; November 23, 2009, review of *Very LeFreak,* p. 59; October 4, 2010, review of *Dash and Lily's Book of Dares,* p. 49.

*School Library Journal,* February, 2002, Gail Richmond, review of *Gingerbread,* p. 129; February, 2003, Maria B. Salvadore, review of *The Steps,* p. 140; March, 2004, Miranda Doyle, review of *Pop Princess,* p. 204; February, 2005, Kelly Czarnecki, review of *Shrimp,* p. 136; May, 2006, Tracy Karbel, review of *Nick and Norah's Infinite Playlist,* p. 120, and Sarah Couri, review of *Two Steps Forward,* p. 122; March, 2007, Caryl Soriano, review of *Cupcake,* p. 206; September, 2007, Kathleen E. Gruver, review of *Naomi and Ely's No Kiss List,* p. 193; March, 2008, Riva Pollard, review of *You Know Where to Find Me,* p. 196; January, 2010, Suzanne Gordon, review of *Very LeFreak,* p. 98; October, 2010, Suanne Roush, review of *Dash and Lily's Book of Dares,* p. 110.

*ONLINE*

*Rachel Cohn Home Page,* http://www.rachelcohn.com (April 1, 2011).

# D'AGNESE, Joseph

## Personal

Born in NJ; married Denise Kiernan (a writer and producer).

## Addresses

*Home*—NC. *Agent*—(children's) Eden Street Literary, P.O. Box 30, 1628 Rte. 55, Billings, NY 12510; (adults) Foundry Literary & Media, 33 W. 17th St., PH, New York, NY 10011. *E-mail*—author@blockheadbook.com.

## Career

Author and journalist. Nutgraf Productions (media company), cofounder.

## Awards, Honors

Educational Press Association awards for children's writing; Notable Children's Book selection, Association for Library Service to Children, Best Science Books for Kids selection, *Smithsonian,* and Noteworthy Books for Children and Teens selection, all 2010, all for *Blockhead.*

## Writings

*FOR CHILDREN*

(With Jack Silbert) *American History Comic Books: Twelve Reproducible Comic Books with Activities Guaranteed to Get Kids Excited about Key Events and People in American History,* illustrated by Mark Zingarelli, Scholastic (New York, NY), 2005.

(With wife, Denise Kiernan) *The Indiana Jones Handbook: The Complete Adventurer's Guide,* Quirk Books (Philadelphia, PA), 2008.

(With Denise Kiernan) *Signing Their Lives Away: The Fame and Misfortune of the Men Who Signed the Declaration of Independence,* Quirk Books (Philadelphia, PA), 2009.

(With Denise Kiernan) *Signing Their Rights Away: The Fame and Misfortune of the Men Who Signed the U.S. Constitution,* Quirk Books (Philadelphia, PA), 2009.

*Blockhead: The Life of Fibonacci,* illustrated by John O'Brien, Henry Holt (New York, NY), 2010.

*OTHER*

(With Denise Kiernan) *The Money Book for Freelancers, Part-time, and the Self-employed: The Only Personal Finance System for People with Not-so-Regular Jobs,* Three Rivers Press (New York, NY), 2010.

Former editor of Scholastic *DynaMath* magazine. Contributor to *The Best American Science Writing 2002,* edited by Matt Ridley, HarperCollins (New York, NY),

2002, and *The Best American Science Writing 2003,* edited by Oliver Sacks, HarperCollins, 2003. Contributor to periodicals, including *Wired, Discover, New York Times, Wall Street Journal, Reader's Digest, Seed,* and *Saveur.*

## Sidelights

Joseph D'Agnese, an award-winning journalist who has written on a wide range of subjects, including medicine, environmental science, and technology, offers a picture-book biography of a groundbreaking medieval mathematician in *Blockhead: The Life of Fibonacci.* D'Agnese, whose work has appeared in such publications as *Wired, Discover,* and the *New York Times,* has also coauthored a number of titles with his wife, Denise Kiernan, including *Signing Their Lives Away: The Fame and Misfortune of the Men Who Signed the Declaration of Independence,* a work for teen history buffs.

The idea for *Blockhead* came to D'Agnese while serving as the editor of *Dynamath,* an educational magazine. As he prepared an article on the Fibonacci Sequence, a recursive number pattern often found in nature, D'Agnese became interested in the man who derived the sequence, a twelfth-century Italian named Leonardo Pisano, or Leonardo, son of Bonaccio. "Fibonacci's tale

is particularly rich and engaging," D'Agnese wrote in a *Cynsations* online essay. "He sailed the Mediterranean, and helped convert the western world from I-II-III to 1-2-3. Some historians argue that without the robust methods of calculation and accounting born out of the Hindu-Arabic numerals he introduced to the west, the Renaissance would not have occurred."

In *Blockhead* D'Agnese offers a fictionalized look at the life of Fibonacci, presenting the man as a day-dreamer who became fascinated by numbers as a child. Later, while working as an accountant for his father's company in Algeria, Fibonacci recognized the superiority of the Hindu-Arabic numeration system and helped popularize it in Europe. His celebrated number pattern grew out of his solution to a word problem about multiplying rabbits. According to *Booklist* critic John Peters, *Blockhead* offers "the clearest explanation to date for younger readers of the numerical sequence," and Lucinda Snyder wrote in *School Library Journal* that "this lighthearted introduction to Fibonacci's ideas will inspire young math lovers and perhaps point them toward more scholarly explorations." A reviewer in *Publishers Weekly* also praised the work, stating that D'Agnese's "colloquial tone . . . lures readers into the story," and *Horn Book* contributor Tanya D. Auger cited the author's "clever tongue-in-cheek humor."

*Joseph D'Agnese's math-centered picture-book biography* Blockhead: The Life of Fibonacci, *features artwork by John O'Brien.* (Illustration copyright © 2010 by John O'Brien. Reproduced with permission of Henry Holt & Company, LLC.)

In *Signing Their Lives Away* D'Agnese and Kiernan chronicle the lives of the fifty-six men who put their names to one the most significant documents in American history. The work includes brief profiles of such celebrated figures as Thomas Jefferson and Benjamin Franklin but also of lesser-known individuals, including William Whipple, a former slave trader, and Caesar Rodney, a Delaware politician who rode his horse eighty miles through a thunderstorm to sign the Declaration. The authors, Brian Odom noted in *School Library Journal*, "present readers with astonishing individual portraits of all the signers," and *Library Journal* critic Jane B. Marino applauded *Signing Their Lives Away* for its "light and breezy tone."

## Biographical and Critical Sources

*PERIODICALS*

*Booklist*, January 1, 2010, John Peters, review of *Blockhead: The Life of Fibonacci*, p. 73.
*Bulletin of the Center for Children's Books*, July-August, 2010, Elizabeth Bush, review of *Blockhead*, p. 478.
*Horn Book*, May-June, 2010, Tanya D. Auger, review of *Blockhead*, p. 105.
*Kirkus Reviews*, February 15, 2010, review of *Blockhead*.
*Library Journal*, June 15, 2009, Jane B. Marino, review of *Signing Their Lives Away: The Fame and Misfortune of the Men Who Signed the Declaration of Independence*, p. 78; April 15, 2010, Poppy Johnson-Renvall, review of *The Money Book for Freelancers, Part-time, and the Self-employed: The Only Personal Finance System for People with Not-so-Regular Jobs*, p. 91.
*New York Times Book Review*, August 15, 2010, Julie Just, review of *Blockhead*, p. 13.
*Publishers Weekly*, February 22, 2010, review of *Blockhead*, p. 64.
*School Library Journal*, August, 2009, Brian Odom, review of *Signing Their Lives Away*, p. 123; March, 2010, Lucinda Snyder, review of *Blockhead*, p. 138.

*ONLINE*

*Blockhead: The Life of Fibonacci Web site*, http://www.blockheadbook.com/ (April 1, 2011).
*Cynsations Web log*, http://cynthialeitichsmith.blogspot.com/ (November 22, 2010), "Guest Post: Joseph D'Agnese on Math Phobia."
*Denise Kiernan and Joseph D'Agnese Web site*, http://www.joedenise.com (April 1, 2011).
*Joseph D'Agnese Home Page*, http://www.josephdagnese.com (April 1, 2011).

\*   \*   \*

# DELINOIS, Alix

## Personal

Born in Saint Marc, Haiti; immigrated to United States at age seven. *Education:* Fashion Institute of Technol-

**Alix Delinois** (Reproduced by permission.)

ogy, A.A.S., 2000; Pratt Institute, B.F.A. (illustration and communication designs), 2003; Brooklyn College, M.A. (art education), 2009.

## Addresses

*Home*—New York, NY. *E-mail*—alix@alixdelinois.com.

## Career

Illustrator and educator. Substitute teacher in New York, NY, public elementary schools, beginning 2004; freelance illustrator, beginning 2006.

## Illustrator

Edwidge Dandicat, *Eight Days: A Story of Haiti*, Orchard Books (New York, NY), 2010.
Walter Dean Myers, *Muhammad Ali: The People's Champion*, Collins Amistad (New York, NY), 2010.

## Sidelights

Alix Delinois is an illustrator whose Haitian roots inject a colorful energy to his paintings and drawings. Delinois's dynamic art, which incorporates oil pastel, acrylics, and collage elements, utilizes stylized contrasts and rich colors. His work appears in several picture books, among them Haitian-born writer Edwidge Dandicat's *Eight Days: A Story of Haiti* and *Muhammad Ali: The People's Champion*, a biography by noted author Walter Dean Myers.

Delinois was born in Saint Marc, Haiti, and moved to New York City with his family when he was seven years old. Exhibiting a passion for art since childhood, he earned a two-year degree at New York's Fashion Institute of Technology before pursuing a bachelor's degree in illustration at the prestigious Pratt Institute. In addition to his training as an artist, Delinois has also earned a master's degree in art education and shares his love of art with elementary-grade students as a substitute teacher in the New York City Public Schools.

In *Muhammad Ali* Myers chronicles the life of the athlete who, as Cassius Clay, rose to prominence as an Olympic gold medalist and world heavyweight boxing champion. One of the best-known athletes of the mid-twentieth century, Clay changed his name to Muhammad Ali when he embraced Islam. His flamboyance both in and out of the boxing ring was balanced by his principled stance on both racism, which he fought, and the Vietnam War, in which he refused to fight. In his text, Myers captures what *Booklist* critic Daniel Kraus described as Ali's "curious mix of bravado and humility," and Delinois "is with Myers ever step" in creating bold images full of energetic "splotches" and "scribbles." "Rendered in a painterly style," according

to *School Library Journal* contributor Blair Christolon, the artwork in *Muhammad Ali* "is dramatic and enhances the boldness of this boxing superstar."

In Dandicat's *Eight Days* readers follow the lengthy ordeal of a seven-year-old boy who was trapped under the wreckage of his home for eight days after the Haitian earthquake hit in 2010. In his determination to survive, the little boy battles his fears and worries and feelings of cold and hunger by using his imagination to play games with friends, sing in the church choir, and visit his father's barber shop. Praising the book as "a true testament to the spirit of the people" of that ravaged island, Susan Lissim added in *School Library Journal* that Delinois's multimedia images of Haiti "are vibrant and share the beauty of the country, not the destruction." The "beautiful, bright artwork" in *Eight Days* "shows how [the boy's] . . . memories and imagination kept him alive," asserted Hazel Rochman in her *Booklist* appraisal of Dandicat's poignant and inspiring picture book. Dubbing *Eight Days* "uplifting," a *Publishers Weekly* contributor praised Delinois's "loose, emotive" paintings, noting that they transcend the boy's tragic circumstances by capturing "the joyful . . . reminiscences that [he] . . . clings to each day."

## Biographical and Critical Sources

*PERIODICALS*

*Booklist,* November 1, 2009, Daniel Kraus, review of *Muhammad Ali: The People's Champion,* p. 50; September 15, 2010, Hazel Rochman, review of *Eight Days: A Story of Haiti,* p. 69.
*Publishers Weekly,* August 30, 2010, review of *Eight Days,* p. 50.
*School Library Journal,* February, 2010, Blair Christolon, review of *Muhammad Ali,* p. 101; November, 2010, Susan Lissim, review of *Eight Days,* p. 91.

*ONLINE*

*Alix Delinois Home Page,* http://alixdelinois.com (March 16, 2011).

*Delinois creates the stylized and light-filled artwork that brings to life Walter Dean Myers story of a famous American athlete in* **Muhammad Ali: The People's Champion.** (Collins/Amistad, 2010. Illustration copyright © 2010 by Alix Delinois. Reproduced with permission of HarperCollins Publishers.)

\*　　\*　　\*

# DIXON, Franklin W.
## See STANLEY, George Edward

# F

## FANCHER, Lou 1960-

### Personal

Born 1960, in MI; married Steve Johnson (a commercial artist and illustrator); children: Nicholas. *Education:* University of Cincinnati, B.F.A. (dance).

### Addresses

*Home*—Moraga, CA. *E-mail*—lou@johnsonandfancher. com.

### Career

Writer, illustrator, children's book designer, ballet mistress, and choreographer. Freelance illustrator with husband, Steve Johnson, c. 1979—; co-creator of pre-production set and character designs for animated films, including *Toy Story,* 1995, and *A Bug's Life,* 1998. Alberta Ballet, former ballet mistress; New Dance Ensemble, former associate artistic director; James Sewell Ballet, Minneapolis, MN, ballet mistress; Company C Contemporary Ballet, Walnut Creek, CA, ballet mistress; choreographer, coach, and instructor to dancers and companies throughout the United States.

### Awards, Honors

(All with Steve Johnson) International Reading Association Children's Book Award, 1989, for *No Star Nights* by Anna Smucker; Minnesota Book Award for Children's Books, 1992, for *The Salamander Room* by Anne Mazer; gold medal, Society of Illustrators, 1993, for *Up North at the Cabin* by Marsha Wilson Chall; Minnesota Book Award finalist for Children's Books, 1993, for *Up North at the Cabin,* 1996, for *Cat, You'd Better Come Home* by Garrison Keillor, 1997, for *My Many Colored Days* by Dr. Seuss, 1998, for *The Lost and Found House* by Michael Cadnum, 1999, for *Coppélia* by Margot Fonteyn, 2002, for both *The Day Ocean Came to Visit* by Diane Wolkstein and *Silver Seeds* by Paul Paolilli and Dan Brewer; Nestlé Children's Book Prize short-list, 2005, for *The Dancing Tiger* by Malachy Doyle; Image Award nomination, National Association for the Advancement of Colored People, 2009, for *Amazing Peace* by Maya Angelou. Solo awards include Minnesota State Arts Board artist fellowship for choreography, 2002.

### Writings

*AND ILLUSTRATOR, WITH HUSBAND STEVE JOHNSON*

*The Quest for the One Big Thing* (based on the animated film *A Bug's Life*), Disney Press (New York, NY), 1998.
(Adapter) Margery Williams, *The Velveteen Rabbit; or, How Toys Become Real*, Atheneum (New York, NY), 2002.
*Star Climbing,* Laura Geringer Books (New York, NY), 2006.

*ILLUSTRATOR, WITH STEVE JOHNSON*

Anna Smucker, *No Star Nights,* Knopf (New York, NY), 1989.
Douglas Hill, *Penelope's Pendant,* Doubleday (New York, NY), 1990.
Anne Mazer, *The Salamander Room,* Knopf (New York, NY), 1991.
Jon Scieszka, *The Frog Prince Continued,* Viking (New York, NY), 1991.
Marsha Wilson Chall, *Up North at the Cabin,* Lothrop, Lee & Shephard (New York, NY), 1992.
B.G. Hennessy, *The First Night,* Viking (New York, NY), 1993.
Sarah S. Kilborne, *Peach and Blue,* Knopf (New York, NY), 1994.
Garrison Keillor, *Cat, You Better Come Home,* Viking (New York, NY), 1995.
Dr. Seuss, *My Many Colored Days,* Knopf (New York, NY), 1996.

Michael Cadnum, *The Lost and Found House,* Viking (New York, NY), 1997.

Margot Fonteyn, *Coppélia,* Harcourt Brace (San Francisco, CA), 1998.

Craig Kee Strete, *The Lost Boy and the Monster,* Putnam's (New York, NY), 1999.

Janet Schulman, adaptor, *Felix Salten's Bambi,* Atheneum (New York, NY), 1999.

Lois Duncan, *I Walk at Night,* Viking (New York, NY), 2000.

Alice Hoffman, *Horsefly,* Hyperion (New York, NY), 2000.

Paul Paolilli and Dan Brewer, *Silver Seeds: A Book of Nature Poems,* Viking (New York, NY), 2001.

Diane Wolkstein, *The Day Ocean Came to Visit,* Harcourt (San Diego, CA), 2001.

Margaret Wise Brown, *Robin's Room,* Hyperion (New York, NY), 2002.

Louise Erdrich, *The Range Eternal,* Hyperion (New York, NY), 2002.

Mary Pope Osborne, *New York's Bravest,* Knopf (New York, NY), 2002.

Mavis Jukes, *You're a Bear,* Knopf (New York, NY), 2003.

Kathleen Krull, *The Boy on Fairfield Street: How Ted Geisel Grew up to Become Dr. Seuss,* Random House (New York, NY), 2004.

Dori Chaconas, *Momma, Will You?,* Penguin (New York, NY), 2004.

H.L. Panahi, *Bebop Express,* Laura Geringer Books (New York, NY), 2005.

Malachy Doyle, *The Dancing Tiger,* Simon & Schuster (New York, NY), 2005.

Karen Hill, *All God's Creatures,* Little Simon (New York, NY), 2005.

Dan Gutman, *Casey Back at Bat,* HarperCollins (New York, NY), 2007.

Margie Palatini, *The Cheese,* Katherine Tegen Books (New York, NY), 2007.

Warren Hanson, *Bugtown Boogie,* Laura Geringer Books (New York, NY), 2008.

Hans Christian Andersen, *The Ugly Duckling,* retold by Stephen Mitchell, Candlewick Press (New York, NY), 2008.

Maya Angelou, *Amazing Peace: A Christmas Poem,* Random House (New York, NY), 2008.

Diane Wright Landolf, *What a Good Big Brother!,* Random House (New York, NY), 2009.

Marcus Hummon, *Anytime, Anywhere: A Little Boy's Prayer,* Atheneum Books for Young Readers (New York, NY), 2009.

Kenneth Oppel, *The King's Taster,* HarperCollins (New York, NY), 2009.

Kathleen Krull, *A Boy Named FDR: How Franklin D. Roosevelt Grew up to Change America,* Knopf (New York, NY), 2010.

Michael McGowan, *Sunday Is for God,* Schwartz & Wade Books (New York, NY), 2010.

Kathleen Krull, *Jim Henson: The Guy Who Played with Puppets,* Random House Children's Books (New York, NY), 2011.

*OTHER*

Contributor of articles to regional newspapers, including the *Walnut Creek Patch, Lamorinda Weekly, Clayton Pioneer,* and *Concordian.*

## Sidelights

Trained in ballet, Lou Fancher has gone on to work on two very different yet equally creative stages. A choreographer and dance teacher, she has served as both artistic director and ballet mistress at many ballet companies in her home state of Minnesota. In addition, Fancher is also one half of the respected artistic collaboration that, with her husband, commercial artist Steve Johnson, produces evocative, vibrantly colored illustrations for dozens of children's books. "We share in the amount of work each of us puts into a painting," the duo stated in a *BWI Titletales* online interview. "It isn't always easy to keep in mind one's own vision, while also being open to input from the other artist. That is the collaborative challenge; the reward is in producing artwork neither of us could produce on our own."

As well as creating art for text by popular writers such as Mavis Jukes, Dr. Seuss, Maya Angelou, Margie Palatini, and Kenneth Oppel, Fancher has also created and co-illustrated the original picture book *Star Climbing.*

*Lou Fancher breathes new life into a classic by co-illustrating a new edition of Margery Williams'* The Velveteen Rabbit *with husband and collaborator Steve Johnson.* (Copyright © 2002 by Steve Johnson and Lou Fancher. Reproduced by permission of Atheneum Books for Young Readers, an imprint of Simon & Schuster Children's Publishing Division.)

Praising the book's "rhythmic, lyrical" verses, which follow a child's make-believe journey up among the constellations on the way to dreamland, a *Publishers Weekly* reviewer predicted that Fancher's "dreamy bedtime poem with its magical, moon-dappled illustrations may well dazzle star-struck young readers." According to a *Kirkus Reviews* contributor, the couple's "lush, rich illustrations highlight [Fancher's] . . . fanciful nighttime adventure," making *Star Climbing* a "peaceful, vivid visual treat" for young listeners.

In their collaborations, Fancher and Johnson work together on all facets of each illustration project: initial conception, drawing, designing, and painting. As a testament to their skill, they were the first illustrators selected by the estate of Theodore Geisel (the man known as Dr. Seuss) to illustrate *My Many-Colored Days,* a manuscript that remained unillustrated and unpublished at Geisel's death. Their work here, which *Booklist* contributor Hazel Rochman dubbed "glowing and lively," is mirrored in a related work, Kathleen Krull's picture-book biography *The Boy on Fairfield Street: How Ted Geisel Grew up to Become Dr. Seuss.* An exploration of Geisel's experiences as a German immigrant in the early twentieth century, Krull's book was deemed a "winner" by Anne Chapman Callaghan, the critic adding in her *School Library Journal* review that Fancher and Johnson's "lovely, full-page illustrations" successfully integrate Seuss's own art. The couple has also created art for posters, business publications, commercial advertising, and periodicals and served as part of the creative team that produced the animated films *Toy Story* and *A Bug's Life.* Fancher's book *The Quest for the One Big Thing*, a counting book, is based on *A Bug's Life.*

Born in Michigan, Fancher took classes in art history at the University of Cincinnati while working toward her B.F.A. in dance. After she met and married Minnesota native Johnson, she relocated to the Minneapolis area, where the couple lived until moving to Moraga, California. "We didn't formally 'decide' we could work together; the process was gradual and instinctive more than planned," the duo stated in their *BWI Titletales* interview. "It evolved over a period of years and continues to change and grow as we mature as visual artists."

Among the many collaborations for which Fancher and Johnson share credit are new versions of some childhood classics. One, Margery Williams' *The Velveteen Rabbit; or, How Toys Become Real,* features a text Fancher adapted for younger readers, while another is Janet Schulman's adaptation of Felix Salten's classic *Bambi.* Commenting on the latter book, Elizabeth Spires wrote in the *New York Times Book Review* that the couple's "luminous paintings" in this "richly illustrated" work "capture, by turns, the radiance of Bambi's forest world, its beauty, terror and stillness." Working again with Johnson, Fancher combines her passions for dance and art in illustrating Margot Fonteyn's picture-book

**New York's Bravest, *a story by Mary Pope Osborne, comes to life in Fancher and Johnson's dramatic paintings.*** (Illustration © 2002 by Steve Johnson and Lou Fancher. Used by permission of Alfred A. Knopf, an imprint of Random House Children's Books, a division of Random House, Inc.)

adaptation of the ballet based on E.T.A. Hoffman's *Coppélia.* Reviewing this work, Carolyn Phelan dubbed it "a rich, visual interpretation and a wonderful introduction to a performance of the ballet" in her *Booklist* review.

Fancher and Johnson's other collaborations include creating illustrations for *I Walk at Night* by Lois Duncan; *New York's Bravest,* Mary Pope Osborne's tribute to heroic firefighters everywhere; *Horsefly* by Alice Hoffman; and Dan Gutman's retelling of a well-known American fable in *Casey Back at Bat.* The unusual media used in illustrating Duncan's story about the world as seen through the eyes of a nocturnal cat—string and oil paint—prompted a *Publishers Weekly* critic to note that the couple's use of "twilight tones" and a textured surface produce an "overall effect [that] is dreamy and atmospheric, and makes for grand bedtime fare." While framed as the story of Moses Humphreys, a volunteer firefighter who, in nineteenth-century New York, heroically saved countless lives before losing his own, *New York's Bravest* is also a timely tribute to the firefighters who lost their lives on September 11, 2001. As a *Publishers Weekly* contributor noted, Fancher and Johnson's oil paintings combine with Osborne's text to "carefully and respectfully balance" the historic and mythic elements of Humphreys' life, resulting in "a loving tribute . . . that may well help youngsters cope with the loss of these brave leaders."

In their illustrations for *Horsefly* the couple "chart the emotional movement" of Hoffman's story about a girl who loses her fear of horses during a magical flight, using what *Booklist* reviewer Connie Fletcher described as "rich artwork" that ranges from "dark and angular. . . . to brightly glowing." Working with author Dan Gutman to revision the American saga of Casey at the Bat, Fancher and Johnson also received critical praise. In *Booklist,* GraceAnne A. DeCandido wrote of the illustrators that "the fab team . . . makes wonderful, nineteenth-century-inspired paintings" that reflect the mood of Gutman's nostalgic tale through "their amber glow, Victorian colors, and newsprint shadows."

Fancher and Johnson also provided the artwork for *Amazing Peace: A Christmas Poem,* a picture-book version of an anti-war poem composed by Maya Angelou for the 2005 White House Christmas tree-lighting ceremony. The mixed-media illustrations "reflect the sentiments of the poem while also telling their own story," Kristen McKulski noted in *Booklist.* In *Anytime, Anywhere: A Little Boy's Prayer* a tale by country music artist Marcus Hummon, young Isaac engages in a thoughtful debate about faith and charity with his father. Fancher and Johnson combine acrylic paintings and collage elements "to create cozy scenes in Isaac's bedroom," maintained a contributor in *Publishers Weekly.* In another religious-themed title, Michael McGowan's *Sunday Is for God,* "Johnson and Fancher expertly layer collaged hymns, Bible verses, and photographs beneath their impressionistic acrylic paintings," according to *School Library Journal* critic Lisa Egly Lehmuller.

*Kenneth Oppel's story in* **The King's Taster** *gets an added dose of whimsy from Fancher and Johnson's art.* (Illustration copyright © 2009 by Steve Johnson and Lou Fancher. Reproduced with permission of HarperCollins Children's Books, a division of HarperCollins Publishers.)

In the picture book *The Cheese* Margie Palatini offers an unusual twist on the favorite children's song "The Farmer in the Dell," with the lively cast of characters questioning the wisdom of allowing a tasty hunk of cheddar to stand alone in the meadow. Fancher and Johnson "pump up the humor" in Palatini's narrative, stated a *Publishers Weekly* contributor, and Susan Moorhead observed in *School Library Journal* that "the cartoon animals are funny and expressive." A youngster discovers a raucous insect dance party in Warren Hanson's *Bugtown Boogie,* a work told in verse. "Vibrant hues and frenetic energy suffuse the artwork," Kirsten Cutler remarked in her *School Library Journal* review of Hanson's story.

Fancher and Johnson's artwork has also graced the pages of *The Ugly Duckling,* Stephen Mitchell's retelling of the classic tale by Hans Christian Andersen. "Every page is spectacular," a contributor in *Kirkus Reviews* observed, and Cutler reported that "the art combines painting with lace to achieve a textural and patterned appearance." Describing the powerful scene in which the duckling realizes it is actually a swan, *Horn Book* critic Deirdre F. Baker noted that the "lacy, luminous art, rich with underwaterlike greens, gives that moment all the visual splendor it deserves."

A tale of sibling bonding, Diane Wright Landolf's *What a Good Big Brother!* concerns a boy's imaginative efforts to soothe his troubled infant sister. Here "Johnson and Fancher's mixed-media collages shimmer with vivid colors and warm emotions," Martha Simpson wrote in *School Library Journal* and a *Publishers Weekly* critic felt that the duo's "use of life-size-and-larger scale is riveting." In Kenneth Oppel's *The King's Taster* Max the dog joins forces with the royal cook to concoct a new menu for a finicky new monarch. Fancher and Johnson's pictures "are deliciously capricious with clever collage details," Julie Cummins stated in her *Booklist* review of *The King's Taster*, and in *School Library Journal* Laura Lutz praised the book's "rich and textured art."

## Biographical and Critical Sources

*PERIODICALS*

*Booklist,* November 1, 1996, Hazel Rochman, review of *My Many Colored Days,* p. 510; October 15, 1998, Carolyn Phelan, review of *Coppélia,* p. 416; December 1, 2000, Connie Fletcher, review of *Horsefly,* p. 721; April 15, 2002, Kay Weisman, review of *Robin's Room,* p. 1406; July, 2002, Ilene Cooper, review of *New York's Finest,* p. 1847; December 1, 2003, Louise Brueggemann, review of *You're a Bear,* p. 684; February 15, 2006, Carolyn Phelan, review of *Star Climbing,* p. 101; January 1, 2007, GraceAnne A. DeCandido, review of *Casey Back at Bat,* p. 114; November 15, 2008, Kristen McKulski, review of *Amaz-*

*ing Peace: A Christmas Poem,* p. 41; February 1, 2009, Hazel Rochman, review of *What a Good Big Brother!,* p. 47; March 15, 2009, Julie Cummins, review of *The King's Taster,* p. 61; April 15, 2009, Ilene Cooper, review of *Anytime, Anywhere: A Little Boy's Prayer,* p. 45.

*Bulletin of the Center for Children's Books,* March, 2004, Krista Hutley, review of *The Boy on Fairfield Street: How Ted Geisel Grew up to Become Dr. Seuss,* p. 284.

*Childhood Education,* winter, 2007, Luisa N. Rodriguez, review of *Casey Back at Bat,* p. 107.

*Horn Book,* November-December, 1993, Mary M. Burns, review of *The First Night,* p. 724; November-December, 2002, Roger Sutton, review of *New York's Bravest,* p. 737; May-June, 2007, Miriam Lang Budin, review of *Casey Back at Bat,* p. 265; January-February, 2008, Deirdre F. Baker, review of *The Ugly Duckling,* p. 67; July-August, 2009, Joanna Rudge Long, review of *The King's Taster,* p. 413.

*Kirkus Reviews,* July 1, 2002, review of *New York's Bravest,* p. 951; August 15, 2002, review of *The Range Eternal,* p. 1222; September 15, 2002, review of *The Velveteen Rabbit,* p. 1389; December 15, 2003, review of *The Boy on Fairfield Street,* p. 1451; April 15, 2005, review of *The Dancing Tiger,* p. 472; June 1, 2005, review of *Bebop Express,* p. 642; February 15, 2006, review of *Star Climbing,* p. 182; November 15, 2007, review of *The Ugly Duckling*; November 1, 2008, review of *Amazing Peace.*

*New York Times Book Review,* November 21, 1999, Elizabeth Spires, review of *Bambi.*

*Publishers Weekly,* September 20, 1993, review of *The First Night,* p. 37; November 7, 1994, review of *Peach and Blue,* p. 77; May 8, 1995, review of *Cat, You Better Come Home,* p. 294; October 13, 1997, review of *The Lost and Found House,* p. 74; November 16, 1998, review of *The Quest for the One Big Thing,* p. 77; January 10, 2000, review of *I Walk at Night,* p. 67; August 13, 2001, review of *The Day Ocean Came to Visit,* p. 311; May 20, 2002, review of *Robin's Room,* p. 65; June 24, 2002, review of *New York's Bravest,* p. 56; September 9, 2002, review of *The Range Eternal,* p. 67; January 23, 2006, review of *Star Climbing,* p. 206; April 2, 2007, review of *The Cheese,* p. 55; January 21, 2008, review of *The Ugly Duckling,* p. 170; November 24, 2008, review of *What a Good Big Brother!,* p. 57; December 8, 2008, review of *Anytime, Anywhere,* p. 57.

*School Library Journal,* April, 1999, review of *The Quest for the One Big Thing,* p. 94; August, 2001, Margaret A. Chang, review of *The Day Ocean Came to Visit,* p. 174; October, 2002, Susan Oliver, review of *The Range Eternal,* p. 104; December, 2003, Laura Scott, review of *You're a Bear,* p. 118; January, 2004, Anne Chapman Callaghan, review of *The Boy on Fairfield Street,* p. 119; November, 2004, Rebecca Sheridan, review of *Momma, Will You?,* p. 94; July, 2005, Grace Oliff, review of *The Dancing Tiger,* p. 88; April, 2006, Susan Weitz, review of *Star Climbing,* p. 105; January, 2007, Marilyn Taniguchi, review of *Casey Back at Bat,* p. 94; June, 2007, Susan Moorhead, review of *The Cheese,* p. 119; January, 2008, Kirsten Cutler, re-

view of *The Ugly Duckling,* p. 80; July, 2008, Kirsten Cutler, review of *Bugtown Boogie,* p. 74; February, 2009, Martha Simpson, review of *What a Good Big Brother!,* p. 76; June, 2009, Laura Lutz, review of *The King's Taster,* p. 97; January, 2010, Lisa Egly Lehmuller, review of *Sunday Is for God,* p. 77.

*ONLINE*

*BWI Titletales Web site,* http://bwibooks.com/ (April 1, 2011), interview with Fancher and Steve Johnson.

*Lou Fancher and Steve Johnson Home Page,* http://www.johnsonandfancher.com (April 1, 2011).*

\*          \*          \*

# FARRELL, Darren

## Personal

Born in Raleigh, NC; married; wife's name Caroline; children: Jonah. *Education:* University of North Carolina, degree (journalism).

## Addresses

*Home*—Hoboken, NJ. *Agent*—Elana Roth, Caren Johnson Literary Agency, 132 E. 43rd St., No. 216, New York, NY 10017; elana@johnsonliterary.com. *E-mail*—df@darrenfarrellcreativetype.com.

## Career

Writer, illustrator, and creative director. Freelance writer, 2005—.

*Darren Farrell's quirky humor is expressed in his equally quirky artwork for his original picture book* **Doug-Dennis and the Flyaway Fib.**

## Writings

(Self-illustrated) *Doug-Dennis and the Flyaway Fib,* Dial Books for Young Readers (New York, NY), 2010.

## Sidelights

Darren Farrell takes a humorous look at the repercussions of telling a lie in his debut picture book, *Doug-Dennis and the Flyaway Fib.* Farrell, a creative director who has written television commercials for the National Football League and the Library of Congress, describes the misadventures of Doug-Dennis, a sneaker-wearing sheep that commits a breach of etiquette and then tries to cover up his misdeed. While attending the circus with his friend, Ben-Bobby the elephant, Doug-Dennis gobbles all of his buddy's popcorn and lies about the incident, disavowing all responsibility and eventually blaming the missing popcorn on monsters. As his lie grows and grows, it literally carries the hapless sheep into the stratosphere, where he meets a host of other fibbers, including unscrupulous salespeople and imaginary friends. Tired of being airborne, Doug-Dennis finally realizes that there is only one way to return home.

Drawing comparisons to the work of author/illustrator Mo Willems, *Doug-Dennis and the Flyaway Fib* earned solid reviews. "Farrell's offhanded humor and the absolute absurdity of the situation and characters make this a fun lesson in truth-telling," Sarah Townsend commented in *School Library Journal,* and a *Publishers Weekly* contributor noted that "the ethically unsteady Doug-Dennis has plenty of Homer Simpson-like appeal." Citing the pen-and-ink and digital illustrations in *Doug-Dennis and the Flyaway Fib, Booklist* reviewer Ilene Cooper observed that Farrell "creates amusing artwork," and a *Kirkus Reviews* critic observed that the author/illustrator's humorous images "move the familiar theme to a story of hilarious and exaggerated lengths."

## Biographical and Critical Sources

*PERIODICALS*

*Booklist,* April 1, 2010, Ilene Cooper, review of *Doug-Dennis and the Flyaway Fib,* p. 46.
*Kirkus Reviews,* February 15, 2010, review of *Doug-Dennis and the Flyaway Fib.*
*Publishers Weekly,* February 15, 2010, review of *Doug-Dennis and the Flyaway Fib,* p. 129.
*School Library Journal,* March, 2010, Sarah Townsend, review of *Doug-Dennis and the Flyaway Fib,* p. 118.

*ONLINE*

*Darren Farrell Home Page,* http://darrenfarrellcreativetype. com (April 1, 2011).
*Darren Farrell Web log,* http://darren-farrell.com (April 1, 2011).
*Fib Factory Web site,* http://www.dougdennis.com (April 1, 2011).*

# FORMENTO, Alison

## Personal

Born in AR; married; has children. *Hobbies and other interests:* Traveling, theatre and film, hiking, tennis.

## Addresses

*Home*—NJ. *Agent*—Courtney Miller-Callihan, Sanford J. Greenburger Associates, 55 5th Ave., New York, NY 10003. *E-mail*—aforment@optonline.net.

## Career

Author and journalist. Experienced presenter at schools, libraries, bookstores, conferences, and festivals. Participant in American Forests Global ReLeafing initiative.

## Member

Society of Children's Book Writers and Illustrators, KidLit Authors Club.

## Awards, Honors

Green Book Award, 2010, and Kids Are Readers, Too Award, and Crystal Kite Award finalist, Society of Children's Book Writers and Illustrators, both 2011, all for *This Tree Counts!*

## Writings

*This Tree Counts!,* illustrated by Sarah Snow, Albert Whitman (Chicago, IL), 2010, abridged version published as *This Tree, 1, 2, 3,* 2011.

*Alison Formento* (Reproduced by permission.)

*Formento's story in* **This Tree Counts!** *is brought to life in child-friendly multi-media artwork by Sarah Snow.* (Reproduced with permission of Albert Whitman & Company.)

*These Bees Count!,* illustrated by Sarah Snow, Albert Whitman (Chicago, IL), 2012.

*These Seas Count!,* illustrated by Sarah Snow, Albert Whitman (Chicago, IL), 2013.

Contributor of essays and articles to periodicals, including the *New York Times, Parenting,* and *Writer.*

## Sidelights

New Jersey author Alison Formento lists some surprising jobs on her resume: hand model, singing telegram delivery girl, and Renaissance Faire queen. Along with these past employment experiences, parenting and a love of nature have melded through her skill as a writer to produce the entertaining picture books *This Tree Counts!*, its preschooler-friendly version, *This Tree, 1,2,3, These Bees Count!,* and *These Seas Count!,* all of which are illustrated with cut-paper art by Sarah Snow. In addition to her books for children, Formento is also a journalist whose work has been published in periodicals such as *Parenting, The New York Times,* and *The Writer.*

In *This Tree Counts!* Formento transports her readers to Oak Lane Elementary School, where Mr. Tate's students worry that the giant oak tree standing alone on the school grounds may feel lonely. Their teacher urges the students not to make assumptions but to study the situation. As they observe the tree, they realize that the lone oak is actually an ecosystem all to itself as a succession of animals—from one owl to two spider, three squirrels, and so forth up to ten earthworms—make homes in and around it, some even relying on the oak for their sustenance. As Formento tells her story, she includes more than just counting; information about tree growth, types of trees, and uses for wood, as well as instructions on sprouting a tree of one's own are covered.

While Formento's text for *This Tree Counts!* encompasses a "theme of cooperation and friendship," according to *School Library Journal* contributor Linda L. Walkins, Snow's "collage illustrations add texture and natural beauty to the story." In *Booklist* Julie Cummins cited the "double meaning of the title" and maintained that the author's "environmental message" is effectively contained within her "concisely written story with a child's point of view." In *This Tree, 1, 2, 3* the story in *This Tree Counts!* is distilled for use as a toddler-friendly concept book where counting from one to ten and introducing basic animals are the focus. "Though the text is pared down," noted *School Library Journal* contributor Laura Butler in reviewing Formento's adaptation, "the important message remains."

## Biographical and Critical Sources

*PERIODICALS*

*American Forests,* summer, 2010, Sarah McVicar, interview with Formento and review of *This Tree Counts!,* both p. 47.

*Booklist,* January 1, 2010, Julie Cummins, review of *This Tree Counts!,* p. 100.

*Kirkus Reviews,* February 15, 2010, review of *This Tree Counts!*

*School Library Journal,* February, 2010, Linda L. Walkins, review of *This Tree Counts!,* p. 84; March, 2011, Laura Butler, review of *This Tree, 1,2,3,* p. 142.

*ONLINE*

*Alison Formento Home Page,* http://www.alisonashley formento.com (March 20, 2011).

*Alison Formento Web log,* http://alisonashleyformento. blogspot.com (March 20, 2011).

*Albert Whitman Web log,* http://www.albertwhitman. wordpress.com/ (July 15, 2010), podcast with Formento and Sarah Snow.

# G

## GAIMAN, Neil 1960-

### Personal

Born November 10, 1960, in Portchester, England; son of David Bernard (a company director) and Sheila (a pharmacist) Gaiman; married Mary Therese McGrath, March 14, 1985 (divorced); married Amanda Palmer (a musician), January 2, 2011; children: (first marriage) Michael Richard, Holly Miranda, Madeleine Rose Elvira. *Education:* Attended Ardingly College, 1970-74, and Whitgift School, 1974-77. *Politics:* "Wooly." *Religion:* Jewish. *Hobbies and other interests:* "Finding more bookshelf space."

### Addresses

*Home*—MN. *Agent*—(literary) Merilee Heifetz, Writer's House, 21 W. 26th St., New York, NY 10010; (film) Jon Levin, Creative Artists Agency, 9830 Wilshire Blvd., Beverly Hills, CA 90212-1825. *E-mail*—cat@gaiman.net.

### Career

Fiction writer, screenwriter, poet, essayist, and journalist. Freelance journalist, 1983-87; full-time writer, 1987—. Director of *A Short Film about John Bolton,* Ska Films, 2004. Songwriter for bands The Flash Girls and One Ring Zero. Fellow, University of Liverpool School of the Arts.

*Neil Gaiman* (Copyright © AP Images.)

### Member

Comic Book Legal Defense Fund (member of board of directors), International Museum of Cartoon Art (member of advisory board), Society of Strip Illustrators (chair, 1988-90), British Fantasy Society, Open Rights Group, Science Fiction Foundation.

### Awards, Honors

Mekon Award, Society of Strip Illustrators, and Eagle Award for Best Graphic Novel, both 1988, both for *Violent Cases;* Eagle Award for Best Writer of American Comics, 1990; Harvey Award for Best Writer, 1990, 1991; Will Eisner Comic Industry Award for Best Writer and Best Graphic Album (Reprint), 1991; World Fantasy Award for Best Short Story, 1991, for "A Midsummer Night's Dream"; Will Eisner Comics Industry Award for Best Writer, 1992, 1993, 1994; Harvey Award for Best Continuing Series, 1992; Will Eisner Comics Industry Award for Best Graphic Album (New), 1993; Gem Award, Diamond Distributors, 1993; Guild Award, International Horror Critics, and World Fantasy Award nomination, both 1994, both for *Angels and Visitations* and short story "Troll Bridge"; SONY Radio Award, for script *Signal to Noise*; GLAAD Award for Best Comic, 1996, for *Death: The Time of Your Life;* Eagle Award for Best Comic, 1996; Lucca Best Writer Prize, 1997; *Newsweek* Best Children's Books designation, 1997, for *The Day I Swapped My Dad for Two Goldfish;* Defender of Liberty Award, Comic Book Legal Defense Fund, 1997; MacMillan Silver Pen Award, 1999, for *Smoke and Mirrors;* Hugo Award nomination, 1999, for *Sandman: The Dream Hunters;* Mythopoeic Award for Best Novel for Adults, 1999, for *Stardust;* Nebula Award nomination, 1999, for screenplay *Princess Mononoke;* Hugo Award for Best Science Fiction/Fantasy Novel, Bram Stoker Award for Best Novel, Horror Writers Association, and British Science Fiction Association (BSFA) Award nomination, all 2002, and Geffen Award, 2004, all for *American Gods;* BSFA Award for Best Short Fiction, Elizabeth Burr/Worzalla Award, Bram Stoker Award, Hugo Award for Best Novella, and Prix Tam Tam, all 2003, all for *Coraline;* World Fantasy Award for Best Short Story, 2003, for "October in the Chair"; BSFA Award for Best Short Fiction, 2004, for *The Wolves in the Walls;* Hugo Award for Best Short Story, 2004, for "A Study in Emerald"; Bram Stoker Award for Best Illustrative Narrative, 2004, for *The Sandman: Endless Nights;* Geffen Award, 2004, for *Smoke and Mirrors;* Locus Award for Best Short Story, 2004, for "Closing Time," 2010, for "An Invocation of Incuriosity"; August Derleth Award, and Best Books for Young Adults selection, American Library Association (ALA), both 2006, both for *Anansi Boys;* Locus Award for Best Short Story, 2007, for "How to Talk to Girls at Parties"; Bob Clampett Humanitarian Award, 2007; Locus Award for Best Collection, 2007, for *Fragile Things;* Hugo Award for Best Novel, British Fantasy Award for Best Novel shortlist, Booktrust Teenage Prize, and John Newbery Medal for outstanding contribution to children's literature, ALA, all 2009, and Carnegie Medal, 2010, all for *The Graveyard Book;* international awards from Austria, Brazil, Canada, Finland, France, Germany, Italy, and Spain.

## Writings

### JUVENILE FICTION

*The Day I Swapped My Dad for Two Goldfish,* illustrated by Dave McKean, Borealis/White Wolf (Clarkson, GA), 1997.

*Coraline* (also see below), illustrated by Dave McKean, HarperCollins (New York, NY), 2002.

*The Wolves in the Walls,* illustrated by Dave McKean, HarperCollins (New York, NY), 2003.

*Mirrormask* (special children's edition; based on the film of the same title; also see below), illustrated by Dave McKean, HarperCollins (New York, NY), 2005.

(With Michael Reaves) *Interworld,* Eos (New York, NY), 2005.

*M Is for Magic,* illustrated by Teddy Kristiansen, HarperCollins (New York, NY), 2007.

*The Graveyard Book,* illustrated by Dave McKean, HarperCollins (New York, NY), 2008.

*The Dangerous Alphabet,* illustrated by Gris Grimly, HarperCollins (New York, NY), 2008.

*Blueberry Girl,* illustrated by Charles Vess, HarperCollins (New York, NY), 2008.

*Crazy Hair,* illustrated by Dave McKean, HarperCollins (New York, NY), 2009.

*Odd and the Frost Giants,* illustrated by Brett Helquist, HarperCollins (New York, NY), 2009.

*Instructions: Everything You'll Need to Know on Your Journey* (originally published in *A Wolf at the Door,* edited by Ellen Datlow and Terri Windling, 2000), illustrated by Charles Vess, HarperCollins (New York, NY), 2010.

### GRAPHIC NOVELS AND COMIC BOOKS

(With others) *Jael and Sisera: Outrageous Tales from the Old Testament,* illustrated by Julie Hollings, Knockabout (London, England), 1987.

*Violent Cases* (originally published in comic-book format, 1987), illustrated by Dave McKean, Titan (London, England), 1987, Tundra (Northampton, MA), 1991, third edition, Kitchen Sink Press (Northampton, MA), 1997.

*Black Orchid* (originally published in comic-book form, 1989), illustrated by Dave McKean, DC Comics (New York, NY), 1991.

*Miracleman, Book 4: The Golden Age,* illustrated by Mark Buckingham, Eclipse (Forestville, CA), 1992.

*Signal to Noise* (also see below), illustrated by Dave McKean, Dark Horse Comics (Milwaukie, OR), 1992.

*The Books of Magic* (originally published in comic-book form), four volumes, illustrated by John Bolton and others, DC Comics (New York, NY), 1993.

*The Tragical Comedy, or Comical Tragedy, of Mr. Punch: A Romance,* illustrated by Dave McKean, VG Graphics (London, England), 1994, Vertigo/DC Comics (New York, NY), 1995.

(Author of text, with Alice Cooper) *The Compleat Alice Cooper: Incorporating the Three Acts of Alice Cooper's The Last Temptation,* illustrated by Michael Zulli, Marvel Comics (New York, NY), 1995, published as *The Last Temptation,* Dark Horse Comics (Milwaukie, OR), 2000.

*Angela,* illustrated by Greg Capullo and Mark Pennington, Image (Anaheim, CA), 1995, published as *Spawn: Angela's Hunt,* 2000.

*Stardust: Being a Romance within the Realms of Faerie,* illustrated by Charles Vess, DC Comics (New York, NY), 1998, text published as *Stardust,* Spike (New York, NY), 1999.

(Author of text, with Matt Wagner) *Neil Gaiman's Midnight Days,* DC Comics (New York, NY), 1999.

*Green Lantern/Superman: Legend of the Green Flame,* DC Comics (New York, NY), 2000.

*Harlequin Valentine,* illustrated by John Bolton, Dark Horse Comics (Milwaukie, OR), 2001.

*Murder Mysteries* (based on play of the same title, also see below), illustrated by P. Craig Russell, Dark Horse Comics (Milwaukie, OR), 2002.

*1602* (originally published comic-book form as *1602,* volumes 1-8), Marvel Comics (New York, NY), 2004.

*The Eternals,* illustrated by John Romita, Jr., Marvel Comics (New York, NY), 2007.

*The Facts in the Case of the Departure of Miss Finch,* illustrated by Michael Zulli, Dark Horse Comics (Milwaukie, OR), 2008.

*Coraline* (graphic novel; based on the children's book of the same title), illustrated by P. Craig Russell, Harper-Collins (New York, NY), 2008.

*Batman: Whatever Happened to the Caped Crusader?; with Other Tales of the Dark Knight,* illustrated by Andy Kubert and others, DC Comics (New York, NY), 2009.

*The Absolute Death,* illustrated by Chris Bachalo and others, DC Comics (New York, NY), 2009.

Also author of *Creatures of the Night,* illustrated by Michael Zulli. Contributor of comics, including "Babycakes" and "The Wheel," to anthologies. Creator of characters for comic-book series, including Lady Justice, Wheel of Worlds, Mr. Hero, Newmatic Man, Teknophage, and Lucifer. Co-editor of *The Utterly Comic Relief Comic* (comic book), UK Comic Relief Charity, 1991.

*"SANDMAN" GRAPHIC-NOVEL SERIES*

*Sandman: The Doll's House* (originally published in comic-book form), illustrated by Mike Dringenberg and Malcolm Jones III, DC Comics (New York, NY), 1990.

*Sandman: Preludes and Nocturnes* (originally published in comic-book form as *Sandman,* volumes 1-8), illustrated by Sam Keith, Mike Dringenberg, and Malcolm Jones III, DC Comics (New York, NY), 1991.

*Sandman: Dream Country* (originally published in comic-book form as *Sandman,* volumes 17-20; contains "A Midsummer's Night's Dream"), illustrated by Kelley Jones, Charles Vess, Colleen Doran, and Malcolm Jones III, DC Comics (New York, NY), 1991.

*Sandman: Season of Mists* (originally published in comic-book form as *Sandman,* volumes 21-28), illustrated by Kelley Jones, Malcolm Jones III, Mike Dringenberg, and others, DC Comics (New York, NY), 1992.

*Sandman: A Game of You* (originally published in comic-book form as *Sandman,* volumes 32-37), illustrated by Shawn McManus and others, DC Comics (New York, NY), 1993.

*Sandman: Fables and Reflections* (originally published in comic-book form as *Sandman,* volumes 29-31, 38-40, 50), illustrated by Bryan Talbot, DC Comics (New York, NY), 1994.

*Death: The High Cost of Living* (originally published in comic-book form in three volumes), illustrated by Dave McKean, Mark Buckingham, and others, DC Comics (New York, NY), 1994.

*Sandman: Brief Lives* (originally published in comic-book form as *Sandman,* volumes 41-49), illustrated by Jill Thompson, Dick Giordano, and Vince Locke, DC Comics (New York, NY), 1994.

*Sandman: World's End* (originally published in comic-book form as *Sandman,* volumes 51-56), illustrated by Dave McKean, Mark Buckingham, Dick Giordano, and others, DC Comics (New York, NY), 1994.

(Author of text, with Matt Wagner) *Sandman: Midnight Theatre,* illustrated by Teddy Kristiansen, DC Comics (New York, NY), 1995.

(Editor, with Edward E. Kramer) *The Sandman: Book of Dreams,* HarperPrism (New York, NY), 1996.

*Sandman: The Kindly Ones* (originally published in comic-book form as *Sandman,* volumes 57-69), illustrated by Marc Hempel, Richard Case, and others, DC Comics (New York, NY), 1996.

*Death: The Time of Your Life,* illustrated by Mark Buckingham and others, DC Comics (New York, NY), 1997.

(Author of commentary and a story) *Dustcovers: The Collected Sandman Covers, 1989-1997,* illustrated by Dave McKean, DC Comics (New York, NY), 1997, published as *The Collected Sandman Covers, 1989-1997,* Watson-Guptill (New York, NY), 1997.

*Sandman: The Wake,* (originally published in comic-book form as *Sandman,* volumes 70-75), illustrated by Michael Zulli, Charles Vess, and others, DC Comics (New York, NY), 1997.

(Reteller) *Sandman: The Dream Hunters,* illustrated by Yoshitaka Amano, DC Comics (New York, NY), 1999, adapted as a graphic novel, illustrated by P. Craig Russell, Vertigo (New York, NY), 2009.

*The Quotable Sandman: Memorable Lines from the Acclaimed Series,* DC Comics (New York, NY), 2000.

*The Sandman: Endless Nights,* illustrated by P. Craig Russell, Milo Manara, and others, DC Comics (New York, NY), 2003.

*The Absolute Sandman,* three volumes, DC Comics (New York, NY), 2006–2008.

*The Absolute Sandman, Volume Two,* DC Comics (New York, NY), 2007.

*The Absolute Sandman, Volume Three,* DC Comics (New York, NY), 2008.

Contributor to *The Sandman Companion,* DC Comics (New York, NY), 1999.

*FICTION*

(With Terry Pratchett) *Good Omens: The Nice and Accurate Prophecies of Agnes Nutter, Witch* (novel), Gollancz (London, England), 1990, revised edition, Workman (New York, NY), 1990.

(With Mary Gentle) *Villains!* (short stories), edited by Mary Gentle and Roz Kaveney, ROC (London, England), 1992.

(With Mary Gentle and Roz Kaveney) *The Weerde: Book One* (short stories), ROC (London, England), 1992.

(With Mary Gentle and Roz Kaveney) *The Weerde: Book Two: The Book of the Ancients* (short stories), ROC (London, England), 1992.

*Angels and Visitations: A Miscellany* (short stories), illustrated by Steve Bissette and others, DreamHaven Books and Art (Minneapolis, MN), 1993.

*Neverwhere* (novel; also see below), BBC Books (London, England), 1996, Avon (New York, NY), 1997.

*Smoke and Mirrors: Short Fictions and Illusions* (short stories), Avon (New York, NY), 1998.

*American Gods* (novel), William Morrow (New York, NY), 2001.

(Reteller) *Snow Glass Apples,* illustrated by George Walker, Biting Dog Press (Duluth, GA), 2003.

*Anansi Boys,* Morrow (New York, NY), 2005.

*Mirrormask* (illustrated film script; based on the film of the same title; also see below), illustrated by Dave McKean, HarperCollins (New York, NY), 2005.

*Fragile Things: Short Fictions and Wonders,* Morrow (New York, NY), 2006.

Author's work has been translated into numerous languages, including Bulgarian, Chinese, Croatian, Czech, Estonian, French, German, Greek, Hebrew, Hungarian, Italian, Japanese, Korean, Polish, Portuguese, Romanian, Russian, Serbian, Spanish, Swedish, and Turkish.

*EDITOR*

(With Kim Newman) *Ghastly beyond Belief,* Arrow (London, England), 1985.

(With Stephen Jones) *Now We Are Sick: A Sampler,* privately published, 1986, published as *Now We Are Sick: An Anthology of Nasty Verse,* DreamHaven (Minneapolis, MN), 1991.

(With Alex Stewart) *Temps,* ROC (London, England), 1991.

(With Alex Stewart) *Euro Temps,* ROC (London, England), 1992.

(With Al Sarrantonio) *Stories: All-New Tales,* William Morrow (New York, NY), 2010.

*SCREENPLAYS*

(With Lenny Henry) *Neverwhere,* BBC2 (London, England), 1996.

*Signal to Noise,* BBC Radio 3 (London, England), 1996.

*Day of the Dead: An Annotated Babylon 5 Script* (episode of television series *Babylon 5,* 1998), DreamHaven (Minneapolis, MN), 1998.

*Princess Mononoke* (English translation of Japanese-language screenplay by Hayao Miyazak), Miramax (New York, NY), 1999.

(And director) *A Short Film about John Bolton,* Ska Films, 2002.

*MirrorMask* (based on the children's book of the same title), Samuel Goldwyn, 2005.

(With Roger Avary) *Beowulf,* Paramount Pictures, 2007.

Author of scripts for films *Avalon, The Confessions of William Henry Ireland, The Fermata, Modesty Blaise,* and others.

*OTHER*

*Duran Duran: The First Four Years of the Fab Five* (biography), Proteus (New York, NY), 1984.

*Don't Panic: The Official Hitch-Hiker's Guide to the Galaxy Companion,* Pocket Books (New York, NY), 1988, revised edition with additional material by David K. Dickson as *Don't Panic: Douglas Adams and the Hitchhiker's Guide to the Galaxy,* Titan (London, England), 1993.

*Warning: Contains Language* (readings; compact disc), music by Dave McKean and the Flash Girls, DreamHaven (Minneapolis, MN), 1995.

(Co-illustrator) *The Dreaming: Beyond the Shores of Night,* DC Comics (New York, NY), 1997.

(Co-illustrator) *The Dreaming: Through the Gates of Horn and Ivory,* DC Comics (New York, NY), 1998.

*Neil Gaiman: Live at the Aladdin* (videotape), Comic Book Legal Defense Fund (Northampton, MA), 2001.

(With Gene Wolfe) *A Walking Tour of the Shambles* (nonfiction), American Fantasy Press (Woodstock, IL), 2001.

*Murder Mysteries* (play), illustrated by George Walker, Biting Dog Press (Duluth, GA), 2001.

*Adventures in the Dream Trade* (nonfiction and fiction), edited by Tony Lewis and Priscilla Olson, NESFA Press (Framingham, MA), 2002.

Works included in numerous anthologies. Contributor of prefaces and introductions to several books. Contributor to newspapers and magazines, including *Knave, Punch,* London *Observer,* London *Sunday Times, Wired, New York Times Book Review, Washington Post Book World,* and *Time Out.*

## Adaptations

*The Books of Magic* was adapted into novel form by Carla Jablonski and others, individual titles include *The Invitation, The Blindings,* and *The Children's Crusade,* HarperCollins (New York, NY). Several of Gaiman's works have been released as audiobooks, including *Neverwhere,* HighBridge Audio, 1997, *American Gods,* Harper Audio, 2001, *Coraline* (read by the author), HarperAudio, 2002, and *Two Plays for Voices* (includes *Snow Glass Apples* and *Murder Mysteries*), Harper Audio, 2003. *Signal to Noise* was adapted as a stage play by NOWtheater (Chicago, IL). *Stardust* was adapted as a major motion picture, Paramount, 2007. *Coraline* was adapted as a major motion picture, Focus Features, and as a musical play, book by David Greenspan, produced on Broadway, both 2009. Several of Gaiman's works have been optioned for film, including *Sandman, The Books of Magic, Death: The High Cost of Living, Good Omens,* and *Chivalry.*

## Sidelights

An author who has developed a cult-like following as well as celebrity status, Neil Gaiman is considered perhaps the most accomplished and influential figure in modern comics as well as one of the most gifted of contemporary fantasists. Characteristically drawing from mythology, history, literature, and popular culture, Gaiman blends the everyday, the fantastic, the frightening, and the humorous to craft works that reveal the mysteries that lie just outside of reality as well as the insights that come from experiencing these mysteries. He is perhaps best known as the creator of the epic "Sandman" comic-book series, a dark fantasy that has remained in print, in graphic-novel form, long after its initial seventy-five-issue run. Among his other works, Gaiman has authored novels, scripted comic books and graphic novels, and crafted plays for film, television, and radio, both original scripts and adaptations of his own works. Throughout his career, he has worked with top artists in the field of comic books and fantasy, including John Bolton, P. Craig Russell, Michael Zulli, Yoshitaka Amaro, Charles Vess, and longtime collaborator Dave McKean. Although much of his work is addressed to adults, Gaiman has written several books for younger readers, among them picture books, the middle-grade novel *Coraline,* a graphic-novel revisioning of the final days of Batman in *What Ever Happened to the Caped Crusader,* and *The Graveyard Book,* winner of both the John Newbery Medal and the Carnegie Medal.

As a prose stylist, Gaiman is known for writing clearly and strongly, using memorable characters and striking images to build his dreamlike worlds. Although his books and screenplays can range from somber to creepy to horrifying, his stories are underscored with optimism and sensitivity and their darkness is balanced with humor and wit. Reviewers have praised Gaiman for setting new standards for comic books as literature and for helping to bring increased popularity to graphic fiction. Despite occasional criticisms regarding his tendency toward self-indulgence, he is considered a brilliant writer and storyteller whose works reflect his inventiveness, originality, and wisdom. According to London *Times* contributor Amanda Craig, Gaiman's "richly imaginative, dark fantasies have the classic element of appealing to the adult in children and the child in adults," while Frank McConnell stated in *Commonweal* that, as perhaps "the most gifted and important storyteller in English," he ranks as the "best and most bound-to-be-remembered writer of fantasy" of his generation.

Born in Portchester, England, Gaiman was raised in an upper-middle-class home. As he recalled in an interview with Ray Olson for *Booklist,* he first read *Alice in Wonderland* "when I was five, maybe, and always kept it around as default reading between the ages of five and twelve, and occasionally picked up and reread since. There are things Lewis Carroll did in *Alice* that are etched onto my circuitry." When he was about fourteen years old, Gaiman began his secondary education at Whitgift School, and in 1977 he left, assured that he was ready to embark on a career as a professional writer.

The receipt of several rejections for short stories convinced Gaiman to become a freelance journalist as a way of learning about the world of publishing. In 1984

he produced his first book, *Duran Duran: The First Four Years of the Fab Five.* Once he had established his credibility as a writer, Gaiman was able to sell the short stories that he had completed earlier in his career, and he decided that he was ready to concentrate on fiction. At this time the comics industry was experiencing a new influx of talent, and this fact inspired Gaiman to consider becoming a contributor to that medium.

In 1983, Gaiman had discovered the work of English comic-strip writer Alan Moore, whose *Swamp Thing* quickly became a favorite. As he later told an interviewer in *Authors and Artists for Young Adults,* "Moore's work convinced me that you really could do work in comics that had the same amount of intelligence, the same amount of passion, the same amount of quality that you could put in any other medium." Three years later he met art student McKean; their first collaboration was the comic-book series "Violent Cases." Around the same time, Gaiman contributed to *Jael and Sisera: Outrageous Tales from the Old Testament,* which is credited with giving him almost instant recognition within the comic-book community. He reteamed with McKean to do a limited-run comic series, "Black Orchid," the first of the author's works to be released by DC Comics. When DC offered him a choice of inactive house characters to rework from the Golden Age of Comics (the 1930s and 1940s), Gaiman chose the Sandman.

As originally presented, millionaire Wesley Dodds—a. k.a. the Sandman—hunted criminals by night wearing a fedora, cape, and a gas mask. When Gaiman began the series in 1988, he changed the whole scope of the character. The Sandman, who is also called Dream, Morpheus, Oneiros, Lord Shaper, Master of Story, and God of Sleep, became a thin, enigmatic figure with a pale face, dark eyes, and a shock of black hair. The Sandman is one of the Endless, a pantheon of immortals that are in charge of individual realms of the human psyche. The Sandman's brothers and sisters in the Endless are (in birth order) Destiny, Death, Destruction, the twins Desire and Despair, and Delirium (formerly Delight). Dream (the Sandman) falls between Death and Destruction.

In the comic-book story arc that was eventually released in graphic-novel form as *Preludes and Nocturnes* Dream (the Sandman) has just returned home after being captured by a coven of wizards and held in an asylum for the criminally insane for seventy-two years. Finding his home in ruins, his powers diminished, and his three tools—a helmet, a pouch of sand, and a ruby stone—stolen, Dream realizes that during his captivity he has become mortal and will eventually die. *The Doll's House,* a subsequent story arc, follows his search for the Arcana, stray dreams and nightmares of the twentieth century that have taken on human form, while *Dream Country* centers on Calliope, a muse and the mother of Dream's son, Orpheus. In *Season of Mists*

Dream meets Lucifer, who has stepped down from his position as ruler of Hell and has left the choice of his successor to Dream.

Other story arcs in the "Sandman" comic-book series include *A Game of You; Fables and Reflections,* a collection of stories featuring the characters from the series; and *Brief Lives. World's End* includes a collection of tales told by a group of travelers who are waiting out a storm in an inn, while in *The Kindly Ones* Hippolyta takes revenge upon Dream for the disappearance of her son with the assistance of the title characters, mythological beings also known as the Furies. In the final "Sandman" chapter, *The Wake,* the Endless attend a ceremony to mark Dream's passing.

Assessing the "Sandman" series, McConnell stated that what Gaiman has done "is to establish the fact that a comic book can be a work of high and very serious art—a story that other storytellers, in whatever medium they work, will have to take into account as an exploration of what stories can do and what stories are for." In the *Dictionary of Literary Biography* Joe Sanders cited Gaiman's "Sandman" saga as "an example of how a serious writer can utilize the comics medium." In addition to using different artists to vary the mood of his works, Sanders noted, the author "utilized the cheeky looseness of comics to bring together an astonishing range of images; *The Sandman* considers, with equal sympathy and assurance, the personal and professional life of Shakespeare and the interpersonal dynamics of a convention of serial killers." Although Gaiman's "Sandman" series ended in 1996, DC Comics has re-released the epic work in a series of deluxe editions.

In his "Sandman" epic, Gaiman features a number of young characters, and this focus on the young remains has remained characteristic of much of his work. His *The Books of Magic* a collection of four comics that predates J.K. Rowling's "Harry Potter" series, features thirteen-year-old Tim Hunter, who is told that he has the capabilities to be the greatest wizard in the world. Tim, a boy from urban London who wears oversized glasses, is taken by the Trenchcoat Brigade—sorcerers with names like The Mysterious Phantom Stranger, the Incorrigible Hellblazer, and the Enigmatic Dr. Occult—on a tour of the universe to learn its magical history. He travels to Hell, to the land of Faerie, and to America, among other places, each place showing him a different aspect of the world of magic. He also searches for his girlfriend Molly, who has been abducted into the fantasy realms; after he finds her, the two teens face a series of dangers as they struggle to return to their own world. *The Books of Magic* also includes cameos by the Sandman and his sister Death. Writing in *Locus,* Carolyn Cushman described the work as "a fascinating look at magic, its benefits and burdens, all dramatically illustrated [by John Bolton, Scott Hampton, Charles Vess, and Paul Johnson], and with a healthy helping of humor."

Also featuring artwork by Vess, Gaiman's novel-length fantasy *Stardust* tells a love story about seventeen-year-old Tristran Thorn, who journeys to the fanciful land of Faerie on a quest to fetch a fallen star far from his village of Wall. Tristran has promised his love, Victoria, this star, and on his journey he has to deal with others who, more powerful and ruthless, also seek the fallen star. Finally, Tristran's journey brings him back to a faerie market near his village where all secrets about his parentage are revealed. Set in nineteenth-century England, *Stardust* "evokes the crisp style of the Brothers Grimm fairy tales," according to Kurt Lancaster writing in the *Christian Science Monitor.* Susan Salpini, reviewing *Stardust* for *School Library Journal,* called it an "old-fashioned fairy tale of mythic images, magic, and lyrical passages." "While the bones of the story—the hero, the quest, the maiden—are traditional," Salpini added, "Gaiman offers a role that is fresh and original." A contributor to *Publishers Weekly* noted of the novel that the author "employs exquisitely rich language, natural wisdom, good humor and a dash of darkness to conjure up a fairy tale in the grand tradition."

*Interworld,* a science-fiction novel coauthored by Gaiman and Michael Reaves, centers on Joey Harker, an ordinary youngster who discovers that he has the ability to travel between dimensions. Once inside the Altiverse, which contains an infinite series of alternate Earths, Joey learns that he is at the center of an epic confrontation pitting the forces of science against the forces of magic. "Filled with bizarre imagery, innovative world-building, and breathless action, *Interworld* is equal parts survival escapade and David-and-Goliath epic," noted *Kliatt* reviewer Claire E. Gross, and John Peters, writing in *Booklist,* described the novel as a "fast-paced, compulsively readable tale."

Along with *Stardust* and *Interworld,* Gaiman has produced several other novels, his first, *Good Omens,* coauthored with writer Terri Pratchett while Gaiman was concluding his "Sandman" saga. The novels *American Gods* and *Anansi Boys* earned him an even broader readership and reached best-seller status with their engaging mix of fantasy and mythology. Further fans were earned through his scripting of the BBC television series *Neverwhere,* which aired in the mid-1990s. In a reflection of its popularity, *American Gods* was selected as the inaugural read in the "One Book, One Twitter" reading program started by *Wired* magazine editor Jeff Howe in 2010.

In 1996 Gaiman and McKean produced their first book specifically geared for children: the picture book *The Day I Swapped My Dad for Two Goldfish.* In this tale, a little boy trades his father for two of his neighbor's goldfish while his little sister stares, horrified. When their mother finds out what has happened, she is furious. She makes the children go and get back their father who, unfortunately, has already been traded for an electric guitar. Writing in *Bloomsbury Review,* Anji Keating called *The Day I Swapped My Dad for Two Goldfish* "fabulously funny" and dubbed the protagonists' journey to fetch their father "delightful." Malcolm Jones, writing in *Newsweek,* predicted that Gaiman and McKean "may shock a few grandparents . . . but in fact the most shocking thing they've done in this droll story is to take the illegible look of cutting-edge magazines like *Raygun* and somehow make it readable."

Gaiman and McKean reteam in the picture books *The Wolves in the Walls* and *Crazy Hair.* In *The Wolves in the Walls* young Lucy insists that she hears the sound of wolves living in the walls of her family home, but no one believes her. The girl is proved correct, however, when the wolves emerge to take over the house, forcing Lucy and her family flee. Because Lucy wants her house back, and misses the beloved pig-puppet that was left behind, she convinces her family to return home, where they move into the walls that have been vacated by the wolves. Turning the tables, the family members create noises that frighten the sharp-clawed usurpers, who are wearing human clothing and eating the family's food. The wolves scatter, and everything seems to go back to normal . . . until Lucy hears another, stranger noise. In her *Booklist* review of *The Wolves in the Walls,* Francisca Goldsmith described the work as "visually and emotionally sophisticated, accessible, and inspired by both literary and popular themes and imagery." Writing in *School Library Journal,* Marian Creamer commented that "Gaiman and McKean deftly pair text and illustration to convey a strange, vivid story," and predicted that "children will delight in the 'scary, creepy tone.'"

In *Crazy Hair* a free-spirited adult narrator extols the virtues of his unkempt locks. When criticized by an uppity but tidily coiffed young girl, the man defends his hair as a sanctuary to creatures of all sorts, from fluttery butterflies to prancing lions and even to a pirate or two. Despite warnings to the contrary, the girl attempts to tackle the offending hairstyle with a comb, with unexpected results. Composed of rhyming couplets, Gaiman's "delightful and glib" text is brought to life by McKean in what *Booklist* critic Ian Chipman described as a "frenzied mix" of colorful collage that is "just on the safe side of nightmarish." The typeset words themselves also play a part in capturing the energy of the titular "crazy hair" as text "curves, spills, vibrates, and dangles, graphically signaling the mood and the message," according to *School Library Journal* contributor Wendy Lukehart. In the London *Times* Amanda Craig praised *Crazy Hair* as "a hymn to the unexpected," while a *Publishers Weekly* contributor predicted that children who relish the "twisted humor" of *The Wolves in the Walls* "will welcome this lighter-than-usual" picture-book fantasy.

Illustrated by Gris Grimly, *The Dangerous Alphabet* is Gaiman's take on the familiar alphabet book, with an eerie twist. In the work, a pair of Victorian children sneaks away from their father and, accompanied by their pet gazelle, journeys to an underworld where hidden treasure awaits. Along the way, however, the girl is captured by evil-doers and her brother must battle pirates, monsters, and trolls to rescue her. The children's story is told through thirteen rhyming couplets which incorporate the twenty-six letters. "Skillful narrative and visual storytelling combine to present a complex adventure that unravels through multilayered text and illustrations," Susannah Richards observed in *School Library Journal,* and *Booklist* contributor Thom Barthelmess reported that in *The Dangerous Alphabet* Gaiman and Grimly "have combined forces to produce an acrid, gothic confection that bubbles with vitriol and wit."

Originally published in a fantasy anthology in 2000, *Instructions* reunites Gaiman and Vess in an unusual picture-book project. Evoking the classic elements of fairy tale and fantasy in its setting, the book follows dapper feline Puss in Boots as he follows the instructions that allow him to pass, unimpeded, through a magical gate and into a garden that leads to a house and thence to a castle surrounded by a dark forest. On his journey, Puss encounters both friends and foes, princesses and witches, and even mythic elements. In illustrations that a *Publishers Weekly* critic explained "are distinguished by elegant, winding lines" and scenes "that evoke moments of gentle wisdom," Vess tracks this journey, echoing Gaiman's message "that the compass used to navigate fairy tales can also guide us in the real world." A *Kirkus Reviews* writer described *Instructions* as "a magical incantatory poem" that "provides a feast of archetypes" in addition to revisiting the many tests and trials encountered by the characters of time-honored fantasy and legend. Describing the book's purpose as a guide for young people turning a new page in their journey toward adulthood, Susan Perren added in her Toronto *Globe & Mail* review of *Instructions* that "it is reassuring to note that its 'usefulness' does not detract from its virtues, one of which is its alluring strangeness."

Gaiman's first story for middle-graders, *Coraline,* outlines how the title character, a young girl who feels that she is being ignored by her preoccupied parents, enters a terrifying, malevolent alternate reality to save them after they are kidnapped. The story begins when Coraline and her parents move into their new house, which is divided into apartments. Left to her own devices, the bored girl explores the house and finds a door in the empty flat next door that leads to a world that is a twisted version of her own. There, Coraline meets two odd-looking individuals who call themselves her "other mother" and "other father." The Other Mother, a woman who looks like Coraline's mom except for her black-button eyes and stiletto fingernails, wants Coraline to stay with her and her husband. Tempted by good food and interesting toys, Coraline considers the offer. However, when the girl returns home, she finds that her parents have disappeared. Coraline discovers that they are trapped in the other world, and she sets out to save them. The Other Mother, who turns out to be a soul-sucking harpy, enters into a deadly game of hide-and-seek with Coraline, and the girl ultimately discovers new qualities of bravery and resolve within herself.

A reviewer in *Publishers Weekly* wrote that Gaiman and illustrator McKean "spin an electrifyingly creepy tale likely to haunt young readers for many moons. . . . Gaiman twines his tale with a menacing tone and crisp prose fraught with memorable imagery . . ., yet keeps the narrative just this side of terrifying." Writing in *School Library Journal,* Bruce Anne Shook commented that "the story is odd, strange, even slightly bizarre, but kids will hang on every word. . . . This is just right for all those requests for a scary book." A critic in *Kirkus Reviews* wrote of the book that, "for stouthearted kids who love a brush with the sinister, *Coraline* is spot on." *Coraline* has won several major fantasy awards and was adapted as a graphic novel and a major motion picture.

Also for middle-grade readers, *Odd and the Frost Giants* has its roots in Norse mythology as it spins a story about the gods Thor, Odin, and Loki and their home in the kingdom of Asgard. Odd is a crippled boy whose widowed mother is now marrying a man with many children to feed. Since he now of age, Odd leaves her home and hikes into the forest, determined to make a home for himself in his father's abandoned hunting cabin. Once there, he is joined by three Norse gods who have been forced from their kingdom of Asgard and now wander the woods in animal form. To help these gods, Odd travels to Asgard and learns that Thor, Odin, and Loki have killed the brother of the powerful Frost Giant and that the vengeful giant now holds goddess Freya captive. Tested by fear, Odd finds himself up to the challenges before him, and his story ends in what *Globe & Mail* critic Perren described as a "final scene [that] is as gratifying as any very good fantasy could be." Noting that Gaiman's young hero proves victorious over his giant adversary "in a way that upholds and yet totally subverts the [mythic] trope," a *Kirkus Reviews* writer added that *Odd and the Frost Giants* "succeeds both as a delightful children's book and an adult collectible," while in *Booklist* Chipman asserted that the book serves as "yet more proof that there isn't much Gaiman can't write well." Illustrated with eight highly detailed color drawings by Brett Helquist that *Horn Book* critic Joanna Rudge Long praised for "deftly evok-[ing] . . . Gaiman's wintry Norse world," *Odd and the Frost Giants* treats readers to what Susan Persson characterized in *School Library Journal* as "a thoughtful and quietly humorous fantasy" that is enriched by "Gaiman's simple and graceful writing."

*M Is for Magic,* a collection of stories also aimed at a young-adult audience, features a number of tales from Gaiman's hard-to-find *Angels and Visitations: A Miscellany.* According to a critic in *Publishers Weekly,* the "volume is an excellent reminder of his considerable talent for short-form prose."

Gaiman's Newbery Medal-winning *The Graveyard Book,* a reimagining of Rudyard Kipling's *The Jungle Book,* was inspired by the cemetery near Gaiman's childhood home in Sussex as well as his memory of a day spent there in the company of his then two-year-old son. Taking root in the author's imagination at age twenty-five, the story actually took more than two decades to write, as Gaiman distilled it down to its core meaning as a story about parenting. *The Graveyard Book* begins with the murder of a family, but the youngest child slips away and finds refuge in a nearby graveyard. Cared for by the ghoulish inhabitants and renamed Nobody Owens, or "Bod" for short, the youngster eventually rejoins the human world, where he is destined to encounter the mysterious killer from his past. Patrick Ness, writing in the London *Guardian,* praised "the outrageous riches of Gaiman's imagination." In the *Scotsman,* Charlie Fletcher called the work "a robust, big-hearted fantasy, tinged with darkness and lit with humour and surprise, and deeper than its genre surface might hint at." As Fletcher added, *The Graveyard Book* "certainly has depth, along with its wide-ranging playfulness, and it has a sureness of tone in terms of precisely what aspects of the dark and macabre to omit, and what to leave in." According to Gross, "Gaiman's assured plotting is as bittersweet as it is action-filled . . . and makes this ghost-story-cum-coming-of-age-novel as readable as it is accomplished."

"Children's fiction is the most important fiction of all," Gaiman noted during his acceptance speech for the 2009 Newbery Medal, transcribed in *Horn Book.* "We who make stories know that we tell lies for a living," he added. "But they are good lies that say true things, and we owe it to our readers to build them as best we can. Because somewhere out there is someone who needs that story. Someone who will grow up with a different landscape, who without that story will be a different person. And who with that story may have hope, or wisdom, or kindness, or comfort.

"And that is why we write."

## Biographical and Critical Sources

*BOOKS*

*Authors and Artists for Young Adults,* Gale (Detroit, MI), Volume 19, 1996, Volume 42, 2002.
*Dictionary of Literary Biography,* Volume 261: *British Fantasy and Science Fiction Writers since 1960,* Gale (Detroit, MI), 2002.
Kwitney, Alisa, *The Sandman: King of Dreams,* introduction by Neil Gaiman, Chronicle Books (San Francisco, CA), 2003.
*Neil Gaiman on His Work and Career: A Conversation with Bill Baker,* Rosen (New York, NY), 2008.
*St. James Guide to Horror, Ghost & Gothic Writers,* St. James Press (Detroit, MI), 1998.

Wagner, Hank, and others, *Prince of Stories: The Many Worlds of Neil Gaiman,* St. Martin's Press (New York, NY), 2008.

*PERIODICALS*

*Bloomsbury Review,* July-August, 1997, Anji Keating, review of *The Day I Swapped My Dad for Two Goldfish,* p. 21.

*Booklist,* August, 2002, Ray Olson, interview with Gaiman, p. 19, and Stephanie Zvirin, review of *Coraline,* p. 1948; August, 2003, Francisca Goldsmith, review of *The Wolves in the Walls,* p. 1989; August, 2005, Ray Olson, review of *Anansi Boys,* p. 1952; September 1, 2007, John Peters, review of *InterWorld,* p. 114; March 1, 2008, Thom Barthelmess, review of *The Dangerous Alphabet,* p. 72; May 15, 2008, Ray Olson, review of *The Facts in the Case of the Departure of Miss Finch,* p. 27; March 15, 2009, Ian Chipman, review of *Crazy Hair,* p. 64; July 1, 2009, Ian Chipman, review of *Odd and the Frost Giants,* p. 61; August 1, 2009, Gordon Flagg, review of *Whatever Happened to the Caped Crusader?,* p. 50.

*Christian Science Monitor,* February 18, 1999, Kurt Lancaster, review of *Stardust,* p. 19.

*Commonweal,* December 2, 1994, Frank McConnell, review of *Mister Punch,* p. 27; October 20, 1995, Frank McConnell, review of *Sandman,* p. 21; June 19, 1998, Frank McConnell, review of *Neverwhere,* p. 21.

*Daily Telegraph* (London, England), October 24, 2009, Susan Perren, review of *Odd and the Frost Giants,* p. F17; July 3, 2010, Nicolette Jones, interview with Gaiman, p. 24.

*Entertainment Weekly,* June 24, 1994, Ken Tucker, review of *Sandman,* pp. 228-229; September 23, 2005, Jennifer Reese, review of *Anansi Boys,* p. 93.

*Globe & Mail* (Toronto, Ontario, Canada), October 14, 2009, Susan Perren, review of *Odd and the Frost Giants,* p. F17; July 17, 2010, Susan Perren, review of *Instructions,* p. F8.

*Guardian* (London, England), July 14, 1999, Nick Hasted, "The Illustrated Man," p. 12; October 25, 2008, Patrick Ness, review of *The Graveyard Book,* p. 11.

*Hollywood Reporter,* September 14, 2005, Gina McIntyre, "Cheap Thrills: Fantasy Author Neil Gaiman Finds Reality a Special Effect, p. 57; July 24, 2007, Noel Murray, interview with Gaiman, p. 1.

*Horn Book,* September-October, 2007, Claire E. Gross, review of *InterWorld,* p. 575; November-December, 2008, Claire E. Gross, review of *The Graveyard Book,* p. 703; July-August, 2009, Neil Gaiman, transcript of Newbery Medal acceptance speech, p. 343, and Elise Howard, "Neil Gaiman," p. 351; November-December, 2009, Joanna Rudge Long, review of *Odd and the Frost Giants,* p. 672.

*Independent* (London, England), October 22, 2007, interview with Gaiman, p. 10.

*Journal of Adolescent & Adult Literacy,* September, 2009, Don L.F. Nilsen, review of *The Graveyard Book,* p. 79.

*Kirkus Reviews,* June 15, 2002, review of *Coraline,* p. 88; July 15, 2006, review of *Fragile Things: Short Fic-*

*tions and Wonders,* p. 691; April 1, 2008, review of *The Dangerous Alphabet;* January 15, 2009, review of *Blueberry Girl;* May 1, 2009, review of *Crazy Hair;* September 15, 2009, review of *Odd and the Frost Giants;* April 15, 2010, review of *Instructions.*

*Kliatt,* July, 2008, George Galuschak, review of *The Facts in the Case of the Departure of Miss Finch,* p. 32; September, 2008, Paula Rohrlick, review of *The Graveyard Book,* p. 10, and George Galuschak, review of *Coraline,* p. 32.

*Library Journal,* September 15, 1990, Keith R.A. DeCandido, review of *The Golden Age,* p. 104.

*Locus,* April, 1993, Carolyn Cushman, review of *The Books of Magic,* p. 29.

*Los Angeles Times,* December 29, 2008, Geoff Boucher, interview with Gaiman.

*Newsweek,* December 1, 1997, Malcolm Jones, review of *The Day I Swapped My Dad for Two Goldfish,* p. 77.

*New York Times,* January 27, 2009, Motoko Rich, "*The Graveyard Book* Wins Newbery Medal," p. C1; July 31, 2009, George Gene Gustines review of *Whatever Happened to the Caped Crusader?,* p. C21.

*New York Times Book Review,* November 9, 2008, Becca Zerkin, review of *The Dangerous Alphabet,* p. 2; February 15, 2009, Monica Edinger, review of *The Graveyard Book,* p. 15; September 12, 2010, Julie Just, review of *Instructions,* p. 19.

*Publishers Weekly,* November 23, 1998, review of *Stardust,* p. 63; June 24, 2002, review of *Coraline,* p. 57; July 18, 2005, review of *Anansi Boys,* p. 180; July 17, 2006, review of *Fragile Things,* p. 131; July 9, 2007, review of *M Is for Magic,* p. 54; December 15, 2008, review of *Blueberry Girl,* p. 52; June 1, 2009, review of *Crazy Hair,* p. 46; July 27, 2009, review of *Batman: Whatever Happened to the Caped Crusader?,* p. 50; August 17, 2009, review of *Odd and the Frost Giants,* p. 62; December 7, 2009, review of *The Sandman: The Dream Hunters,* p. 40; May 10, 2010, review of *Instructions,* p. 41.

*School Library Journal,* February, 1999, Susan Salpini, review of *Stardust,* p. 142; August, 2002, Bruce Anne Shook, review of *Coraline,* p. 184; September, 2003, Marian Creamer, review of *The Wolves in the Walls,* p. 178; August, 2007, Beth Wright, review of *M Is for Magic,* p. 116; May, 2008, Susannah Richards, review of *The Dangerous Alphabet,* p. 98; October, 2008, Megan Honig, review of *The Graveyard Book,* p. 144; January, 2009, Wendy Lukehart, review of *Blueberry Girl,* p. 74; March, 2009, Roger Sutton, interview with Gaiman, p. 30; June, 2009, Wendy Lukehart, review of *Crazy Hair,* p. 86; October, 2009, Lauralyn Persson, review of *Odd and the Frost Giants,* p. 126; March, 2010, Andrea Lipinski, review of *The Sandman: The Dream Hunters,* p. 185.

*Scotsman* (Edinburgh, Scotland), November 8, 2008, Charlie Fletcher, interview with Gaiman.

*Star Tribune* (Minneapolis, MN), November 16, 2007, Colin Covert, "Gaiman's Take on *Beowulf:* Beyond Heroics," p. 13F.

*Sunday Times* (London, England), July 15, 1990, Nicolette Jones, review of *Violent Cases;* November 2, 2008,

Nicolette Jones, review of *The Graveyard Book,* p. 57; August 15, 2009, Allan Brown, "It's a Fantastical Life" (profile), p. 11.

*Times* (London, England), November 1, 2008, Amanda Craig, interview with Gaiman, p. 8; August 15, 2009, Amanda Craig, review of *Crazy Hair,* p. 12.

*USA Today,* July 31, 2007, Anthony Breznican, "Storyteller Gaiman Wishes upon a Star," p. 1D.

*Washington Post Book World,* April 7, 2002, Michael Swanwick, "Reel Worlds," p. 3.

*ONLINE*

*Neil Gaiman Home Page,* http://www.neilgaiman.com (March 15, 2011).

*Neil Gaiman Web log,* http://journal.neilgaiman.com (March 15, 2011).

*Time Online,* http://www.time.com/ (September 25, 2005), Lev Grossman, interview with Gaiman and Joss Whedon.

\*　　\*　　\*

# GAL, Susan

## Personal

Born in San Diego, CA. *Education:* Art Center College of Design, B.F.A., 1986

## Addresses

*Home*—Berkeley, CA. *Agent*—Morgan Gaynin, 194 3rd. Ave., New York, NY 10003. *E-mail*—susan@galgirl studio.com.

## Career

Author and illustrator. O.S.P. Publishing, Inc., poster and calendar artist, 1986-89; Disney Animation, FL, "in-between" animator, 1989-91; currently freelance illustrator.

## Member

Society of Children's Book Writers and Illustrators.

## Writings

*SELF-ILLUSTRATED*

*Night Lights,* Alfred A. Knopf (New York, NY), 2009.
*Please Take Me for a Walk,* Alfred A. Knopf (New York, NY), 2010.

*ILLUSTRATOR*

Jake Miller, *On the Job with an Architect, Builder of the World,* Barron's (Hauppauge, NY), 2001.

Jake Miller and Jonathan Rubinstein, *On the Job with an Astronomer, Explorer of the Universe,* Barron's (Hauppauge, NY), 2001.

Jamie Kyle McGillian, *On the Job with a Firefighter, Neighborhood Guardian,* Barron's (Hauppauge, NY), 2001.

Jonathan Rubinstein, *On the Job with a Police Officer, Protector of the Peace,* Barron's (Hauppauge, NY), 2001.

Carolyn Crimi, *Mystery in the Wings,* Rigby Publishing, 2001.

*Susan Gal creates a child-friendly night-time read aloud in her self-illustrated picture book* **Night Lights.** (Copyright © 2009 by Susan Gal. Used with permission of Alfred A. Knopf, an imprint of Random House Children's Books, a division of Random House, Inc.)

Contributor to periodicals, including *Baltimore Sun, Barron's, Better Homes & Gardens, Bride Guide Magazine, Girl's Life, Guideposts, Harvard Magazine, Her Nashville, New York Life, San Francisco Chronicle, Saturday Evening Post, Scholastic Storyworks, Wall Street Journal, Washington Post,* and *Woman's World.*

## Sidelights

As a graduate of Pasadena's prestigious Art Center College of Design, Susan Gal worked as an "inbetweener" (animator's assistant) for Disney Studios in Florida before returning to her native California and pursuing a career as a freelance illustrator. In addition to creating art for a number of corporate and publishing clients, Gal's illustrations have appeared in a number of books for children, including stories by Jake Miller, Jonathan Rubinstein, and Jamie Kyle McGillian. In 2009 she expanded her creativity to writing, and the picture books *Night Lights* and *Please Take Me for a Walk* have been the result.

In *Night Lights* Gal helps tuck readers in for the night with illuminated illustrations that capture a child's evening ritual. As the sun lowers in the west, a girl, her mother, and the family dog return home, grill a summer dinner that doubles as the dog's birthday celebration, and enjoy nightfall until a summer rainfall herds them inside and into cozy pajamas. With each illustration, Gal's simple text identifies a different kind of light, from the sunlight of late afternoon and the glow of a bedside table lamp to the hazy light of the moon and the reassuring glimmer of a nightlight. "Young children will enjoy . . . the rich details" the author/illustrator incorporates into her colorful digitally enhanced collage-and-oil-pastel images, wrote *School Library Journal* contributor Martha Simpson, and in *Booklist* Diane Foote maintained that Gal's "snapshot of one calm evening is appealing" and "will send young ones off to sleep gently." A *Kirkus Reviews* writer concluded of Gal's picture-book debut that "the many warm renderings of light. . ." in *Night Lights* "reveal the loveliness of a night spent with an affectionate family."

As the book's title implies, a dog is the star of *Please Take Me for a Walk.* In this story, a scruffy, gray-furred terrier makes the titular request to the reader and then imagines all the fun it will have on a walk through the small town that is part of its doggy domain. Within Gal's colorful multimedia collages are "a riot of texture and color," asserted Susan Weitz, the critic adding in her *School Library Journal* review that *Please Take Me for a Walk* allows readers to "enjoy many aspects of their own world" from an eager pup's perspective. "Even cat people may be hard pressed to resist the polite pleadings" of Gal's canine hero, admitted Andrew Medlar in *Booklist,* and in a *Publishers Weekly* review of the book a critic noted the infectiously upbeat energy that emanates from Gal's "fresh and inviting . . . illustrations of a hip, multicultural community."

"I've dreamed of writing and illustrating children's books since I was in the second grade," Gal told *SATA.* "An author, Al Perkins, came to speak at my elementary school. Some of his titles include *The Digging-est Dog* and *Hand, Hand, Fingers Thumb.* My teacher, Miss Bryan, assigned our class to write and illustrate their own individual stories, and make them into a little book. Some of us lucky students were then chosen to spend an afternoon with Mr. Perkins and share our 'books' with him. Years later, when I received a contract to publish my first book, I was shocked to discover my publisher, Random House, was the same publisher as Mr. Perkins'!

"To anyone out there that has a book inside of them . . . just do it! I'm proof that, with hard work and determination, you can make your dream career come true."

## Biographical and Critical Sources

*PERIODICALS*

*Booklist,* December 1, 2009, Diane Foote, review of *Night Lights,* p. 51; April 1, 2010, Andrew Medlar, review of *Please Take Me for a Walk,* p. 48.
*Kirkus Reviews,* October 15, 2009, review of *Night Lights.*
*Publishers Weekly,* November 30, 2009, review of *Night Lights,* p. 47; April 12, 2010, review of *Please Take Me for a Walk,* p. 48.
*School Library Journal,* November, 2009, Martha Simpson, review of *Night Lights,* p. 78; May, 2010, Susan Weitz, review of *Please Take Me for a Walk,* p. 84.

*ONLINE*

*Susan Gal Home Page,* http://www.galgirlstudio.com (February 16, 2011).

*        *        *

# GAUCH, Patricia Lee 1934-

## Personal

Born January 3, 1934, in Detroit MI; daughter of William Melbourne (an investor) and Muriel Lee; married Ronald Raymond Gauch (a scientist and administrator) August 27, 1955; children: Sarah, Christine, John. *Education:* Miami University (Oxford, OH), B.A. (English literature), 1956; Manhattanville College, M.A.T., 1970; Drew University, Ph.D. (English literature), 1988.

## Addresses

*Home*—Hyde Park, NY. *Agent*—Dorothy Markinko, Mcintosh & Otis, Inc., 18 E. 41st St., New York, NY 10014.

## Career

Author, editor, and educator. *Louisville Courier-Journal,* Louisville, KY, reporter, 1957-59; Coward-McCann & Geoghegan, New York, NY, publisher-writer, beginning 1969; Philomel Books, New York, NY, editor, beginning 1985, vice president and editorial director, 2003-09. Gill-St. Berhards School, Gladstone, NJ, teacher, 1972-83; part-time professor at Drew University, Madison, NJ, and Rutgers University, New Brunswick, NJ, 1984-85; Chairman, Rutgers University advisory council on children's literature, 1984-86; consultant, American Library Association "Lets Read about It" program, 1986. Lecturer; presenter at conferences.

## Member

Society of Children's Book Writers and Illustrators.

## Awards, Honors

Writers of Children's Books of the Year citation, New Jersey Institute of Technology, 1971, for both *Christina Katerina and the Box* and *A Secret House,* 1972-73, for both *Grandpa and Me* and *Aaron and the Green Mountain Boys,* and 1983, for *Night Talks;* Notable Children's Trade Book in the Field of Social Studies designation, National Council for the Social Studies/Children's Book Council, 1974, for *This Time, Tempe Wick?;* inducted into New Jersey Hall of Fame, 1993.

## Writings

*FOR CHILDREN*

*My Old Tree,* illustrated by Doris Burn, Coward, McCann (New York, NY), 1970.
*A Secret House,* illustrated by Margot Tomes, Coward, McCann (New York, NY), 1970.
*Aaron and the Green Mountain Boys,* illustrated by Margot Tomes, Coward, McCann (New York, NY), 1972.
*Grandpa and Me,* illustrated by Symeon Shimin, Coward, McCann (New York, NY), 1972.
*This Time, Tempe Wick?,* illustrated by Margot Tomes, Coward, McCann (New York, NY), 1974, reprinted, Boyds Mills Press (Honesdale, PA), 2003.
*Thunder at Gettysburg,* illustrated by Stephen Gammell, Coward, McCann (New York, NY), 1975, reprinted, Boyds Mill Press (Honesdale, PA), 2003.
*The Impossible Major Rogers,* illustrated by Robert Andrew Parker, Putnam (New York, NY), 1977.
*Once upon a Dinkelsbuhl,* illustrated by Tomi de Paola, Putnam (New York, NY), 1977.
*On to Widecombe Fair,* illustrated by Trina Schart Hyman, Putnam (New York, NY), 1978.
*The Little Friar Who Flew,* illustrated by Tomie de Paola, Putnam (New York, NY), 1980.
*Uncle Magic,* illustrated by Deborah Kogan Ray, Holiday House (New York, NY), 1992.
*Noah,* illustrated by Jonathan Green, Philomel (New York, NY), 1994.

*Poppy's Puppet,* illustrated by David Christiana, Henry Holt (New York, NY), 1999.
*The Knitting of Elizabeth Amelia,* illustrated by Barbara Lavallee, Henry Holt (New York, NY), 2009.

*FOR CHILDREN; "CHRISTINA KATERINA" SERIES*

*Christina Katerina and the Box,* illustrated by Doris Burn, Coward, McCann (New York, NY), 1971.
*Christina Katerina and the First Annual Grand Ballet,* illustrated by Doris Burn, Coward, McCann (New York, NY), 1973.
*Christina Katerina and the Time She Quit the Family,* illustrated by Elise Primavera, Putnam (New York, NY), 1987.
*Christina Katerina and the Great Bear Train,* illustrated by Elise Primavera, Putnam (New York, NY), 1990.
*Christina Katerina and Fats and the Great Neighborhood War,* illustrated by Stacey Schuett, Putnam's (New York, NY), 1997.

*FOR CHILDREN; "TANYA" SERIES*

*Dance, Tanya,* illustrated by Satomi Ichikawa, Philomel (New York, NY), 1989.
*Bravo, Tanya,* illustrated by Satomi Ichikawa, Philomel (New York, NY), 1992.
*Tanya and Emily in a Dance for Two,* illustrated by Satomi Ichikawa, Philomel (New York, NY), 1994.
*Tanya Steps Out,* illustrated by Satomi Ichikawa, Philomel (New York, NY), 1996.
*Tanya and the Magic Wardrobe,* illustrated by Satomi Ichikawa, Philomel (New York, NY), 1997.
*Presenting Tanya, the Ugly Duckling,* illustrated by Satomi Ichikawa, Philomel (New York, NY), 1999.
*The Tanya Treasury,* illustrated by Satomi Ichikawa, Philomel (New York, NY), 2002.
*Tanya and the Red Shoes,* illustrated by Satomi Ichikawa, Philomel (New York, NY), 2002.

*YOUNG-ADULT NOVELS*

*The Green of Me,* Putnam (New York, NY), 1978.
*Fridays,* Putnam (New York, NY), 1979.
*Kate Alone,* Putnam (New York, NY), 1980.
*Morelli's Game,* Putnam (New York, NY), 1981.
*Night Talks,* Putnam (New York, NY), 1983.
*The Year the Summer Died,* Putnam (New York, NY), 1985.

*OTHER*

Contributor to periodicals, including *Writer.*

## Sidelights

Patricia Lee Gauch transformed an early love of people and stories into a career as a journalist, but her unflagging interest in stories inspired her to eventually write and edit children's books. As a respected editor at New

York City publisher Philomel Books for many years, Gauch had the chance to work with noteworthy writers such as Andrew Clements, Judith St. George, Brian Jacques, David Small, and Jane Yolen. Her contributions as an author range from whimsical retellings of folk songs and legends for young children to accessible, history-themed stories for older children to young-adult novels that present serious treatments of painful, real-life subjects. Throughout her career, Gauch has been praised for the quality of her prose, the sensitivity of her approach to her subjects, and the realism that provides the backbone for her characterizations. "With both her fiction and nonfiction," Karen M. Klockner wrote in *Horn Book,* "the author is effective at capturing the immediacy of a scene through fragments of dialogue and flashes of thought on the part of characters."

Raised in southeastern Michigan, Gauch enjoyed camping with her family in the Great Lakes region and places from her childhood have found their way into several of her books. After completing her English degree at Ohio's Miami University, she spent several years learning to work to deadline as a journalist, first for Louisville, Kentucky's *Courier-Journal* and later the *Detroit Free Press.* Gauch also continued her education, earning a teaching degree as well as a Ph.D. in English literature. She began to write for children while raising her own family, and as her children grew older Gauch's audience matured accordingly. Her early picture hooks, such as *A Secret House, My Old Tree,* and *Grandpa and Me,* celebrate the simple childhood pleasures of daydreaming and make believe. Reviewing the former, in which a little girl daydreams about a perfect, old-fashioned house, a *Publishers Weekly* critic described the work as "a story with universal appeal." In *My Old Tree* a little boy daydreams of having a huge tree he can play in and around, as well as of a special friend to play with him, while *Grandpa and Me* evokes the special relationship between a man and his grandson in what a *Publishers Weekly* contributor described as "a beguiling story."

Gauch's "Christina Katerina" stories were inspired by her own children. In the first, *Christina Katerina and the Box,* readers meet a boisterous young girl as she plays in a huge refrigerator box with her friend Fats. Reviewing *Christina Katerina and the Box,* a *Bulletin of the Center for Children's Books* writer commented that the "idea of imaginative play is convincing if elaborately . . . pursued." *Christina Katerina and the First Annual Grand Ballet* comically portrays an ambitious backyard performance that is "nothing new but good fun," according to *School Library Journal* contributor Amy Keliman. In *Christina Katerina and the Time She Quit the Family* Gauch's main character is frustrated by the injustices in her home and decides to change her' name and leave the family. Although *New York Times Book Review* contributor Ellen Schecter praised Gauch's "sprightly heroine," she found the book's ending somewhat predictable. In *Christina Katerina and the Great Bear Train,* which Judith Gloyer described in *School*

*Library Journal* as "written with both skill and flair," Gauch's heroine runs away from home rather than face the prospect of the arrival of a new sibling.

The American Revolution provides the backdrop for *Aaron and the Green Mountain Boys,* a picture book for slightly older children that features artwork by Margot Tomes. In this story, nine-year-old Aaron yearns to join Vermont's Green Mountain Boys and ride against the British redcoats, but instead he is assigned to chop wood to keep the bread ovens going for his grandfather. When the colonial militia men arrive and hungrily consume the freshly baked bread, Aaron realizes the importance of his contribution. A *Booklist* reviewer praised *Aaron and the Green Mountain Boys,* citing the story's "action, excitement, and . . . very believable nine-year-old central character."

Another collaboration with Tomes, Gauch's *This Time, Tempe Wick?,* is also set during the American Revolution. Temperance, a courageous young girl, rescues her beloved horse from a band of mutinous American soldiers that wants to steal it. Anita Silvey praised the book for presenting a "realistic and humane view of the war and the people who fought it" in her review of the story in *Horn Book,* and a *Publishers Weekly* critic recommended *This Time, Tempe Wick?* as a tale "told with wit as well as drama." While Pauline Maier did not find Temperance Wick's feat "particularly impressive or convincing," she nonetheless noted in her *New York Times Book Review* appraisal that *This Time, Tempe Wick?* is "valuable" due to Gauch's focus on a female hero.

Illustrated by Robert Andrew Parker, *The Impossible Major Rogers* introduces Robert Rogers, a man who was both a hero in the French and Indian Wars and an outlaw. In her review of the picture-book biography for *Horn Book,* Mary M. Burns commented that Gauch "underscores the ambivalence of his [Rogers'] character, thus providing a solid framework for a vivid biographical sketch, which neither enlarges nor diminishes his personality." Ralph Adams Brown praised the author's prose style in his *School Library Journal* review, predicting that the intriguing hero of *The Impossible Major Roger* is one who "will captivate young readers."

In *Thunder at Gettysburg* Gauch turns to the U.S. Civil War, drawing on Tillie Pierce's eyewitness account of the long and bloody battle near Gettysburg, Pennsylvania, in her story. While "the scenes of bloodshed are handled with restraint and a minimum of sentimentality," according to a *Kirkus Reviews* writer, Joe Bearden remarked in his *School Library Journal* review of *Thunder at Gettysburg* that "the horror of the situation comes through" in Gauch's text "with a startling clarity."

"There is an infectious lilt to the language" of Gauch's *On to Widecombe Fair,* according to *New York Times Book Review* contributor Selma G. Lanes. This picture book is based on an English folk ballad about seven village men who ride an old horse to death on their way home from the fair and then are condemned to ride through the moors for eternity as punishment for their cruelty. Although some critics found that the leap from song to story makes for a thin plot, a reviewer for the *Bulletin of the Center for Children's Books* concluded that Gauch's story "has the same jaunty, rollicking tone" as the folk song. Another fanciful story that features artwork by David Christiana, *Poppy's Puppet*, relates Gauch's tale about a toymaker whose creations carry the spirit of the wood each is carved from. Praising this story as "gracefully written," Carolyn Phelan added in *Booklist* that Gauch weaves within it "a gentle allegory for artists of many kinds," and a *Publishers Weekly* critic dubbed *Poppy's Puppet* a "lucid and eloquent" tale that "gains a measure of mystery and magic from the ethereal illustrations."

Another allegory, *The Knitting of Elizabeth Amelia*, focuses on a doll that is knitted all of wool. Elizabeth Amelia is no ordinary doll, however; like a human girl, she eventually grows up and gets married. Wishing for children, Elizabeth begins to unravel bits of herself and eventually produces four woolen youngsters, even unraveling enough to knit them clothes and other necessaries. When her husband comments that there is not much of his wife left, a fresh supply of yarn is found and soon Elizabeth has knitted herself together again. Commenting on the "stylized and exuberant" folk-art-style water-color illustrations contributed by Barbara Lavallee, a *Publishers Weekly* critic dubbed *The Knitting of Elizabeth Amelia* "an unusual but touching story." In *Kirkus Review* a critic also praised the book, noting that Gauch's "whimsical original fairy tale about motherhood" is enlivened by both "humor and a dash of wisdom"

In the late 1980s Gauch began a series of picture books that focus on a young girl who loves to dance. In the first, *Dance, Tanya*, Tanya, a preschooler, finally convinces her mother that she is old enough for dance lessons. As Kay MacPherson wrote in *School Library Journal*, this "charming family story" exhibits "strong and loving relationships all around." *Booklist* critic Denise Wilms remarked that, although Gauch and illustrator Satomi Ichikawa intend to amuse the reader with Tanya's exploits, "a wholehearted respect for Tanya's earnest dedication is evident" in the tale. *Bravo, Tanya* finds the young girl having a difficult time at her first ballet lessons until the kindly accompanist helps her to focus on the music. Phelan, writing in *Booklist*, predicted of *Bravo, Tanya*, that Gauch's "sympathetic story will speak to every young ballerina whose dreams have exceeded her skill."

In *Tanya and Emily in a Dance for Two* Tanya makes a new friend and the girls teach each other "that there is room for more than one style of expression," as Cheri Estes stated in her *School Library Journal* review. Other stories following Tanya through her development as a dancer include *Tanya and the Magic Wardrobe, Presenting Tanya, the Ugly Duckling,* and *Tanya and the Red Shoes,* the last in which the girl is ready to transition to toe shoes. Brought to life in what *School Library Journal* contributor Dorian Chong described as Ichikawa's "loose and vibrant watercolors," *Tanya and the Red Shoes* "is "a rewarding picture book for the many young girls who take ballet classes or dream of dancing," according to Phelan.

In addition to picture books, Gauch has also produced several novels for teen readers. Her first, *The Green in Me,* centers on a train trip taken by seventeen-year-old Jennifer to meet her boyfriend. Through extensive use of flashback, the author conveys a sense of what brought Jennifer to the emotional crossroads she approaches as the train nears its destination, producing what a *Publishers Weekly* critic dubbed a "sensitive, wholly involving story." Although *New York Times Book Review* contributor Georgess MeHargue maintained that Gauch's narrative occasionally loses focus, *The Green in Me* treats young-adult readers to "an ambitious and often appealing book whose ending . . . is entirely appropriate," according to the critic.

In *Kate Alone* Gauch takes on the subject of responsibility in her story about a girl who must decide whether to put her best friend, the family dog, to sleep after it begins biting people. Another teen novel, *Morelli's Game,* chronicles a grueling bicycle trip from Pennsylvania to Washington state that almost parallels the adventures characters encounter in J.R.R. Tolkien's popular "Lord of the Rings" fantasy novels. In *Night Talks* three wealthy young women decide to enroll in summer camp and end up bunking with a tough urban teen who declines to join in many of the camp's activities. Encouraged by their counselor, the friends attempt to help the outsider but end up causing more problems than they are prepared to handle by themselves. Gauch's "intriguing idea . . . is skillfully explored through well-developed plot and characters," wrote *New York Times Book Review* critic E.A. Hass in an appraisal of *Night Talks,* and a *Publishers Weekly* critic asserted that the author "moves the reader with this arresting novel."

Also for young adults, Gauch's *The Year the Summer Died* takes on the problem of long-time friends who move into adolescence at different rates of maturity. Erin's idyllic summers spent with her grandfather in his cottage on a lake in Michigan are spoiled the year the elderly man becomes obsessed with protecting his property against local vandals. Meanwhile, best friend Laurie is too busy with her boyfriend to play the games that used to occupy both girls all summer long. Gauch fully explores this painful stage of growing up in *The Year the Summer Died;* as Cynthia Percak Infantino noted in *School Library Journal,* her story's "underlying themes of change and growth, fantasy and reality lend depth to Erin's story."

Discussing her writing, Gauch once told *SATA:* "A story is in my head long before it ever finds its way to paper.

By the time it finally makes it that far, I have spent sleepless nights with it, washed dishes with it, walked in the snow with it. When I finally write the story down, however, I will probably write it in [my office in] Lexington, Michigan, where my parents still have a red farmhouse on Lake Huron. I have a window there that looks out on the lake. It is a time of being alone, but I am alone with my characters and my story, and by then I am ready."

As an editor of picture books for many years, Gauch has watched the genre bloom under the work of writers such as Jane Yolen, Kevin Henkes, Rosemary Welles, Loren Long, and Mo Willems. Now retired and devoting her time primarily to her writing, she continues to offer her insights and advice at writer's conferences and workshops. "Readers do not want what is straightforward, understandable, four square, typical, sturdy, easy, predictable," she stated at a Highlights Foundation writers workshop, as quoted on the National Writing for Children Center Web site. "No, I believe character and plot and setting and language—on a slant—is what readers thirst for. They are intrigued with what is odd, aberrant, offbeat, strange—for goodness' sake. And praise be!"

## Biographical and Critical Sources

*PERIODICALS*

*Booklist,* November 15, 1972, review of *Aaron and the Green Mountain Boys,* p. 300; September 1, 1989, Denise Wilms, review of *Dance, Tanya,* pp. 70-71; May 1, 1992, Carolyn Phelan, review of *Bravo, Tanya,* p. 1610; November 1, 1997, Carolyn Phelan, review of *Tanya and the Magic Wardrobe,* p. 481; July, 1999, Carolyn Phelan, review of *Presenting Tanya, the Ugly Duckling,* p. 1943; September 15, 1999, Carolyn Phelan, review of *Poppy's Puppet,* p. 267; March 1, 2002, review of *Tanya and the Red Shoes,* p. 1141.

*Bulletin of the Center for Children's Books,* October, 1971, review of *Christina Katerina and the Box,* p. 25; October, 1978, review of *On to Widecombe Fair,* p. 28; June, 1997, review of *Christina Katerina and Fats and the Great Neighborhood War,* p. 357.

*California Kids!,* February, 2005, Patricia Newman, "Who Wrote That?" (profile of Gauch).

*Horn Book,* October, 1974, Anita Silvey, review of *This Time, Tempe Wick?,* p. 147; April, 1978, Mary M. Burns, review of *The Impossible Major Rogers,* p. 174; October, 1980, Karen M. Klockner, review of *Kate Alone,* p. 519.

*Kirkus Reviews,* December 1, 1975, review of *Thunder at Gettysburg,* p. 1337; September 15, 1992, review of *Uncle Magic,* p. 1186; September 1, 2009, review of *The Knitting of Elizabeth Amelia.*

*New York Times Book Review,* November 3, 1973, Pauline Maier, "Re-creating the Revolution," p. 26; June 19, 1977, Joyce Milton, review of *Once upon a Dinkelsbuhl,* p. 28; July 2, 1978, Selma G. Lanes, review of *On to Widecombe Fair,* p. 11; March 25, 1979, Gerogess McHargue, review of *The Green of Me,* p. 30; November 8, 1987, Ellen Schecter, "Declaring War at Home, p. 51; September 18, 1983, E.A. Hass, review of *Night Talks,* p. 38.

*Publishers Weekly,* September 14, 1970, review of *A Secret House,* p. 70; September 18, 1972, review of *Grandpa and Me,* p. 74; September 23, 1974, review of *This Time, Tempe Wick?,* p. 155; March 28, 1977, review of *Once upon a Dinkelsbuhl,* p. 79; October 30, 1978, review of *The Green of Me,* p. 50; October 31, 1980, review of *The Little Friar Who Flew,* p. 85; March 4, 1983, review of *Night Talks,* p. 99; January 25, 1999, review of *Noah,* p. 98; July 19, 1999, review of *Poppy's Puppet,* p. 194; October 19, 2009, review of *The Knitting of Elizabeth Amelia,* p. 51.

*School Library Journal,* January, 1976, Joe Bearden, review of *Thunder at Gettysburg,* p. 37; December, 1977, Amy Kellman, "For Very Young Dancers," p. 35; January, 1978, Ralph Adams Brown, review of *The Impossible Major Rogers,* p. 88; March, 1986, Cynthia Percak Infantino, review of *The Year the Summer Died,* p. 174; October, 1989, Kay MacPherson, review of *Dance, Tanya,* p. 78; November, 1990, Judith Gloyer, review of *Christina Katerina and the Great Bear Train,* p. 92; September, 1994, Cheri Estes, review of *Tanya and Emily in a Dance for Two,* p. 184; October, 1997, Dawn Amsberry, review of *Tanya and the Magic Wardrobe,* p. 95; June, 1999, Susan Pine, review of *Tanya, the Ugly Duckling,* p. 95; March, 2002, Dorian Chong, review of *Tanya and the Red Shoes,* p. 187; October, 2009, Ieva Bates, review of *The Knitting of Elizabeth Amelia,* p. 92.

*ONLINE*

*National Writing for Children Center Web site,* http://writingforchildrencenter.com/ (January 29, 2008), "A Tip from Philomel Editor Patricia Lee Gauch."*

\*        \*        \*

## GODOWN, Jan
### See ANNINO, Jan Godown

# H

## HALL, Melanie 1949-
### (Melanie W. Hall)

### Personal

Born November 20, 1949, in Gloucester, MA; daughter of Edward A. (a doctor) and Doris (a homemaker) Winsten; married Ronald Hall (an artist and musician), 1982. *Education:* Attended Rhode Island School of Design, 1967-70; Pratt Institute, B.F.A., 1978; Marywood College, M.A., 1993. *Hobbies and other interests:* Archery, reading, meditation.

### Addresses

*Home and office*—Cat's Paw Studio, 22 Krom Rd., Olivebridge, NY 12461. *E-mail*—mhallart@netstep.net.

### Career

Artist and illustrator. Worked variously as a painter, museum curator, printer's assistant, editorial illustrator, graphic designer, and fashion illustrator. Freelance illustrator and painter, 1978—; children's book illustrator, 1991—. Lecturer at Pratt Institute and Marywood University; workshop leader at Highlights Foundation, Honesdale, PA, and Boards of Cooperative Educational Services, Port Ewen, NY. *Exhibitions:* Work included in Original Art Show, Society of Illustrators, New York, NY, 1992.

### Member

Society of Illustrators, Society of Children's Book Writers and Illustrators.

### Awards, Honors

Award for work exhibited at Original Art Show, Society of Illustrators, 1992; Don Freeman grant, Society of Children's Book Writers and Illustrators, 1993; Parents' Choice Award; Sydney Taylor Book Award, 2008, for *Goodnight Sh'ma* by Jacqueline Jules.

*Melanie W. Hall* (Reproduced by permission.)

### Illustrator

Charles Temple, *On the Riverbank,* Houghton (Boston, MA), 1992.

Washington Irving, *The Legend of Sleepy Hollow,* adapted by Freya Littledale, Scholastic (New York, NY), 1992.

Lee Bennett Hopkins, selector, *Weather,* HarperCollins (New York, NY), 1994.

Charles Temple, *Shanty Boat,* Houghton (Boston, MA), 1994.

(Under name Melanie W. Hall) Patrick Lewis, *July Is a Mad Mosquito,* Atheneum (New York, NY), 1994.

(Under name Melanie W. Hall) Cathy Goldberg Fishman, *On Passover,* Atheneum (New York, NY), 1997.

(Under name Melanie W. Hall) Cathy Goldberg Fishman, *On Rosh Hashanah and Yom Kippur,* Atheneum (New York, NY), 1997.

(Under name Melanie W. Hall) Cathy Goldberg Fishman, *On Hanukkah,* Atheneum (New York, NY), 1998.

Nancy Sohn Swartz, *In Our Image: God's First Creatures,* Jewish Lights (Woodstock, VT), 1998.

(Under name Melanie W. Hall) Cathy Goldberg Fishman, *On Purim,* Atheneum (New York, NY), 2000.

(Under name Melanie W. Hall) Cathy Goldberg Fishman, *On Shabbat,* Atheneum (New York, NY), 2001.

Ivy O. Eastwick, *I Asked a Tiger to Tea, and Other Poems,* compiled by Walter B. Barbe, Wordsong/Boyds Mills Press (Honesdale, PA), 2002.

Melinda Kay Busch, *Born on Christmas Morn: The Story of Jesus' Birth, Luke 2:1-20 for Children,* Concordia (St. Louis, MO), 2003.

Nancy Sohn Swartz, *How Did the Animals Help God?,* SkyLight Paths (Woodstock, VT), 2004.

Rebecca Kai Dotlich, *Over in the Pink House: New Jump Rope Rhymes,* Wordsong/Boyds Mills Press (Honesdale, PA), 2004.

Lee Bennett Hopkins, selector, *Christmas Presents: Holiday Poetry,* HarperCollins (New York, NY), 2004.

Lee Bennett Hopkins, selector, *Hanukkah Lights: Holiday Poetry,* HarperCollins (New York, NY), 2004.

Deborah Bodin Cohen, *The Seventh Day,* Kar-Ben Publishing (Minneapolis, MN), 2005.

(Under name Melanie W. Hall) Cathy Goldberg Fishman, *On Sukkot and Simchat Torah,* Kar-Ben Publishing (Minneapolis, MN), 2005, published under name Melanie Hall, 2006.

William Shakespeare, *Winter Song,* introduction by Alice Provensen, Wordsong (Honesdale, PA), 2006.

Jacqueline Jules, *Goodnight Sh'ma,* Kar-Ben Publishing (Minneapolis, MN), 2008.

Peninnah Schram, *The Magic Pomegranate: A Jewish Folktale,* Millbrook Press (Minneapolis, MN), 2008.

Christine San José and Bill Johnson, editors, *Every Second Something Happens: Poems for the Mind and Senses,* Wordsong (Honesdale, PA), 2009.

Work included in *The Very Best of Children's Book Illustration,* Society of Illustrators/Northlight Books, 1993.

## Sidelights

Melanie Hall is a painter and illustrator of children's books who is noted for her use of mixed media, from watercolors to crayons. Hall's artwork can be both folksy and vibrant, even flashy, depending on the theme of the material she is illustrating. Working in collaboration with authors such as Charles Temple, Cathy Goldberg Fishman, and Peninnah Schram, she has illustrated books dealing with a wide range of subjects, from a day on the river to Elizabethan England to the Jewish holidays.

"Illustrating children's books is a dream come true for me," Hall once told *SATA*. "When I was a little girl I made a series of books called 'The Fun Book,' which came out seasonally and were filled with illustrations, rebuses, puzzles, and stories. I laugh to myself remembering how I sat on the beach with colored pencils and paper finishing up the latest fun book so I wouldn't be late for the deadline. I didn't know that was a taste of what was to come."

After attending the prestigious Rhode Island School of Design from 1967 to 1970, Hall worked in a variety of careers allied to the visual and studio arts. "I've had a checkered career as a painter, museum curator, printer's assistant, editorial illustrator, graphic designer, and fashion illustrator," she once recalled to *SATA*. She returned to school to earn her B.F.A. at the Pratt Institute, but still did not discover her niche. "I wasn't very happy. One day, while sitting at my drawing table doing my umpteenth fashion illustration, I wondered, 'Will I be doing this boring stuff when I'm sixty?' I complained to my girlfriend, 'I want to do children's books!' She replied, 'Well, why don't you?' At that moment, lights flashed and bells rang. I said to myself, 'Yeah, why don't I? What's stopping me?' Everything fell into place. I went back to school and learned how to do children's books.

"The day I got my first book contract changed my life forever. After my editor, Matilda Welter of Houghton Mifflin, offered me *On the Riverbank* [by Charles Temple], I jumped up and down and whooped for joy. I tried to sound calm, cool, and collected but failed

*Hall's whimsical art is a perfect match for the quirky verses created by well-known writer Ivy O. Eastwick and collected in* I Asked a Tiger to Tea, and Other Poems. *(Illustration copyright © 2002 by Melanie Hall. Reprinted with the permission of Boyds Mills Press, Inc.)*

miserably. Matilda chuckled appreciatively at my delight. I told her, 'This is the day all my dreams come true,' quoting Bob Dylan's song 'New Morning.' Afterward, I called up every member of my family and every friend to crow about the news."

*On the Riverbank* is a story of a family of three who are out for a fishing trip on the shores of a river lit by moonlight. Daddy and Mama bring along a picnic basket and all the assorted gear necessary for an evening of catfishing. Together the young narrator and his father bait the lines and eagerly await the first bites. Told in pulsing, rhythmic stanzas, Temple's story details the simple joys of catching fish and swapping tall tales around a campfire. Hall adds to the down-home feel, contributing "rustic-looking, mixed-media paintings [that] call to mind colored woodblock prints," according to a reviewer for *Publishers Weekly*. The artist's "cool palette of blues, purples and shimmering whites winningly matches the story's setting of a June night steeped in moonglow," the critic added. *Booklist* contributor Denia Hester called attention to Hall's technique, noting that "the several applications of paint give the art a textured look." "This effect sometimes roughens the art, occasionally obscuring a facial detail," Hester added, "but it also gives the book a unique look." Anne Connor, reviewing *On the Riverbank* in *School Library Journal,* observed that the "soft, mixed media illustrations have a verve that echoes the text and adds a romanticized dimension of a fond reminiscence to this story of an African-American family that has spent a winter anticipating such an outing."

Hall also collaborated with Temple on *Shanty Boat,* a picture book recalling the life of a boatman who plies his trade on the Mississippi River. Uncle Sheb spent his whole life on the river, never settling down or having a family. In fact, Sheb's home WAS the river, and after his death people reported seeing him and his ramshackle little boat when the moon shines brightly. Hall paced her paintings to Temple's hard-driving textual rhythms, and her "mixed-media illustrations . . . portray the bucolic existence of this solitary oarsman," according to *Booklist* critic Kay Weisman. A *Publishers Weekly* reviewer called Hall and Temple's picture-book collaboration "part ballad, part ghost story and part tall tale," noting that the book's "collagraphs bustle with a tone of joyous confusion." Reviewing the same title in *School Library Journal,* Lisa S. Murphy commented: "The art is luminous with light ranging from the warmth of the morning sun to the mysterious glow of the moon."

Among her illustration projects, Hall has crafted art for an adaptation of the classic *The Legend of Sleepy Hollow,* and her artwork has appeared in the anthology *The Very Best of Children's Book Illustration,* compiled by the Society of Illustrators. Hall's inclusion in the latter stands as a compliment to the illustrator; at the time of this volume's 1993 publication she had only two books to her credit.

*Hall's pastel and colored-pencil drawings capture the magic in the verses collected by well-known anthologist Lee Bennett Hopkins in his simply titled* **Weather.** (Illustration copyright © 1994 by Melanie Hall. Reproduced by permission of HarperCollins Children's Books, a division of HarperCollins Publishers.)

To accompany Lewis's twelve poems about the months of the year, collected and publoished as *July Is a Mad Mosquito,* Hall contributes "zippy collagraphs," according to a critic for *Publishers Weekly*. If the text falters, "Hall's literal interpretations should clear up any confusion," the same reviewer decided. Judy Greenfield, writing in *School Library Journal,* called attention to the "full-color, double-spread impressionistic painting" in *July Is a Mad Mosquito,* which are designed to interpret the central motif of each poem, while in *Booklist* Carolyn Phelan cited "Hall's lively illustrations, fanciful scenes in popsicle-bright pastels and muted blues and browns."

Hall's work also brings to life the poetry in *Weather,* a book of verses edited by Lee Bennett Hopkins, that features the poems of both famous—such as Carl Sandburg and Ogden Nash—and lesser-known versifiers. "The dominant colors are pink and orange—more sunny than rainy," noted Ruth K. MacDonald in her *School Library Journal* review of the book, the critic going on to observe that "the overall impression is of brightness, lightheartedness, and fun." In *Horn Book* Margaret A. Bush noted that Hall's work for *Weather* includes "pastel sketches, warmly energetic views of children and simple nature scenes."

Other collaborations between Hall and Hopkins include *Christmas Presents: Holiday Poetry* and *Hanukkah Lights: Holiday Poetry,* both which feature poetry and illustrations that tie in with the season. Reviewing both books, a *Horn Book* reviewer noted that Hall's paintings "accent the verses without overwhelming them." In *Kirkus Reviews* a contributor wrote of *Christmas Presents* that the artist's "attractive illustrations eschew traditional Christmas colors" and give the collection "a lively flair." In the same periodical, a reviewer noted of *Hanukkah Lights* that "whimsical paintings full of swirls and curves . . . complete the Judaic settings for each poem," while a *Publishers Weekly* critic wrote that Hall's paintings "combine visual flights of fancy with cozy scenes of Jewish domesticity."

Hall has worked with author Cathy Goldberg Fishman on several other books dealing with Jewish holidays. Passover is the subject of their first collaborative effort, *On Passover,* which *Booklist* critic Ilene Cooper called "more attractive and lyrical than many other Passover books." Here the story is told by a young girl who asks a series of questions of her family as they prepare for the traditional Jewish holiday. There is the ritual dinner, the Seder plate, and the Passover service, among other parts of the ceremonial aspects of the holiday. A *Publishers Weekly* reviewer concluded of *On Passover* that "Hall's rich mixed-media creations bustle with energy." In *On Rosh Hashanah and Yom Kippur* the High Holidays are explored, with particular focus on Rosh Hashanah, again employing a little girl's voice to get to the heart of the celebration. Once more, Fishman's text explores both the meaning of the holiday as well as the common holiday practices and food, while "Hall's beautiful, rosy, expressionistic pictures are a fine complement," according to Stephanie Zvirin in *Booklist.*

Reviewing *On Hanukkah* in *Booklist,* Julie Corsaro wrote that Hall's "fanciful, mixed-media paintings feature strong texturing and glowing, gilt-edged colors." Another collaboration with Fishman, *On Shabbat,* explains the weekly celebration of the Sabbath. Here "Hall's marbled, multilayered collagraphs are alive with intriguingly textured images," wrote Ellen Mandel in her *Booklist* review, adding that "they radiate the warmth, comfort, and refreshing strength" symbolized by Shabbat. According to *School Library Journal* contributor Martha Link, "the illustrations are the highlight of this book." In *On Sukkot and Simchat Torah* Fishman describes a Jewish family's preparation for two significant fall holidays. "The lovely, muted pastel illustrations are an excellent accompaniment to the lyrical text," Lisa Silverman commented in reviewing this work for *School Library Journal,* and *Booklist* reviewer Cooper praised Hall's artwork as "ethereal yet full of sweet, everyday detail."

A traditional Jewish tale is the focus of *The Seventh Day,* written by Rabbi Deborah Bodin Cohen. The author combines the creation story with a prayer that names God an artist, a potter, and a musician. "The

mixed-media illustrations are quite lovely, with a Chagall-like feel," complimented Amy Lilien-Harper in a review for *School Library Journal.* A *Publishers Weekly* critic felt that Hall's illustrations for Cohen's story "swirl with color and energy. Her palette balances purple sunsets, fluffy white clouds and verdant fields and mountains all in a vibrant, appealing rainbow of life." In Peninnah Schram's *The Magic Pomegranate: A Jewish Folktale* three brothers travel the globe in search of rare and unusual items. After ten years, the siblings reunite and reveal their discoveries: a crystal ball, a magic carpet, and a pomegranate. When a beautiful princess falls desperately ill, the brothers use their gifts to restore her to health, and the grateful princess decides to choose one as her husband. "Hall's imaginative illustrations in jewel tones add to the fairy-tale qualities of the story," a contributor in *Kirkus Reviews* observed.

Hall turns to biblical stories in illustrating Nancy Sohn Swartz's picture book *In Our Image: God's First Creatures.* This "nondenominational, nonsectarian retelling of the creation story . . . focuses on the period before man and woman were created," as Yapha Nuss-

*Hall's illustration projects include creating the artwork for Peninnah Schram's retelling of a Jewish folktale in* **The Magic Pomegranate.** (Illustration copyright © 2008 by Lerner Publishing Group, Inc. Reprinted with the permission of Millbrook Press, a division of Lerner Publishing Group, Inc. All rights reserved. No part of this excerpt may be used or reproduced in any manner whatsoever without the prior written permission of Lerner Publishing Group, Inc.)

baum Mason described the book in a *School Library Journal* review. In Swartz's tale, a group of animals informs God of the gifts they would like to present to humans, including the chimps who think curiosity would be a fine thing, and the ostriches who opt for humans minding their own business. Worried when God tells them that humans will have dominion over them, the animals are finally reassured when God further informs them that the humans will not abuse this sacred trust. "The vibrantly colored illustrations nearly leap off the page in this delightful interpretation," concluded Mason. In *Booklist* Ilene Cooper deemed Hall's artwork "particularly nice," noting that her illustrations both extend and elaborate Swartz's text, and "capture the feeling of life that is the essence of the story." A reviewer for *Publishers Weekly* concluded of the combination of soft watercolor with sharper, black and neon images that "the effect is both complex and magical."

Ivy O. Eastwick's poems, collected in *I Asked a Tiger to Tea, and Other Poems,* and playground rhymes collected by Rebecca Kai Dotlich in *Over in the Pink House: New Jump Rope Rhymes,* have each provided Hall with unique subjects for her illustrations. The poetry in Eastwick's compilation is based on the poet's childhood in early 1900's England. The verses "are in concert with Hall's richly textured, lushly colored art," according to Ellen Mandel in *Booklist.* Kathleen Whalin, writing in *School Library Journal,* observed that, while Eastwick's poems have been better collected in other compilations, "Hall's bright, impressionistic paintings do much to enliven the book." The traditional rhymes of *Over in the Pink House* contain elements of folklore and fantasy, as well as realistic imagery woven together by a steady jump-rope beat. "The style of each picture perfectly captures the tone of the accompanying poem," wrote Sally R. Dow in her *School Library Journal* review of Dotlich's book, and Hazel Rochman noted in *Booklist* that "Hall's clear, colorful illustrations . . . keep the scenarios open, whether realistic or magical."

*Winter Song,* a picture-book version of a poem composed for the end of William Shakespeare's early comedy *Love's Labor's Lost,* is also enriched by Hall's art. "The illustrations artfully capture the temper of the text while helping readers to comprehend unfamiliar language," a contributor noted in *School Library Journal,* and *New York Times Book Review* critic Julie Just felt that "Hall's images, evocative of the Elizabethan era, add charm and detail to Shakespeare's playful poem." *Every Second Something Happens: Poems for the Mind and Senses,* a collection edited by Christine San José and Bill Johnson, includes selections from such acclaimed writers as Eileen Spinelli, Joy Cowley, and John Ciardi. Here "Hall's clear colorful illustrations never overwhelm the words," wrote Rochman, and a *Kirkus Reviews* critic observed that the "eclectic artwork . . . reflects the individual mood and theme for each poem."

## Biographical and Critical Sources

*PERIODICALS*

*Booklist,* November 15, 1992, Denia Hester, review of *On the Riverbank,* p. 64; June 1, 1994, Kay Weisman, review of *Shanty Boat,* p. 1846; July, 1994, Carolyn Phelan, review of *July Is a Mad Mosquito,* p. 1950; March 1, 1997, Ilene Cooper, review of *On Passover,* p. 1165; October 1, 1997, Stephanie Zvirin, review of *On Rosh Hashanah and Yom Kippur,* p. 322; September 1, 1998, Julie Corsaro, review of *On Hanukkah,* p. 132; October 1, 1998, Ilene Cooper, review of *In Our Image: God's First Creatures,* p. 345; April, 1, 2001, Ellen Mandel, review of *On Shabbat,* p. 1474; December 15, 2002, Ellen Mandel, review of *I Asked a Tiger to Tea, and Other Poems,* p. 756; May 1, 2004, Hazel Rochman, review of *Over in the Pink House: New Jump Rope Rhymes,* p. 1560; August, 2004, Jennifer Mattson, review of *Christmas Presents: Holiday Poetry,* p. 1938; October 1, 2006, Ilene Cooper, review of *On Sukkot and Simchat Torah,* p. 66; September 1, 2009, Hazel Rochman, review of *Every Second Something Happens: Poems for the Mind and Senses,* p. 94.

*Children's Bookwatch,* May, 2005, review of *Over in the Pink House.*

*Horn Book,* July-August, 1994, Margaret A. Bush, review of *Weather,* p. 468; November-December, 2004, review of *Christmas Presents* and *Hanukkah Lights: Holiday Poetry,* p. 661.

*Kirkus Reviews,* March 15, 2004, review of *Over in the Pink House,* p. 267; November 1, 2004, reviews of *Christmas Presents,* and *Hanukkah Lights,* p. 1050; September 15, 2006, review of *Winter Song,* p. 967; July 15, 2008, review of *The Magic Pomegranate: A Jewish Folktale;* July 1, 2009, review of *Every Second Something Happens.*

*New York Times Book Review,* December 17, 2006, Julie Just, review of *Winter Song.*

*Publishers Weekly,* October 5, 1992, review of *On the Riverbank,* p. 70; February 14, 1994, reviews of *Shanty Boat,* p. 87, and *July Is a Mad Mosquito,* p. 89; February 24, 1997, review of *On Passover,* p. 83; September 28, 1998, review of *In Our Image,* p. 95; February 14, 2005, review of *The Seventh Day,* p. 78; July 31, 2006, review of *On Sukkot and Simchat Torah,* p. 78.

*School Library Journal,* November, 1992, Anne Connor, review of *On the Riverbank,* p. 79; March, 1994, Ruth K. MacDonald, review of *Weather,* p. 216; April 1994, Judy Greenfield, review of *July Is a Mad Mosquito,* p. 120; July, 1994, Lisa S. Murphy, review of *Shanty Boat,* p. 98; March, 1999, Yapha Nussbaum Mason, review of *In Our Image,* p. 202; February, 2000, Amy Lilien-Harper, review of *On Purim,* p. 110; August, 2001, Martha Link, review of *On Shabbat,* p. 168; November, 2002, Kathleen Whalin, review of *I Asked a Tiger to Tea, and Other Poems,* p. 142; April, 2004, Sally R. Dow, review of *Over in the Pink House,* p. 130; August, 2005, Amy Lilien-Harper, review of *The Seventh Day,* p. 86; September, 2006, Lisa Silverman, review of *On Sukkot and Simchat Torah,* p. 192; November, 2006, Marily Taniguchi, review of *Winter Song,* p. 124; October, 2007, Lisa Silverman, review of *The Magic Pomegranate,* p. 139; September, 2009, Margaret Bush, review of *Every Second Something Happens,* p. 147.

*ONLINE*

*ispot.com,* http://www.theispot.com/ (April 1, 2011), "Melanie Hall."
*Melanie Hall Home Page,* http://www.mhallillustration. com (April 1, 2011).*

\*          \*          \*

# HALL, Melanie W.
## See HALL, Melanie

\*          \*          \*

# HALL, Michael 1954-

## Personal

Born 1954; married; children: two daughters. *Education:* University of Michigan, B.S. (biochemistry and psychology).

## Addresses

*Home*—MN. *Office*—Hall Kelley, Inc., 661 Nason Hill Rd., Marine on Saint Croix, MN 55047. *Agent*—Anna Olswanger, Liza Dawson Associates, 350 7th Ave., Ste. 2003, New York, NY 10001. *E-mail*—mfhall@me.com; michael@hallkelley.com.

## Career

Author, illustrator, and graphic designer. Formerly worked in biomedical research; Hall Kelley, Inc., owner and principal designer, 1984—. Trustee for nonprofit organizations. Presenter at schools.

## Member

American Institute of Graphic Arts, Society for Environmental Graphic Design.

## Awards, Honors

Numerous design awards.

## Writings

*SELF-ILLUSTRATED PICTURE BOOKS*

*My Heart Is like a Zoo,* Greenwillow Books (New York, NY), 2010.

*Perfect Square,* Greenwillow Books (New York, NY), 2011.

*OTHER*

Work has appeared in industry publications, including *American Institute of Graphic Arts Annual, Communication Arts,* and *Print.*

## Sidelights

Decades ago, as a student in college, Michael Hall focused his attention on biochemistry and psychology. This choice of curriculum has proved to be very unusual for someone who, like Hall, is now a professional illustrator and graphic designer. As it happened, Hall did work in the field of biomedical research for several years, but then decided to change course and pursue his interest in art. This choice led to his career as a successful graphic designer as well as to his creation of the self-illustrated picture books *My Heart Is like a Zoo* and *Perfect Square,* the latter which finds a perfect square transformed into a variety of non-square objects.

Praised by *School Library Journal* contributor Anne Beier as "an outstanding choice for one-on-one sharing," *My Heart Is like a Zoo* mixes a toddler-friendly introduction to animals children can meet at the zoo with an identification guide to basic colors and human emotions. Hall pairs his boldly colored digital illustrations with a rhyming text that takes readers on a tour of a twenty-animal menagerie that ends with a meeting the zoo keeper: a small sleeping boy who is surrounded by

*Michael Hall creates the graphic-style art that fills the pages of his picture book* **My Heart Is like a Zoo.** (Copyright © 2010 by Michael Hall. Reproduced with permission of HarperCollins Children's Books, a division of HarperCollins Publishers.)

his favorite stuffed-animal toys. Paired with what Beier described as a "crisp, succinct," and "carefully crafted" text, the illustrations in *My Heart Is like a Zoo* are composed of geometric shapes along with hearts of various sizes—over 300 in all. A *Kirkus Reviews* critic likened Hall's illustration style to that of collage artist Lois Ehlert and described the overall effect of the book as "bright" and "appealing," and in *Booklist* Hazel Rochman predicted that Hall's "simple rhymes about feelings will have preschoolers savoring the words" and "joining in." "Children just learning about shapes will revel in these pages," predicted a *Publishers Weekly* contributor, citing the "masterful blending of bright, saturated colors" in *My Heart Is like a Zoo*.

## Biographical and Critical Sources

*PERIODICALS*

*Booklist*, November 15, 2009, Hazel Rochman, review of *My Heart Is like a Zoo*, p. 43.
*Kirkus Reviews*, December 15, 2009, review of *My Heart Is like a Zoo*.
*Publishers Weekly*, December 7, 2009, review of *My Heart Is like a Zoo*, p. 46.
*School Library Journal*, February, 2010, Anne Beier, review of *My Heart Is like a Zoo*, p. 86.

*ONLINE*

*Hall Kelley Inc. Web site*, http://www.hallkelly.com (February 20, 2011).
*Michael Hall Home Page*, http://www.myheartislikeazoo.com (February 20, 2011).*

\*　　\*　　\*

## HAWKINS, Rachel 1979-

### Personal

Born 1979, in VA; husband a geologist; children: one son. *Education:* Auburn University, B.A. (English). *Hobbies and other interests:* Reading, traveling, knitting.

### Addresses

*Home*—AL. *Agent*—Holly Root, Waxman Literary Agency, 80 5th Ave., Ste. 1101, New York, NY 10011. *E-mail*—rachel@rachel-hawkins.com.

### Career

Writer. Taught high school English in Harvest, AL, for three years.

### Writings

*"HEX HALL" SERIES*

*Hex Hall*, Disney/Hyperion Books (New York, NY), 2010.

*Demonglass*, Disney/Hyperion Books (New York, NY), 2011.

### Sidelights

A former high school English teacher, Rachel Hawkins is the creator of the "Hex Hall" series of middle-grade novels featuring the exploits of a budding teenaged witch. A longtime fan of such celebrated authors as Lois Duncan and Anne Rice, Hawkins notes that her books—including *Hex Hall* and its sequel, *Demonglass*—also mix elements of humor, horror, and the supernatural. "I've always had a deep love for The Spooky," she remarked to *Cynsations* online interviewer Cynthia Leitich Smith. "I think there's something about the heightened emotions of paranormal stories that really resonates with me, both as a writer and a reader."

In *Hex Hall* Hawkins introduces Sophie Mercer, the sixteen-year-old offspring of an often-absent warlock father. When one of Sophie's love spells goes awry, she is exiled to Hecate Hall, a reformatory for unruly adolescent Prodigium, including witches, vampires, were-

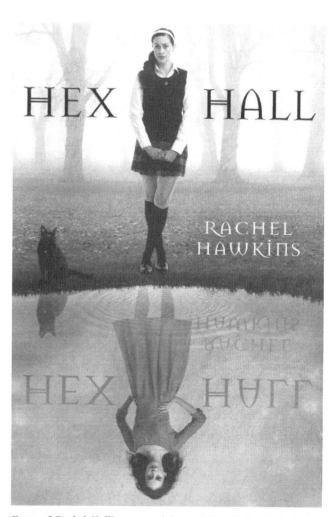

*Cover of Rachel Hall's young-adult novel* Hex Hall, *which finds a young witch whose missteps find her enrolled at a reform school for the supernaturally inclined.*

wolves, and shapeshifters. Almost immediately, the teen makes enemies of a trio of powerful witches, falls for a good-looking warlock classmate, and bonds with her vampiric roommate, Jenna. When a number of Prodigium are found drained of their blood and suspicion falls upon Jenna, the loyal Sophie begins an investigation to determine the identity of the true culprit. "What makes this fast-paced romp work is Hawkins' wry humor and sharp eye for teen dynamics," observed Debbie Carton in *Booklist.* A reviewer in *Publishers Weekly* also complimented *Hex Hall,* stating that "Hawkins's proficient and entertaining debut is jam-packed with magical creatures and mystery."

Sophie faces a momentous decision about her future in *Demonglass,* a follow-up. After surviving an assassination attempt at the hands of Archer Cross, a member of The Eye, a group bent on destroying Prodigium, Sophie ventures to England under the protective watch of her warlock father. As she discovers more about her heritage, she considers undergoing a procedure that will destroy her magical powers. Writing in *Voice of Youth Advocates,* Stacey Hayman praised the "engaging, entertaining story" in *Demonglass,* and Carton observed that "the many action scenes lend a cinematic feel" to Hawkins' middle-grade novel.

## Biographical and Critical Sources

*PERIODICALS*

*Booklist,* March 15, 2010, Debbie Carton, review of *Hex Hall,* p. 38; February 15, 2011, Debbie Carton, review of *Demonglass,* p. 76.

*Bulletin of the Center for Children's Books,* May, 2010, Kate Quealy-Gainer, review of *Hex Hall,* p. 379.

*Kirkus Reviews,* February 15, 2010, review of *Hex Hall.*

*Publishers Weekly,* January 18, 2010, review of *Hex Hall,* p. 49.

*Voice of Youth Advocates,* June, 2010, Sherrie Williams, review of *Hex Hall,* p. 164; December, 2010, Stacey Hayman, review of *Demonglass,* p. 471.

*ONLINE*

*Cynsations Web log,* http://cynthialeitichsmith.blogspot. com/ (March 1, 2010), Cynthia Leitich Smith, interview with Hawkins.

*Rachel Hawkins Web log,* http://readingwritingrachel. blogspot.com (April 1, 2011).

*Rachel Hawkins Home Page,* http://www.rachel-hawkins. com (April 1, 2011).*

\*          \*          \*

# HILDEBRANDT, Greg, Jr. 1970-

## Personal

Born 1970; son of Greg (an illustrator) and Diana Hildebrandt; married; wife's name Jane. *Education:* Raritan Valley Community College, earned degree.

## Addresses

*Home*—NJ. *E-mail*—greg@creativebonzinc.com.

## Career

Writer. Fox 5 News, New York, NY, aerial cameraman; Eastern Effects, Inc., New York, NY, coordinator; production assistant on films, 2000-01; personal assistant to screenwriter David Milch; cinematographer on *In a Single Bound* (documentary short), 2006; writer for Martini Studios and Creative Bonz (creative media companies).

## Writings

*Greg and Tim Hildebrandt: The Tolkien Years,* Watson-Guptill (New York, NY), 2001.

(With Justin Boring) *War on Flesh* (graphic novel), TokyoPop (Los Angeles, CA), 2005.

*Realm of the Rodent: Blood Brother* (novel), illustrated by Alex Horley and Dean Robinson, Sourcebooks Jabberwocky (Naperville, IL), 2009.

Coauthor, with Ross Marroso, of *Osama Bin Latte* (short comedy). Coauthor and co-illustrator, with Greg and Tim Hildebrandt, of comic strip "The Emerald Seven," in *Frank Frazetta Fantasy Illustrated,* 1998-99.

## Sidelights

In *Realm of the Rodent: Blood Brother,* his debut novel for young readers, Greg Hildebrandt, Jr., follows the adventures of Crycket and Sylan, mouse cousins that embark on a perilous journey through the land of Brystal to combat forces led by power-hungry Lord Elnack. Hildebrandt is no stranger to the creation of imaginary realms: his father, Greg Hildebrandt, and uncle, Tim Hildebrant, produced some of the most memorable works of fantasy art of the twentieth century, including the original poster for the groundbreaking 1977 film *Star Wars* as well as bestselling calendars featuring scenes from J.R.R. Tolkien's *Lord of the Rings.*

In his heavily illustrated profile of his illustrious relatives, *Greg and Tim Hildebrandt: The Tolkien Years,* Hildebrandt, Jr., recounts the efforts of his father and uncle to create their Tolkien-inspired art, often using family members as models for the characters of Middle-Earth. Writing in *Booklist,* Ray Olson praised "Gregory's companionable I-was-there anecdotes," and *School Library Journal* reviewer Patricia White-Williams noted that *Greg and Tim Hildebrandt* "gives insight into the younger Hildebrandt's unorthodox childhood." According to *January* online contributor Sue Bursztynski, Hildebrandt "recalls those years with enormous affection and conveys beautifully that same sense of wonder he felt during his childhood. The painting process he witnessed was, for a little boy, a magical journey in its own right."

## Biographical and Critical Sources

*PERIODICALS*

*Booklist,* July, 2001, Ray Olson, review of *Greg and Tim Hildebrandt: The Tolkien Years,* p. 1967.
*Kirkus Reviews,* October 15, 2009, review of *Realm of the Rodent: Blood Brother.*
*Library Journal,* August, 2001, review of *Greg and Tim Hildebrandt,* p. 99.
*Publishers Weekly,* June 8, 2001, review of *Greg and Tim Hildebrandt,* p. 65.
*School Library Journal,* April, 2002, Patricia White-Williams, review of *Greg and Tim Hildebrandt,* p. 189; February, 2010, Eric Norton, review of *Realm of the Rodent,* p. 112.
*Voice of Youth Advocates,* April, 2002, review of *Greg and Tim Hildebrandt,* p. 62.

*ONLINE*

*January Online,* http://januarymagazine.com/ (December, 2002), Sue Bursztynski, review of *Greg and Tim Hildebrandt.*
*Sourcebooks Web site,* http://www.sourcebooks.com/ (April 15, 2011), "Greg Hildebrandt, Jr."*

\*　　\*　　\*

## HOBERMAN, Mary Ann 1930-

***Mary Ann Hoberman*** (Photograph by Helen Neafsey. Reproduced by permission.)

### Personal

Born August 12, 1930, in Stamford, CT; daughter of Milton (a salesman) and Dorothy Freedman; married Norman Hoberman (an architect, ceramist, and illustrator), February 4, 1951; children: Diane, Perry, Charles, Margaret. *Education:* Smith College, B.A. (magna cum laude), 1951; Yale University, M.A., 1985, postgraduate work in English literature. *Hobbies and other interests:* Biking, gardening, dancing.

### Addresses

*Home*—Greenwich, CT. *Agent*—Gina Maccoby, Gina Maccoby Literary Agency, P.O. Box 60, Chappaqua, NY 10514.

### Career

Poet and author. Little, Brown, Boston, MA, editor of children's books, c. 1950s; writer, 1955—. Speaker, consultant, and artist-in-the-schools, 1955—Fairfield University, Fairfield, CT, adjunct professor, 1980-83; C.G. Jung Center, New York, NY, program coordinator, 1981; former newspaper reporter and. Pocket People (children's theater group), founder and member, 1968-75. Greenwich Library, trustee, 1986-91; Literacy Volunteers of America, Greenwich/Stamford Chapter, member of board, 1997—.

### Awards, Honors

Book Week Poem award, Children's Book Council, 1976; American Book Award, 1983, for *A House Is a House for Me;* Best Book in Language Arts selection, Society of School Librarians International, 1998, for *One of Each;* Gold Award, National Parenting Publications Awards, 1998, and Children's Books of Distinction listee, *Riverbank Review,* 1999, both for *The Llama Who Had No Pajama;* Parents' Choice Award, 2001, for *It's Simple, Said Simon;* Notable Children's Book selection, American Library Association, 2001, for *You Read to Me, I'll Read to You: Very Short Stories to Read Together;* Excellence in Poetry for Children Award, National Council of Teachers of English (NCTE), 2003; National Outdoor Book Award, 2004, for *Whose Garden Is It?;* Gryphon Award Honor Book selection, Center for Children's Books, 2004, and Notable Children's Book in the Language Arts, NCTE, 2005, both for *You Read to Me, I'll Read to You: Very Short Fairy Tales to Read Together;* named U.S. children's poet laureate, 2008-10.

### Writings

*CHILDREN'S FICTION AND POETRY*

*All My Shoes Come in Two's,* illustrated by husband, Norman Hoberman, Little, Brown (Boston, MA), 1957.

*How Do I Go?,* illustrated by Norman Hoberman, Little, Brown (Boston, MA), 1958.

*Hello and Good-by,* illustrated by Norman Hoberman, Little, Brown (Boston, MA), 1959.

*What Jim Knew,* illustrated by Norman Hoberman, Little, Brown (Boston, MA), 1963.

*Not Enough Beds for the Babies,* illustrated by Helen Spyer, Little, Brown (Boston, MA), 1965.

*A Little Book of Little Beasts,* illustrated by Peter Parnall, Simon & Schuster (New York, NY), 1973.

*The Looking Book,* illustrated by Jerry Joyner, Viking (New York, NY), 1973.

*The Raucous Auk: A Menagerie of Poems,* illustrated by Joseph Low, Viking (New York, NY), 1973.

*Nuts to You and Nuts to Me: An Alphabet of Poems,* illustrated by Ronni Solbert, Knopf (New York, NY), 1974.

*I Like Old Clothes,* illustrated by Jacqueline Chwast, Knopf (New York, NY), 1976, illustrated by Patricia Barton, Knopf (New York, NY), 2012.

*Bugs,* illustrated by Victoria Chess, Viking (New York, NY), 1976.

*A House Is a House for Me,* illustrated by Betty Fraser, Viking (New York, NY), 1978.

*Yellow Butter, Purple Jelly, Red Jam, Black Bread,* illustrated by Chaya Burstein, Viking (New York, NY), 1981.

*The Cozy Book,* illustrated by Tony Chen, Viking (New York, NY), 1982, illustrated by Betty Fraser, Browndeer Press (San Diego, CA), 1985.

*Mr. and Mrs. Muddle,* illustrated by Catharine O'Neill, Little, Brown (Boston, MA), 1988.

*A Fine Fat Pig, and Other Animal Poems,* illustrated by Malcah Zeldis, HarperCollins (New York, NY), 1991.

*Fathers, Mothers, Sisters, Brothers: A Collection of Family Poems,* illustrated by Marilyn Hafner, Joy Street Books (Boston, MA), 1991.

(Editor) *My Song Is Beautiful: Poems and Pictures in Many Voices,* Little, Brown (Boston, MA), 1994.

*The Seven Silly Eaters,* illustrated by Marla Frazee, Harcourt Brace (San Diego, CA), 1997.

*The Llama Who Had No Pajama: 100 Favorite Poems,* illustrated by B. Fraser, Harcourt Brace (San Diego, CA), 1997.

*One of Each,* illustrated by Marjorie Priceman, Little, Brown (Boston, MA), 1997.

(Adapter) *Miss Mary Mack: A Hand-clapping Rhyme,* illustrated by Nadine Bernard Westcott, Little, Brown (Boston, MA), 1998.

*And to Think That We Thought That We'd Never Be Friends,* illustrated by Kevin Hawkes, Crown (New York, NY), 1999.

*The Marvelous Mouse Man,* illustrated by Laura Forman, Harcourt Brace (San Diego, CA), 2000.

*The Two Sillies,* illustrated by Lynne Cravath, Harcourt Brace (San Diego, CA), 2000.

(Adapter) *The Eensy Weensy Spider,* illustrated by Nadine Bernard Westcott, Little, Brown (Boston, MA), 2000.

*"It's Simple,"* Said Simon, illustrated by Meilo So, Knopf (New York, NY), 2001.

*The Looking Book: A Hide-and-Seek Counting Story,* illustrated by Laura Huliska-Beith, Little, Brown (Boston, MA), 2001.

(Adapter) *There Once Was a Man Named Michael Finnegan,* illustrated by Nadine Bernard Westcott, Little, Brown (Boston, MA), 2001.

*You Read to Me, I'll Read to You: Very Short Stories to Read Together,* illustrated by Michael Emberley, Little, Brown (Boston, MA), 2001.

(Adapter) *Bill Grogan's Coat,* illustrated by Nadine Bernard Westcott, Little, Brown (Boston, MA), 2002.

(Adapter) *The Marvelous Mouse Man,* illustrated by Laura Forman, Harcourt Brace (San Diego, CA), 2002.

*Right outside My Window,* illustrated by Nicholas Wilton, Mondo (New York, NY), 2002.

(Adapter) *Mary Had a Little Lamb,* illustrated by Nadine Bernard Westcott, Little, Brown (New York, NY), 2003.

*Whose Garden Is It?,* illustrated by Jane Dyer, Harcourt (San Diego, CA), 2004.

(Adapter) *Yankee Doodle,* illustrated by Nadine Bernard Westcott, Little, Brown (New York, NY), 2004.

*You Read to Me, I'll Read to You: Very Short Fairy Tales to Read Together,* illustrated by Michael Emberley, Little, Brown (New York, NY), 2004.

*You Read to Me, I'll Read to You: Very Short Mother Goose Tales to Read Together,* illustrated by Michael Emberley, Little, Brown (New York, NY), 2005.

*Sing-along Stories Three: More Favorite Songs to Sing Together,* illustrated by Nadine Bernard Westcott, Little, Brown (New York, NY), 2005.

*I'm Going to Grandma's,* illustrated by Tiphanie Beeke, Harcourt (Orlando, FL), 2007.

(Adapter) *Mrs. O'Leary's Cow,* illustrated by Jenny Mattheson, Little, Brown (New York, NY), 2007.

*You Read to Me, I'll Read to You: Very Short Scary Tales to Read Together,* illustrated by Michael Emberley, Little, Brown (New York, NY), 2007.

*All Kinds of Families,* illustrated by Marc Boutavant, Little, Brown (New York, NY), 2009.

(Selector, with Linda Winston; and contributor) *The Tree That Time Built: A Celebration of Nature, Science, and Imagination,* illustrated by Barbara Fortin, Sourcebooks Jabberwocky (Napperville, IL), 2009.

*Strawberry Hill* (novel), illustrated by Wendy Anderson Halperin, Little, Brown (New York, NY), 2009.

*You Read to Me, I'll Read to You: Very Short Fables to Read Together,* illustrated by Michael Emberley, Little, Brown (New York, NY), 2010.

*OTHER*

Contributor of poems to numerous anthologies, textbooks, and magazines in the United States and abroad, including *Southern Poetry Review, Small Pond,* and *Harper's.* Contributor of travel articles to *New York Times* and *Boston Globe.*

## Sidelights

Mary Ann Hoberman "is a consummate channeler of children's sensibilities," Michael Atkinson declared in an essay on the Poetry Foundation Web site, announcing Hoberman's selection as U.S. children's poet laureate in 2008. Hoberman employs playful rhythms and rhymes in her picture books, which include such popular tales as *The Seven Silly Eaters* and *All Kinds of Families,* as well as the works in the "You Read to Me, I'll Read to You" series. "It's a measure of Hoberman's writerly sensibility that her work has remained remarkably consistent in tone and craft," Atkinson added, "and her voice timelessly unfaddish; she knows that although the culture may change, children in the first half-dozen years of life don't really."

Celebrating the everyday lives and concerns of children, Hoberman's picture books deal with animals, pesky little brothers and other family relationships, growing up, the idea of home, and a myriad of other commonplace subjects, though her handling of such themes is far from commonplace. In her critically acclaimed *A House Is a House for Me,* for example, she takes the concept of house and home to the generic level, investigating rabbit hutches, mule sheds, and garages—houses for cars. "Hoberman's own imagination entices the reader/listener to use his imagination, to add more houses for more things," commented Mary Lystad in a critical analysis of the poet's work in the *St. James Guide to Children's Writers.* It is this teasing of imagination for which Hoberman is best known; her many books attest to an imagination ever at work. As a contributor to *Riverbank Review* noted in its 1999 Children's Books of Distinction awards list, Hoberman's "overriding theme is the joy of playing with words."

Born in 1930, in Stamford, Connecticut, Hoberman grew up in various towns in the Northeast before returning to Stamford and the house "that is the locus and

*In* **The Two Sillies** *Hoberman tells a humorous rural tale that gains added levity from Lynne Cravath's nostalgic-themed art.* (Illustration copyright © 2000 by Lynne Cravath. Reprinted by permission of Houghton Mifflin Harcourt Publishing Company.)

inspiration for most of my writing for children," as she more-recently noted in an essay for the *Something about the Author Autobiography Series* (SAAS). The older of two children, she was often put in charge of her younger brother, and this sibling relationship later found expression in her writing. One thing was certain: "I have always wanted to be a writer," Hoberman explained in *SAAS.* "This conviction saved me a lot of career counseling later on in life, but it has always puzzled me. How did I know so early on that that was what I wanted to do with my life?"

Books and words were among Hoberman's best friends as a young girl and adolescent. She made up rhymes everywhere, especially on the swing where the natural physical rhythm encouraged word play. Graduating from Stamford High School, she went on to Smith College on the advice of one of her teachers, a Smith alumna. On one of the first postwar junior-year-abroad programs, Hoberman travelled to France to study in the company of young women from other prestigious schools, among them Jacqueline Bouvier, the future Mrs. John F. Kennedy. Her year in France was a revelation and only reluctantly did she return to America and her senior year at Smith. Soon she met Norman Hoberman, a senior at Harvard Law School and the two were married within four months.

During the Korean War, both Hoberman and her husband finished school before Norman was sent off to the military. As luck would have it, he was ultimately stationed in Canada where Hoberman could join him, and there the couple had their first baby. After military service, Norman decided to return to college to study architecture. During his studies, Hoberman became a freelance editor at Little, Brown in Boston and also had two more children. It was during this time, after giving birth to three children in three years, that Hoberman began playing with rhymes once again. Wheeling her children in the park one day, she came up with a short couplet—"All my shoes/ Come in two's"—that she turned into her first rhyming picture book, illustrated by her husband. It was a sudden inspiration and something of a lark to put the book together; then she sent it off to an editor at Little, Brown and forgot about it. Months later came the acceptance. Writing in the *New York Times Book Review,* C. Elta Van Norman called *All My Shoes Come in Two's* "a unique treatment of a subject fascinating to the small child." Hoberman was on her way to becoming a children's author.

The Hobermans went on to collaborate on several books, looking at modes of transport in *How Do I Go?,* at greetings in *Hello and Good-by,* and at fantasy worlds in *What Jim Knew.* Generally well received, their books of verses for young and very young children won a receptive readership as Hoberman experimented with poetic techniques and forms ranging from free verse to metered poems, from internal rhyme to end rhyme, and from alliteration to the tongue twister. More recently teaming up with other illustrators, she has gone on to create several award-winning picture books, and has also penned the chapter book *Mr. and Mrs. Muddle,* about a horse couple who learn the art of compromise, as well as the novel *Strawberry Hill.*

Of Hoberman's early works, her American Book Award-winning *A House Is a House for Me* is one of her most popular. Collaborating with illustrator Betty Fraser, the author employs "alternating lines of anapestic trimeter and tetrameter with lots of end and internal rhyme," according to Sharon Elswit in *School Library Journal.* Hoberman created "a rich book," and one that should inspire kids to "reach for the colors and chorus the refrain," according to Elswit, while Harold C.K. Rice called *A House Is a House for Me* "an astonishing picture book, one of the best of the year," in his review for the *New York Times Book Review.* Twenty years later, Hoberman reteamed with Fraser on *The Llama Who Had No Pajama: 100 Favorite Poems,* prompting a *Publishers Weekly* reviewer to note that this "inventively illustrated" collaboration "brims with enough wordplay and silliness to please a room full of young wordsmiths."

After taking a hiatus from writing during the 1980s to return to college and completed an advanced degree, Hoberman came back to writing with renewed vigor. As she noted in *SAAS:* "My sabbatical had done its work; after all those years of academic papers, I was eager to write for children once more." *A Fine Fat Pig and Other Animal Poems* features a favorite Hoberman motif: description of animals. Mary Jo Salter, writing in the *Washington Post Book World,* found the verses in this collection to be "irresistibly memorizable." Reviewing *Fathers, Mothers, Sisters, Brothers,* a collection of Hoberman's poems dealing with the family, a writer for *Kirkus Reviews* called the work "wise, witty, and neatly constructed."As Hoberman commented in *SAAS,* the idea for *Fathers, Mothers, Sisters, Brothers* "had been evolving over a lifetime. In the poems I write about many of the feelings I had as a child, of the relationships I experienced and observed, as well as of new kinds of family life and configurations."

Finicky gourmands get the Hoberman treatment in *The Seven Silly Eaters,* "a highly comic rhyming romp," according to Barbara Elleman writing in *School Library Journal.* Mrs. Peters, eternally pregnant, would like nothing better than to play her cello in peace, but she is continually at work catering to the likes and dislikes of her children, some who like milk, some who like lemonade—but not from a can. Another wants homemade bread, while only creamy oatmeal will satisfy other tiny taste buds. "The combination of food and farce makes for an affectionate rhyming picture book," observed *Booklist* critic Rochman, and Ann A. Flowers concluded in *Horn Book* that *The Seven Silly Eaters* will be a "pleasure for parent and child."

Hoberman returns to the animal kingdom for *One of Each,* featuring a hound dog, and *Miss Mary Mack,*

starring a clumsy pachyderm. In the former title, Oliver Tolliver—described as "a dapper and bewhiskered hound" by Carol Ann Wilson in *School Library Journal*—is happy with his home and possessions, of which he has one of each. Inviting the cat, Peggoty Small, to enjoy his home, Oliver is surprised when his guest finds it all too predictable and boring. Readjusting his singular possessions, Oliver invites Peggoty back, and she suddenly enjoys the new dual-item household. Wilson dubbed *One of Each* "a 'peachy' offering from a talented team," while Elizabeth Bush advised in the *Bulletin of the Center for Children's Books* that teachers should "run this by the preschool or primary students when it's time to lay down the classroom laws: sharing and caring." Susan Dove Lempke, reviewing the same book in *Booklist,* called *One of Each* a "surefire storytime hit."

*Miss Mary* is definitely surprised to find an elephant crashing her backyard barbecue in *Miss Mary Mack,* an adaptation of "a favorite hand-clapping rhyme," according to *Booklist* reviewer Stephanie Zvirin. Escaping from the zoo, a rambunctious pachyderm has a great time when it invites itself to a local barbecue cum tea party. "Hands will be clapping and toes will be tapping to this spunky rendition of a favorite schoolyard rhyme," predicted a reviewer for *Publishers Weekly.* Jane Marino echoed these sentiments in *School Library Journal* by noting thatHoberman's "high-flying package of fun, complete with music and hand instructions, will have children clapping along in no time."

Hoberman has adapted several other familiar songs into picture books, including *There Once Was a Man Named Michael Finnegan, Bill Grogan's Coat,* and *Yankee Doodle.* In *The Marvelous Mouse Man* she adapts the legend of the Pied Piper of Hamelin by focusing on a small town overrun by mice in which residents turn to a mysterious stranger for help. Using an enticing array of cheesy odors, the stranger soon rids the village of its mouse problem, but when their cats, dogs, and children also begin to disappear, the townspeople devise a clever solution to restore order. "Hoberman's agile and comical verse cleverly contorts a classic," noted a reviewer in *Publishers Weekly,* while a *Kirkus Reviews* critic judged *The Marvelous Mouse Man* to be "a rollicking, readable remake from one of the best versifiers in the business."

A young boy faces a series of unusual challenges in *"It's Simple," Said Simon,* described as an "agreeable picture book" by a critic in *Publishers Weekly.* While out for a walk, Simon meets a dog that challenges him to growl, a cat that challenges him to stretch, and a horse that challenges him to jump. Simon completes each task with ease, but he appears to meet his match when a sly tiger that plans to eat the boy for dinner issues its own challenges. Reviewing *"It's Simple," Said Simon, Horn Book* contributor Christine Heppermann deemed the tale "delectable," and *Booklist* reviewer Shelley Townsend-Hudson called Hoberman's work a "simple, winning fable."

The first book in a popular read-aloud series designed for two voices, *You Read to Me, I'll Read to You: Very Short Stories to Read Together* collects twelve brief poems that allow participants to read both individually and as partners. "Each poem bounces back and forth between readers beautifully," noted *Horn Book* reviewer Roger Sutton, and Mary Ann Carcich praised the book in *School Library Journal* as a "delightful choreography of rhythm, rhyme, and repetition that begs to be read aloud in tandem by children and adults." *You Read to Me, I'll Read to You: Very Short Fairy Tales to Read Together* features offbeat, humorous versions of eight classic tales; *You Read to Me, I'll Read to You: Very Short Mother Goose Tales to Read Together* features stories that are "sure to draw giggles from the most reluctant young readers," according to a *Kirkus Reviews* critic; and *You Read to Me, I'll Read to You: Very Short Scary Tales to Read Together* was described as "a must for Halloween sharing" by Hazel Rochman in *Booklist*.

Hoberman examines the wonders of nature in her verse picture books *Right outside My Window* and *Whose Garden Is It?* In *Right outside My Window* a young girl observes the changes that occur during the four seasons as she peers through a window in her home, resulting in a "lyrical offering . . . just right any time of the year," according to a *Publishers Weekly* critic. In *Whose Garden Is It?* Mrs. McGee and her young companion happen upon a wonderful garden full of vegetables and flowers. Although a rather surly gentleman claims sole ownership of the plot, Mrs. McGee learns that the garden belongs to many creatures, including a rabbit, a woodchuck, and a honeybee. "Hoberman's creative words and upbeat rhythms cheerfully introduce some basic players in the garden web of life," observed *Booklist* contributor Gillian Engberg of the book.

In *The Tree That Time Built: A Celebration of Nature, Science, and Imagination* Hoberman and coeditor Linda Winston, a cultural anthropologist, collect more than one hundred poems that explore the mysteries of the natural world. Inspired by the work of evolutionist Charles Darwin and featuring selections by such esteemed writers as Rainer Maria Rilke, Emily Dickinson, X.J. Kennedy, Alice Schertle, and Jelaluddin Rumi, *The Tree That Time Built* was described as an "attractive and unusual hybrid of poetry and science" by Engberg. "From the playful to the profound," Shawn Brommer wrote in *School Library Journal*, "the poems invite reflection and inspire further investigation."

A young girl prepares for an overnight visit without her parents in *I'm Going to Grandma's,* another work told in rhyme. Although the cheery narrator has a fine time dressing up in an old wedding gown, hosting a tea party, and playing with her grandparent's puppy, she feels a twinge of anxiety as night falls. Fortunately, her wise and understanding grandmother steadies the youngster's nerves by sharing a host of family stories. Writing in *Booklist,* Ilene Cooper remarked of *I'm Going to Grandma's* that "the incidents recounted are sweet and famil-

*A farm family's busy life is captured in Wendy Anderson Halperin's colored-pencil artwork for Hoberman's picture-book story in* **Strawberry Hill**. (Illustration copyright © 2009 by Wendy Anderson Halperin. Reproduced with permission of Little, Brown & Company, a division of Hachette Book Group, Inc.)

iar," and a *Publishers Weekly* contributor noted that "the grand-parents' doting feels utterly real, as does the comfort and security that the girl draws from their presence." In *All Kinds of Families* Hoberman toys with the notion of belonging, suggesting ways to organize a variety of inanimate objects into harmonious groups. According to *School Library Journal* reviewer Joan Kindig, the book's narrative implies that "making a family is about seeing the likenesses, not the differences," and a *Kirkus Reviews* critic noted that the story's "singsong cadence . . . begs to be read aloud."

In *Mrs. O'Leary's Cow* Hoberman offers a rollicking, contemporary version of the popular 1890's song "There'll be a Hot Time in the Old Town Tonight." Her story centers on the eponymous bovine, whose careless kick upends a lantern and starts a conflagration that soon engulfs the entire barn. Luckily, a team of firefighters manages to douse the flames and rescue the mischievous cow, which ends up tucked cozily in bed, all according to plan, apparently. "This is definitely a book that requires a sing-a-long," Mary Elam declared in *School Library Journal,* and a contributor in *Kirkus*

*Reviews* noted that the popular tune "with a shadowy past now translates to one of bravery and love, with a dash of impishness."

Hoberman turns from writing to editing in *My Song Is Beautiful,* a collection of multicultural poems from around the world. Included are Eskimo chants, a Chippewa song, a verse from ancient Mexico, as well as lines from poems by A.A. Milne and Nikki Giovanni. A *Publishers Weekly* reviewer called the collection an "outstanding multicultural anthology," and concluded that "this eclectic and joyful volume underscores Hoberman's conviction that 'Every you everywhere in the world is an I;/ Every I in the world is a you!'" *Booklist* reviewer Rochman wrote that this "small anthology celebrates diversity, not only in culture, but also in mood and genre," while in *School Library Journal,* Dot Minzer ranked *My Song Is Beautiful* as a "first-rate collection that definitely deserves consideration."

More than fifty years after the publication of her first children's book, Hoberman completed her debut novel, *Strawberry Hill,* a work of historical fiction that is set during the Great Depression of the 1930s. When the father of ten-year-old Allie Sherman lands a new job, he moves his family to the Strawberry Hill section of Stamford, Connecticut. As she adjusts to her unfamiliar surroundings, Allie finds herself drawn to two very different friends: Martha, a wealthy and popular neighbor who attends Catholic school, and Mimi, a pudgy Jewish girl who is scorned by Martha. "Allie's plight will be utterly relatable to contemporary readers and the resolution is both satisfying and realistic," a contributor maintained in *Publishers Weekly.* Cooper remarked that the "story lines . . . are simple but never simplistic," and Maria B. Salvadore, writing in *School Library Journal,* called *Strawberry Hill* "a gentle story with the sensibility of a novel written in an earlier time."

Reflecting on her decades-long career, Hoberman stated in a Harcourt Trade Publishers online interview: "Words are my world; and in my writing for children, I have been able to wallow in my love of language, of rhyme and of rhythm, and to use as my subject matter the things I care most about: family, friendship, animals, nature, our beautiful fragile earth. And to have had as my audience generations of young children who grow up to read my poems and stories to children and even grandchildren of their own—I have been blessed!"

## Biographical and Critical Sources

### BOOKS

*Authors of Books for Young People,* Scarecrow Press (Metuchen, NJ), 1990.
*Children's Books and Their Creators,* edited by Anita Silvey, Houghton Mifflin (Boston, MA), 1995.

*Children's Literature Review,* Volume 22, Gale (Detroit, MI), 1991.
*St. James Guide to Children's Writers,* edited by Sara Pendergast and Tom Pendergast, St. James Press (Detroit, MI), 1999.
*Something about the Author Autobiography Series,* Volume 18, Gale (Detroit, MI), 1994.

### PERIODICALS

*Booklist,* June 1, 1994, Hazel Rochman, review of *My Song Is Beautiful: Poems and Pictures in Many Voices,* p. 1828; March 1, 1997, Hazel Rochman, review of *The Seven Silly Eaters,* p. 1172; November 1, 1997, Susan Dove Lempke, review of *One of Each,* p. 466; March 15, 1998, Stephanie Zvirin, review of *Miss Mary Mack,* p. 1245; April 1, 2001, Hazel Rochman, review of *There Once Was a Man Named Michael Finnegan,* p. 1475, and Shelley Townsend-Hudson, review of *"It's Simple," Said Simon,* p. 1478; August, 2001, John Peters, review of *You Read to Me, I'll Read to You: Very Short Stories to Read Together,* p. 2124; July, 2002, Hazel Rochman, review of *The Looking Book: A Hide-and-Seek Counting Story,* p. 1859; August, 2002, Julie Cummins, review of *Right outside My Window,* p. 1972; April 15, 2004, Carolyn Phelan, review of *Yankee Doodle,* pp. 1443-1444, and Gillian Engberg, review of *Whose Garden Is It?,* p. 1446; July, 2004, Hazel Rochman, review of *You Read to Me, I'll Read to You: Very Short Fairy Tales to Read Together,* p. 1840; April 1, 2007, Ilene Cooper, review of *I'm Going to Grandma's* and John Peters, review of *Mrs. O'Leary's Cow,* both p .57; May 1, 2007, Hazel Rochman, review of *You Read to Me, I'll Read to You: Very Short Scary Tales to Read Together,* p. 92; June 1, 2009, Ilene Cooper, review of *Strawberry Hill,* p. 66; December 15, 2009, Gillian Engberg, review of *The Tree That Time Built: A Celebration of Nature, Science, and Imagination,* p. 38.
*Bulletin of the Center for Children's Books,* October, 1997, Elizabeth Bush, review of *One of Each,* p. 53.
*Christian Science Monitor,* January 22, 2008, Joan Russell, "For Kids, Anytime Is a Good Time to Rhyme," p. 18.
*Early Years,* January, 1985, Allen Raymond, "Mary Ann Hoberman: Fun-loving Poet, Student of Literature," pp. 23-24.
*Horn Book,* January-February, 1974, Paul Heins, review of *The Raucous Auk: A Menagerie of Poems,* pp. 59-60; January-February, 1996, Hanna B. Zeiger, review of *The Cozy Book,* p. 98; May-June, 1997, Ann A. Flowers, review of *The Seven Silly Eaters,* p. 308; March, 2001, Christine Heppermann, review of *"It's Simple," Said Simon,* p. 196; November-December, 2001, Roger Sutton, review of *You Read to Me, I'll Read to You: Very Short Stories to Read Together,* p. 766; May-June, 2004, Roger Sutton, review of *You Read to Me, I'll Read to You: Very Short Fairy Tales to Read Together,* pp. 315-316.
*Kirkus Reviews,* October 1, 1991, review of *Fathers, Mothers, Sisters, Brothers: A Collection of Family Poems,* p. 1295; October 15, 1995, review of *The Cozy Book,*

p. 1493; April 1, 2002, review of *The Marvelous Mouse Man,* p. 493; May 1, 2002, review of *Right outside My Window,* p. 657; June 15, 2005, review of *You Read to Me, I'll Read to You: Very Short Mother Goose Tales to Read Together,* p. 684; March 1, 2007, review of *Mrs. O'Leary's Cow,* p. 223; July 1, 2007, review of *You Read to Me, I'll Read to You: Very Short Scary Tales to Read Together;* June 15, 2009, review of *Strawberry Hill;* July 15, 2009, review of *All Kinds of Families!.*

*New York Times Book Review,* May 26, 1957, C. Elta Van Norman, "Slippers with Zippers," p. 26; December 10, 1978, Harold C.K. Rice, "Good Looking," pp. 72-73, 93; April 15, 2001, review of *It's Simple, Said Simon,* p. 24; January 20, 2002, review of *You Read to Me, I'll Read to You: Very Short Stories to Read Together,* p. 14.

*Publishers Weekly,* May 9, 1994, review of *My Song Is Beautiful,* p. 73; April 20, 1998, review of *Miss Mary Mack,* p. 65; November 23, 1998, review of *The Llama Who Had No Pajama: 100 Favorite Poems,* p. 97; March 19, 2001, review of *"It's Simple," Said Simon,* p. 99; August 6, 2001, review of *You Read to Me, I'll Read to You: Very Short Stories to Read Together,* p. 89; March 18, 2002, review of *The Marvelous Mouse Man,* p. 102; April 15, 2002, review of *The Looking Book,* p. 63; April 29, 2002, review of *Right outside My Window,* p. 68; April 5, 2004, *Whose Garden Is It?,* p. 61; March 5, 2007, review of *I'm Going to Grandma's,* p. 60; July 6, 2009, review of *Strawberry Hill,* p. 52; July 20, 2009, review of *All Kinds of Families!,* p. 138; November 30, 2009, review of *The Tree That Time Built,* p. 49.

*Riverbank Review,* spring, 1999, review of *The Llama Who Had No Pajama,* p. 22.

*School Library Journal,* October, 1978, Sharon Elswit, review of *A House Is a House for Me,* p. 133; June, 1994, Dot Minzer, review of *My Song Is Beautiful,* p. 119; March, 1997, Barbara Elleman, review of *The Seven Silly Eaters,* p. 160; September, 1997, Carol Ann Wilson, review of *One of Each,* p. 183; May, 1998, Jane Marino, review of *Miss Mary Mack,* p. 117; May, 2001, Piper L. Nyman, review of *There Once Was a Man Named Michael Finnegan,* p. 142; August, 2001, Mary Ann Carcich, review of *You Read to Me, I'll Read to You: Very Short Stories to Read Together,* p. 153; April, 2002, Carol Schene, review of *Bill Grogan's Goat,* p. 132; May, 2002, Wendy Luke- hart, review of *The Marvelous Mouse Man,* p. 117; June, 2002, Dona Ratterree, review of *The Looking Book,* p. 97; November, 2002, Sally R. Dow, *Right outside My Window,* p. 126; May, 2004, Janet M. Bair, review of *Whose Garden Is It?,* p. 114, and Shelley B. Sutherland, review of *You Read to Me, I'll Read to You: Very Short Fairy Tales to Read Together,* pp. 132-133; September, 2005, Shawn Brommer, review of *You Read to Me, I'll Read to You: Very Short Mother Goose Tales to Read Together,* p. 193; March, 2007, Mary Elam, review of *Mrs. O'Leary's Cow* and Susan Moorehead, review of *I'm Going to Grandma's,* p. 173; September, 2007, Catherine Threadgill, review of *You Read to Me, I'll Read to You: Very Short Scary Tales to Read Together,* p. 183; July, 2009,

Maria B. Salvadore, review of *Strawberry Hill,* p. 64; August, 2009, Joan Kindig, review of *All Kinds of Families,* p. 77; January, 2010, Shawn Brommer, review of *The Tree That Time Built,* p. 121.

*Washington Post Book World,* May 12, 1991, Mary Jo Salter, "Peaceable Kingdom," p. 18.

ONLINE

*Harcourt Trade Publishers Web site,* http://www. harcourtbooks.com/ (May, 2004), interview with Hoberman and Jane Dyer.

*Hachette Book Group Web site,* http://www.hachettebook group.com/ (April 15, 2011), "Mary Ann Hoberman."

*Mary Ann Hoberman Home Page,* http://www.maryann hoberman.com (April 15, 2011).

*Poetry Foundation Web site,* http://www.poetryfoundation. org/ (October 8, 2008), Michael Atkinson, "Mary Ann Hoberman Named Children's Poet Laureate."

*School Library Journal Web site,* http://www.school libraryjournal.com/ (September 25, 2007), Joan Oleck, interview with Hoberman.*

\*　　\*　　\*

# HOPE, Laura Lee
## See STANLEY, George Edward

\*　　\*　　\*

# HOSTETTER, Joyce Moyer 1952-

## Personal

Born July 18, 1952; married. *Religion:* Mennonite. *Hobbies and other interests:* Reading, writing, history, gardening.

## Addresses

*Home*—NC. *E-mail*—moyergirl@twave.net.

## Career

Writer. Former special education teacher and preschool program director.

## Awards, Honors

International Reading Association Children's Book Award, Parents' Choice Silver Honor, and North Carolina Juvenile Literature Award, all for *Blue.*

## Writings

(With Jim Egli) *Life to Share: Leader's Guide: Discovering a Biblical Vision for Evangelism,* Faith and Life Press (Newton, KS), 1991.

*Best Friends Forever,* illustrated by Eddie Ross, Friendship Press (New York, NY), 1995.

*Blue,* Boyds Mills Press (Honesdale, PA), 2006.

*Healing Water: A Hawaiian Story,* Calkins Creek (Honesdale, PA), 2008.

*Comfort,* Calkins Creek (Honesdale, PA), 2009.

Author of Web log *Three R's.*

## Sidelights

Joyce Moyer Hostetter is the author of several well-received books of historical fiction for young readers. An avid reader as a youngster, Hostetter had to retreat to the bathroom to be able to enjoy books in her family of four brothers and three sisters. A teacher in the seventh grade let Hostetter know that she had talent as a writer, but she worked for many years as a special education teacher and director of a preschool before she had the time and inclination to begin a career as an author. Hostetter's first juvenile novel, *Best Friends Forever,* appeared in 1995 and was written as an entry in a contest to explore diversity in America. She employs her own Mennonite heritage in this work, which deals with the unlikely friendship between a young Mennonite girl and a girl from the Greek Orthodox faith.

With her novel *Blue,* as well as its sequel, *Comfort,* Hostetter deals in more detail with historical events. As part of her course work for a history-writing workshop, she was advised to research an incident from local history. While doing so, she discovered an outbreak of polio in her hometown in 1944 that prompted the creation of an emergency polio hospital in three days. From this germ of an idea, she created the story of Ann Fay Honeycutt, a thirteen year old who is admonished to be the man of the house and take care of her younger siblings when her father goes off to fight in World War II. In *Blue* Ann Fay dons the pair of blue overalls her father gave her before his departure and assumes her new responsibility bravely. She already has her hands full when a polio outbreak takes the life of her younger brother, and then Ann Fay also contracts the dreaded disease. *Booklist* reviewer Jennifer Matson praised *Blue* as "heartfelt fiction" that is "marked by an agreeable, vernacular narrative and unobtrusive symbolism surrounding the color blue." *School Library Journal* reviewer Kathryn Childs also commended Hostetter's juvenile novel, terming it "a compelling story of resourcefulness, loss, and the healing power of friendship," and a *Kirkus Reviews* contributor praised *Blue* as "chock full of life, history and character development." Reviewing *Comfort,* in which Alice Fay visits a polio center in Georgia, Kim Dare concluded in *School Library Journal* that "Hostetter's beautiful story about rebuilding, with [its] absorbing back matter about post-traumatic stress disorder and disability rights, is exceptional historical fiction."

In *Healing Water: A Hawaiian Story* Hostetter again deals with illness in an historical setting. This time Hansen's Disease, or leprosy, is at the center of "a memorable story of hope in the most desperate of circumstances," as a *Kirkus Reviews* writer noted. Pia is a thirteen-year-old Hawaiian whose life is turned upside down in 1860 when he is diagnosed with leprosy and sent to the island of Molokai, where a settlement isolates people with the disfiguring disease. Once there, Pia must rely on his own wits and spirit to survive. His struggle is aided by a Catholic missionary who tends to the sick on Molokai. Hostetter's novel was inspired by the real-life work of Belgian Catholic priest Father Damien, who devoted his life to working with the ill on Molokai. Writing for *School Library Journal,* Denise Moore lauded *Healing Water* for sharing "timeless themes . . . presented in a powerful way."

Hostetter once commented: "As an educator, I've always worked with young people, so writing for them is a natural. I don't consciously think about why I write for middle graders and young adults. The stories themselves seem to dictate the age of my protagonists and therefore my readers.

"My books tend to be about serious subjects—disease in particular. I'm not a medically inclined person but I've discovered that the emotional impact of disease and epidemics is enormously interesting to me. It's important to me to write about things that matter. To explore the hard questions of life and to try to understand why bad things happen in the world.

"I'm beginning to think that I write to find an answer to the question, 'Why me?' or actually, 'Why not me? How did I get so lucky as to be born in this place and in this time to this family? And if I had been heir to a much more difficult life, how would I have handled it?' Or maybe I'm trying to figure out how I will handle disease or disaster when it does come to me. Will I be up to the task?

"In addition to the 'What if it were me?' questions there is the question of 'How will I respond to those in need of compassion?' *Blue* is about a polio epidemic in North Carolina and *Healing Water* is about leprosy in Hawai'i. Both polio and leprosy were mysterious and therefore frightening diseases. Both provided opportunities for the communities to shun or embrace the afflicted. The call to a compassionate response is at the heart of my stories. And the call is most definitely to myself!

"These stories always seem to be lodged in the past. I love finding bits of someone's personal history—stories that have been largely forgotten for various reasons. At the heart of each are truths that connect with today's readers. It's a thrill to sit in an archive and find some tiny bit of evidence that lends authenticity to my story. And I've learned to treasure the experts—those individuals who have lived the story or done more research than I'll be able to do. They give me copious amounts of info and generously critique my work before it goes to publication.

"It is an honor for me to collaborate with them and with history in writing for young people."

## Biographical and Critical Sources

*PERIODICALS*

*Booklist,* February 15, 2006, Jennifer Mattson, review of *Blue,* p. 109.

*Bulletin of the Center for Children's Books,* June, 2006, Karen Coats, review of *Blue,* p. 457; May, 2008, Karen Coats, review of *Healing Water: A Hawaiian Story,* p. 388.

*Children's Bookwatch,* June, 2006, review of *Blue.*

*Hickory Daily Record* (Hickory, NC), June 6, 2007, "Author Shares Her Writing Process with Students."

*Kirkus Reviews,* March 1, 2006, review of *Blue,* p. 232; April 1, 2008, review of *Healing Water.*

*School Library Journal,* June, 2006, Kathryn Childs, review of *Blue,* p. 159; July, 2008, Denise Moore, review of *Healing Water,* p. 100; May, 2009, Kim Dare, review of *Comfort,* p. 108.

*Voice of Youth Advocates,* December, 2006, Sherrie Williams, review of *Blue,* p. 424; August, 2008, Hillary Crew, review of *Healing Water,* p. 244.


*ONLINE*

*Joyce Moyer Hostetter Home Page,* http://www.joyce moyerhostetter.com (April 15, 2011).

\*     \*     \*

# HUANG, Nathan 1982(?)-

## Personal

Born c. 1982.

## Addresses

*Home*—Brooklyn, NY. *E-mail*—nathan@nathanhuang. com.

## Career

Illustrator and comics artist. Freelance illustrator, beginning 2005.

## Illustrator

Derrick Niederman, *Inspector Forsooth's Mini-Mysteries,* Sterling (New York, NY), 2009.

Sandra Alonzo, *Riding Invisible: An Adventure Journal,* Hyperion (New York, NY), 2010.

Contributor to periodicals, including *Esquire, Los Angeles Times, New York Times, Time out New York,* and *Washington Post.*

## Biographical and Critical Sources

*PERIODICALS*

*Booklist,* February 1, 2010, Ian Chipman, review of *Riding Invisible: An Adventure Journal,* p. 38.

*Kirkus Reviews,* February 15, 2010, review of *Riding Invisible.*

*Publishers Weekly,* February 8, 2010, review of *Riding Invisible,* p. 52.


*ONLINE*

*Nathan Huang Home Page,* http://www.nathanhuang.com (February 20, 2011).\*

# J-K

## JACKSON, Alison 1953-

### Personal

Born August 22, 1953, in Alhambra, CA; daughter of Samuel (a physician) and Lorayne (a musician) Coombs; married Stephen Jackson (a computer analyst), September 10, 1983; children: Kyle (son), Quinn (daughter). *Education:* University of California, Irvine, B.A., 1975; San Jose State University, M.L.S., 1977. *Politics:* Democrat. *Religion:* Protestant. *Hobbies and other interests:* Travel, snow skiing, waterskiing.

### Addresses

*Home and office*—6213 Wynfield Ct., Orlando, FL 32819. *E-mail*—pieauthor@aol.com.

### Career

Writer and librarian. Long Beach Public Library, Long Beach, CA, children's librarian, 1977-80; Newport Beach Public Library, Newport Beach, CA, children's librarian, 1980-87; Fullerton Public Library, Fullerton, CA, children's librarian, 1987-97; Seminole County Public Library, Longwood, FL, children's librarian, 1997—; writer. Presenter at schools.

### Member

American Library Association, Society of Children's Book Writers and Illustrators, California Library Association, Southern California Council on Literature for Children and Young People, Florida Library Association.

### Writings

*My Brother the Star,* illustrated by Diane Dawson Hearn, Dutton (New York, NY), 1990.
*Crane's Rebound,* illustrated by Diane Dawson Hearn, Dutton (New York, NY), 1991.

**Alison Jackson** (Reproduced by permission.)

*Blowing Bubbles with the Enemy,* Dutton (New York, NY), 1993.
*I Know an Old Lady Who Swallowed a Pie,* illustrated by Judith Byron Schachner, Dutton (New York, NY), 1997.
*If the Shoe Fits,* illustrated by Karla Firehammer, Henry Holt (New York, NY), 2001.
*Turkey's Best Thanksgiving* (reader), illustrated by Patrick Girouard, Troll Communications (Mahwah, NJ), 2001.
*The Ballad of Valentine,* illustrated by Tricia Tusa, Dutton (New York, NY), 2002.
*Over in the Desert* (reader), illustrated by Ka Botsiz, Troll Communications (Mahwah, NJ), 2002.
*Rainmaker,* Boyd Mills Press (PA), 2005.
*Thea's Tree,* illustrated by Janet Pederson, Dutton Children's Books (New York, NY), 2008.

*Desert Rose and Her Highfalutin' Hog,* illustrated by Keith Graves, Walker Books for Young Readers (New York, NY), 2009.

*Eggs over Evie,* illustrated by Tuesday Mourning, Henry Holt (New York, NY), 2010.

## Sidelights

Alison Jackson's career as a children's librarian—she has worked in both California and Florida—has made her aware that there are still books for young people that need to be written. As a writer, she has set about to fill such voids, producing a variety of humorous picture books, beginning readers, and chapter books. *The Ballad of Valentine,* for example, came about when Jackson realized that Valentine's Day was under-represented on the library's book shelves, and her middle-grade novels *Crane's Rebound* and *My Brother the Star* address the continual need for engaging fiction that appeals to boys as well as girls.

Raised in southern California, Jackson gained a strong interest in writing while serving on the staff of her high school newspaper and yearbook. During her college years at the University of California, Irvine, she took creative-writing courses and produced several short stories while also focusing on a future career as a librarian. As Jackson once recalled to *SATA,* "I certainly wouldn't have dared to send anything in for publication. I didn't think I had enough talent!"

After working as a children's librarian for ten years, Jackson finally returned to writing and her first book, *My Brother the Star,* was published by Dutton Children's Books in 1990. Reviewing the novel, which focuses on a preteen's brief career in television, *School Library Journal* contributor Trish Ebbatson deemed it "nicely written" and described Jackson's protagonist, Leslie, as "a likable and believable central character." Jackson created a sequel to *My Brother the Star* titled *Crane's Rebound,* and here she recounts Leslie's adventures at summer basketball camp. In addition to competition on the court, Leslie is saddled with an obnoxious roommate, who also happens to be the best player on the team. Another problem for Les is found in feisty basketball-playing tomboy Bobby Lorimer, who develops a major crush on her. In *Booklist* Kay Weisman called Jackson's portrayal of Leslie's insecurities "right on target," and noted of *Crane's Rebound* that the author's "comic touch . . . will appeal to sports fans and problem-novel enthusiasts alike."

Bobby Lorimer returns in *Blowing Bubbles with the Enemy,* which focuses on the tomboy's drop in social standing when she decides to try out for the boys' basketball team at her middle school. Although she makes a few enemies among the boys who view her as competition, Bobby also finds allies in her female classmates after she is unfairly turned down by the coach. A *Kirkus Reviews* critic predicted that female readers will "enjoy Bobby's breezy voice, admire her gumption, and share her confusion over the awkwardness of boy-girl relationships." *School Library Journal* contributor Renee Steinberg also appreciated the "likeable, well-drawn heroine" in *Blowing Bubbles with the Enemy,* adding that Jackson's "smooth prose style and believable characters make this an enjoyable read."

A thirteen year old dealing with a fragmenting family is the focus of *Eggs over Evie,* a chapter book illustrated with whimsical pen-and-ink drawings by Tuesday Mourning. In the story, Evie Carson's parents are divorced and her dad is starting a new family. Not only did he leave her and her mom alone, he even took the family dog, the loss of which is still keenly felt a year later. During the summer before her freshman year of high school, Evie has the opportunity to deal with all the changes in her family, and in the process she begins to be more understanding toward the adults around her: her lonely mom, her elderly neighbor, her overworked celebrity-chef dad, and her pregnant stepmother. A summer cooking class rewards the teen with a new skill as well as a new friend, and Jackson's text is salted with cooking terms and even a few recipes. "Relationships are at the heart of this appealing, illustrated chapter books," concluded Carolyn Phelan in her *Booklist* review of *Eggs over Evie,* and in *School Library Journal* Teri Markson recommended the novel on the strength of Evie's "authentic [narrative] voice, particularly when discussing the upheaval and discomfort caused by divorce."

In *Rainmaker* Jackson turns to history and the lives of central Florida farmers during the Great Depression of the 1930s. The novel focuses on Pidge, a thirteen year old who watches as her home town faces its longest drought in forty years. As crops wilt and wells run dry, a miracle is surely in order, and Pidge's father hopes that sending for a "rainmaker" will provide one. In *School Library Journal,* Diana Pierce noted that Jackson's story expresses a cohesive theme: "accepting change as a part of life, even when one doesn't like it," while in *Booklist* Shelle Rosenfeld described Pidge as a "well-characterized, sympathetic protagonist that readers will connect with." In a *Kirkus Reviews* appraisal of *Rainmaker* the critic concluded that Pidge's "candid and earnest voice will linger, just as the rain clouds after the rainmaker's departure."

Jackson began alternating picture-books with longer fiction in the late 1990s, beginning with a humorous riff on a folk-song classic in 1997's *I Know an Old Lady Who Swallowed a Pie.* The elderly lady introduced in this story seems to have one interest: eating. In her parody of the traditional rhyme about the old woman who swallowed a fly, Jackson chronicles her rotund heroine as she attends a family's Thanksgiving Day feast and proceeds to devour not only a pie, but the entire meal, right down to the roasting pan. The result is "an amusingly successful variation" on the original, as Gahan Wilson remarked in his review for the *New York Times Book Review.* Several critics complimented Jack-

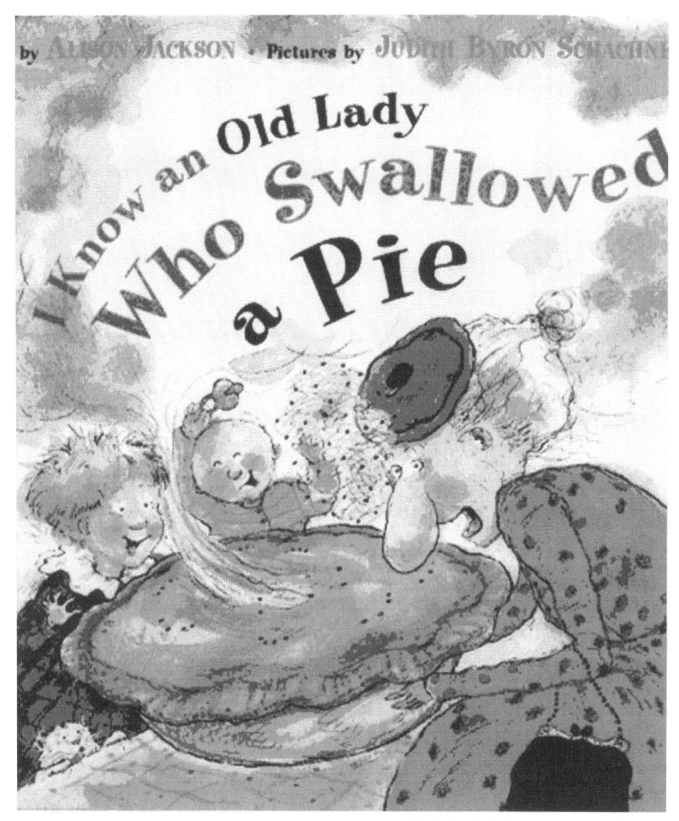

*Jackson presents a humorous take on a well-known cumulative song in her Thanksgiving-themed picture book* **I Know an Old Lady Who Swallowed a Pie,** *featuring artwork by Judith Byron Schachner.* (Illustration copyright © 1997 by Judith Byron Schachner. Reproduced by permission of Dutton Children's Books, a division of Penguin Young Readers Group, a member of Penguin Group (USA) Inc.)

son on her inventive, holiday-appropriate conclusion, in which the family finally trusses up the old lady with ropes and throws her out the door, where she floats

away among the other enormous balloons in the Thanksgiving Day parade. Told in whimsical rhymes that mimic the original, *I Know an Old Lady Who Swal-*

*lowed a Pie* prompted *Bulletin of the Center for Children's Books* critic Elizabeth Bush to predict: "Sing it once, and kids'll beg for seconds."

Inspired by another well-known story, *If the Shoe Fits* begins with a premise familiar to nursery-rhyme fans: An elderly woman living in a large shoe finds space at a premium due to her many children. In Jackson's version, rather than not knowing what to do, the woman takes immediate action and moves her brood to, first the teacup used by Miss Muffett on her tuffet, then the woolen coat worn by Jack Horner while sitting in his corner. Other encounters include watching the demise of Humpty Dumpty, being chased by twenty-four blackbirds (none too pleased about being baked in a pie), and even trying out the well-heeled boot of the Duke of York. Ultimately, the old woman learns the lesson—If the shoe fits then wear it—in a book that a *Kirkus Reviews* contributor described as a "romp through the world of nursery rhymes." *School Library Journal* contributor Piper L. Nyman praised Jackson's "deft touch for humor," while in *Booklist* Kathy Broderick dubbed *If the Shoe Fits* a "clever story" recounted in a "brisk pace perfect for energetic toddlers and preschoolers."

*The Ballad of Valentine* does dual duty, providing a Valentine's Day storybook and also parodying the folk song "My Darling Clementine." In her update to the old song, Jackson retains the rhythm but alters the words to tell the story of a pair of lovers whose communication is continually thwarted. Valentine's suitor produces love letters, but has a difficult time actually getting them to his beloved. As he grows increasingly frustrated and flustered, finding problems with everything from the

U.S. Postal Service to homing pigeons to smoke signals, Valentine calmly finishes up her chores, bakes a special pie, and arrives at her suitor's door with a smile. "This inspired treatment of an age-old tale communicates plenty about love," a *Publishers Weekly* contributor noted, while in *Kirkus Reviews* a reviewer praised Jackson's sing-song text as "funny and satisfying without being too sugary." Recommending *The Ballad of Valentine* as "ideal for Valentine's Day programs," *School Library Journal* contributor Shawn Brommer also praised Tricia Tusa's "quirky watercolor illustrations" for the book, in which the artist "portray[s] a simpler time."

Another story told with old-timey flair, *Desert Rose and Her Highfalutin' Hog* is brought to life in illustrations by Keith Graves and focuses on a tough-minded pig farmer. When Desert Rose finds a nugget of gold, she buys the biggest, roundest hog she can find, certain that it will be a prize winner. Unfortunately, in addition to being big and fat, the hog is also stubborn when it comes to crossing water, as Rose finds out while making her way to the Texas State Fair. Desert Rose is not shy about asking for help, but soon she has a chain of incapable critters to deal with. Fortunately, Armadillo comes to the rescue in a story where Jackson's "lively prose" is "sprinkled with Rose's alliterative exclamations," according to *Booklist* critic Shelle Rosenfeld. In *School Library Journal* Mary Jean Smith predicted that the "over-the-top" storytelling in *Desert Rose and Her Highfalutin' Hog* "makes it a surefire hit for storytime."

A little girl's science project morphs into a version of "Jack and the Beanstalk" in *Thea's Tree,* a picture book illustrated by Janet Pederson. For a science project, Thea plants a strange purple bean in her backyard, expecting a week to pass before she needs to record its visible growth in her science journal. This is no everyday bean, however, and within hours the new plant has bubbled up the soil and started to sprout. Soon Thea's house is covered in the bean's prolific vine, prompting the interest of a number of botanical experts as well as the concern of her parents when the vegetation grows so tall that it blocks the sun. In Pederson's illustrations, readers will recognize the golden egg, pile of gold, and giant-sized footprints that signify this particular vine as the one memorialized in the well-known fairy tale. Jackson employs an unusual storytelling method—her text is composed of the increasingly desperate letters Thea writes to various scientists—resulting in "a funny story that kids will love," according to Lee Bock in *School Library Journal.* Noting the "deadpan humor" in both the story and art, Phelan predicted in *Booklist* that while young children will "figure out the plant's identity" early on in the story, "anyone can enjoy the chaos created in this amusing picture book."

Discussing her career as a writer, Jackson once told *SATA* that "a number of sources have influenced my writing. One University of California, Irvine professor in particular, by the name of Oakley Hall, gave me

*Illustrator Karla Firehammer teams up with Jackson to present a fresh and humorous take on an old story in* **If the Shoe Fits.** (Illustration copyright © 2001 by Karla Firehammer. Reprinted by permission of Henry Holt & Company, LLC. All rights reserved.)

*Jackson's story about a nature-loving young girl in* **Thea's Tree** *features engaging watercolor art by Janet Pederson.* (Dutton Children's Books, 2008. Illustration copyright © 2008 by Janet Pedersen. Reproduced with permission of Penguin Young Readers Group.)

much encouragement and advice. He taught me some of the finer points of plotting and characterization, and he continually emphasized the use of realistic detail." Other sources of inspiration include her children, as well as "the students who come into the library every day, either to do homework or just to chat with each other. I find that children will talk about almost anything, if I simply stay in the background. And I have already used quite a few of their inspirational conversations in my books."

"I think this is the real reason why I want to continue writing for children," Jackson added. "They are so uninhibited and funny that I find them irresistible, not only as subjects in my work, but as members of my potential audience. So I feel safe in saying that as long as kids keep on reading . . . I will continue writing books for them."

## Biographical and Critical Sources

*PERIODICALS*

*Booklist,* January 1, 1990, Denise Wilms, review of *My Brother the Star,* p. 917; September 15, 1991, Kay Weisman, review of *Crane's Rebound,* pp. 151-152; October 1, 2001, Kathy Broderick, review of *If the Shoe Fits,* p. 325; November 15, 2002, Julie Cummins, review of *The Ballad of Valentine,* p. 602; March 15, 2005, Shelle Rosenfeld, review of *Rainmaker,* pp. 1292-1293; July 1, 2008, Carolyn Phelan, review of *Thea's Tree,* p. 74; August 1, 2009, Shelle Rosenfeld, review of *Desert Rose and Her Highfalutin' Hog,* p. 77; December 15, 2010, Carolyn Phelan, review of *Eggs over Evie,* p. 52.

*Bulletin of the Center for Children's Books,* November, 1997, Elizabeth Bush, review of *I Know an Old Lady Who Swallowed a Pie,* p. 87; December, 2010, Hope Morrison, review of *Eggs over Evie,* p. 190.

*Kirkus Reviews,* September 1, 1989, review of *My Brother the Star,* p. 1328; November 1, 1993, review of *Blowing Bubbles with the Enemy,* p. 1392; August 15, 2001, review of *If the Shoe Fits,* p. 1214; December 1, 2002, review of *The Ballad of Valentine,* p. 1769; March 15, 2005, review of *Rainmaker,* p. 353; April 15, 2008, review of *Thea's Tree*; August 1, 2009, review of *Desert Rose and Her Highfalutin' Hog.*

*New York Times Book Review,* November 16, 1997, Gahan Wilson, "Perhaps She'll Die," p. 56.

*Publishers Weekly,* August 27, 2001, review of *If the Shoe Fits,* p. 83; December 2, 2002, review of *The Ballad of Valentine,* p. 52.

*School Library Journal,* January, 1990, Trish Ebbatson, review of *My Brother the Star,* p. 104; January, 1994, Renee Steinberg, review of *Blowing Bubbles with the Enemy,* p. 114; December, 2001, Piper L. Nyman, review of *If the Shoe Fits,* p. 104; December, 2002, Shawn Brommer, review of *The Ballad of Valentine,* p. 98; April, 2005, Diana Pierce, review of *Rainmaker;* April, 2008, Lee Bock, review of *Thea's Tree,* p. 112; November, 2009, Mary Jean Smith, review of *Desert Rose and Her Highfalutin' Hog,* p. 82; January, 2011, Teri Markson, review of *Eggs over Evie,* p. 108.

*ONLINE*

*Alison Jackson Home Page,* http://www.alison-jackson.com (March 20, 2011).

\*      \*      \*

## JEROME, Elaine

### Personal

Female. *Education:* San Francisco Academy of Art, degree.

### Addresses

*Home*—Lake Tahoe, CA. *E-mail*—elaine@jerome illustration.com.

### Career

Artist, illustrator, and restauranteur. Java Sushi, Truckee, CA, co-owner. *Exhibitions:* Work exhibited at Riverside Gallery, Truckee, CA.

## Illustrator

Lupe Ruiz-Flores, *The Woodcutter's Gift/El regalo del leñador,* Spanish translation by Gabriela Baeza Ventura, Piñata Books (Houston, TX), 2007.

Amy Costales, *Sundays on Fourth Street/Los domingos en la calle Cuatro,* Piñata Books (Houston, TX), 2009.

## Biographical and Critical Sources

*PERIODICALS*

*Kirkus Reviews,* November 1, 2009, review of *Sundays on Fourth Street/Los domingos en la calle Cuatro.*

*School Library Journal,* October, 2009, Rebecca Hickman, review of *Sundays on Fourth Street/Los domingos en la calle Cuatro,* p. 116.

*ONLINE*

*Elaine Jerome Home Page,* http://jeromeillustration.com (February 20, 2011).*

\* \* \*

## KADOHATA, Cynthia 1956-

## Personal

Born 1956, in Chicago, IL; married (divorced, 2000); children: Sammy (adopted). *Education:* Attended Los Angeles City College; University of Southern California, B.A. (journalism); graduate study at University of Pittsburgh and Columbia University.

## Addresses

*Home*—Long Beach, CA. *Agent*—Andrew Wylie, Wylie, Aitken & Stone, Inc., 250 W. 57th St., Ste. 2106, New York, NY 10107.

## Career

Writer. Worked variously as a department-store clerk and waitress.

## Awards, Honors

Whiting Writer's Award, Mrs. Giles Whiting Foundation; Chesterfield Writer's Film Project screenwriting fellowship; National Endowment for the Arts grant; Newbery Medal, 2005, and APALA Award for Young-Adult Literature, 2006, both for *Kira-Kira;* Jane Addams Children's Book Award for Older Readers, 2007, for *Weedflower.*

## Writings

*The Floating World,* Viking (New York, NY), 1989.

**Cynthia Kadohata** (Copyright © AP/Wide World Photos.)

*In the Heart of the Valley of Love,* Viking (New York, NY), 1992.

*Kira-Kira,* Atheneum (New York, NY), 2004.

*Weedflower,* Atheneum (New York, NY), 2006.

*Cracker!: The Best Dog in Vietnam,* Atheneum (New York, NY), 2007.

*Outside Beauty,* Atheneum Books for Young Readers (New York, NY), 2008.

*A Million Shades of Gray,* Atheneum Books for Young Readers (New York, NY), 2010.

Contributor of short stories to periodicals, including *Horn Book, New Yorker, Grand Street, Ploughshares,* and *Pennsylvania Review.*

## Adaptations

Several of Kadohata's novels have been adapted as audiobooks, including *Kira-Kira,* read by Elaina Erika Davis, 2005; *Cracker!,* read by Kimberly Farr, Random House Audio, 2007; *Outside Beauty,* read by Sue Jean Kim, Simon & Schuster Audio, 2008; *Weedflower,* read by Farr, Random House Audio, 2009; and *A Million Shades of Gray,* Simon & Schuster Audio, 2010.

## Sidelights

Cynthia Kadohata is an award-winning novelist and short-story writer. Her short fiction has appeared in the *New Yorker, Grand Street,* and the *Pennsylvania Review,* and her adult novels include *The Floating World, Outside Beauty,* and *In the Heart of the Valley of Love.*

In 2005 Kadohata received the prestigious Newbery Medal for *Kira-Kira,* a semi-autobiographical tale about a Japanese-American girl growing up in a small town in rural Georgia. With this first story geared for younger readers, she has gone on to craft other books for younger readers, among them *Weedflower, Cracker!: The Best Dog in Vietnam,* and *A Million Shades of Gray.*

Kadohata's novels are interwoven with clearly autobiographical features and her tales have frequently been lauded for their striking imagery and hauntingly lyrical narratives. Her writing has been compared to that of Raymond Carver, Bobbie Ann Mason, Mark Twain, and J.D. Salinger. Like authors such as Amy Tan, Kadohata has also been viewed by some as a literary spokesperson for Asian Americans, but this is a distinction about which she is ambivalent. As the author told *Publishers Weekly* interviewer Lisa See, "There's so much variety among Asian-American writers that you can't say what an Asian-American writer is."

Although Kadohata was born in Chicago, Illinois, she lived in Michigan, Georgia, Arkansas, and California while her parents were searching for work. A voracious reader but an indifferent student, she dropped out of high school during her senior year, opting instead to go to work in a department store and a restaurant before enrolling in Los Angeles City College. From there, Kadohata transferred to the University of Southern California, where she earned a degree in journalism in 1977. After an accident in which an automobile jumped a curb and severely injured her arm, Kadohata moved to Boston and concentrated on her writing career. "I started looking at short stories," the author told See. "I had always thought that nonfiction represented the 'truth.' Fiction seemed like something that people had done a long time ago, and wasn't very profound. But in these short stories I saw that people were writing now, and that the work was very alive. I realized that you could say things with fiction that you couldn't say any other way."

Taking a practical approach, Kadohata set herself the goal of writing one story each month, using money from temporary jobs and her insurance settlement to support herself. After submitting dozens of stories and receiving numerous rejections, she sold a work of short fiction to the *New Yorker* in 1986; that tale, along with two others also published by that prestigious magazine, would later become part of her debut novel, *The Floating World.* Meanwhile, after briefly attending graduate-level writing courses at the University of Pittsburgh, Kadohata transferred to Columbia University's writing program. After finding a publisher for *The Floating World,* however, she abandoned her pursuit of an M.A. and set about the actual business of writing.

*The Floating World* is narrated by twelve-year-old Olivia and follows the journey of a Japanese-American family searching for economic and emotional security in post-World War II America. Kadohata uses Olivia's character to portray the family dynamics and interactions that occur as they travel, eat, and even sleep in the same room together. In addition to the physical journey, Kadohata illustrates Olivia's internal journey in *The Floating World.* Due to the close quarters of her family's living arrangement, the preteen is exposed to adult issues at an early age, witnessing tensions between her parents, their quiet arguments, and even their love making. In addition, Olivia is constantly subjected to her eccentric grandmother's abusive behavior. Finally the family finds a stable home in Arkansas where the girl matures through her teen years, learns to understand the ways of her parents and grandmother, and develops her own values.

Reviewing *The Floating World,* Diana O'Hehir wrote in the *New York Times Book Review* that Kadohata's "aim and the book's seem to be one: to present the world affectionately and without embroidery. To notice what's there. To see it as clearly as you can." Caroline Ong, a *Times Literary Supplement* contributor, described Olivia's narrative as "haunting because of its very simplicity and starkness, its sketchy descriptions fleshing out raw emotions and painful truths." Susanna Moore maintained in the *Washington Post Book World* that, while the novel might have been more effective presented in the style of a memoir, "Kadohata has written a book that is a child's view of the floating world, a view that is perceptive, unsentimental and intelligent." *New York Times* critic Michiko Kakutani praised the first-time novelist's ability to handle painful moments with humor and sensitivity, concluding that such "moments not only help to capture the emotional reality of these people's lives in a delicate net of images and words, but they also attest to Ms. Kadohata's authority as a writer." Kakutani concluded the review by noting that *The Floating World* marks the debut of a luminous new voice in fiction."

Family issues are also at the center of *Outside Beauty,* a novel set during the 1980s that, while focusing on twelve-year-old Shelby, also features sophisticated themes. Almost thirteen, Shelby is the second-oldest daughter of a Japanese-born mother who has borne each of her children with a different father. The sisters have learned from their mother, Helen, how to use their beauty to survive in the world, but they question these lessons after a terrible automobile accident leaves the woman disfigured and hospitalized. Sent to live with their respective fathers while Helen recovers, the sisters have differing experiences, and the youngest, six-year-old Maddie, may be in an unsafe situation while living with the stern Mr. Bronson. Reviewing *Outside Beauty* in *Kliatt,* Janice Flint-Ferguson noted that "older readers will appreciate the characters' resilience and determination to stay together" as a family, while a *Kirkus Reviews* writer dubbed Kadohata's novel "quirky and disarming." Praising in particular the second half of *Outside Beauty, School Library Journal* critic Johanna Lewis cited the "smooth, snappy, and believable" conversations between sisters and observed that "Shelby's running commentary on beauty is smart and poignant, as is her portrayal of a mother she both loves and reviles." Kadohata's "gifts for creating and containing drama and for careful definition of character prove as powerful as ever in this wise, tender and compelling novel," asserted a reviewer in appraising *Outside Beauty* for *Publishers Weekly.*

In the fictional future world Kadohata creates in *In the Heart of the Valley of Love* the year is 2052 and the place is Los Angeles, as the haves and have-nots are divided into gun-toting communities without morals, law, or order. Amid this chaos, the main character, a nineteen-year-old orphan of Asian and African descent named Francie, relates her story of endurance. For Kakutani, while the novel falls somewhere between "futuristic writing, and an unconvincing tale of coming of age," Kadohata's prose remains "lucid and finely honed, often lyrical and occasionally magical." Praising *In the Heart of the Valley of Love, Los Angeles Times Book Review* contributor Susan Heeger lauded the author as "masterful in her evocation of physical, spiritual and cultural displacement," adding that "the message of this marvelous though often painful book is that our capacity to feel deep emotion . . . just might bind us together, and save us from ourselves."

The Newbery Medal-winning *Kira-Kira,* Kadohata's first book for a young-adult audience, "tells the tender story of a Japanese-American family that moves from Iowa to rural Georgia in the 1950s," according to *School Library Journal* contributor Susan Faust. The work concerns the complex relationship between Katie Takeshima and her older sister, Lynn, who often cares for Katie while their parents work long hours at the town's poultry plants. Katie worships her older sister, who taught Katie the Japanese word "kira-kira," which means "glittering" and which Katie uses to describe everything she loves. When Lynn falls ill and is diagnosed with lymphoma, the sisters' roles are reversed; Katie becomes Lynn's caretaker, an exhausting and heart-wrenching ordeal that ends with her sister's death. Through Katie's narration, *Kira-Kira* "stays true to the child's viewpoint," the "plain, beautiful prose . . . barely contain[ing] the [narrator's] passionate feelings," noted *Booklist* critic Hazel Rochman. "The family's devotion to one another, and Lynn's ability to teach Katie to appreciate the 'kira-kira,' or glittering, in everyday life makes this novel shine," added a *Publishers Weekly* critic.

Also for young adults, *Weedflower* is set in the aftermath of Pearl Harbor and chronicles the growing friendship between Sumiko Yamaguchi, a Japanese-American girl living in an internment camp, and a Native-American boy who lives on nearby reservation lands. Noting that the work is loosely based on the childhood experiences of her father, Kadohata explained on her home page: "My father and his family were interned in the Poston camp on the Colorado River Indian Reservation in the Sonoran desert. One source claims the thermometer in 1942 hit more than 140 degrees in the Pos-

ton area." In the novel, Sumiko's uncle and grandfather are sent to North Dakota after the United States declares war on Japan, while the rest of her family is transported to a camp in the Arizona desert. Despite the harsh living conditions and her frustrations at being imprisoned, "Sumiko finds hope and a form of salvation" by creating a garden, observed a contributor for *Publishers Weekly.* A reviewer in *Kliatt* also praised *Weedflower,* calling it "a haunting story of dramatic loss and subtle triumphs."

The author's love of dogs is the inspiration for *Cracker!* which captures the deep friendship between a bomb-sniffing German shepherd and Rick Hanski, a young G.I. stationed in Vietnam during wartime. When the two are assigned together and tasked with rescuing prisoners of war held in enemy encampments, man and dog must learn to build trust and work as a team to ensure the safety of both. In addition to giving voice to Cracker's thoughts upon meeting his new comrade, Kadohata

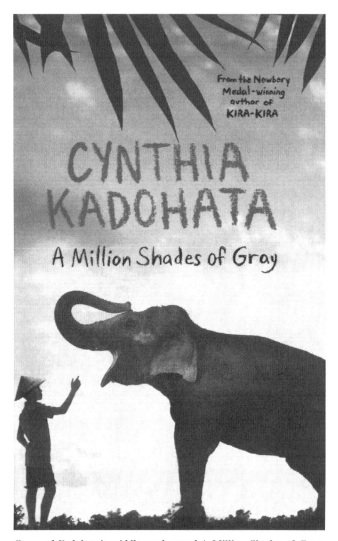

*Cover of Kadohata's middle-grade novel* **A Million Shades of Gray,** *which focuses on a young elephant trainer living in war-torn Vietnam.*
(Atheneum Books for Young Readers, 2010. Jacket design and photo-illustration by Russell Gordon. Jacket photograph of boy, copyright © 2010 by Michael Frost. Jacket photograph of elephant by DLILLC / Corbis. Reproduced with permission of Michael Frost and Corbis.)

captures in Rick's narrative "the confusion and growing paranoia of soldiers living in a land where friends and foes are hardly distinguishable," according to a *Publishers Weekly* contributor. In *Booklist* Hazel Rochman deemed *Cracker!* "a stirring, realistic story of America's war in Vietnam," while in *School Library Journal* Vicki Reutter wrote that Kadohata's story "is filled with action and accurately re-creates the experience of the military canine program, from aspects of training to the battlefield." Middle-school readers "without much familiarity with the Vietnam War will find an easy intro via Rick and Cracker in this emotionally resonant tale," predicted Anita L. Burkham in her review of *Cracker!* for *Horn Book.*

The Vietnam war also provides the backdrop for *A Million Shades of Gray*, as thirteen-year-old elephant trainer Y'Tin copes with war's aftermath in his South Vietnamese village. As supporters of U.S. troops prior to their withdrawal, the Dega people of the central highlands region are now being targeted by the Vietcong. To avoid being killed or forced into a work camp, Y'Tin, his friend Y'Juen, and Y'Tin's pet wild elephant, Lady, flee into the jungle. While managing to survive and also keep Lady safe, the teens attempt to discover the whereabouts of their other family members as well as the fate of their other friends. Based on the author's interviews with Dega refugees who encountered harsh treatment at the hands of North Vietnamese forces, *A Million Shades of Gray* highlights "political history that is seldom explored . . . in books for youth," according to *Booklist* critic Rochman. Kadohata "shows that truth has as many shades of gray as an elephant in this emotionally taut survival story," asserted a *Publishers Weekly* critic, and in *School Library Journal* Terrie Dorio praised Y'Tin as "a thoughtful young man searching for clear answers [about life] where there are none."

Kadohata maintains that literature has the power to nurture and transform an individual. This has been her own experience, she explained in her Newbery acceptance speech (as published in *Horn Book*). "I sought out the library near my home," she recalled of the period of her life after she quit high school. "Seeking it out was more of an instinct, really, not a conscious thought. I didn't think to myself, I need to start reading again. I felt it. I rediscovered reading—the way I'd read as a child, when there was constantly a book I was just finishing or just beginning or in the middle of. I rediscovered myself." She continued, "I look back on 1973, the year I dropped out of school, with the belief that libraries can not just change your life but save it. Not the same way a Coast Guardsman or a police officer might save a life, not all at once. It happens more slowly, but just as surely."

## Biographical and Critical Sources

### BOOKS

*Listen to Their Voices: Twenty Interviews with Women Who Write*, Norton (New York, NY), 1993.
*Notable Asian Americans*, Gale (Detroit, MI), 1995.

*PERIODICALS*

*Amerasia Journal*, winter, 1997, Lynn M. Itagaki, review of *In the Heart of the Valley of Love*, p. 229.
*America*, November 18, 1989, Eve Shelnutt, review of *The Floating World*, p. 361.
*Antioch Review*, winter, 1990, review of *The Floating World*, p. 125.
*Belles Lettres*, spring, 1993, review of *In the Heart of the Valley of Love*, p. 46.
*Booklist*, June 15, 1992, Gilbert Taylor, review of *In the Heart of the Valley of Love*, p. 1807; January 1, 2004, Hazel Rochman, review of *Kira-Kira*, p. 858; April 15, 2006, Hazel Rochman, review of *Weedflower*, p. 59; February 15, 2007, Hazel Rochman, review of *Cracker!: The Best Dog in Vietnam*, p. 76; June 1, 2008, Cindy Dobrez, review of *Outside Beauty*, p. 67; December 1, 2009, Hazel Rochman, review of *A Million Shades of Gray*, p. 36.
*Globe & Mail* (Toronto, Ontario, Canada), August 5, 1989.
*Horn Book*, March-April, 2004, Jennifer M. Brabander, review of *Kira-Kira*, pp. 183-184; July-August, 2005, Cynthia Kadohata, "Newbery Medal Acceptance," pp. 409-417, and Caitlyn M. Dlouhy, "Cynthia Kadohata," pp. 419-427; March-April, 2007, Anita L. Burkam, review of *Cracker!*, p. 195; July-August, 2008, Jennifer M. Brabander, review of *Outside Beauty*, p. 451.
*Journal of Adolescent & Adult Literacy*, December, 2006, Alleen Pace Nilsen, review of *Weedflower* and interview with Kadohata, both p. 310.
*Kirkus Reviews*, March 15, 2006, review of *Weedflower*, p. 293; December 15, 2006, review of *Cracker!*, p. 1270; May 15, 2008, review of *Outside Beauty*; December 1, 2009, review of *A Million Shades of Gray*.
*Kliatt*, March, 2006, Janis Flint-Ferguson, review of *Weedflower*, pp. 12-13; July, 2008, Janis Flint-Ferguson, review of *Outside Beauty*, p. 16.
*Library Journal*, June 15, 1992, Cherry W. Li, review of *In the Heart of the Valley of Love*, p. 102.
*Los Angeles Times Book Review*, May 2, 1993, review of *The Floating World*, p. 10.
*MELUS*, summer, 2007, Hsiu-chuan Lee, interview with Kadohata, p. 165.
*New York Times*, June 30, 1989, Michiko Kakutani, review of *The Floating World*, p. B4; July 28, 1992, Michiko Kakutani, review of *In the Heart of the Valley of Love*, p. C15.
*New York Times Book Review*, July 23, 1989, Diana O'Hehir, review of *The Floating World*, p. 16; August 30, 1992, Barbara Quick, review of *In the Heart of the Valley of Love*, p. 14.
*Publishers Weekly*, May 12, 1989, review of *The Floating World*, p. 279; June 1, 1992, review of *In the Heart of the Valley of Love*, p. 51; August 3, 1992, Lisa See, interview with Kadohata, pp. 48-49; February 9, 2004, review of *Kira-Kira*, pp. 81-82; February 27, 2006, review of *Weedflower*, p. 62; January 15, 2007, review of *Cracker!*, p. 52; May 12, 2008, review of *Outside Beauty*, p. 54; December 14, 2009, review of *A Million Shades of Gray*, p. 60.

*School Library Journal,* January, 1990, Anne Paget, review of *The Floating World,* p. 127; March, 2004, Ashley Larsen, review of *Kira-Kira,* pp. 214-215; May, 2005, Susan Faust, "The Comeback Kid," pp. 38-40; July, 2006, Marilyn Taniguchi, review of *Weedflower,* p. 106; February, 2007, Vicki Reutter, review of *Cracker,* p. 120; July, 2008, Johanna Lewis, review of *Outside Beauty,* p. 100; March, 2010, Terrie Dorio, review of *A Million Shades of Gray,* p. 160.

*Time,* June 19, 1989, review of *The Floating World,* p. 65.

*Times Literary Supplement,* December 29, 1989, Caroline Ong, review of *The Floating World,* p. 1447.

*U.S. News & World Report,* December 26, 1988, Miriam Horn and Nancy Linnon, "New Cultural Worlds," p. 101.

*ONLINE*

*Cynthia Kadohata Home Page,* http://www.kira-kira.us (April 15, 2011).

*Time for Kids Web site,* http://www.timeforkids.com/ (February 28, 2005), Aminah Sallam, "TFK Talks with Cynthia Kadohata."

*OTHER*

*Good Conversation! A Talk with Cynthia Kahodata* (film), Tim Podell Productions, 2005.*

\*      \*      \*

# KAGAWA, Julie

## Personal

Born in Sacramento, CA; married. *Hobbies and other interests:* Playing video games.

## Addresses

*Home*—Louisville, KY. *E-mail*—juliekagawa@juliekagawa.com.

## Career

Writer. Also worked in bookstores and as a professional dog trainer for several years.

## Writings

*"IRON FEY" NOVEL SERIES*

*The Iron King,* Harlequin Teen (New York, NY), 2010.
*The Iron Daughter,* Harlequin Teen (New York, NY), 2010.
*The Iron Queen,* Harlequin Teen (New York, NY), 2011.

Also author of e-novella *Winter's Passage.*

## Sidelights

Julie Kagawa is the creator of the "Iron Fey" series of fantasy tales about an ordinary teen who learns that she is the daughter of a faery king. "Faeries, the old, ancient fey, not the glittery winged sprites, have always fascinated me," Kagawa stated on her home page. "But I wanted to write a book that was different than other faery books." Knowing that in some folklore faeries have an aversion to iron, the author decided to create a new breed of fey. "What if they weren't only immune to iron, their existence was slowly poisoning and corrupting the lands of the traditional fey?," she wrote. "And I realized we already have 'monsters' in machines: gremlins, bugs, viruses, etc. And from that thought, the Iron fey were born."

Born in Sacramento, California, and raised in Hawai'i, Kagawa developed an intense love of literature while growing up, especially of fantasy fiction. As she told *Fantasy* interviewer Alethea Kontis, "My favorite children's book was *Where the Wild Things Are* by Maurice

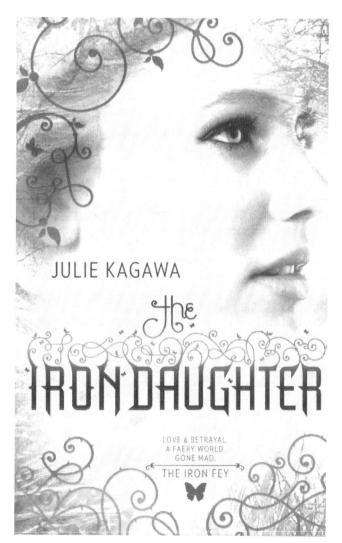

*Cover of Julie Kagawa's young-adult fantasy* **The Iron Daughter,** *which focuses on the adventures and loves of a girl who is half faery and half human.* (Copyright © 2010 by Julie Kagawa. Reproduced with permission of Harlequin Enterprises Limited.)

Sendak. (My fascination with monsters started early.) I went through a 'horse phase' in junior high, where everything I read was about horses. . . . But I always came back to fantasy, even then. Terry Brooks's 'Sword of Shannara' series was one that I remember most fondly." Kagawa also used books as an escape from her painful experiences at school. "I was a loner who didn't fit in anywhere, who wore only black, and who didn't have but one or two friends," she related to Kontis. "I was constantly getting into fights, hid novels behind my textbooks in class, and generally drove my poor teachers insane."

After graduation, Kagawa worked in a number of bookstores and as a professional dog trainer while writing her own fiction. Her debut novel, *The Iron King,* introduces Meghan Chase, a high-school misfit who, on the eve of her sixteenth birthday, finds herself at the center of an otherworldly conflict. Trailed by a mysterious stranger and alarmed by her younger half-brother Ethan's transformation into a snarling beast, Meghan turns to her best friend, Robbie, for assistance, only to discover that Robbie is actually Robin Goodfellow, a.k.a. the mischievous sprite Puck. Transported to the faery world of Nevernever, Meghan learns that her real father is Oberon, king of the Seelie Court, and that she must undertake a perilous mission to rescue her kidnapped brother, who has been taken to the Unseelie Court. According to a *Publishers Weekly* critic, in reviewing *The Iron King,* "Kagawa is a talented writer and her descriptions are lush." Ginny Collier, writing in *School Library Journal,* also praised the author's debut, writing that "Meghan is a likable heroine and her quest is fraught with danger and adventure."

In *The Iron Daughter,* the second work in Kagawa's "Iron Fey" series, Meghan finds herself accused of stealing the powerful Scepter of the Seasons and escapes from the Unseelie Court with the help of Ash, a Winter prince with whom she has fallen in love. "Written in vivid language that allows the reader to visualize the faery realms and driven by well-developed characters," according to *Voice of Youth Advocates* contributor Gina Bowling, *The Iron Daughter* ranks as "a solid choice" for readers of fantasy literature.

## Biographical and Critical Sources

*PERIODICALS*

*Bulletin of the Center for Children's Books,* April, 2010, Kate Quealy-Gainer, review of *The Iron King,* p. 340.

*Kirkus Reviews,* January 15, 2010, review of *The Iron King.*

*Publishers Weekly,* January 11, 2010, review of *The Iron King,* p. 49.

*School Library Journal,* April, 2010, Ginny Collier, review of *The Iron Fey,* p. 161; November 2010, Ginny Collier, review of *The Iron Daughter,* p. 118.

*Voice of Youth Advocates,* April, 2010, Kim Carter, review of *The Iron King,* p. 70; December, 2010, Gina Bowling, review of *The Iron Daughter,* p. 472.

*ONLINE*

*Fantasy Magazine Online,* http://www.fantasy-magazine. com/ (April 1, 2011), Alethea Kontis, interview with Kagawa.

*Iron Fey Web site,* http://enterthefaeryworld.com/ (April 1, 2011).

*Julie Kagawa Home Page,* http://www.juliekagawa.com (April 1, 2011).

*Julie Kagawa Web log,* http://juliekagawa.blogspot.com (April 1, 2011).*

\*      \*      \*

## KEENE, Carolyn
## See STANLEY, George Edward

# L

## LAIRD, Elizabeth 1943-

### Personal

Born October 21, 1943, in Wellington, New Zealand; daughter of John MacLelland (a general secretary) and Florence Marion (a homemaker) Laird; married David Buchanan McDowall (a writer), April 19, 1975; children: Angus John, William Alistair Somerled. *Education:* University of Bristol, B.A. (with honors), 1966; London University, Certificate of Education, 1967; Edinburgh University, M.Litt., 1971. *Religion:* Church of England (Anglican). *Hobbies and other interests:* Chamber music, gardening.

### Addresses

*Home*—London, England; Edinburgh, Scotland. *Agent*—Hilary Delamere, The Agency, 24 Pottery Ln., Holland Park, London W11 4LZ, England; hd-office@theagency.

### Career

Writer, 1980—. Bede Mariam School, Addis Ababa, Ethiopia, teacher, 1967-69; Pathway Further Education Centre, Southall, London, England, lecturer, 1972-77.

### Member

Society of Authors and Illustrators, Anglo-Ethiopian Society.

### Awards, Honors

Carnegie Medal Award runner-up, British Library Association, 1988, for *Red Sky in the Morning;* Children's Book Award, Federation of Children's Book Groups, and Sheffield Children's Book Award, both 1992, and Glazen Globe prize, Royal Dutch Geographical Society, 1993, all for *Kiss the Dust;* Smarties Young Judges Award, 1994, for *Hiding Out;* Carnegie Medal shortlist, 1996, for *Secret Friends;* Lancashire Book Award, 1997, for *Jay;* Carnegie Medal shortlist, and London *Guardian* Children's Fiction Prize shortlist, both 2002, both

*Elizabeth Laird* (Reproduced by permission.)

for *Jake's Tower;* Hampshire Book Award, 2004, Middle East Outreach Council Youth Literature Award, 2006, and Outstanding International Book Award, U.S. Board on Books for Young People, 2007, all for *A Little Piece of Ground;* Scottish Arts Council Children's Book of the Year Award, Carnegie Medal shortlist, and BBC Blue Peter shortlist, all 2004, and Stockport Schools Book Award, 2005, all for *The Garbage King;* Royal

Mail Scottish Children's Book Award shortlist, and Costa Children's Book Award shortlist, both 2007, and Carnegie Medal shortlist, 2008, all for *Crusade;* numerous awards from reading associations in the United Kingdom.

## Writings

*Anna and the Fighter,* illustrated by Gay Galsworthy, Heinemann Educational (London, England), 1977.

*The House on the Hill,* illustrated by Gay Galsworthy, Heinemann Educational (London, England), 1978.

*The Garden,* illustrated by Peter Dennis, Heinemann Educational (London, England), 1979.

*The Big Green Star,* illustrated by Leslie Smith, Collins (London, England), 1982.

*The Blanket House,* illustrated by Leslie Smith, Collins (London, England), 1982.

*The Doctor's Bag,* illustrated by Leslie Smith, Collins (London, England), 1982.

*Jumper,* illustrated by Leslie Smith, Collins (London, England), 1982.

(With Abba Aregawi Wolde Gabriel) *The Miracle Child: A Story from Ethiopia,* Holt (New York, NY), 1985.

*The Dark Forest,* illustrated by John Richardson, Collins (London, England), 1986.

*The Long House in Danger,* illustrated by John Richardson, Collins (London, England), 1986.

*Henry and the Birthday Surprise,* illustrated by Mike Hibbert, photographs by Robert Hill, British Broadcasting Corporation (London, England), 1986.

*The Road to Bethlehem: An Ethiopian Nativity,* foreword by Terry Waite, Holt (New York, NY), 1987.

*Prayers for Children,* illustrated by Margaret Tempest, Collins (London, England), 1987.

*Wet and Dry,* Pan Books (London, England), 1987.

*Hot and Cold,* Pan Books (London, England), 1987.

*Light and Dark,* Pan Books (London, England), 1987.

*Heavy and Light,* Pan Books (London, England), 1987.

*Busy Day,* illustrated by Carolyn Scrace, Children's Press Choice, 1987.

*Happy Birthday! A Book of Birthday Celebrations,* illustrated by Satomi Ichikawa, Collins (London, England), 1987.

*Hymns for Children,* illustrated by Margaret Tempest, Collins (London, England), 1988.

*Sid and Sadie,* illustrated by Alan Marks, Collins (London, England), 1988.

(With Olivia Madden) *The Inside Outing,* illustrated by Deborah Ward, Barron's Educational Services (Woodbury, NY), 1988.

*Red Sky in the Morning,* Heinemann (London, England), 1988, published as *Loving Ben,* Delacorte (New York, NY), 1989.

*Graces for Children,* Collins (London, England), 1989.

*Crackers,* Heinemann (London, England), 1989.

*Fireman Sam and the Missing Key,* Heinemann (London, England), 1990.

*Rosy's Garden: A Child's Keepsake of Flowers,* illustrated by Satomi Ichikawa, Philomel (New York, NY), 1990.

*Kiss the Dust,* Dutton (New York, NY), 1991, reprinted, Macmillan (London, England), 2007.

*The Pink Ghost of Lamont,* Heinemann (London, England), 1991.

*Pandemonium,* Little Mammoth (London, England), 1992.

*Dolly Rockers,* Little Mammoth (London, England), 1992.

*Hiding Out,* Heinemann (London, England), 1993.

(With Susan Hellard) *Stinker Muggles and the Dazzle Bug,* Collins (London, England), 1995.

*Secret Friends,* Hodder & Stoughton (London, England), 1996, Putnam (New York, NY), 1999.

*Jay,* Heinemann (London, England), 1997.

*Forbidden Ground,* Hamish Hamilton (London, England), 1997.

*Rosy's Winter: A Child's Fireside Book,* illustrated by Satomi Ichikawa, Heinemann (London, England), 1997.

*The Listener,* illustrated by Pauline Hazelwood, A. & C. Black (London, England), 1997.

*A Funny Sort of Dog,* illustrated by Russell Ayto, Heinemann (London, England), 1997.

*On the Run,* illustrated by Carrie Herries, Mammoth (London, England), 1997.

(Editor) *Me and My Electric,* illustrated by Polly Dunbar, Mammoth (London, England), 1998.

*Gabriel's Feather: The Story of the Nativity,* illustrated by Bettina Patterson, Scholastic (New York, NY), 1998.

*King of the Supermarket,* illustrated by Ailie Busby, Scholastic (New York, NY), 1999.

*A Book of Promises,* illustrated by Michael K. Frith, Dorling Kindersley (New York, NY), 2000.

*When the World Began: Stories Collected in Ethiopia,* Oxford University Press (New York, NY), 2000.

*Jake's Tower,* Macmillan (London, England), 2001, Macmillan (New York, NY), 2002.

*The Garbage King,* Macmillan (New York, NY), 2003.

(With Sonia Nmir) *A Little Piece of Ground,* Macmillan (London, England), 2003, Haymarket Books (Chicago, IL), 2006.

*Ice Cream Swipe,* illustrated by Ted Dewan, Oxford University Press (Oxford, England), 2003.

*Beautiful Bananas,* Peachtree Publishers (Atlanta, GA), 2004.

*Paradise End,* Macmillan (London, England), 2004.

*Hot Rock Mountain,* Egmont (London, England), 2004.

*Secrets of the Fearless,* Macmillan (London, England), 2005.

(With Roz Davison) *Jungle School,* illustrated by David Sim, Crabtree Publishing (New York, NY), 2006.

*Oranges in No Man's Land,* illustrated by Gary Blythe, Macmillan (London, England), 2006, Haymarket Books (Chicago, IL), 2008.

*Crusade,* Macmillan (London, England), 2007.

*Lost Rider,* Macmillan (London, England), 2008.

(Reteller) *Fistful of Pearls, and Other Tales from Iraq,* illustrated by Shelley Fowles, Frances Lincoln (London, England), 2008.

(Reteller) *The Ogress and the Snake, and Other Stories from Somalia,* illustrated by Shelley Fowles, Frances Lincoln (London, England), 2009.

(Reteller) *Pea Boy and Other Tales from Iran,* illustrated by Shirin Adl, Frances Lincoln (London, England), 2009.

*Witching Hour,* Macmillan (London, England), 2009.

*The Betrayal of Maggie Blair,* Houghton Mifflin (Boston, MA), 2011.

Author of school readers for Longman and Penguin, including *Anita's Big Day, Australia, Dead Man's River, The Storm, Simon the Spy, Karen and the Artist, Americans on the Move, The Earthquake, Clara, Ask Me Again, Sugar and Candy, Americans at Home, Faces of the U.S.A.,* and *Faces of Britain.*

### *"CUBBY BEARS" SERIES*

*The Cubby Bears' Birthday Party,* illustrated by Carolyn Scrace, Collins (London, England), 1985.

*The Cubby Bears Go Camping,* illustrated by Carolyn Scrace, Collins (London, England), 1985.

*The Cubby Bears Go on the River,* illustrated by Carolyn Scrace, Collins (London, England), 1985.

*The Cubby Bears Go Shopping,* illustrated by Carolyn Scrace, Collins (London, England), 1985.

### *"LITTLE RED TRACTOR" SERIES*

*The Day The Ducks Went Skating,* illustrated by Colin Reeder, Tambourine Books (New York, NY), 1991.

*The Day Veronica Was Nosy,* illustrated by Colin Reeder, Tambourine Books (New York, NY), 1991.

*The Day Sidney Ran Off,* illustrated by Colin Reeder, Tambourine Books (New York, NY), 1991.

*The Day Patch Stood Guard,* illustrated by Colin Reeder, Tambourine Books (New York, NY), 1991.

### *"TOUCAN 'TECS" SERIES*

*The Grand Ostrich Ball,* illustrated by Peter Lawson, Heinemann (London, England), 1989.

*Arctic Blues,* illustrated by Peter Lawson, Heinemann (London, England), 1989.

*Gopher Gold,* illustrated by Peter Lawson, Heinemann (London, England), 1989.

*High Flyers,* illustrated by Peter Lawson, Heinemann (London, England), 1989.

*Going Cuckoo,* illustrated by Peter Lawson, Heinemann (London, England), 1989.

*Fine Feathered Friends,* illustrated by Peter Lawson, Heinemann (London, England), 1989.

*Kookaburra Cackles,* illustrated by Peter Lawson, Heinemann (London, England), 1989.

*Peacock Palace Scoop,* illustrated by Peter Lawson, Heinemann (London, England), 1989.

*Highland Fling,* Buzz Books, 1991.

*The Big Drip,* Buzz Books, 1991.

*Desert Island Ducks,* Buzz Books, 1991.

*The Snail's Tale,* Buzz Books, 1991.

### *"WILD THINGS" SERIES*

*Leopard Trail,* Macmillan (New York, NY), 1999.

*Baboon Rock,* Macmillan (New York, NY), 1999.

*Elephant Thunder,* Macmillan (New York, NY), 1999.

*Rhino Fire,* Macmillan (New York, NY), 1999.

*Red Wolf,* Macmillan (New York, NY), 1999.

*Zebra Storm,* Macmillan (New York, NY), 1999.

*Turtle Reef,* Macmillan (New York, NY), 2000.

*Parrot Rescue,* Macmillan (New York, NY), 2000.

*Chimp Escape,* Macmillan (New York, NY), 2000.

*Lion Pride,* Macmillan (New York, NY), 2000.

### *"LET'S READ" SERIES*

*Tina the Detective/Tina la detective,* illustrated by Jenny Vincent, French text by Marie-Thérèse Bougard, Barron's Educational Series (Hauppauge, NY), 2009, published as *Tina the Detective/Tina, la détective,* illustrated by Martin Ursell, Spanish text by Rosa María Martín, 2009.

*Where Is Toto?/¿Dónde está Toto?,* illustrated by Leighton Noyes, Spanish text by Rosa María Martín, Barron's Educational Series (Hauppauge, NY), 2009, published as *Where Is Toto?/Ou est Toto?,* illustrated by Martin Ursell, French text by Marie-Thérèse Bougard, 2009.

### *FOR ADULTS*

*English in Education,* Oxford University Press (Oxford, England), 1977.

*Arcadia,* Macmillan (New York, NY), 1990.

## Sidelights

A prolific and versatile writer of picture books, easy readers, and young-adult novels, Elizabeth Laird is best known for her works for teen readers, among them *Jake's Tower, The Garbage King,* and *Crusade.* Laird has earned a host of honors for her issue-oriented stories; one of her most widely read books, *Loving Ben*—published in England as *Red Sky in the Morning*—tells about a young girl caring for her hydrocephalic baby brother. "I simply write the stories that come to me," Laird told *Books for Keeps* interviewer Nicholas Tucker. "What I really like doing is exploring emotional and psychological issues, creating characters who feel like real people, even to the extent of not always doing what I want them to do."

Laird has paired a love of travel with a love of writing in her stories about Muslim countries, the Middle East, and East Africa. *Kiss the Dust* deals with the realities of the Kurdish rebellion in modern-day Iraq; *A Little Piece of Ground* examines the Israeli-Palestinian conflict; and *Pea Boy, and Other Tales from Iran* collects seven fables from that nation. The works in Laird's "Wild Things" series are set in Kenya and Ethiopia and feature a core cast of characters who deal with wildlife issues in each volume.

*Cover of Laird's novel* Kiss the Dust, *a story set in Iraq that focuses on the longstanding conflict between Kurds and Arabs.* (Illustration copyright © 1994 by Diana Zelvin. Reproduced by permission of Puffin Books, a division of Penguin Young Readers Group, a member of Penguin Group (USA) Inc.)

Born in New Zealand to Scottish parents, Laird has gained inspiration from her experiences as a traveler and teacher. She was particularly motivated to adapt Ethiopian Christian folklore for a European audience after spending two years in Ethiopia. "I always had a burning desire to travel," Laird once told *SATA,* "and as soon as I possibly could, at the age of eighteen, I took off from home (with my parents' blessing!) and went to Malaysia where I spent a year as a teacher's aide in a boarding school for Malay girls. That experience only gave me a taste for more, so after I had graduated in French (which involved a wonderful spell as a student in Paris) I headed off to Ethiopia, and worked for two years in a school in Addis Ababa. In those days the country was at peace, and it was possible to travel to the remotest parts by bus and on horseback."

That experience provided the background for a series of easy readers for teaching purposes, as well as for *The Miracle Child: A Story from Ethiopia,* which was writ-

ten in collaboration with Abba Aregawi Wolde Gabriel. The book recounts the life of Takla Haymanot, a thirteenth-century Ethiopian saint who is revered for the miracles of healing the sick and raising the dead. The text is accompanied by reproductions of eighteenth-century paintings by Ethiopian monks. Vincent Crapanzano, writing in the *New York Times Book Review,* asserted that the reproductions in *The Miracle Child* are "informative and explain many of the artistic conventions of Ethiopian painting in a manner so simple as to be understandable to a child, yet interesting to an adult."

Laird's second adaptation of Ethiopian religious folklore follows the same format. *The Road to Bethlehem: An Ethiopian Nativity* is an Ethiopian-focused account of the events surrounding the birth of Jesus. The tale presents a more earthly account of the nativity than the standard Christian version and credits Mary with an active role as a healer and saint. "Mary is no ordinary woman in these stories, and not just because she is the mother of Jesus," observed Rosemary L. Bray in the *New York Times Book Review.* "As the Holy Family flees Herod into Egypt, Mary embarks on a ministry of healing: 'The dumb spoke, the lame ran, the deaf heard, and the blind could see.'" A reviewer for the *Bulletin of the Center for Children's Books* concluded that *The Road to Bethlehem* combines familiar themes of the New Testament "with popular legends and miracles into a cohesive narrative."

Laird's first novel for young adults was inspired by the birth and death of a younger brother. *Loving Ben* tells the story of twelve-year-old narrator Anna, whose brother, Ben, is born brain damaged. Through Anna, Laird recreates the family struggle of raising a handicapped child and the confusing feelings of pain and release experienced when that child dies. "Anna's voice rings true throughout as she moves from awkwardness and judgmental statements to a more mature empathy," wrote Barbara Chatton in a *School Library Journal* review. Critics also praised the author's rendering of the adult characters outside Anna's family. The adults who help Anna to understand new aspects of human nature "are sufficiently real, and the story homely and natural enough for the wisdom of the moral lessons conveyed to be palatable," wrote a *Junior Bookshelf* reviewer.

Laird's interest in foreign places has also inspired *Kiss the Dust.* Set in Iraq, this novel tells the story of Tara Khan, a twelve-year-old Kurdish girl whose family is forced to relocate when the Iraqi government attempts to suppress the Kurds. Tara's family escapes first to Iran, where she is forced to adopt a highly conservative Muslim lifestyle, and finally to England, where she must confront the shock of an entirely new, secular culture. Critics have commented on the graphic depiction of violence in the story, and although some found the detail unnecessary, others deemed it appropriate to, and accurate for, the wartime situations in which Tara is embroiled and fleeing. "*Kiss the Dust* is filled with wonderfully researched ethnographic details about both Kurdish and refugee culture, and opens a door to a foreign world," wrote Elizabeth Cohen, a *New York Times Book Review* contributor. This is particularly the case, observed Cohen, when Tara makes comparisons between her journey's beginning in urban Sulaimaniya and its end in a working-class neighborhood in London. A critic for *Kirkus Reviews* wrote that Laird "builds a sympathetic portrait of the embattled Kurds and a compelling portrait of Tara" and cited *Kiss the Dust* as an "important contribution to the growing number of refugee stories."

While *Secret Friends* does not borrow an exotic locale, it does look at a newly immigrated family in England. Rafaella feels an outsider at school, except for Lucy, the one girl who befriends her. Lucy does not want to risk being a social outcast herself, however, and she gives her "secret friend" Rafaella the pejorative nickname "Earwig" because of the girl's large ears. Taunted and teased on the playground for this physical anomaly, Rafaella finally undergoes corrective surgery. When she dies of heart failure during the operation, Lucy is haunted with guilt for her behavior. "The power of the story," noted *Booklist* reviewer Hazel Rochman, "is the honesty of Lucy's first-person narrative, her uneasiness as a bystander to the bullying, torn between shame and pity." Rochman added that what gives "unexpected depth to the outsider theme" is Lucy's envy of Rafaella's happy home life, a stark contrast to her own.

With *Forbidden Ground* Laird focuses on a love story that challenges conventions and is set in an unnamed North African country. Hannah has just moved to the city from a more-traditional rural culture and finds it difficult adjusting to the cosmopolitan moral values she encounters there. These internal conflicts increase when she meets Sami, who may or may not be sincere in his professed love for her. George Hunt noted in *Books for Keeps* that the novel "is a romantic, but realistic and unsentimental story; its cultural and geographic settings are vividly evoked, but the universality of the emotional dilemmas it describes gives the story a very wide relevance and appeal." Sarah Mears concluded in *School Librarian* that Laird's book presents a "readable story which provides a view of life in a modern Islamic community."

Another unnamed foreign country is the backdrop for *On the Run,* a "feel-good" novel about a resourceful but lonely child, according to Chris Stephenson in *School Librarian.* Hania is left behind with her grandfather when her parents flee the country to avoid being conscripted to the nationalist cause in the current civil war. Hania finds consolation feeding the chickens until a wounded freedom fighter comes her way and she nurses him back to health in the barn, her activities hidden from her gruff grandfather. Finally she discovers that her grandfather also supports the freedom movement and has actually been looking for the wounded soldier all along. Stephenson concluded that *On the Run* is "somewhat far-fetched, but ultimately a heart-warming moral tale."

A popular project for Laird has been the "Wild Things" series of books, with their cast of three main recurring characters: an English boy, a Kenyan boy, and an Ethiopian-American girl. Set in East Africa, the short novels deal with the troubles the three encounter each time they find a wild species at risk. In *Leopard Trail* Tom, Joseph, and Afra learn about the difficulty involved in re-locating wild leopards. In *Baboon Rock* Afra is confronted with the knowledge that adopting an injured baby baboon might not be the smartest thing to do. Tom intercedes between humans and pachyderms in *Elephant Thunder,* while Joseph confronts a band of illegal hunters in *Rhino Fire.* Deadly rabies is at the heart of *Red Wolf,* and a drought parches the plains in *Zebra Storm.* All the while, the trio of characters must also deal with the usual childhood dilemmas of growing up.

Laird's novel *Jake's Tower* is set in England and concerns a young boy who lives in fear of his mother's abusive boyfriend. To escape his misery, Jake often dreams of a secret hideaway, and he also creates a fantasy involving Danny, his biological father, who, as a teenager, abandoned Jake's mother, Marie. After a particularly violent beating from the boyfriend, mother and son realize that they need help. They now move in with Danny's mother, who has always denied that her son is Jake's father. As Jake and his grandmother forge a strong bond, the boy also learns to deal with some uncomfortable truths about his father. Jennifer Ralston, reviewing *Jake's Tower* in *School Library Journal,* praised Laird for creating "believable characters" in a story that "conveys the tension and terror of living with abuse."

In her young-adult novel *The Garbage King* Laird focuses on the street children of Ethiopia. Dani, a wealthy, spoiled boy who runs away from home, and Mamo, an orphan who escapes after being sold into slavery, meet in a cemetery in Addis Ababa. The pair soon joins a gang of homeless children led by Million, a young tough who teaches them the ways of the street, including how to beg for money and scavenge food from the garbage. According to *School Library Journal* reviewer Genevieve Gallagher, "the boys become a family and both their tragedies and triumphs are painted in vivid, authentic, and often horrific detail." Although some critics faulted Laird's upbeat ending, most found her tale compelling and praised the authenticity of the characters in *The Garbage King.* In the words of *Booklist* critic Rochman, "It's the elemental friendship story of fear and hope that will draw in readers."

The folktale *Beautiful Bananas* follows the adventures of Beatrice, a little girl who travels through the African jungle to present a bunch of bananas to her grandfather. Along the way, she loses the fruit after a giraffe accidentally bumps into her; the giraffe replaces the bananas with a gift of flowers that are soon damaged by a group of bees, who replace the flowers with a gift of honey. As her journey continues, Beatrice is involved in a number of other mishaps when she encounters other animals, but by the time she arrives at her grandfather's home the bananas are safely back in her arms. Reviewing *Beautiful Bananas* in *Booklist,* John Peters complimented the story's "direct action and elegantly circular structure."

One of Laird's most controversial books *A Little Piece of Ground* was coauthored with Sonia Nmir. "An unflinchingly grim description of life in Palestine under Israeli occupation," according to *Books for Keeps* interviewer Tucker, the novel centers on Karim, a twelve-year-old Palestinian living in Ramallah who has often witnessed his family's harsh treatment at the hands of Israeli soldiers. In an attempt to escape the violence that surrounds him, Karim enlists his friends to help him transform an abandoned lot into a soccer field. Caught outdoors after curfew, however, the boy risks his life by hiding near his "little piece of ground." Criticized by some critics for presenting an unbalanced view of the Israeli-Palestinian conflict in her novel, Laird still received the Outstanding International Book Award for her work, which "deserves serious attention and discussion," As Cooper Renner maintained in *Booklist.* "A classic story of the pain and growth of adolescence, *A Little Piece of Ground* is one of a very few good books written for young readers about the Arab world at all, and Palestine in particular," Sara Powell concluded in the *Washington Report on Middle East Affairs.*

A work of historical fiction set during the Napoleonic Wars and based on the experiences of Laird's great-great grandfather, *Secrets of the Fearless* follows the adventures of John Barr, a twelve year old who is forced into the British Navy. Working as a powder monkey aboard the HMS *Fearless,* a man o' war that patrols the high seas, Barr is aboard when the ship is sent on a covert mission into France. There he is separated from his shipmates and left, wounded, behind enemy lines. In the London *Times,* Amanda Craig described *Secrets of the Fearless* as "an enjoyable period romp," and Tom Adair noted in *Scotland on Sunday* that the "action scarcely draws breath in 300-odd pages of rowdy doings and closet skullduggery."

*Crusade* focuses on the unlikely relationship between a Christian and a Muslim who meet at the Siege of Acre in the late twelfth century. Adam, a British serf hoping to travel to Jerusalem, finds work as a squire for a knight serving under Richard the Lionheart. His counterpart, Salim, serves as an assistant to Saladin's personal physician. "Laird uses a series of encounters between the two boys as a chance to confound mutual misapprehensions," Kathryn Hughes stated in the London *Guardian,* further noting that *Crusade* is "a sturdy attempt to show young teenagers that their Muslim contemporaries come from a culture that is as civilised and peaceable as their own—or perhaps more civilised." "The moral of looking to understand another world-view, particularly between Christians and Muslims, is

timely in spite of its historical context," Alana Joli Abbott, concluded in her *School Library Journal* review of the book.

Laird was inspired to create *When the World Began: Stories Collected in Ethiopia* by her travels to Ethopia, where she came in contact with traditional storytellers. As she told interviewer Joseph Pike on the Jubilee Books Web site: "The storytellers would tell the stories absolutely straight, very much like the style of the Bible. In the African oral tradition there's a wonderful spareness: they don't bother with adjectives, they don't dress it up, they tell the bare bones of the story and do a lot of colour with the voice." In the twenty stories included in *When the World Began,* Laird continued, "I tried to reproduce the simplicity of the original narrators. Very often you have to listen to the story several times . . . unpack them and really be able to make the narrative work." According to reviewers, many of the tales in *When the World Began* are reminiscent of Aesop's fables or stories by the Brothers Grimm. According to *School Library Journal* contributor Ann Welton, the "tales, myths, and extended jokes paint a picture of a vibrant culture, open to the world around it." "The straightforward prose and the brevity of the tales make them good for reading aloud or story times," noted Shelle Rosenfeld in *Booklist.*

Laird, who lived in Iraq when she was first married, offers retellings of nine fables in *Fistful of Pearls, and Other Tales from Iraq,* a work flavored by "flavored with humor and cultural details," according to Carolyn Angus in *School Library Journal.* The collection also garnered praise from London *Sunday Times* critic Nicolette Jones for "its variety of characters' voices and its clear and lively style." In *The Ogress and the Snake, and Other Stories from Somalia* Laird retells "a pleasing variety" of tales she learned during her travels in Ethiopia, according to a contributor in *Kirkus Reviews.* A number of trickster stories highlight Laird's anthology *Pea Boy and Other Tales from Iran,* a book featuring what Rochman described as "stories [that] are universal with their . . . themes of betrayal, love, and redemption."

In a change of pace, Laird's *Rosy's Garden: A Child's Keepsake of Flowers* is a collection of flower lore and legend dispensed within the framework of Rosy's visits to her garden-loving grandmother's house. In addition to the story-telling, Rosy's grandmother teaches her to make such garden trifles as rose water, potpourri, and herb sandwiches. *Rosy's Garden* is an "unusual treasury of flower lore" according to Carolyn Phelan in *Booklist.* Laird has also written the text for several picture books, including the "Cubby Bears" and "Little Red Tractor" series. In the latter, a tractor and its driver, Stan, come to the rescue of farmers and livestock in need of assistance. While Duncan, the tractor, is never given human thoughts or actions, it still becomes something of a character in these gentle stories. According to *School Library Journal* contributor Nancy Seiner, "child appeal is assured by the winning personalities of the animals and the major role played by the tractor." Writing in *Magpies*, Lyn Linning commented that both series "are appealing pictures books for preschoolers." Linning went on to comment about Laird's writing for very young readers in general, claiming that the author "knows how to entertain middle primary readers while extending their facility with books and language."

Commenting on her varied literary output to *SATA*, Laird once wrote: "I feel immensely privileged to be able to earn my living as a writer. I cherish the freedom. I enjoy working on my own thing in my own time. I also love the unexpectedness. I never know where the inspiration will strike next, or into what exciting byways it will lead me."

## Biographical and Critical Sources

*PERIODICALS*

*Booklist,* March 15, 1990, Carolyn Phelan, review of *Rosy's Garden: A Child's Keepsake of Flowers,* p. 1446; January 1, 1999, Hazel Rochman, review of *Secret Friends,* p. 878; February 15, 2001, Shelle Rosenfeld, review of *When the World Began: Stories Collected in Ethiopia,* p. 1148; December 1, 2003, Hazel Rochman, review of *The Garbage King,* p. 667; May 1, 2004, John Peters, review of *Beautiful Bananas,* p. 1563; October 15, 2006, Hazel Rochman, review of *A Little Piece of Ground,* p. 40; September 15, 2010, Hazel Rochman, review of *Pea Boy and Other Stories from Iran,* p. 62.

*Books for Keeps,* January, 1998, George Hunt, review of *Forbidden Ground,* pp. 19-20; March, 2010, Nicholas Tucker, "Authorgraph No. 181: Elizabeth Laird."

*Bulletin of the Center for Children's Books,* January, 1988, review of *The Road to Bethlehem.*

*Guardian* (London, England), February 3, 1998, Joanna Carey, "Out of Africa," p. 5; January 18, 2005, Lindsey Fraser, review of *Hot Rock Mountain,* p. 11; October 10, 2006, Kate Agnew, review of *Oranges in No Man's Land,* p. 7; July 28, 2007, Kathryn Hughes, review of *Crusade,* p. 16; March 1, 2008, Julia Eccleshare, review of *A Fistful of Pearls and Other Tales from Iraq,* p. 20.

*Horn Book,* September-October, 2009, Madelyn Travis, "A Bit of a Snake Pit: The Middle East Conflict in British Children's Books," p. 515.

*Junior Bookshelf,* August, 1988, review of *Red Sky in the Morning,* p. 197.

*Kirkus Reviews,* April 15, 1992, review of *Kiss the Dust,* p. 539; February 1, 2004, review of *Beautiful Bananas,* p. 135; November 15, 2009, review of *The Ogress and the Snake, and Other Stories from Somalia.*

*Kliatt,* January, 2007, Amanda MacGregor, review of *A Little Piece of Ground,* p. 24.

*Magpies,* July, 1999, Lyn Linning, "Know the Author: Elizabeth Laird," pp. 14-15.

*New York Times Book Review,* November 10, 1985, Vincent Crapanzano, "Takla the Wonderworker," p. 38; December 6, 1987, Rosemary L. Bray, review of *The Road to Bethlehem,* p. 80; October 4, 1992, Elizabeth Cohen, review of *Kiss the Dust,* p. 22.

*Publishers Weekly,* November 10, 2003, review of *The Garbage King,* p. 63; March 15, 2004, review of *Beautiful Bananas,* p. 74.

*Race and Class,* July-September, 2004, Imman Laksari-Adams, review of *A Little Piece of Ground,* p. 139.

*School Librarian,* spring, 1997, Chris Stephenson, review of *On the Run,* p. 34; November, 1997, Sarah Mears, review of *Forbidden Ground,* p. 21.

*School Library Journal,* September, 1989, Barbara Chatton, review of *Loving Ben,* p. 252; September, 1991, Nancy Seiner, reviews of *The Day Patch Stood Guard* and *The Day Sidney Ran Off,* both p. 236; November, 2000, Ann Welton, review of *When the World Began,* p. 172; October, 2002, Jennifer Raiston, review of *Jake's Tower,* p. 168; December, 2003, Genevieve Gallagher, review of *The Garbage King,* p. 156; April, 2004, Margaret R. Tassia, review of *Beautiful Bananas,* p. 118; December, 2006, Coop Renner, review of *A Little Piece of Ground,* p. 148; February, 2007, Kathleen Pavin, review of *Jungle School,* p. 90; April, 2009, Carolyn Angus, review of *A Fistful of Pearls, and Other Tales from Iraq,* p. 123; December, 2010, Alana Joli Abbott, review of *Crusade,* p. 117.

*Scotland on Sunday* (Edinburgh, Scotland), August 21, 2005, Tom Adair, review of *Secrets of the Fearless,* p. 8.

*Sunday Times* (London, England), February 24, 2008, Nicolette Jones, review of *A Fistful of Pearls, and Other Tales from Iraq,* p. 48.

*Times* (London, England), August 20, 2005, Amanda Craig, review of *Secrets of the Fearless,* p. 17.

*Washington Report on Middle East Affairs,* November, 2006, Sara Powell, review of *A Little Piece of Ground,* p. 42.

*ONLINE*

*Elizabeth Laird Home Page,* http://www.elizabethlaird. co.uk (April 15, 2011).

*Elizabeth Laird Web log,* http://lairdelizabeth.blogspot.com (April 15, 2011).

*Jubilee Books Web site,* http://www.jubileebooks.co.uk/ (June, 2002), Joseph Pike, interview with Laird.

*Macmillan Readers Web site,* http://www.macmillan readers.com/ (April 15, 2011), interview with Laird.*

\*        \*        \*

# LATHAM, Irene 1971-

## Personal

Born 1971, in GA; married; children: three sons. *Education:* University of Alabama at Birmingham, degree (social work); University of Alabama, degree (social work). *Hobbies and other interests:* Travel, quilting.

## Addresses

*Home*—Birmingham, AL. *E-mail*—irene@irenelatham.com.

## Career

Poet, novelist, and editor.

## Member

Society of Children's Book Writers and Illustrators, Alabama Writers Forum, Big Table Poets (cofounder).

## Awards, Honors

Named Alabama Poet of the Year, 2006; Book of the Year, Alabama State Poetry Society, 2007, and Independent Publishers Book Award, 2008, both for *What Came Before;* Children's Book Award, Alabama Library Association, and Notable Children's Book, American Library Association, both 2011, both for *Leaving Gee's Bend.*

## Writings

*Leaving Gee's Bend* (novel), Putnam (New York, NY), 2010.

Also author of *The Color of Lost Rooms* (poetry), Blue Rooster Press (Birmingham, AL), and *What Came Before* (poetry), Churn Dash Press (Birmingham, AL). Poetry editor for *Birmingham Arts Journal.* Contributor to *Poems from the Big Table* and *Einstein at the Odeon Café: Poems from the Big Table,* Churn Dash Press.

## Sidelights

Irene Latham's debut novel, a work of historical fiction titled *Leaving Gee's Bend,* was inspired by the author's 2003 visit to the Whitney Museum of American Art. An award-winning poet who lives and works in Alabama, Latham traveled to New York City to view "The Quilts of Gee's Bend," a celebrated exhibit featuring bold, vibrant work created by four generations of women living in the isolated African-American community of Gee's Bend, Alabama. The experience proved to be a surprisingly emotional one and left the author with a host of unanswered questions. "Something happened to me as I walked through those rooms . . . I was moved by the quilts and by the voices of the quilt makers," Latham recalled on her home page. "The more I learned, the more I wanted to know: What if your community was so remote and isolated that it didn't have a doctor, and your mother was seriously ill? What if you were black and you saw a white person for the very first time? What if you thought the whole world was just like what you saw from your front porch and found out it wasn't?"

Latham was an avid reader while growing up, devouring childhood classics such as the "Little House" books by Laura Ingalls Wilder as well as *The Black Stallion,*

*Sounder,* and *Old Yeller.* "So, from the get-go, my reading life has been about those early, powerful experiences of love," she remarked to *Cynsations* online interview Cynthia Leitich Smith. "In fact, I'm still drawn to stories like that—classic stories, simple stories, before life gets complicated by sexual relationships and responsibilities and the pressures and demands of early adulthood. So, it really is no mystery where *Leaving Gee's Bend* comes from. What I've written is my favorite kind of story."

Set in 1932, *Leaving Gee's Bend* focuses on Ludelphia Bennett, a ten year old from an impoverished sharecropping family who displays a gift for quilting, despite being blind in one eye. When her mother falls seriously ill, Ludelphia decides she must leave her small hamlet of Gee's Bend and venture to Camden, some forty miles away, to find a doctor. During her often-difficult journey, the youngster stitches together a quilt that chronicles her experiences, including her first encounters with white people. When Ludelphia discovers a planned raid on Gee's Bend by a vengeful widow, she

*Cover of* Leaving Gee's Bend, *Irene Latham's story about a young black girl's first journey into a white community in 1930s Alabama.*
(G.P. Putnam's Sons, 2010. Cover photo © 2009 by David Sacks/Getty Images. Jacket design by Jeanine Henderson. Reproduced with permission from Penguin Young Reader's Group.)

must take action to save her friends and family. "Ludel-phia's voice is authentic and memorable," Hazel Rochman stated in *Booklist,* and Joanna K. Fabicon noted in *School Library Journal* that through her narrative "Latham pays homage to the community spirit that historically fostered a heritage of artisan quilt-makers."

One of the keys to the success of *Leaving Gee's Bend,* Latham notes, was discovering a way to identify with her fictional characters. As she recalled to Smith, the research and writing of the novel "became an exercise first in imagination, then in empathy." What the author learned through the process, she concluded, "is that we have the power as writers to create a more compassionate world. We can awaken mercy in our readers by first awakening mercy within ourselves."

## Biographical and Critical Sources

*PERIODICALS*

*Booklist,* February 1, 2010, Hazel Rochman, review of *Leaving Gee's Bend,* p. 61.
*Bulletin of the Center for Children's Books,* March, 2010, Kate Quealy-Gainer, review of *Leaving Gee's Bend,* p. 293.
*Chicago Tribune,* March 6, 2010, Mary Harris Russell, review of *Leaving Gee's Bend,* p. 16.
*Kirkus Reviews,* December 15, 2009, review of *Leaving Gee's Bend.*
*Publishers Weekly,* January 11, 2010, review of *Leaving Gee's Bend,* p. 48.
*School Library Journal,* January, 2010, Joanna K. Fabicon, review of *Leaving Gee's Bend,* p. 106.
*Voice of Youth Advocates,* February, 2010, KaaVonia Hinton-Johnson, review of *Leaving Gee's Bend,* p. 496.

*ONLINE*

*Cynsations Web log,* http://cynthialeitichsmith.blogspot.com/ (August 4, 2010), Cynthia Leitich Smith, "New Voice: Irene Latham on *Leaving Gee's Bend.*"
*Irene Latham Home Page,* http://www.irenelatham.com (April 1, 2011).
*Irene Latham Web log,* http://www.irenelatham.blogspot.com (April 1, 2011).

\*      \*      \*

## LAYBURN, Joe

### Personal

Born in London, England. *Education:* College degree.

### Addresses

*Home*—London, England.

### Career

Journalist, teacher, and author. Former television journalist for British Broadcasting Corporation, ITV, and Channel 4, for fifteen years; primary-grade teacher in London, England, beginning 2002.

### Awards, Honors

Royal Television Society Home Current Affairs Award nomination.

### Writings

*Ghostscape,* illustrated by John Williams, Frances Lincoln (London, England), 2008.
*Street Heroes,* illustrated by John Williams, Frances Lincoln (London, England), 2010.
*Runaways,* illustrated by John Williams (Frances Lincoln (London, England), 2011.

### Biographical and Critical Sources

*PERIODICALS*

*Kirkus Reviews,* October 15, 2009, review of *Ghostscape.*
*School Library Journal,* December, 2009, Kathleen Isaacs, review of *Ghostscape,* p. 126.

*ONLINE*

*Joe Layburn Web log,* http://joelayburn.blogspot.com (April 1, 2011).
*Frances Lincoln Web site,* http://www.franceslincoln.co.uk/ (April 1, 2005).\*

\*      \*      \*

## LINTERN, Tom

### Personal

Born in Stow, OH. *Education:* Kent State University, degree, 2000. *Hobbies and other interests:* Visiting friends and family, exploring New York City, drawing.

### Addresses

*Home*—New York, NY. *Agent*—Shannon Associates, 333 W. 57th St., Ste. 809, New York, NY 10019. *E-mail*—tom.lintern@gmail.com.

### Career

Designer, illustrator, and storyboard artist. Worked as a Web site designer; storyboard artist for independent films and television commercials, Los Angeles CA, for five years; storyboard artist and illustrator in New York, NY, 2006—.

## Illustrator

René Colato Laínez, *The Tooth Fairy Meets El Ratón Pérez,* Tricycle Press (Berkeley, CA), 2010.

Yannick Murphy, *The Cold Water Witch,* Tricycle Press (Berkeley, CA), 2010.

## Sidelights

A designer and storyboard artist based in New York City, Tom Lintern has provided the artwork for *The Tooth Fairy Meets El Ratón Pérez,* a picture book by René Colato Laínez, as well as *The Cold Water Witch,* a story by Yannick Murphy. A frightful tale with an amusing twist, *The Cold Water Witch* finds a young girl outwitting an evil sorceress who hopes to lure the child into her icy realm. Here Lintern's pastel illustrations "glow with cold light, like computer screens," as a reviewer in *Publishers Weekly* reported.

In *The Tooth Fairy Meets El Ratón Pérez* two legendary characters have an unexpected encounter as they attempt to fulfill their duties. When Miguelito, a Mexican-American boy, loses his tooth and places it beneath his pillow one night, he is visited not only by the Tooth Fairy but also by her Latino counterpart, El Ratón Pérez. At first, both claim possession of the tooth, but when their tug-of-war sends the tooth flying across the room, they realize that they must cooperate to retrieve the treasured object. Colato Laínez's tale of cultural identity garnered praise from reviewers, Mary Landrum commenting in *School Library Journal* that Lintern's colored-pencil illustrations have "a sparkly, ethereal quality that perfectly suits this modern fairy tale." A contributor in *Publishers Weekly* also praised the illustrations in *The Tooth Fairy Meets El Ratón Pérez,* writing that they create "a sense of nocturnal whimsy."

## Biographical and Critical Sources

*PERIODICALS*

*Kirkus Reviews,* February 15, 2010, review of *The Tooth Fairy Meets El Ratón Pérez.*

*Tom Lintern's illustration projects include creating the artwork for René Colato Lainez's story in* **The Tooth Fairy Meets El Ratón Pérez.**
(Illustration copyright © 2010 by Tom Lintern. Reproduced with permission of Tricycle Press, an imprint of Random House Children's Books, a division of Random House, Inc.)

*Publishers Weekly,* March 15, 2010, review of *The Tooth Fairy Meets El Ratón Pérez,* p. 52; July 5, 2010, review of *The Cold Water Witch,* p. 40.

*School Library Journal,* March, 2010, Mary Landrum, review of *The Tooth Fairy Meets El Ratón Pérez,* p. 124; September, 2010, Margaret Bush, review of *The Cold Water Witch,* p. 132.

*ONLINE*

*Tom Lintern Home Page,* http://www.tomlintern.com (April 15, 2011).*

# M

## MADDEN, Colleen
### (Colleen M. Madden)

### Personal

Married; huband's name Patrick (a writer); children: Sean, Gabe. *Education:* B.A. (illustration and English literature). *Hobbies and other interests:* Gardening, distance running.

### Addresses

*Home*—PA. *Agent*—Mela Bolinao, MB Artists, 775 6th Ave., Ste. 6, New York, NY 10001.

### Career

Illustrator and author.

### Awards, Honors

Louie Award, International Greeting Card.

### Illustrator

Jacqueline H. Blumenstock and David C. Pool, *Making New Friends,* new edition, Big Brown Box (Douglassville, PA), 2005.

Dotti Enderle, *The Library Gingerbread Man,* Upstart-Books (Janesville, WI), 2010.

Edith Hope Fine and Angela Demos Halpin, *Water, Weed, and Wait,* Tricycle Press (Berkeley, CA), 2010.

Ellen Javernick, *What If Everybody Did That?,* Marshall Cavendish Children (Tarrytown, NY), 2010.

### Biographical and Critical Sources

*PERIODICALS*

*School Library Journal,* June, 2010, Barbara Auerbach, review of *The Library Gingerbread Man,* p. 68; September, 2010, Margaret Bush, review of *Water, Weed, and Wait,* p. 137.

*ONLINE*

*Colleen M. Madden Home Page,* http://www.greenfro graphics.com (February 20, 2011).

*Colleen M. Madden We blog,* http://unofroblog.blogsppot. com (February 20, 2011).

*M.B. Artists Web site,* http://www.mbartists.com/ (February 21, 2011), "Colleen Madden."\*

\*        \*        \*

## MADDEN, Colleen M.
### See MADDEN, Colleen

\*        \*        \*

## MADDOX, Jake
### See TRUMBAUER, Lisa

\*        \*        \*

## MANDINE, Selma 1973-

### Personal

Born 1973, in Hong Kong. *Education:* B.A. (with honors).

### Addresses

*Home*—France. *E-mail*—contact@petiteselma.com.

### Career

Illustrator and graphic designer. Worked as graphic designer for museums, and for a publishing company in Hong Kong; children's book illustrator, 2003—.

## Writings

*SELF-ILLUSTRATED*

*Bisous bisous,* Éditions Philippe Auzou (Paris, France), 2008, translated by Michelle Williams as *Kiss Kiss,* Golden Books (New York, NY), 2009.

*Mon premier cauchemar,* Éditions Chocolat (Brésilley, France), 2009.

*ILLUSTRATOR*

Régine Joséphine, *La clé des songes,* Éditions Gecko (Rouen, France), 2006.

Régine Joséphine, *Le roi qui désirait le Temps,* Éditions Gecko (Rouen, France), 2006.

Sandrine Lévy, *Raphie Rasibus, une histoire de taille!,* Éditions Gecko (Rouen, France), 2007.

Guo, *Pince-coeur,* HongFei Cultures (Champs-sur-Marne, France), 2008.

Fabienne Roulié, *Les secrets de Pétronille,* Éditions Chocolat (Brésilley, France), 2008.

Régine Joséphine *Les ailes du vent,* Éditions Gecko (Rouen, France), 2008.

Virginie Hanna, *Il y a quelque chose dans l'air!,* Éditions Gecko (Rouen, France), 2009.

Sandrine Lévy, *Les coquilles de Mikado l'escargot,* Éditions Micmac (France), 2010.

## Sidelights

A native of Hong Kong who lives and works in France, Selma Mandine is the author and illustrator of *Bisous bisous,* a kindhearted tale published in the United States as *Kiss Kiss.* The work centers on a young boy's efforts to describe a kiss to his inquisitive teddy bear, noting that a kiss is as unique as the person (or pet) who delivers it. A kiss from a stubbly-faced father, as the lad tells his bear, resembles a prickly cactus, while the ones delivered by Rex, the family dog, are wet and sloppy.

Mandine's artwork for *Kiss Kiss* earned her substantial critical praise, a *Publishers Weekly* reviewer citing the "doll-like adorableness" of the characters as a highlight of the work. According to a a contributor in *Kirkus Re-*

***Selma Mandine captures the gentle relationship between a mother and child in her engagingly titled self-illustrated picture book* Kiss Kiss.** (Copyright © 2008 by Éditions Philippe Auzou, Paris. Reproduced with permission of Random House Children's Books.)

views, Mandine's "warm palette and soft-edged, just-surreal-enough digital illustrations beckon" young readers, and in *School Library Journal* Donna Atmur similarly commented that the artist's pictures for her original story "emphasize the sweetness of this tale."

## Biographical and Critical Sources

*PERIODICALS*

*Kirkus Reviews,* December 15, 2009, review of *Kiss Kiss.*
*Publishers Weekly,* November 30, 2009, review of *Kiss Kiss,* p. 47.
*School Library Journal,* December, 2009, Donna Atmur, review of *Kiss Kiss,* p. 87.

*ONLINE*

*Selma Mandine Home Page,* http://www.petiteselma.free.fr (April 1, 2011).*

\*    \*    \*

## McCAFFREY, Kate 1970-

### Personal

Born 1970, in Liverpool, England; immigrated to Australia, 1972; partner's name Jason; children: Savannah, Willow. *Education:* University of Western Australia, B.A. (English and fine art), 1990, Dip.Ed., 1991. *Hobbies and other interests:* Travel.

### Addresses

*Home*—Mariginiup, Western Australia, Australia. *E-mail*—jn-arts@oceanbroadband.net.

### Career

Educator and author. High-school teacher of English and art, beginning 1992; St. Stephen's School, Carramar, part-time teacher of English; freelance author and presenter at schools.

### Awards, Honors

Western Australian Premier's Book Award for Young-Adult Fiction, 2006, and Western Australian Young Reader's Book Award, Australian Family Therapists' Book Awards Highly Commended designation, and Notable Book selection, Children's Book Council of Australia (CBCA), all 2007, all for *Destroying Avalon;* Australian Family Therapists' Book Award in Young Adult category, 2008, for *In Ecstasy;* White Raven Award, 2011, for *Beautiful Monster.*

### Writings

*YOUNG-ADULT NOVELS*

*Destroying Avalon,* Fremantle Arts Centre Press (North Fremantle, Western Australia, Australia), 2006.

*In Ecstasy,* Fremantle Press (North Fremantle, Western Australia, Australia), 2008.
*Beautiful Monster,* Fremantle Press (North Fremantle, Western Australia, Australia), 2010.

### Sidelights

An award-winning author based in Western Australia, Kate McCaffrey writes novels for children who do not enjoy reading, children like those she encountered during her years teaching English at the high-school level. Rather than pulling readers into her stories through humor and hijinks, McCaffrey explores the darker side of modern adolescence, addressing cyber bullying in *Destroying Avalon,* drug addiction in *In Ecstasy,* and anorexia in *Beautiful Monster.*

Born in England, McCaffrey became an Australian at age two when her family immigrated to Perth, in Western Australia. After graduating from high school with lots of ideas but no clear career plans, she earned a double major in fine arts and English at the University of Western Australia and also minored in history. Before starting her family, McCaffrey started her teaching career and also took time to fulfill her long-held desire to travel in Europe. She began to devote serious time to her writing when her children were infants, eventually juggling parenting, writing, and teaching. Her first novel, *Destroying Avalon,* was written in 2005 and published the following year.

In *Destroying Avalon* McCaffrey's teen heroine is off to a rocky start at her new school, if her first day is any indication. Dismissed by the popular clique, Avalon soon discovers that she is the target of an attack via text messages and e-mails. As the harassment escalates, its target shifts from Avalon to Marshall, one of Avalon's few friends and a teen who is far less emotionally equipped to handle the unpleasant situation. Reviewing McCaffrey's debut in *Magpies,* Tina Cavanough called *Destroying Avalon* "a thought provoking" look at cyber bullying that ranks as "a must have for school and public libraries."

Although Sophie and Mia have been friends since elementary school, when readers meet the fifteen year olds in *In Ecstasy* the social stresses of high school threaten to pull them apart. Outgoing Sophie always seems to have a boy in tow, and shy Mia feels out of place until she experiments with the drug Ecstasy and becomes flirtatious and uninhibited. While Mia's experiences with drugs bolster her attractiveness to the party crowd, Sophie is sexually assaulted after someone slips her a "roofie," a date-rape drug. Soon the girls' roles are reversed as Sophie gives up partying and Mia continues to discard her inhibitions, ignoring the concerns of her longtime friend. "Told in alternating voices and chapters, the girls' divergent paths unfold," explained *School Library Journal* contributor Roxanne Myers Spencer, "each filled with poignant hope, illusion, and ultimately pain and peril." To a *Kirkus Reviews* writer,

*In Ecstasy* seems "oddly old-fashioned," although the teens' "pitch-perfect" narratives effectively capture "Mia's descent into addiction." "McCaffrey is gifted with a wining and eminently readable style," asserted Daniel Kraus in his *Booklist* review of the novel, and the parallel narratives of the two teens "are distinct and vibrant."

After her family is torn apart by the death of her younger brother, teenager Tessa focuses on her body image as a way to take control of her life in *Beautiful Monster.* As her parents withdraw into their sorrow, Tessa feels adrift, until Ned comes into her life and becomes her closest friend and biggest supporter. Ned sees her potential and constantly challenges her to rise to meet it, whether it is at school, in a social setting, or in achieving her best on a physical level. As McCaffrey draws readers into Tessa's inner world, where Ned seems real rather than a manifestation of her insecurities, she illustrates the realities of a person suffering from anorexia, a determination to control their eating to the point where they risk their health and sometimes their life. Praising *Beautiful Monster* as "a topical and moving story of an all-too-familiar problem" among adolescents, Margot Hillel added in her *Reading Time* review that McCaffrey also includes "a strong message . . . asking family and friends not to ignore the problem."

## Biographical and Critical Sources

*PERIODICALS*

*Booklist,* December 1, 2009, Daniel Kraus, review of *In Ecstasy,* p. 36.
*Kirkus Reviews,* November 15, 2009, review of *In Ecstasy.*
*Magpies,* November, 2006, Tina Cavanough, review of *Destroying Avalon.*
*Reading Time,* August, 2010, Margot Hillel, review of *Beautiful Monster,* p. 37.
*School Library Journal,* January, 2010, Roxanne Myers Spencer, review of *In Ecstasy,* p. 108.
*Voice of Youth Advocates,* June, 2009, Laura Woodruff, review of *In Ecstasy,* p. 140.

*ONLINE*

*Fremantle Press Web site,* http://www.fremantlepress.com.au/ (February 20, 2011), "Kate McCaffrey."
*Kate McCaffrey Home Page,* http://www.katemccaffrey.com (February 20, 2011).

\*       \*       \*

## McGUIGAN, Mary Ann 1949-

## Personal

Surname pronounced "Mick-*gwig*-in"; born August 3, 1949, in New York, NY; daughter of Jame and Mary McGuigan; children: Matthew Pritchard, Douglas Pritchard. *Education:* St. Peter's College, A.B., 1972; Trenton State College, graduate study. *Politics:* "Left of Venus." *Religion:* Roman Catholic.

## Addresses

*Home*—Old Bridge, NJ. *Office*—Bloomberg Financial Markets, 100 Business Park Dr., P.O. Box 888, Princeton, NJ 08542-0888. *Agent*—Charlotte Sheedy, 65 Bleecker St., 12th Fl., New York, NY 10012. *E-mail*—heddagab@aol.com; maryann@ maryannmcguigan.com.

## Career

Author and editor. Teacher of English and reading at elementary, junior high, and high schools in Jersey City, NJ, 1972-75, Old Bridge, NJ, 1975-79, Trenton, NJ, 1979-80, and Middletown, NJ, 1980-81; Moody's Investors Service, New York, NY, editor of financial publications, 1981-84; Vantage Press, Inc., New York, editor of fiction and nonfiction, 1981-84; A. Foster Higgins, Inc., Princeton, NJ, communications consultant, 1984-93; Bloomberg Financial Markets, Princeton, managing editor of *Wealth Manager,* 1993—.

## Awards, Honors

Best Books for the Teen Age selection, New York Public Library, 1995, for *Cloud Dancer,* and 1998, for *Where You Belong;* finalist, National Book Award, 1997, for *Where You Belong;* finalist, National Magazine Award, American Society of Magazine Editors, 1995, editorial excellence award, *Folio,* 1996, and Business Award, New York Press Club, 1996, all for *Bloomberg* magazine; finalist, Excellence in Video Award, Michigan Advertising Group, for a Kellogg Company videotape; first place award, *Business Insurance,* for a Reader's Digest communication project; two recognition awards, New York chapter of International Association of Business Communicators.

## Writings

*YOUNG-ADULT NOVELS*

*Cloud Dancer,* Scribner (New York, NY), 1994.
*Where You Belong,* Atheneum (New York, NY), 1997.
*Morning in a Different Place* (sequel to *Where You Belong*), Front Street (Honesdale, PA), 2009.

Contributor to the anthology *Lost and Found: A Collection of Stories by Award-winning Authors,* edited by M. Jerry Weiss, Forge, 2000. Contributor of essays and stories for adults to magazines and newspapers, including *New York Times, Image, Dawn, New York Sunday, Newsday,* and *Bloomberg.*

## Sidelights

Young-adult novelist Mary Ann McGuigan earned fame with her second published work, *Where You Belong,* and its sequel, *Morning in a Different Place.* The latter story is set in November of 1963, and follows fourteen-year-old Fiona O'Doherty. She and her siblings are constantly moving because of their father's alcoholism, but now they have found refuge with Fiona's friend Yolanda Baker. Aside from dealing with the everyday pains of adolescence and her unfortunate domestic situation, Fiona must also contend with the racial bigotry of the day and the shockwave emanating from the assassination of U.S. President John F. Kennedy. Critics applauded *Morning in a Different Place* as a well-written sequel able to stand on its own. Praising the novel in *Kirkus Reviews,* a contributor commended "the author's portrait of the chameleonic nature of teenage girls" in a story that "builds aggressively to a powerful finale." Daniel Kraus, writing in *Booklist,* declared that McGuigan presents "a classic moral battle, but the results are never didactic" and her "writing is spare and low-key." As Renee Steinberg pointed out in *School Library Journal,* "Fiona's voice reverberates through a range of emotional highs and lows in this story of friendship, loyalty, trust, racism, and coping."

McGuigan once commented: "The creator must have been on a bender the day he was supposed to hand me the blueprints for my earth plane debut, because it looks as if central casting took over instead and gave me the starring role in a 'B' movie—a corny one. In real life, the shy, skinny kid from a poor, wacko Irish family in the Bronx doesn't get to have her dreams come true. All I ever wanted to be was a writer. By age fourteen—having attended thirteen different grammar schools in a free-fall flight from landlords who wanted their rent—I knew I wasn't Ivy League material. I thought writers were well educated, well traveled, knew which fork to use, and had parents who spent the majority of their time sober. I thought I'd try anyway.

"I had the good sense to keep the first stories I wrote to myself. They were awful. I didn't have a clue what good writing was until college, when the Jesuits introduced me to all the dead white men who had already said everything there was to say better than anyone else could hope to say it. Nowhere in the required reading, however, could I find anything that quite captured what it was like to grow up the way I did. So I respectfully concluded the Jesuits were wrong.

"Still, it took me another twenty years to find the courage and the voice to get some stories told. That came together as soon as I knew who my audience would be: it would be me—and all the kids like me who grew up looking for a way out. I wanted *Where You Belong* to be a story about courage, not the kind that soldiers draw on or the kind that astronauts and adventurers need, but the kind that ordinary people must summon when they believe they are alone and without hope.

"Fiona and Yolanda are growing up in the Bronx, where circumstances can easily conspire to make life seem hopeless. Fiona has much to contend with: poverty, violence, a family whose center cannot hold. But these desperate conditions are not what threaten Fiona most. It is instead the knowledge that it has become pointless to seek comfort—or even safety—from those she loves. She has been set adrift. What finally anchors her is a friend. In Yolanda's strength, Fiona witnesses the courage needed to see the joys that wait beyond the day, and in her friendship, she finds the right to believe that she deserves them. As they find their place in the world, young people—and the not so young—may often feel lost. I offer Fiona's journey to all those struggling to find their way home."

## Biographical and Critical Sources

*PERIODICALS*

*Booklist,* June 1, 1997, Michael Cart, review of *Where You Belong,* p. 1695; February 1, 2009, Daniel Kraus, review of *Morning in a Different Place,* p. 50.

*Bulletin of the Center for Children's Books,* May, 1997, review of *Where You Belong,* p. 328; March, 2009, Karen Coats, review of *Morning in a Different Place,* p. 290.

*Kirkus Reviews,* January 15, 2009, review of *Morning in a Different Place.*

*School Library Journal,* July, 1997, Linda Greengrass, review of *Where You Belong,* p. 96; March 1, 2009, Renee Steinberg, review of *Morning in a Different Place,* p. 146.

*Voice of Youth Advocates,* October, 1994, review of *Cloud Dancer,* p. 212; August, 1997, review of *Where You Belong,* p. 187; August, 2009, Matthew Weaver, review of *Morning in a Different Place,* p. 228.

*ONLINE*

*Mary Ann McGuigan Home Page,* http://maryannmcguigan .com (April 15, 2011).*

*          *          *

# MILLS, Adam
## See STANLEY, George Edward

*          *          *

# MORLEY, Ben

## Personal

Born in London, England; married; wife's name Heloise (a designer); children: Lyra, Rocco. *Education:* Durham University, B.A. (education). *Hobbies and other interests:* Soccer, snakes, going on adventures.

## Addresses

*Home*—Singapore. *Office*—EtonHouse International Pre-School, 2 Orchard Blvd., Singapore 248643.

## Career

Educator and writer. Early childhood educator in United Kingdom, Poland, Brunei, and China for more than ten years; EtonHouse International Pre-School, Singapore, currently teacher and director.

## Awards, Honors

Red Dot Award shortlist, 2009-10, for *The Silence Seeker.*

## Writings

*The Silence Seeker,* illustrated by Carl Pearce, Tamarind Books (London, England), 2010.

## Sidelights

Ben Morley draws on his experiences as an inner-city educator in writing *The Silence Seeker,* a picture book that explores the issues confronting refugee families. Morley has taught in Poland, Brunei, and China, as well as in Singapore, where he now lives, but it was his work at a primary school in England, where several students were immigrants seeking asylum, that inspired him to write. As Morley recalled in a *Today's Motherhood* online interview, "It was incredible to hear these children share their stories with their newfound friends. These stories were often hard to fathom, frequently desperately sad but what I sensed time and again in the children was hope. It was this *sense of hope* that inspired me to write a story about asylum seekers. However, it is not necessarily about asylum seekers, it is more about belonging and the possibilities of friendship."

*The Silence Seeker* concerns the brief but touching relationship between two boys from vastly different backgrounds. When young Joe inquires about his new neighbors, he mis-hears his mother's reference to asylum seekers, and infers that the newcomers simply want peace and quiet. Touring the chaotic city with the family's teenage son, who does not speak English, Joe realizes that silence may be impossible to find, but his efforts earn a simple, heartfelt reward. A critic in *Kirkus Reviews* applauded the "cacophonous, tense urban atmosphere" in the story, and Jane Doonan remarked in *School Library Journal* that *The Silence Seeker* "could certainly encourage worthwhile discussion about several kinds of 'difference' and being tolerant and open to strangers."

## Biographical and Critical Sources

*PERIODICALS*

*Kirkus Reviews,* February 15, 2010, review of *The Silence Seeker.*

*Resource Links,* spring, 2010, Jane Doonan, review of *The Silence Seeker,* p. 36.

*Ben Morley's evocative story about the experiences of refugees is captured in Carl Pearce's art for* The Silence Seekers. (Tamarind Books, 2009. Illustration copyright © 2009 by Carl Pearce. Reproduced with permission of Random House Children's Books.)

*School Library Journal,* April, 2010, Joan Kindig, review of *The Silence Seeker,* p. 136.

*ONLINE*

*AsianParent.com,* http://sg.theasianparent.com/ (December 4, 2009), interview with Morley.
*Today's Motherhood Web site,* http://www.todaysmother hood.com/ (April 15, 2011), interview with Morley.*

*      *      *

# MORRISON, Slade 1964-2010

## Personal

Born 1964, in Lorain, OH; died December 22, 2010; son of Harold (an architect) and Toni (an author and educator) Morrison; has children. *Education:* Purchase College—State University of New York, degree.

## Career

Fine-art painter and writer.

## Writings

*WITH MOTHER, TONI MORRISON*

*The Big Box,* illustrated by Giselle Potter, Hyperion Books for Children/Jump at the Sun (New York, NY), 1999.
*The Book of Mean People,* illustrated by Pascal Lemaître, Hyperion Books for Children (New York, NY), 2002.
*My Book of Mean People Journal,* illustrated by Pascal Lemaître, Hyperion Books for Children (New York, NY), 2002.
*Peeny Butter Fudge,* illustrated by Joe Cepeda, Simon & Schuster Books for Young Readers (New York, NY), 2009.
*Little Cloud and Lady Wind,* illustrated by Sean Qualls, Simon & Schuster Books for Young Readers (New York, NY), 2010.
*The Tortoise or the Hare,* illustrated by Joe Cepeda, Simon & Schuster Books for Young Readers (New York, NY), 2010.

*"WHO'S GOT GAME?" SERIES; WITH TONI MORRISON*

*The Ant or the Grasshopper?,* illustrated by Pascal Lemaître, Scribner (New York, NY), 2003.
*The Lion or the Mouse?,* illustrated by Pascal Lemaître, Scribner (New York, NY), 2003.
*Poppy or the Snake?,* illustrated by Pascal Lemaître, Scribner (New York, NY), 2003.
*The Mirror or the Glass?,* illustrated by Pascal Lemaître, Scribner (New York, NY), 2004.
*Who's Got Game?: Three Fables* (contains *The Ant or the Grasshopper?, The Lion or the Mouse?,* and *Poppy or the Snake?*) illustrated by Pascal Lemaître, Scribner (New York, NY), 2007.

## Adaptations

The "Who's Got Game?" series was adapted as an audiobook, Simon & Schuster Audio.

## Sidelights

An accomplished painter prior to his untimely death at age forty-five, Slade Morrison also cowrote a host of children's books with his mother, Nobel Prize-winning author Toni Morrison, including the works in the well-received "Who's Got Game?" series. *The Big Box,* the debut picture book for both mother and son, is based on a story Slade wrote when he was just nine years old. Told in verse, the work concerns a group of children who are forced to live in a large, brown box, imprisoned there by adults who feel threatened by the youngsters' imaginative, nonconformist attitudes. Although a critic in the *Journal of Adolescent & Adult Literacy* noted that the Morrisons' "seemingly humorous book has a haunting message" about accepting differences, a number of reviewers maintained that the sophisticated themes of *The Big Box* are best suited for an adult audience.

*The Book of Mean People* marked the Morrisons' first collaboration with illustrator Pascal Lemaître, who would also provide the artwork for their "Who's Got Game?" titles. Focusing on a young bunny's reactions to a number of frightful and frustrating experiences, such as an encounter with a bully, *The Book of Mean People* is valuable "as a springboard to discuss anger and shouting," as Judith Constantinides suggested in *School Library Journal.* Hazel Rochman, writing in *Booklist,* predicted that "small kids will recognize the

*Slade Morrison's picture-book collaborations with his mother, author Toni Morrision, include* Little Cloud and Lady Wind, *a story featuring stylized art by Sean Qualls.* (Illustration copyright © 2010 by Sean Qualls. Reprinted with permission of Simon & Schuster Books for Young Readers, an imprint of Simon & Schuster Children's Publishing Division.)

angry scenarios," and a *Publishers Weekly* reviewer commented that the "bittersweet volume takes meanness in stride and advocates kindness as the antidote."

Three children spend an exuberant and fun-filled day playing with their grandmother—while ignoring their mother's strict rules—in *Peeny Butter Fudge,* another of the Morrisons' collaborative efforts. "This is a vision of family life that many kids . . . will regard with envy," observed a contributor in *Publishers Weekly.* In *Little Cloud and Lady Wind* mother and son offer a meditation on individuality. Unlike her fellow clouds, who want to storm and thunder, Little Cloud wishes to live in harmony with the earth, finding an unexpected ally in Lady Wind. A tribute to Aesop's fable "The Bundle of Sticks," *Little Cloud and Lady Wind* "will resonate with anyone who has been caught in the tempest of mean or unfriendly behavior," Andrew Medlar predicted in *Booklist.*

Slade and Toni Morrison also present contemporary, rhyming versions of Aesop's stories in their "Who's Got Game?" series, which includes *The Ant or the Grasshopper?* In that work, the urban-dwelling Kid A refuses to assist Foxy G, his melodious companion, when the grasshopper comes looking for food during the cold winter, despite Foxy G's insistence that his musical talents have worth. According to *School Library Journal* reviewer Steven Engelfried, young readers "are neatly led to a conclusion that encourages them to ponder and discuss the value and importance of art."

A rodent becomes drunk with power in *The Lion or the Mouse?,* another "Who's Got Game?" story that also serves as a "farce about the triumph, the bombast, and the failure of a small creature," as Rochman observed. In *Poppy or the Snake?* a wise man teaches his grandson the value of preparation when he injures and then brings home a fast-talking serpent. Writing in *Booklist,* Francisca Goldsmith declared that this tale "will be a hit with both children and the adults who read to them."

## Biographical and Critical Sources

*PERIODICALS*

*Black Issues Book Review,* November-December, 2002, Evette Porter, review of *The Book of Mean People,* p. 39; May-June, 2003, Suzanne Rust, review of *The Ant or the Grasshopper?,* p. 57.

*Booklist,* August, 1999, Hazel Rochman, review of *The Big Box,* p. 2067; October 15, 2002, Hazel Rochman, review of *The Book of Mean People,* p. 412; May 15, 2003, Francisca Goldsmith, review of *The Ant or the Grasshopper?,* p. 1660; November 15, 2003, Hazel Rochman, review of *The Lion or the Mouse?,* p. 598; February 15, 2004, Francisca Goldsmith, review of *Poppy or the Snake?,* p. 1077; July 1, 2009, Daniel Kraus, review of *Peeny Butter Fudge,* p. 68; December 15, 2009, Andrew Medlar, review of *Little Cloud and Lady Wind,* p. 46.

*Horn Book,* September, 1999, Roger Sutton, review of *The Big Box,* p. 598.

*Journal of Adolescent & Adult Literacy,* May, 2002, review of *The Big Box,* p. 795.

*Kirkus Reviews,* September 1, 2002, review of *The Book of Mean People,* p. 1316; February 15, 2010, review of *Little Cloud and Lady Wind.*

*New York Times Book Review,* December 22, 2002, review of *The Book of Mean People,* p. 18.

*Publishers Weekly,* July 12, 1999, review of *The Big Box,* p. 95; September 2, 2002, review of *The Book of Mean People,* p. 68; November 11, 2002, review of *My Book of Mean People Journal,* p. 66; June 2, 2003, review of *The Ant or the Grasshopper?* and *The Lion or the Mouse?,* p. 50; February 2, 2004, review of *Poppy or the Snake?,* p. 79; August 24, 2009, review of *Peeny Butter Fudge,* p. 61; January 4, 2010, review of *Little Cloud and Lady Wind,* p. 45; August 23, 2010, review of *The Tortoise or the Hare,* p. 47.

*School Library Journal,* November, 2002, Judith Constantinides, review of *The Book of Mean People,* p. 132; September, 2003, Steven Engelfried, review of *The Ant or the Grasshopper?,* p. 204; December, 2003, John Peters, review of *The Lion or the Mouse?,* p. 138; September, 2009, Meg Smith, review of *Peeny Butter Fudge,* p. 130; January, 2010, review of *Little Cloud and Lady Wind,* p. 79; October, 2010, Mary Jean Smith, review of *The Tortoise or the Hare,* p. 103.

*ONLINE*

*Slade Morrison Home Page,* http://slademorrison.com (April 15, 2011).*

# N-O

## NADOL, Jen

### Personal

Born in Reading, PA; married; children: three sons. *Education:* American University, B.A. (literature).

### Addresses

*Home*—Westchester County, NY. *E-mail*—jennadol@ verizon.net.

### Career

Writer. Worked in human resources for twelve years.

### Awards, Honors

Best Children's Books of the Year, Bank Street College of Education, 2010, for *The Mark.*

### Writings

*The Mark,* Bloomsbury (New York, NY), 2010.
*The Vision,* Bloomsbury (New York, NY), 2011.

### Sidelights

In *The Mark,* her debut novel for young adults, Jen Nadol offers "a thoughtful exploration of fate and free will," according to a *Publishers Weekly* critic. In the work, Nadol, who cites Stephen King as one of her literary influences, introduces Cassie Renfield, a sixteen year old with the extraordinary ability to foretell an individual's imminent death. For years, Cassie has noticed an aura, or "mark," surrounding people, but the teen does not realize its significance until she witnesses the demise of a marked man. After her beloved grandmother dies, Cassie begins to question her responsibility to those who bear this mark, and she decides to use her foreknowledge to save the life of her "marked" boyfriend, Lucas. With Lucas's encouragement, Cassie explores the full extent of her powers, intervening in the lives of strangers, even as she often doubts the wisdom and morality of her actions.

Writing in *Horn Book,* Claire E. Cross described *The Mark* as "a thoughtful dramatization of a fascinating philosophical conundrum," and *Booklist* reviewer Cindy Welch similarly commented that "Nadol has interwoven an absorbing and thoughtful philosophical dilemma with a YA romance." *School Library Journal* contributor Leah J. Sparks applauded the author's portrayal of Cassie, stating that "her dilemma and emotions feel genuine and believable." According to a *Kirkus Reviews* writer, Nadol's protagonist in *The Mark* deals with ethical dilemmas that are "heartwrenching."

### Biographical and Critical Sources

*PERIODICALS*

*Booklist,* December 15, 2009, Cindy Welch, review of *The Mark,* p. 36.
*Bulletin of the Center for Children's Books,* April, 2010, Kate Quealy-Gainer, review of *The Mark,* p. 347.
*Horn Book,* May-June, 2010, Claire E. Cross, review of *The Mark,* p. 87.
*Kirkus Reviews,* January 15, 2010, review of *The Mark.*
*Publishers Weekly,* January 11, 2010, review of *The Mark,* p. 50.
*School Library Journal,* February, 2010, Leah J. Sparks, review of *The Mark,* p. 120.
*Voice of Youth Advocates,* June, 2010, Amy Fiske, review of *The Mark,* p. 168.

*ONLINE*

*AuthorsNow! Web site,* http://www.authorsnow.com/ (January 19, 2010), "Jen Nadol."

*Jen Nadol Home Page,* http://www.jennadolbooks.com (April 15, 2011).*

\* \* \*

## NEWMAN, Jeff 1976-

### Personal

Born 1976, in Ashland, MA; married; wife's name Jodi. *Education:* Art Institute of Boston.

### Addresses

*Home*—Milwaukee, WI. *E-mail*—jeff@newmanpictures. com.

### Career

Animator, author, and illustrator.

### Writings

*SELF-ILLUSTRATED*

*Reginald,* Random House Children's Books (New York, NY), 2003.
*Hippo! No, Rhino,* Little, Brown (New York, NY), 2006.
*The Boys,* Simon & Schuster Books for Young Readers (New York, NY), 2010.
*Hand Book,* Simon & Schuster Books for Young Readers (New York, NY), 2011.

*ILLUSTRATOR*

James and Joseph Bruchac, *Rabbit's Snow Dance,* Dial (New York, NY), 2011.
Aaron Reynolds, *The Carnivore Club,* Chronicle Books (San Francisco, CA), 2012.

### Sidelights

The line and water-color art of author/illustrator Jeff Newman has appeared in several of his own picture-book stories in addition to bringing to life texts by Aaron Reynolds and the father-son writing team of James and Joseph Bruchac. Growing up with an appreciation for the picture-book art of James Marshall, illustrator of Harry Allard's "Miss Nelson" stories, Newman captures the same wry humor in self-illustrated books that include *Reginald, Hippo! No, Rhino, The Boys,* and *Hand Book.*

Newman grew up in Ashland, Massachusetts, and studied illustration at the Art Institute of Boston. He got his start in book illustration after a move to New York City in 2000. A friend, who was then working in publishing, told him that Random House was in the market for an

illustrator for their ongoing "Harriet the Spy" books, and that Newman should apply for the job. In order to mimic the style of the original illustrator, Louise Fitzhugh, Newman created a new portfolio of Fitzhugh-like renderings, and got the job, althogh the project was eventually shelved. He released his first self-illustrated book, *Reginald,* a few years later to a positive critical reception. Discussing Newman's story—in which a friendly bull attempts to befriend the many dangerous creatures that are his neighbors in his new Amazon jungle home—Marianne Saccardi noted in *School Library Journal* that "humor abounds in both text and . . . cartoon illustrations," making *Reginald* a good choice "for a great storyhour."

A lackadaisical zookeeper named Randy is responsible for the humor in *Hippo! No, Rhino,* as a captive rhinoceros becomes disconcerted when a sign painted with the word "Hippo" is placed near its cage. After several zoo visitors read the sign and make the wrong identification, the rhino tries to remove the sign, with the help of a pair of purple birds. Fortunately, a little boy also realizes the zookeeper's error, and he quickly sorts out the problem. Newman's entertaining art, featuring black lines and brilliant hues of opaque watercolor, was characterized by a *Publishers Weekly* critic as featuring "a '70s retro vibe," while in *Horn Book* Kitty Flynn described Newman's "off-beat" and "color-mad" art as rendered "in a retro style reminiscent of Roger Duvoisin." A *Kirkus Reviews* writer praised the same work as an "oddball but ultimately tender zoo episode" in which "the pictures carry most of the plot and humor." In *School Library Journal* Carol L. MacKay cited *Hippo! No, Rhino* for its "colorful, graphic-style illustrations" and recommended Newman's book as "a clever exercise in promoting visual literacy."

Described by *Fuse 8 Productions* Web log reviewer Betsy Bird as the "magnificent best-wordless-book-I've-seen-in-years," *The Boys* follows a young lad as he moves to a new city and takes his baseball bat and glove to a nearby park in the hopes of making new friends. Shyly, he sits on a bench and watches the neighborhood children play, while a group of old men seated nearby observe him. Every day the boy returns, making small moves toward fitting in, until the old men decide to get up off their park benches and start a baseball game of their own. In addition to a minimal text—the days of the week—Newman's story is brought to life in what *Booklist* critic Todd Morning described as "retro-style pictures" featuring a minimalist palette. Although several critics noted that the unsaid story in *The Boys* might be better appreciated by adults that by children, a *Kirkus Reviews* writer asserted that Newman's evocative story captures "sports' deep truths about acceptance" and "a willingness to try." *The Boys* "shows a mastery of art and heart that would be difficult for any author/illustrator to capture in just 40 pages," concluded Bird, the critic deeming the book "Brilliant brilliant brilliant."

In an interview with Julia Donaldson on the *Seven Impossible Things before Breakfast* Web log, Newman explained that *The Boys* "started with a drawing of a boy dressed as an old man. Based on that character, I wrote a rough draft of a story that vaguely resembles the one in the published book. Except that it had words. Lots of words, and they weren't very good. So, I decided to take all of them out. And that made it much better."

## Biographical and Critical Sources

### PERIODICALS

*Booklist*, December 15, 2009, Todd Morning, review of *The Boys*, p. 43.
*Horn Book*, July-August, 2006, Kitty Flynn, review of *Hippo! No, Rhino*, p. 427.
*Kirkus Reviews*, June 1, 2006, review of *Hippo! No, Rhino*, p. 577; February 15, 2010, review of *The Boys*.
*Publishers Weekly*, November 17, 2003, review of *Reginald*, p. 62; July 10, 2006, review of *Hippo! No, Rhino!*, p. 80; January 11, 2010, review of *The Boys*, p. 47.
*School Library Journal*, December, 2003, Marianne Saccardi, review of *Reginald*, p. 122; July, 2006, Carol L. Mackay, review of *Hippo! No, Rhino*, p. 84; January, 2010, Ieva Bates, review of *The Boys*, p. 80.

### ONLINE

*Fuse 8 Production Web log*, http://blog.schoollibrary journal.com/afuse8production/ (January 28, 2010), Betsy Bird, review of *The Boys*.
*Jeff Newman Home Page*, http://www.newmanpictures. com (March 20, 2011).
*Jeff Newman Web log*, http://newmanpicturesblog.blogspot. com (March 20, 2011).
*Seven Impossible Things Web log*, http://blaine.org/seven imposssiblethings/ (February 15, 2010), Julia Danielson, interview with Newman.*

\*            \*            \*

## O'CONNOR, George 1973-

### Personal
Born November 5, 1973, in NY.

### Addresses
*Home*—Brooklyn, NY. *E-mail*—geooco@gmail.com.

### Career
Author and cartoonist.

### Writings

#### SELF-ILLUSTRATED

*Kapow!*, Simon & Schuster (New York, NY), 2004.
*Ker-Splash!*, Simon & Schuster (New York, NY), 2005.

*Sally and the Some-Thing*, Roaring Brook Press (New Milford, CT), 2006.
*Uncle Bigfoot*, Roaring Book Press (New Milford, CT), 2008.

#### SELF-ILLUSTRATED; "OLYMPIANS" SERIES

*Zeus: King of the Gods*, First Second (New York, NY), 2010.
*Athena: Grey-eyed Goddess*, First Second (New York, NY), 2010.
*Hera: The Goddess and Her Glory*, First Second (New York, NY), 2011.
*Hades: The Wealthy One*, First Second (New York, NY), 2011.

#### ILLUSTRATOR

Deborah Abela, *Spyforce Revealed* ("Max Remy, Super Spy" series), Random House Australia (Milsons Point, New South Wales, Australia), 2002, published as *Mission: Spyforce Revealed*, Simon & Schuster (New York, NY), 2005.
Deborah Abela, *The Nightmare Vortex* ("Max Remy, Super Spy" series), Random House Australia (Milsons Point, New South Wales, Australia), 2003, published as *Mission: The Nightmare Vortex*, Simon & Schuster (New York, NY), 2005.
Deborah Abela, *In Search of the Time and Space Machine* ("Max Remy, Super Spy" series), Random House Australia (Milsons Point, New South Wales, Australia), 2003, published as *Mission: In Search of the Time and Space Machine*, Simon & Schuster (New York, NY), 2005.
Deborah Abela, *Hollywood* ("Max Remy, Super Spy" series), Random House Australia (Milsons Point, New South Wales, Australia), 2003, published as *Mission: Hollywood*, Simon & Schuster (New York, NY), 2007.
(And adaptor) H.M. van den Bogaert, *Journey into Mohawk Country*, First Second (New York, NY), 2006.
Michael Simmons, *Alien Feast: Chronicles of the First Invasion*, Roaring Brook Press (New York, NY), 2009.
Adam Rapp, *Ball Peen Hammer*, First Second (New York, NY), 2009.

### Sidelights
Brooklyn-based artist George O'Connor is a cartoonist and illustrator whose work has been featured in graphic novels such as "Adam Rapp's surreal *Ball Peen Hammer* and Michael Simmons' humorous *Alien Feast: Chronicles of the First Invasion*, as well as in Australian author Deborah Abela's "Max Remy, Super Spy" novel series. In addition to bringing to life stories by other writers, O'Connor has also produced original picture books such as *Kapow!, Sally and the Some-Thing*, and *Uncle Bigfoot*. In his twelve-volume "Olympians" graphic-novel series, he also takes on a particularly ambitious goal: inspiring a generation tuned to television and computer games with an interest in classical Greek myths.

*George O'Connor follows a group of energetic siblings during an busy day in his self-illustrated* **Ker-Splash!** (Copyright © 2005 by George O'Connor. Reprinted with the permission of Simon & Schuster Books for Young Readers, an imprint of Simon & Schuster's Children's Publishing Division.)

Rooted in O'Connor's love of comic books, *Kapow!* and *Ker-Splash!* introduce a trio of imaginative youngsters who realize their dreams of becoming superheroes. Transforming themselves into American Eagle, Rubber Bandit, and Bug Lady, the three siblings seek out challenges wherever they find them. In a review of *Kapow!* for the *New York Times,* Jake Coburn praised O'Connor's story as a "lush, rambunctious ride through a hyperactive young mind," and noted of the book's colorful illustrations: "After seeing these enchanting watercolors and explosive acrylic action scenes, young readers may decide to turn in their capes for crayons." O'Connor "draws dramatic comics with authority and humor," asserted a *Publishers Weekly* contributor, while Steven Engelfried wrote in *School Library Journal* that *Kapow!* gives readers "an appealing splash of adventure, neatly placed within the recognizable world of children's daily lives."

*Ker-Splash!,* which finds the three secret superheroes spending a day at the beach, shares the same imaginative dual narrative. "The switches between daily life and a vividly realized imaginary world are easy to follow," wrote *School Library Journal* critic Joy Fleishhacker of the sequel, "and the action-packed presentation eases the lesson on sibling relationships."

O'Connor tells other fanciful stories in his comic-book-style picture books *Sally and the Some-Thing* and *Uncle Bigfoot.* In the first work, when a pragmatic young girl meets . . . , well, some thing, during her trip to a local fishing pond, she decides to overlook the creature's monstrous appearance and blue tongue and appreciate its company. The young boy who stars in *Uncle Bigfoot* must decide what to do after he becomes convinced that his uncle Bernie is actually a Bigfoot-type monster. "Young listeners are sure to enjoy Sally's tentative first steps toward friendship," predicted Kay Weisman in a *Booklist* review of *Sally and the Some-Thing*, and in *School Library Journal* Julie Roach noted that O'Connor's "snappy text and comic pacing make this an ideal read-aloud for generating laughs." Noting the humor in *Uncle Bigfoot,* Susan Weitz wrote in the same periodical that "O'Connor is a sardonic, imaginative, and exuberant illustrator" whose "homey artwork is filled with delightful touches," and in *Booklist* Jesse Karp dubbed the picture book "a lighthearted, enjoyable read for all."

In his "Olympians" books, O'Connor hooks young readers with the premise that the Greek pantheon of gods was actually the world's first roster of super heroes. His own interest in Greek myths was sparked during middle school, as he explained on his Olympians Web site. "I was home sick from school one day, and my parents brought me a copy of 'The Mighty Thor,' published by

*A feisty but lonely young girl meets an unusual new friend in O'Connor's self-illustrated graphic novel* **Sally and the Some-Thing.** (Roaring Brook Press, 2006. Illustration © 2006 by George O'Connor. Reproduced by permission of Henry Holt & Company, LLC. All rights reserved.)

Marvel Comics. The art was weird and wonderful, and I remember staring at it, trying to comprehend whether I loved it or hated it. The story was full of all those enormous, bigger-than-life beasts I remembered from my copy of Edith Hamilton's *Mythology*. I had always loved comics, but that copy of 'Thor,' with its gods and monsters and lightning and drama, changed what comics could be for me."

In each book in his "Olympians" series, O'Connor focuses on a separate god, retelling his or her story in a unique version based on his research into primary documents. In *Zeus: King of the Gods*, for example, readers follow the chief god of Olympus from his childhood to his rise to power. The goddess of war and wisdom is brought to life in *Athena: Grey-eyed Goddess*, while the other inhabitants of Mount Olympus are introduced in books that include *Hera: The Goddess and Her Glory* and *Hades: The Wealthy One*. Reviewing the ongoing series in *Booklist*, Ian Chipman praised O'Connor's approach to his time-honored characters as "well researched, synthesized and presented," adding that with the "superhero appeal" of the "Olympians" books

*O'Connor introduces young readers to the world of Greek myth in a series of graphic novels that include Zeus,* **King of the Gods.** (Copyright © 2010 by George O'Connor. Reprinted by permission of Henry Holt & Company, LLC.)

"can't come out fast enough." His "necessarily episodic" tale in *Athena* transitions "lightly from one narrative to another," according to a *Publishers Weekly* critic, while "endnotes . . . give concise and clear explanations of the myths and their characters." In *School Library Journal* Paula Willey cited O'Connor's use of a "sophisticated color palette" and wrote that his "drawings, full of energetic diagonals and expressive faces, are nicely balanced by spare settings and minimalistic backgrounds." Dubbing *Zeus* the "ultimate superhero story," Barbara M. Moon predicted in her *School Library Journal* review that the opening "Olympians" graphic novel "will appeal to anyone who enjoys Greek mythology or great comic art."

In *Journey into Mohawk Country* O'Connor combines his talent for art with yet another interest: the history of his native New York. Based on the 1634 narrative of Harmen Meyndertsz van den Bogaert, a twenty-three-year-old Dutch surgeon, *Journey into Mohawk Country* recounts Bogaert's trek from the southern tip of Manhattan Island through the lands controlled by the Mohawk tribe and considered the most important trade routes in the region. Together with his companions, the Dutchman exchanges tools, knives, and guns for furs as well as the necessary food and shelter, while also attempting to develop trade relationships between the Dutch and Native Americans living in what is now New York State.

The task of transforming the seventeenth-century journal into a graphic novel required O'Connor to not only create original characters, but also to research the clothing, weapons, lifestyle habits, and setting of actual historic characters. "More than simply illustrating the account, O'Connor fills it with a new life," concluded Karp in a review of *Journey into Mohawk Country* for *Booklist*, and a *Kirkus Reviews* writer called the graphic novel "an example of the kind of work that will engage younger teens and spark interest in a potentially dull and little-known segment of American history."

A collaboration with playwright and filmmaker Adam Rapp, *Ball Peen Hammer* allowed O'Connor to stretch as an artist, adopting a more highly detailed, realistic style of drawing to capture the horrific claustrophobia of Rapp's apocalyptic story. *Ball Been Hammer* takes place in New York City after a plague hits, leaving human society in shambles and with few survivors. One man, the musician Welton, has survived by isolating himself in the basement of his apartment building, emerging only to dispose of the corpses of children who have been murdered. Now infected with the disease, Welton longs for news of Exley, the woman he loves, not realizing that she is alive and living several floors above him. Other characters include Aaron, an author, the half-wild preadolescent Horlick, and a journalist named Underjohn. In bringing to life Rapp's "thought provoking" story, O'Connor creates what a *Publishers Weekly* contributor praised as "sinister, stunning artwork" that serves as "the most haunting aspect of the book." "Eminently suited to Rapp's grim and demanding vision, O'Connor's full-color art meshes with the spare text and conveys portions of the tale all by itself," maintained Francisca Goldsmith in her *Booklist* review of *Ball Peen Hammer.* In *School Library Journal* Mark Flowers asserted that, with lengthy sections that "unfold entirely in images," Rapp and O'Connor's collaborative tale "hit[s] home with the taut force of a good short story."

## Biographical and Critical Sources

*PERIODICALS*

*Booklist,* June 1, 2005, John Green, review of *Ker-Splash!,* p. 1822; June 1, 2006, Kay Weisman, review of *Sally and the Some-Thing,* p. 88; October 15, 2006, Jesse Karp, review of *Journey into Mohawk Country,* p. 38; May 1, 2008, Kesse Karp, review of *Uncle Bigfoot,* p. 94; March 1, 2009, Francisca Goldsmith, review of *Ball Peen Hammer,* p. 33; May 15, 2009, Shelle Rosenfeld, review of *Alien Feast: Chronicles of the First Invasion,* p. 54; January 1, 2010, Ian Chipman, review of *Zeus: King of the Gods,* p. 76; May 1, 2010, Ian Chipman, review of *Athena: Grey-eyed Goddess,* p. 80.

*Bulletin of the Center for Children's Books,* November, 2006, Elizabeth Bush, review of *Journey into Mohawk Country,* p. 116.

*Horn Book,* May-June, 2009, Betty Carter, review of *Alien Feast,* p. 307.

*Kirkus Reviews,* July 1, 2004, review of *Kapow!,* p. 635; June 1, 2005, review of *Ker-Splash!,* p. 641; July 1, 2005, review of *Mission: In Search of the Time and Space Machine,* p. 729; July 15, 2005, review of *Mission: Spy Force Revealed,* p. 785; March 15, 2006, review of *Sally and the Some-Thing,* p. 297; March 1, 2008, review of *Uncle Bigfoot;* April 1, 2009, review of *Alien Feast;* December 15, 2009, review of *Zeus.*

*Kliatt,* November, 2006, George Galuschak, review of *Journey into Mohawk Country,* p. 32.

*New York Times,* January 15, 2005, Jake Coburn, review of *Kapow!*

*Publishers Weekly,* July 19, 2004, review of *Kapow!,* p. 160; July 25, 2005, review of *Mission: In Search of the Time and Space Machine,* p. 77; May 29, 2006, review of *Sally and the Some-Thing,* p. 58; February 25, 2008, review of *Uncle Bigfoot,* p. 78; May 11, 2009, review of *Alien Feast,* p. 51; August 10, 2009, review of *Ball Peen Hammer,* p. 42; February 1, 2010, review of *Zeus,* p. 52; May 3, 2010, review of *Athena,* p. 55.

*School Library Journal,* August, 2004, Steven Engelfried, review of *Kapow!,* p. 92; June, 2005, Joy Fleishacker, review of *Ker-Splash!,* p. 123; December, 2005, Terrie Dorio, review of *Mission: In Search of the Time and Space Machine,* p. 136; March, 2006, Julie Roach, review of *Sally and the Some-Thing,* p. 200; April 2006, Walter Minkel, review of *Mission: The Nightmare*

*Vortex,* p. 133; June, 2008, Susan Weitz, review of *Uncle Bigfoot,* p. 112; August, 2008, Kristin Anderson, review of *Alien Feast,* p. 133; November, 2009, Mark Flowers, review of *Ball Peen Hammer,* p. 143; March, 2010, Barbara M. Moon, review of *Zeus,* p. 186; May, 2010, Paula Willey, review of *Athena,* p. 141.

*Voice of Youth Advocates,* February, 2007, Snow Wildsmith, review of *Journey into Mohawk Country,* p. 557.

*ONLINE*

*Comic Book Resources Web site,* http://www.comicbook resources.com/ (November 27, 2009), Kiel Phegley, "Hammer-cracking Sci-Fi and Lightning-cracking Mythology."

*Comics Reporter Online,* http://www.comicsreporter.com/ (March 28, 2007), review of *Journey into Mohawk Country.*

*First Second Book Web site,* http://www.firstsecondbooks. typepad.com/ (March 28, 2007), interview with O'Connor.

*George O'Connor Web log,* http://geooco.blogspot.com (April 15, 2011).

*Macmillan Web site,* http://us.macmillan.com/ (April 15, 2011), "George O'Connor."

*Olympians Web site,* http://www.olympiansrule.com (April 15, 2011).*

\*   \*   \*

# OLIVER, Lauren 1982-

## Personal

Born November 8, 1982, in New York, NY. *Education:* University of Chicago, B.A. (philosophy and literature), 2004; New York University, M.F.A. (creative writing), 2008. *Hobbies and other interests:* Travel, cooking, writing.

## Addresses

*Home*—Brooklyn, NY. *Agent*—Stephen Barbara, Foundry Literary + Media, 33 W. 17th St., PH, New York, NY 10011. *E-mail*—laurenoliverbooks@gmail. com.

## Career

Novelist and editor. Penguin, New York, NY, editorial assistant then assistant editor of Razorbill imprint, 2007-08; freelance writer. Paper Lantern Lit (literary development company), cofounder, with Lexa Hillyer, 2010. Speaker at conferences.

## Writings

*Before I Fall,* Harper (New York, NY), 2010.
*Delirium,* HarperCollins (New York, NY), 2011.

***Lauren Oliver*** (Photograph by Jonathan Alpeyrie. Reproduced by permission.)

Author's works have been translated into over two dozen languages, including French and German.

## Adaptations

*Before I Fall* was adapted for audiobook, read by Sarah Drew, Listening Library, 2010. Both *Before I Fall* and *Delirium* were optioned for film by Fox 2000 Pictures, 2011.

## Sidelights

Lauren Oliver worked for Razorbill, a New York City publisher, just long enough to realize that what she really wanted to do was write for teen readers. With her first novel, *Before I Fall,* Oliver proved her instinct correct; the novel quickly attracted positive reviews as well as interest from the film industry. The Brooklyn-based writer has followed the success of her YA fiction debut with *Delirium,* the first novel in a proposed trilogy that includes *Pandemonium* and *Requiem.*

Oliver grew up in a household where reading and writing were part of everyday life and writing could be done just about anywhere. "As a child, after finishing a book, I would continue to write a sequel for its characters," she admitted on the HarperTeen Web site, "because I did not want to have to give them up. Somehow, this did not get me ridiculed (too badly) at school, and I managed to make real friends as well as imaginary ones." At the University of Chicago Oliver majored in philosophy and literature, and then completed the MFA program at New York University. "I've had dozens of books in various stages of completion," the writer admitted to *Publishers Weekly* interviewer Donna Freitas, "and I wrote two full adult novels, one of which had absolutely no plot. It was in the YA world where I learned about narrative tension."

Oliver demonstrates her grasp of narrative tension in *Before I Fall*, a story in which a teen spends seven days in a revolving cycle of life and death, dying at the end of every day and waking to the same opportunities that initial day provided. Senior Samantha Kingston is part

of the popular clique at Thomas Jefferson High School when she dies in a car accident on her way home from a Friday-night party. When Friday morning begins again, presenting the same possibilities and the same ultimate tragedy, Sam realizes that to be dead is to be invulnerable. During her first few go-rounds, she acts outlandishly, breaking all the rules she formerly upheld and with no regard for consequences. As the rotation continues, she begins to look beyond her clique to the other people who used to just be background noise. As Sam learns to make other choices with her final hours, she moves from what *School Library Journal* contributor Amy J. Chow described as a "snobbish, obnoxious, . . . and just plain mean" teen to a person willing to sacrifice "in order to save another life." *Before I Fall* "is a compelling book with a powerful message" about redemption, according to *Booklist* critic Krista Hutley, and in *Publishers Weekly* a reviewer deemed Oliver's debut "raw, emotional, and, at times, beautiful" as well as "heartbreaking." Praising the story as "unexpectedly rich," a *Kirkus Reviews* writer added that Oliver avoids predictability in her "quietly lyrical story of selfhood and friendship."

Oliver takes readers to the isolated coastal community of Portland, Maine, in *Delirium*, but the world that seventeen-year-old Lena Haloway inhabits is a future world in which the emotional turmoil known as romantic love has been identified by the government as a disease. Amor deliria nervosa brings myriad emotions, making those affected with it unpredictable, and society is more stable now that everyone receives a "cure" for such love the day they turn eighteen. For those who do not—the Invalid—the only choice is exile to a barren wasteland known as the Wilds. Lena lives a quiet life with her aunt, and she welcomes the cure until a meeting with the handsome and passionate Alex (an Invalid) convinces her that being exiled to the Wilds might be well worth the feelings she now has for him. With its "deft blend of realism and fantasy," *Delirium* is "irresistible," according to Daniel Kraus, the *Booklist* contributor adding that Oliver's ability to see parallels between love and other modern behavior disorders is a "masterstroke."

## Biographical and Critical Sources

*PERIODICALS*

*Booklist,* October 15, 2009, Krista Hutley, review of *Before I Fall,* p. 58; November 15, 2010, Daniel Kraus, review of *Delirium,* p. 41.
*Bookseller,* November 12, 2010, Alice O'Keeffe, interview with Oliver, p. 24.
*Bulletin of the Center for Children's Books,* April, 2010, Karen Coats, review of *Before I Fall,* p. 348.
*Kirkus Reviews,* February 15, 2010, review of *Before I Fall.*

*Publishers Weekly,* January 25, 2010, review of *Before I Fall,* p. 121; June 28, 2010, Donna Freitas, "Flying Starts," p. 22.

*School Library Journal,* April, 2010, Amy J. Chow, review of *Before I Fall,* p. 164.

*Voice of Youth Advocates,* April, 2010, Teri S. Lesesne, review of *Before I Fall,* p. 60.

*ONLINE*

*Harper Teen Web site,* http://www.harperteen.com/ (March 20, 2011), "Lauren Oliver."

*Lauren Oliver Home Page,* http://www.laurenoliverbooks. com (March 20, 2011).

*Lauren Oliver Web log,* http://laurenoliverbooks.blogspot. com (March 20, 2011).

# P

## PASQUALOTTO, Chiara 1976-

### Personal

Born 1976, in Padua, Italy. *Education:* University of Padova, degree (humanistic studies), 2000; M.A. (teaching Italian as a second language); attended Ŝkola Umêlecko-Promyslová (Academy of Arts, Architecture, and Design, Prague, Czech Republic).

### Addresses

*Home*—Padua, Italy. *E-mail*—Clairepas@yahoo.fr.

### Career

Illustrator and educator. Teacher of Italian in Paris, France, Ann Arbor, MI, and Prague, Czech Republic. *Exhibitions:* Works exhibited in Italy.

### Illustrator

M.T. Dinale and E. Duso, retellers, *Storie per imparare*, Carrocci (Rome, Italy), 2004.
Claire Hawcock, *Mine, All Mine!*, Boxer Books (London, England), 2009.

### Biographical and Critical Sources

*PERIODICALS*

*Kirkus Reviews,* October 15, 2009, review of *Mine, All Mine!*
*Publishers Weekly,* November 23, 2009, review of *Mine, All Mine!*, p. 54.
*School Library Journal,* December, 2009, Donna Atmur, review of *Mine, All Mine!*, p. 84.

*ONLINE*

*Chiara Pasqualotto Home Page,* http://www.clairepas.it (February 20, 2011).

*Chiara Pasqualotto Web log,* http://chiarapasqualotto. blogspot.com (April 1, 2011).
*Frances Lincoln Web site,* http://www.franceslincoln.com/ (April 1, 2011), "Chiara Pasqualotto."*

\* \* \*

## PEARSON, Michael Parker
## See PEARSON, Mike Parker

\* \* \*

## PEARSON, Mike Parker 1957-
## (Michael Parker Pearson)

### Personal

Born 1957, in England; partner of Karen Godden (an archaeologist). *Education:* Southampton University, B.A., 1979; Cambridge University, Ph.D., 1985.

### Addresses

*Home*—Sheffield, England. *Office*—Department of Archaeology, University of Sheffield, Northgate House, West St., Sheffield S1 4ET, England. *E-mail*—M.Parker-Pearson@Sheffield.ac.uk.

### Career

Archaeologist and educator. English Heritage, former staff archaeologist; University of Sheffield, Sheffield, England, assistant professor, beginning 1990, currently professor of archaeology. Archaeologist at digs, including Stonehenge Riverside Project; guest on television programs including *Time Team,* Channel 4, and *Stonehenge Decoded,* National Geographic Channel, and *Nova: Secrets of Stonehenge.*

### Member

Institute of Field Archaeologists, Prehistoric Society (vice president), Society of Antiquaries (fellow, beginning 1991).

## Awards, Honors

Named Archaeologist of the Year, 2010; (with others) Archaeological Research Project of the Year award, 2010, for Stonehenge Riverside Project.

## Writings

*FOR CHILDREN*

(With Marc Aronson) *If Stones Could Speak: Unlocking the Secrets of Stonehenge,* National Geographic (Washington, DC), 2010.

*OTHER*

(Editor with Colin Richards) *Architecture and Order: Approaches to Social Space,* Routledge (New York, NY), 1994.

(With Niall Sharples and others) *Between Land and Sea: Excavations at Dun Vulan, South Uist,* Sheffield Academic (Sheffield, England), 1999.

*The Archaeology of Death and Burial,* Texas A & M University Press (College Station, TX), 1999.

(With Andrew T. Chamberlain) *Earthly Remains: The History and Science of Preserved Human Bodies,* Oxford University Press (New York, NY), 2001.

(With Karen Godden) *In Search of the Red Slave: Shipwreck and Captivity in Madagascar,* Sutton (Stroud, England), 2002.

(With Naomi Field) *Fiskerton: An Iron Age Timber Causeway with Iron Age and Roman Votive Offerings: The 1981 Excavations,* Oxbow (Oakville, CT), 2003.

(Editor) *Food, Culture, and Identity in the Neolithic and Early Bronze Age* (conference proceedings), Hadrian Books (Oxford, England), 2003.

(With Niall Sharples and Jim Symonds) *South Uist: Archaeology and History of a Hebridean Island,* Tempus (Stroud, England), 2004.

(Editor with I.J.N. Thorpe) *Bronze Age Britain,* revised edition, Sterling (London, England), 2005.

(Editor with I.J.N Thorpe) *Warfare, Violence, and Slavery in Prehistory* (conference proceedings), Archaeopress (Oxford, England), 2005.

(Editor with Mats Larsson) *From Stonehenge to the Baltic: Living with Cultural Diversity in the Third Millennium BC,* Hadrian Books (Oxford, England), 2007.

Contributor to scholarly works, including *Pastoralists, Warriors, and Colonists: The Archaeology of Southern Madagascar,* Archaeopress (Oxford, English), 2010, and *Indigenous Archaeologies: A Reader on Decolonization,* edited by Margaret M. Bruchac, Sioban M. Hart, and H. Martin Wobst, Left Coast (Walnut Creek, CA), 2010. Contributor to periodicals, including *Antiquity.*

## Sidelights

Nobody can claim a more intimate knowledge of England's Salisbury Plain than can Mike Parker Pearson, an archeologist and a professor at the University of Sheffield whose work excavating Stonehenge has revealed new insights into a monument that dates to 250 BCE. In addition to appearing in films discussing his work—which includes numerous other archeological sites in Great Britain and elsewhere—Pearson has authored several scholarly books relevant to his field, such as *Earthly Remains: The History and Science of Preserved Human Bodies* and *Bronze Age Britain.* In *In Search of the Red Slave: Shipwreck and Captivity in Madagascar,* a collaborative project with partner and fellow archaeologist Karen Godden, Pearson attempts to verify the assertions in a book first published in 1729 that purported to be the journal of a shipwrecked English sailor, while a collaboration with writer Marc Aronson produce the children's book *If Stones Could Speak: Unlocking the Secrets of Stonehenge.*

After completing his degrees at Southampton and Cambridge universities, where he earned his B.A. and Ph.D. respectively, Pearson worked for English Heritage on excavations of sites dating to Great Britain's later prehistory. As a professor at the University of Sheffield, he now oversees directs student field projects and training excavations in England and Scotland. In 2009 his Stonehenge Riverside Project uncovered "Bluestonehenge," the remains of a second stone circle close to Stonehenge. This supports Pearson's 2005 findings placing Stonehenge within a larger complex of memorials constructed in Neolithic times, likely as a means of honoring deceased ancestors.

Aronson discusses Pearson's work at Stonehenge in *If Stones Could Speak,* a book that not only describes the known history and present theories regarding the circular stone monument but also encourages middle-graders interested in archaeology to consider how many sites are still left to be discovered and explored. Although Stonehenge had long been viewed as some sort of temple due to its orientation with the heavens, Pearson started to consider another use after conversing with a colleague from Madagascar. On that island, dual temples were constructed in ancient times: a stone structure built to honor ancestors was paired with a wooden structure to honor the living. In his text, Aronson fully details Pearson's hypothesis and describes the findings that support it. His "casual style . . . effectively conveys the excitement of this research," noted *School Library Journal* contributor Caroline Tesauro, the critic adding that a wealth of colored photographs "complement the text and . . . capture what archaeology in progress looks like." *If Stones Could Speak* conveys a "sense of wonder and excitement," wrote a *Kirkus Reviews* critic, and by noting that Pearson's is but one of several theories, Aronson "urges readers to question what they see and always keep an open mind." In his *Horn Book* review of *If Stones Could Speak,* Jonathan Hunt praised the coauthors' text as both "clear and succinct," and their example of the scientific method—ask a question, construct a hypothesis, test the hypothesis, generate a theory—"should lead curious readers to more fully investigate" the work of modern-day archeologists.

## Biographical and Critical Sources

*PERIODICALS*

*Horn Book,* May-June, 2010, Jonathan Hunt, review of *If Stones Could Speak: Unlocking the Secrets of Stonehenge,* p. 102.
*Kirkus Reviews,* February 15, 2010, review of *If Stones Could Speak.*
*School Library Journal,* March, 2010, Caroline Tesauro, review of *If Stones Could Speak,* p. 171.

*ONLINE*

*National Geographic News Web site,* http://news.national geographic.com/news/ (January, 2007), Mike Parker Pearson, "Stonehenge Builders' Village: An Inside Look" (video).
*University of Sheffield Web site,* http://www.shef.ac.uk/ (March 20, 2011), "Michael Parker Pearson."*

\*  \*  \*

# PECK, Richard 1934-
## (Richard Wayne Peck)

## Personal
Born April 5, 1934, in Decantur, IL; son of Wayne Morris (a merchant) and Virginia (a dietician) Peck. *Education:* Attended University of Exeter, 1955-56; DePauw University, B.A., 1956; Southern Illinois University, M.A., 1959; further graduate study at Washington University, 1960-61. *Politics:* Republican. *Religion:* Methodist.

## Addresses
*Home and office*—New York, NY. *Agent*—Sheldon Fogelman, 155 E. 72nd St., New York, NY 10021.

## Career
Author. Southern Illinois University at Carbondale, instructor in English, 1958-60; Glenbrook North High School, Northbrook, IL, teacher of English, 1961-63; Scott, Foresman Co., Chicago, IL, textbook editor, 1963-65; Hunter College of the City University of New York and Hunter College High School, instructor in English and education, 1965-71; writer, 1971—. Assistant director, Council for Basic Education, Washington, DC, 1969-70; English-speaking Union fellow to Jesus College, Oxford, 1973; adjunct professor at Louisiana State University School of Library and Information Sciences. *Military service:* U.S. Army, 1956-58; served in Stuttgart, Germany.

## Member
Authors Guild, Authors League of America, Delta Chi.

**Richard Peck** (Photograph by Don Gallo. Reproduced by permission of Richard Peck.)

## Awards, Honors
Child Study Association of America Children's Book of the Year citations, 1970, for *Sounds and Silences,* 1971, for *Mindscapes,* and 1986, for *Blossom Culp and the Sleep of Death;* writing award, National Council for the Advancement of Education, 1971; Edgar Allan Poe Award runner-up, Mystery Writers of America, 1974, for *Dreamland Lake;* Friends of American Writers Award (older category), 1976, for *The Ghost Belonged to Me;* Edgar Allan Poe Award for best juvenile mystery novel, 1976, and Author's Award, New Jersey Institute of Technology, 1978, both for *Are You in the House Alone?; New York Times* Outstanding Book of the Year citation, 1977, for *Ghosts I Have Been;* Illinois Writer of the Year citation, Illinois Association of Teachers of English, 1977; American Library Association (ALA) Young Adult Services Division's Best of the Best Books 1970-1983 citations, for both *Are You in the House Alone?* and *Ghosts I Have Been;* Margaret A. Edwards Award for lifetime achievement in writing for young adults, 1990; Newbery Medal honorable mention, 1998, for *A Long Way from Chicago;* Newbery Medal, 2001, for *A Year down Yonder;* National Humanities Medal, 2001; National Book Award nomination, 2003, and Scott O'Dell Award for Historical Fiction, 2004, both for *The River between Us;* Jeremiah Ludington Memorial Award, 2004; *ALAN* Award, 2005; numerous selections as ALA Best Books for Young Adults, *School Library Journal* Best Books for Young Adults, and New York Library Books for the Teen Age.

# Writings

*FICTION; FOR CHILDREN AND YOUNG ADULTS*

*Don't Look and It Won't Hurt,* Holt (New York, NY), 1972.

*Through a Brief Darkness,* Viking (New York, NY), 1973.

*Dreamland Lake,* Holt (New York, NY), 1973, reprinted, Dell (New York, NY), 1990.

*Representing Super Doll,* Viking (New York, NY), 1974.

*The Ghost Belonged to Me,* Viking (New York, NY), 1975.

*Are You in the House Alone?* (with teacher's guide), Viking (New York, NY), 1976.

*Ghosts I Have Been* (sequel to *The Ghost Belonged to Me*), Viking (New York, NY), 1977.

*Monster Night at Grandma's House,* illustrations by Don Freeman, Viking (New York, NY), 1977.

*Father Figure,* Viking (New York, NY), 1978.

*Secrets of the Shopping Mall,* Delacorte (New York, NY), 1979.

*Close Enough to Touch,* Delacorte (New York, NY), 1981.

*The Dreadful Future of Blossom Culp,* Delacorte (New York, NY), 1983.

*Remembering the Good Times,* Delacorte (New York, NY), 1985.

*Blossom Culp and the Sleep of Death,* Delacorte (New York, NY), 1986.

*Princess Ashley,* Delacorte (New York, NY), 1987.

*Those Summer Girls I Never Met,* Delacorte (New York, NY), 1988.

*Unfinished Portrait of Jessica,* Delacorte (New York, NY), 1991.

*Bel-Air Bambi and the Mall Rats,* Delacorte (New York, NY), 1993.

*The Last Safe Place on Earth,* Delacorte (New York, NY), 1995.

*Lost in Cyberspace,* Dial Books (New York, NY), 1995.

*The Great Interactive Dream Machine: Another Adventure in Cyberspace,* Dial Books (New York, NY), 1996.

*A Long Way from Chicago: A Novel in Stories,* Dial Books (New York, NY), 1998.

*Strays like Us,* Dial Books (New York, NY), 1998.

*A Year down Yonder,* Dial Books (New York, NY), 2000.

*Fair Weather,* Dial Books (New York, NY), 2001.

*The River between Us,* Dial Books (New York, NY), 2003.

*The Teacher's Funeral: A Comedy in Three Parts,* Dial Books (New York, NY), 2004.

*Here Lies the Librarian* (sequel to *The Teacher's Funeral*), Dial Books (New York, NY), 2006.

*On the Wings of Heroes,* Dial Books (New York, NY), 2007.

*A Season of Gifts,* Dial Books for Young Readers (New York, NY), 2009.

*Three-quarters Dead,* Dial Books (New York, NY), 2010.

*ADULT NOVELS*

*Amanda/Miranda,* Viking (New York, NY), 1980.

*New York Time,* Delacorte (New York, NY), 1981.

*This Family of Women,* Delacorte (New York, NY), 1983.

*Voices after Midnight,* Dell (New York, NY), 1990.

*London Holiday,* Viking (New York, NY), 1998.

*EDITOR*

(With Ned E. Hoopes) *Edge of Awareness: Twenty-five Contemporary Essays,* Dell (New York, NY), 1966.

*Sounds and Silences: Poetry for Now,* Delacorte (New York, NY), 1970.

*Mindscapes: Poems for the Real World,* Delacorte (New York, NY), 1971.

*Leap into Reality: Essays for Now,* Dell (New York, NY), 1972.

*Urban Studies: A Research Paper Casebook,* Random House (New York, NY), 1973.

*Transitions: A Literary Paper Casebook,* Random House (New York, NY), 1974.

*Pictures That Storm inside My Head* (poetry anthology), Avon (New York, NY), 1976.

*OTHER*

(With Norman Strasma) *Old Town, A Complete Guide: Strolling, Shopping, Supping, Sipping,* 2nd edition, [Chicago, IL], 1965.

(With Mortimer Smith and George Weber) *A Consumer's Guide to Educational Innovations,* Council for Basic Education (Washington, DC), 1972.

(With Stephen N. Judy) *The Creative Word 2,* Random House (New York, NY), 1974.

*Write a Tale of Terror,* Book Lures, 1987.

*Anonymously Yours* (autobiography), Messner (Englewood Cliffs, NJ), 1991.

*Life and Death at the Mall: Teaching and Writing for the Literate Young,* Delacorte (New York, NY), 1994.

*Invitations to the World: Reflections on Teaching and Writing for Young Adults,* Dial Books (New York, NY), 2002.

*Past Perfect, Present Tense: New and Collected Stories,* Dial Books (New York, NY), 2004.

Author of column on historic architecture for *New York Times.* Contributor to books, including *Literature for Today's Young Adults,* edited by Kenneth L. Donelson and Alleen Pace Nilsen, Scott, Foresman, 1980; *Sixteen: Short Stories by Outstanding Young Adult Writers,* edited by Donald R. Gallo, Delacorte, 1984; *Visions: Nineteen Short Stories by Outstanding Writers for Young Adults,* edited by Gallo, Delacorte, 1987; and *Connections: Short Stories by Outstanding Writers for Young Adults,* edited by Gallo, Delacorte, 1989. Contributor of poetry to anthologies and to *Saturday Review* and *Chicago Tribune Magazine.* Contributor of articles to periodicals, including *American Libraries, PTA Magazine,* and *Parents' Magazine.*

A collection of Peck's papers from 1972-91 are housed at the University of Southern Mississippi.

# Adaptations

Audiocassette versions of Peck's books include *The Ghost Belonged to Me,* Live Oak Media, 1976, *Don't Look and It Won't Hurt* (filmstrip with cassette), Random House, *Remembering the Good Times* (cassette), Listening Library, 1987, and *Here Lies the Librarian,* Puffin, 2007. Television movies based on his books include *Are You in the House Alone?,* CBS, 1977; *Child of Glass* (based on *The Ghost Belonged to Me*), Walt Disney Productions, 1979; *Father Figure,* Time-Life Productions, 1980; and *Gas Food Lodging* (based on *Don't Look and It Won't Hurt,* 1991.

## Sidelights

The author of young-adult novels that have won critical praise for their realism and emotional power, Richard Peck focuses on such important adolescent issues as suicide, unwanted pregnancy, the death of a loved one, and rape. In award-winning stories that include *The River between Us, A Long Way from Chicago: A Novel in Stories,* and *A Year down Yonder,* Peck introduces characters whos ability to face challenges help young readers develop their own self-confidence. He has also written adult novels that show men and women who are not confined to roles that traditionally belong to their gender.

When writing for young adults, Peck thinks about potential readers. "As I'm typing I'm trying to look out over the typewriter and see faces," he told Roger Sutton in a *School Library Journal* interview. "I don't certainly want to 'write for myself' because I'm trying to write across a generation gap." As he told Jean F. Mercier in *Publishers Weekly,* he tries to "give readers leading characters they can look up to and reasons to believe that problems can be solved." The excellence of Peck's work has been recognized by numerous awards, including the 1990 American Library Association's Young-Adult Author Achievement Award, the 2001 National Humanities Medal, and the 2001 Newbery Medal, the last two for *A Year down Yonder.*

Peck became familiar with contemporary adolescent problems while teaching high school. He liked his students, but after several years became discouraged and quit; teaching "had begun to turn into something that looked weirdly like psychiatric social work," as he later recalled. Peck decided instead to write books for teenagers that featured the problems he had seen. "Ironically, it was my students who taught me to be a writer, though I had been hired to teach *them,*" he said in a speech published in *Arkansas Libraries.* "They taught me that a novel must entertain first before it can be anything else." He observed that young adults are most concerned with winning approval from their peers and they seek reassurance from their reading material. He believes that, in an effective young-adult novel, typically "the reader meets a worthy young character who takes one step nearer maturity, and he or she takes that step independently."

Peck's first novel, *Don't Look and It Won't Hurt,* is about adolescent pregnancy. Knowing that teens do not identify with main characters they view as losers, he tells his story of alienation and healing from the viewpoint of the teen mother's younger sister. This fifteen year old manages to keep her troubled family together, "parenting" her parents in a role reversal that appeals to readers of this age group. She is also helpful in supporting her sister's decision to give her baby up for adoption. *Don't Look and It Won't Hurt* received much critical praise and became a popular success.

Peck's controversial novel about a teenage girl who is raped, *Are You in the House Alone?,* received the Edgar Allan Poe Award in 1976. Zena Sutherland, writing in the *Bulletin of the Center for Children's Books,* was impressed by the novel's scope, writing that the author "sees clearly both society's problem and the victim's: the range of attitudes, the awful indignity, the fear and shame that is part of this kind of crime." Peck recalled in his Newbery Medal acceptance speech (as published in *Horn Book*), "I did not write the novel to tell the young about rape. They already know what that is." Instead, he wrote *Are You in the House Alone?* to warn

*Cover of Peck's middle-grade thriller* Are You in the House Alone?, *winner of the Edgar Allan Poe Mystery Award.* (Cover copyright © 1989 by Dell Books. Reproduced by permission of Dell Books, a division of Random House, Inc.)

the young that criminals are regrettably sometimes treated with more respect than victims even though victims of crime live in the shadow of that experience for the rest of their lives. Alix Nelson, writing in the *New York Times Book Review,* commended Peck for reaching his audience and for teaching them about a topic that most adults in their lives likely avoid.

In his "Blossom Culp" books Peck mixes humor and the supernatural. Set in the years 1913 and 1914, the series features spirited young Blossom Culp, who makes her own rules for life and has psychic powers. In both *The Ghost Belonged to Me* and *Ghosts I Have Been* Blossom is revealed as a strong and resourceful young heroine. Through the use of time-travel devices, readers are introduced to ancient Egypt and the women's suffrage movement in *Blossom Culp and the Sleep of Death.* The ghost characters in the "Culp" books are "distinct and memorable," wrote a contributor in the *St. James Guide to Young-Adult Writers.* Past and future are also blended with ease in Peck's science-fiction-influenced novels *Lost in Cyberspace* and *The Great Interactive Dream Machine: Another Adventure in Cyberspace.*

*Close Enough to Touch,* a love story written in response to a young man's request that Peck should write a book about dating, is "*told by a boy,*" as the author noted in his Newbery acceptance speech. "It might please some boys to be given this voice. It might surprise some girls that boys have emotions too. Mother never told them. Mothers are still telling daughters that boys only want one thing. How wrong they are. Boys want a great deal." When the teen narrator's first-ever girlfriend dies, he suddenly has to cope with the fact that, just as no one had prepared him for intimacy with the opposite sex, no one has prepared him to face grief. "There is no sexual content in this book," Peck continued. "This is a novel about the emotions, not the senses."

Peck believes that American attitudes about public education have discouraged young people instead of equipping them for survival in the real world. He asserted in his speech that, fortunately, another America exists—an America revealed through its literature. "This America is one of self-reliance and coming from behind," he noted; "of characters who learn to accept the consequences of their actions; of happy endings worked for and almost achieved; of being young in an old world and finding your way in it; of a nation of people hasty and forgetful but full still of hope; of limitless distances and new beginnings and starting over; of dreams like mountaintops, and rivers that run to the sea. We owe our young this record of our dreams."

Peck's sense of responsibility for conveying such dreams energizes his novels *A Long Way from Chicago* and its companion volumes *A Year down Yonder* and *A Season of Gifts,* all which realistically portray women in periods of social change and fluctuating social roles. In the seven related short stories in *A Long Way from*

*Cover of Peck's historical novel* **A Long Way from Chicago,** *featuring artwork by Steve Cieslawski.* (Illustration copyright © 1998 by Steve Cieslawski. Used by permission of Dial Books for Young Readers, a division of Penguin Young Readers Group, a member of Penguin Group (USA) Inc.)

*Chicago,* Chicago residents Joey and his younger sister travel each summer from 1929 to 1935 to visit their grandmother in a small Illinois town. Rifle-toting Grandma Dowdel, Peck's central character, is a strong and memorable figure who poaches catfish, brews her own beer, and delights in outsmarting her adversaries. Narrated by fifteen-year-old Mary Alice, Grandma's granddaughter, *A Year down Yonder* offers an engaging mix of "wit, gentleness, and outrageous farce," according to *Booklist* contributor Hazel Rochman. As Gerry Larson wrote in his review of the Newbery Medal-winning book for *School Library Journal,* in *A Year down Yonder* "Peck has created a delightful, insightful tale that resounds with a storyteller's wit, humor, and vivid description."

Two decades pass in Grandma Dowel's life between *A Year down Yonder* and *A Season of Gifts,* but at age ninety the woman is still as feisty and outspoken as ever. She is captured this time through the narration of her young neighbor, eleven-year-old Bobby Barnhart. The son of the town's new Methodist minister, Bobby quicky attracted the attention of a group of young bullies, and he is returning from a humiliating taunting when he encounters the elderly Mrs. Dowel. In addition to giving the young boy practical and time-honored advice—get even—Mrs. Dowel impresses Bobby and his sisters with her outspokenness, independence, and determination. Praising *A Season of Gifts* in *Booklist,* Carolyn Phelan cited the author's "vivid character portrayals, dry wit, economical writing style, and convincing depictions" of life in small-town Midwest America, while a *Publishers Weekly* critic wrote that Grandma Dowel's "actions exude as much warmth and wisdom as they do hilarity." Noting the pleasure of encountering Peck's engaging elderly character once more, Teri Markson added in *School Library Journal* that *A Season of Gifts* welcomes readers to "a place where the folksy wisdom and generosity of one gruff old woman can change lives."

Peck's strong sense of community has consistently infused his works of historical fiction, and it has only become stronger as time has distanced him from the world of his childhood. "I'm reaching the age of nostalgia now," the author told *Publishers Weekly* interviewer Jennifer M. Brown, "when my beginnings are more vivid to me than all the years between. I realize now

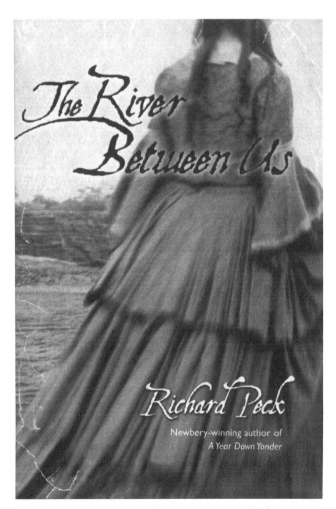

*Cover of Peck's historical novel* The River between Us, *featuring artwork by Kim McGillivray.* (Cover illustration copyright © 2003 by Kim McGillivray. Used by permission of Dial Books for Young Readers, a division of Penguin Young Readers Group, a member of Penguin Group (USA) Inc.)

what a tremendous advantage it was to grow up where and when I did, with all races, ethnicities, and age groups jumbled together. It was the most nearly democratic place I ever lived." Capturing the mix of cultures of this earlier time, *Fair Weather* follows the Beckett family on its whirlwind visit to the 1893 Chicago World's Columbian Exposition. "Peck's unforgettable characters, cunning dialogue and fast-paced action will keep readers of all ages in stitches as he captures a colorful chapter in American history," concluded a *Publishers Weekly* critic in reviewing *Fair Weather.*

A young man explores his family's complex history in *The River between Us.* The novel opens in 1916, as Howard Hutchings travels with his family to Grand Tower, Illinois, where Howard's paternal grandparents, great-aunt, and great-uncle all await them. The narrative then shifts to 1861, as Tilly Pruitt, Howard's grandmother, recalls the day two enigmatic women arrived in Grand Tower via steamboat, encountering a local population divided by the events of the U.S. Civil War. The wealthy and beautiful Delphine Duval and her companion, the younger, darker-skinned Calinda, are taken in by the Pruitt family, although the women's relationship confounds the townspeople. When Noah Pruitt, Tilly's brother, joins the Union army and is wounded in battle, Tilly and Delphine are sent to bring him home, a secret is revealed, and the journey changes both their lives forever. In *The River between Us* "Peck masterfully describes the female Civil War experience, the subtle and not-too-subtle ways the country was changing, and the split in loyalty that separated towns and even families," noted *School Library Journal* contributor Connie Tyrell Burns. Hazel Rochman, reviewing the work in *Booklist,* stated that the author's "spare writing has never been more eloquent than in this powerful mystery in which personal secrets drive the plot and reveal the history." For this effort, Peck received the Scott O'Dell Award for Historical Fiction.

In *The Teacher's Funeral: A Comedy in Three Parts* "Peck fully and gracefully describes the family life of an era gone by," observed *Kliatt* reviewer Janis Flint-Ferguson. Set in 1904, the story is narrated by Russell Culver, a rural Indiana teen whose older sister, Tansy, takes charge of Russell's one-room schoolhouse after the death of the local schoolteacher. Despite the chaos created by her energetic young charges—including a fire in the privy and a snake hidden in her desk—Tansy manages the classroom effectively and offers her students hope for the future. "Following the tradition of Mark Twain, Peck gently pokes fun at social manners and captures local color while providing first-rate entertainment," stated a reviewer in *Publishers Weekly.* "Best of all," remarked *Booklist* contributor Phelan, "the dry wit and unpretentious tone" in *The Teacher's Funeral* "make the story's events comical, its characters memorable, and its conclusion unexpectedly moving."

Peck returns to the rural Midwest setting of *The Teacher's Funeral* in *Here Lies the Librarian.* The year is now 1914 and newfangled automobiles are taking the place of the horse and buggy. Gas-station operator Jake McGrath and his fourteen-year-old tomboy sister Eleanor—called PeeWee—are particularly aware of the growing popularity of the new invention. PeeWee takes little notice when a group of do-gooders decides to rebuild the town's library following a tornado; she is much more interested in helping Jack build his racing car. Soon, the pretty young women who come to staff the new library begin introducing the motherless girl to flouncy dresses and feminine airs, and although PeeWee rethinks her own self-image as a girl, she maintains her independence from typical roles when her brother needs her. Calling *Here Lies the Librarian* a "lively story," *Kliatt* reviewer Carol Reich added that the author's "feminist message won't be lost on readers, who will enjoy the [plot's] action." In *School Library Journal,* Tricia Melgaard called Peck "a master at creating enchanting characters," noting that "even his dead librarian has personality."

Peck casts *On the Wings of Heroes* with his typical multigenerational cast of colorful characters. Set in the Midwest during World War II, the novel introduces Davy Bowman and his hard-working family. The patriotic Bowmans join many of their fellow Americans in living modestly during wartime, and Davy collects tin cans and other scrap metal to recycle into armaments. He also collects milkweed pods for use inside life jackets. His efforts to gather materials to support the war effort lead Davy into relationships with several elderly neighbors, and these new friendships, as well as his brother's Bill's deployment to Europe as an Air Force cadet, causes the boy to change his view of the world. "Chock full of eccentric characters and poignant moments, *On the Wings of Heroes* "will be embraced by children and grownups alike," according to a *Publishers Weekly* contributor, while in *School Library Journal* Lee Bock deemed it "an absolute delight." Noting that "no one does nostalgia better than Peck," *Booklist* critic Michael Cart explained that Peck's "abundant, affectionate references" to the popular culture of the War era "help evoke . . . a time very different from today."

Peck turns to the paranormal in his novel *Three-quarters Dead,* a story that "captures the extremes of joy and dread, belonging and ostracism that are at the core of the high-school experience," according to a *Publishers Weekly* critic. The novel is also notable as the first story by Peck that is set in the contemporary world of his readers. In the story, fifteen-year-old narrator Kerry Williamson and her family have just moved to the suburbs. As the new girl at Pondfield High School, Kerry is pleasantly surprised when she is accepted into the clique of most popular upper-grade girls. Soon she finds herself the acolyte of seniors Natalie, Tanya, and Makenzie, a trio that basically controls Pondfield's social life through their good looks and bad attitudes. After the three queen bees are killed in a car accident, Kerry mourns the loss of being a somebody, until her life—and Peck's story—takes a dark and surprising

turn. In *Publishers Weekly* the critic predicted that *Three-quarters Dead* will keep teens transfixed "to the very end," while in *Horn Book* Dean Schneider maintained that by melding Kerry's problems "in the shrouds of a ghost story" Peck transforms the novel into "a creepy tale middle-school girls will die for . . . if they put down their cell phones long enough to read it."

In his Newbery Medal acceptance speech Peck observed: "Powerful forces divorce the young from their roots and traditions. . . . We writers and librarians, we people of the word, spot for survivors in a generation who have learned the wrong lesson from their elementary-school years; that yes, you should be able to read and write; yes, you should be literate. But if you're not, you will be accommodated."

When asked about what he hopes to accomplish with his writing for young adults, Peck told Sutton: "I don't know what books can do, except one point is that I wish every kid knew that fiction can be truer than fact, that it isn't a frivolous pastime unless your reading taste

*Peck takes readers on an enjoyable ride in his middle-grade novel* **A Season of Gifts,** *featuring artwork by Chris Riddell.* (Puffin Books, 2010. Cover art and lettering © by Chris Riddell. Reproduced with permission of Penguin Young Readers Group.)

is for the frivolous. I wish they knew that being literate is a way of being successful in any field. I wish they all wanted to pit their own experience against the experiences they see in books." "But in books you reach an awful lot of promising kids who write back good literate letters and give you hope," Peck concluded. "So that's the hope I have."

## Biographical and Critical Sources

*BOOKS*

*Beacham's Guide to Literature for Young Adults,* Beacham (Osprey, FL), Volume 1, 1990, Volume 6, 1994, Volume 8, 1994, Volume 11, Gale (Detroit, MI), 2001.

*Children's Literature Review,* Volume 15, Gale (Detroit, MI), 1988.

*St. James Guide to Young-Adult Writers,* St. James Press (Detroit, MI), 1999.

*Something about the Author Autobiography Series,* Volume 2, Gale (Detroit, MI), 1986.

*Writers for Young Adults,* Scribner (New York, NY), 1997.

*PERIODICALS*

*Arkansas Libraries,* December, 1981, Richard Peck, "People of the Word," pp. 13-16.

*Book,* January, 2001, Kathleen Odean, review of *A Year down Yonder,* p. 83.

*Booklist,* September 1, 1998, Hazel Rochman, review of *A Long Way from Chicago: A Novel in Stories,* p. 113; November 15, 1999, Frances Bradburn, review of *Amanda/Miranda,* p. 615; October 15, 2000, Hazel Rochman, review of *A Year down Yonder,* p. 436; April 2001, Barbara Wysocki, review of *A Year down Yonder,* p. 92; September 1, 2001, Carolyn Phelan, review of *Fair Weather,* p. 110; September 15, 2003, review of *The River between Us,* p. 239; April 1, 2004, Hazel Rochman, review of *Past Perfect, Present Tense: New and Collected Stories,* p. 1361; October 1, 2004, Carolyn Phelan, review of *The Teacher's Funeral: A Comedy in Three Parts,* p. 326; August 1, 2006, Patricia Austin, review of *Here Lies the Librarian,* p. 101; December 1, 2006, Michael Cart, review of *On the Wings of Heroes,* p. 48; July 1, 2007, Anna Rich, review of *On the Wings of Heroes,* p. 74; August 1, 2009, Carolyn Phelan, review of *A Season of Gifts,* p. 68.

*Bulletin of the Center for Children's Books,* March, 1977, Zena Sutherland, review of *Are You in the House Alone?,* pp. 111-112.

*Christian Science Monitor,* December 1, 2009, Yvonne Zipp, review of *A Season of Gifts,* p. 25.

*Horn Book,* January, 2000, review of *Amanda/Miranda,* p. 82; November, 2000, Kitty Flynn, review of *A Year down Yonder,* p. 761; July, 2001, Richard Peck, Newbery Medal acceptance speech, p. 397, and Marc Talbert, "Richard Peck," p. 403; November-December, 2001, Kitty Flynn, review of *Fair Weather,* p. 757; September-October, 2003, Peter D. Sieruta, review of

*The River between Us,* p. 616; March-April, 2004, Betty Carter, review of *Past Perfect, Present Tense,* p. 187; September-October, 2004, Peter D. Sieruta, review of *The Teacher's Funeral,* p. 595; May-June, 2007, Betty Carter, review of *On the Wings of Heroes,* p. 287; November-December, 2007, Richard Peck, transcript of Zena Sutherland lecture, p. 617; September-October, 2009, Jonathan Hunt, review of *A Season of Gifts,* p. 573; March-April, 2010, Jennifer M. Brabander, review of *A Season of Gifts,* p. 84; September-October, 2010, Dean Scneider, review of *Three Quarters Dead,* p. 89.

*Kirkus Reviews,* August 1, 2009, review of *A Season of Gifts.*

*Kliatt,* September, 2006, Carol Reich, review of *Here Lies the Librarian,* p. 57.

*New York Times Book Review,* November 14, 1976, Alix Nelson, "Ah, Not to Be Sixteen Again," p. 29; March 11, 2001, Jim Gladstone, review of *A Year down Yonder,* p. 27; November 18, 2001, Ilene Cooper, review of *Fair Weather,* p. 45.

*Publishers Weekly,* March 14, 1980, Jean F. Mercier, interview with Peck; July 6, 1998, review of *A Long Way from Chicago,* p. 61; September 25, 2000, review of *A Year down Yonder,* p. 118; July 23, 2001, review of *Fair Weather,* p. 77; July 14, 2003, review of *The River between Us,* p. 77; July 21, 2003, Jennifer M. Brown, "A Long Way from Decatur" (interview), pp. 169-170; November 10, 2003, review of *The River between Us,* p. 38; November 1, 2004, review of *The Teacher's Funeral,* p. 63; January 8, 2007, review of *On the Wings of Heroes,* p. 52; July 13, 2009, review of *A Season of Gifts,* p. 59; September 13, 2010, review of *Three Quarters Dead,* p. 46.

*Reading Today,* October-November, 2005, Donna Marie Pocius, interview with Peck, p. 27.

*School Library Journal,* June, 1990, Roger Sutton, interview with Peck, pp. 36-40; October, 1998, Shawn Brommer, review of *A Long Way from Chicago,* p. 144; September, 2000, Gerry Larson, review of *A Year down Yonder,* p. 236; September, 2001, Kit Vaughan, review of *Fair Weather,* p. 231; September, 2003, Connie Tyrrell Burns, review of *The River between Us,* p. 218; November, 2003, Carol Fazioli, review of *Anonymously Yours,* p. 83; April, 2004, Karen Hoth, review of *Past Perfect, Present Tense,* p. 160; August, 2004, Jane P. Fenn, review of *The River between Us,* p. 78; November, 2004, Susan Riley, review of *The Teacher's Funeral,* p. 152; September, 2006, Tricia Melgaard, review of *Here Lies the Librarian,* p. 70; April, 2007, Lee Bock, review of *On the Wings of Heroes,* p. 146; July, 2007, Charlie Osborne, review of *On the Wings of Heroes,* p. 57; October, 2009, Teri Markson, review of *A Season of Gifts,* p. 134.

*ONLINE*

*Carol Hurst Children's Literature Web site,* http://www.carolhust.com/ (April 15, 2011), "Richard Peck."

*Children's Book Council Web site,* http://www.cbcbooks.org/ (July 15, 2008), "Richard Peck."

*Scholastic Web site,* http://www2.scholastic.com/ (April 15, 2011), "Richard Peck."

\*      \*      \*

## PECK, Richard Wayne
### See PECK, Richard

\*      \*      \*

## PERDOMO, Willie

### Personal

Born in New York, NY. *Education:* Attended Ithaca College.

### Addresses

*Home*—New York, NY. *E-mail*—willie@willieperdomo. com.

### Career

Spoken-word poet and author. Cypher Books, New York, NY, cofounder and publisher. Teacher at Friends Seminary and Bronx Academy of Letters; Woolrich fellow in creative writing, Columbia University; artist-in-residence at Workspace, Lower Manhattan Cultural Council.

### Awards, Honors

New York Foundation for the Arts poetry fellowship, 2001; Coretta Scott King Honor Book in Illustration designation, 2002, for *Visiting Langston* illustrated by Bryan Collier; Beyond Margins Award, PEN American Center, 2003, for *Smoking Lovely;* New York Foundation for the Arts fiction fellowship, 2006; Pushcart Prize nomination; Urban Arts Initiative grant.

### Writings

*Where a Nickel Costs a Dime* (with CD), Norton (New York, NY), 1996.
*Postcards of El Barrio* (bilingual English/Spanish text), Isla Negra Editores (San Juan, PR), 2002.
*Visiting Langston,* illustrated by Bryan Collier, Henry Holt (New York, NY), 2002.
*Smoking Lovely* (with CD), Rattapallax, 2003.
*Clemente!,* illustrated by Bryan Collier, Henry Holt (New York, NY), 2010.

Contributor to periodicals, including *Bomb, New York Times Magazine,* and *Rattapallax.* Work included in anthologies *Poems of New York, The Harlem Reader, Metropolis Found,* and *Pick-up Game: A Full Day of Full Court,* edited by Marc Aronson and Charles R. Smith, Candlewick Press (Somerville, MA), 2011.

### Sidelights

Incorporating hip-hop rhythms, Spanish words, and his experiences growing up in New York's East Harlem neighborhood, Willie Perdomo is a slam poetry performer and the author of adult poetry collections such as *Smoking Lovely* and *Where a Nickel Costs a Dime,* both of which include CD recordings of his verbal performance. With its urban focus, *Where a Nickel Costs a Dime* "bristles with congas, timbales, police sirens and wino oracles," wrote a *Publishers Weekly* critic. *Smoking Lovely* features the "pitch-perfect intonation" that makes Perdomo "a necessary and insistent voice in the current American literary scene," asserted another contributor to the periodical. In addition to his works for adults, Perdomo has also turned his generous talents to writing for younger readers, teaming with artist Bryan Collier on the picture books *Visiting Langston* and *Clemente!*

Raised in Harlem, New York, Perdomo left public school in the sixth grade when he earned a scholarship to Friends Seminary, a private Quaker school. He found establishing his place within the school's predominately white, upper-class Quaker culture to be a challenge and ended up in several schoolyard confrontations before he found mentors among the school's staff. Fortunately, a receptionist at Friends Seminary introduced the young teen to poetry and also helped him hone and refine his writing. By the time Perdomo graduated from high school and prepared for his first year at Ithaca College, his work had been acknowledged by the New York Public Library, which included his poems in one of their publications. Within the city, where he still lives, Perdomo is known through his participation on local poetry slams, competitions in which poet performers recite their works and are judged by their fellow contestants.

Illustrated by award-winning illustrator Collier, *Visiting Langston* has personal roots for Perdomo: he grew up only blocks away from the house where jazz-age poet Langston Hughes once lived. In his text he follows a young writer as she dresses up in preparation for a trip with her father to visit the Hughes house. Perdomo's rhyme is "powerful in its simplicity" as it "explores the child's special connection to the famous man," noted Alicia Eames in her *School Library Journal* review of *Visiting Langston,* while a *Publishers Weekly* critic deemed the book "an inspired—and inspiring—introduction to the legendary writer." Explaining that Perdomo's book "celebrates Hughes' legacy rather than the events of his life," Gillian Engberg noted in *Booklist* that *Visiting Langston* pairs Collier's "vibrant, sophisticated images" and the poet's "strong voice," and a *Kirkus Reviews* contributor asserted that Perdomo's "admiration for Hughes's artistry and accomplishments is clearly felt in the voice of" his "glorious child" narrator.

In *Clemente!* the poet introduces another young narrator, Clemente, whose father idolizes the Puerto-Rican-

*Willie Perdomo's picture-book biography* Clemente! *brings to life the story of baseball great Roberto Clemente in artwork by Bryan Collier.* (Illustration copyright © 2010 by Bryan Collier. Reproduced with permission from Henry Holt & Company, LLC. All rights reserved.)

born Hall-of-Fame baseball player Roberto Clemente, after whom the boy is named. Salted with evocative Spanish words, Perdomo's rhyming text captures the energy and enthusiasm of the young Clemente's family as the boy shares everything he has been told of the late athlete's life. In doing so, *Clemente!* "warmly illustrates the parent-child bond that is one of the finer by-products of sports fandom," according to *Booklist* critic Ian Chipman, while a *Kirkus Reviews* writer deemed it an "infectiously energetic tribute" to an admirable man. Marilyn Taniguchi cited Perdomo's "joyful prose" in her *School Library Journal* of the book, adding that "Collier's watercolor and collage illustrations teem with detail and vibrancy." "The joy of hero worship is on full display in this [picture-book] tribute," announced a *Publishers Weekly* contributor, and in *Clemente!* Perdomo "convey[s] a people's enormous pride in one of their own."

## Biographical and Critical Sources

### PERIODICALS

*Booklist,* February 15, 2002, Gillian Engberg, review of *Visiting Langston,* p. 1033; February 15, 2010, review of *Clemente!,* p. 73.

*Kirkus Reviews,* February 1, 2002, review of *Visiting Langston,* p. 186; February 15, 2010, review of *Clemente!*

*Publishers Weekly,* January 22, 1996, review of *Where a Nickel Costs a Dime,* p. 69; January 21, 2002, review of *Visiting Langston,* p. 89; December 22, 2003, review of *Smoking Lovely,* p. 55; May 3, 2010, review of *Clemente!,* p. 49.

*School Library Journal,* April, 2002, Alicia Eames, review of *Visiting Langston,* p. 140; April, 2010, Marilyn Taniguchi, review of *Clemente!,* p. 147.

*ONLINE*

*Willie Perdomo Home Page,* http://www.willieperdomo. com (March 20, 2011).
*Writers at Cornell Web log,* http://writersatcornell.blogspot. com/ (August 30, 2007), podcast interview with Willie Perdomo.*

*    *    *

# POON, Janice

## Personal

Born in Alberta, Canada. *Education:* Holds an art degree.

## Addresses

*Home*—Toronto, Ontario, Canada.

## Career

Graphic designer and writer. Has designed movie sets, created storyboards for animation, and worked as a fashion designer. Fine-art painter and sculptor.

## Awards, Honors

Merit Award, Annual International Cook Books and Culinary Arts, 2007, for *The Cocktail Chef;* Best Books for Kids and Teens designation, Canadian Children's Book Centre, 2009, for *Claire and the Water Wish.*

## Writings

*FOR CHILDREN*

*Claire and the Bakery Thief* (graphic novel), Kids Can Press (Tonawanda, NY), 2008.
*Claire and the Water Wish* (graphic novel), Kids Can Press (Tonawanda, NY), 2009.

*OTHER*

(With Dinah Koo) *The Dinah's Cupboard Cookbook: Recipes and Menus for Elegant Home Entertaining,* Totem Books (Toronto, Ontario, Canada), 1986.
(With Dinah Koo) *The Cocktail Chef: Entertaining in Style,* Douglas & McIntyre (Toronto, Ontario, Canada), 2007.

## Sidelights

After attending art college in Washington state, Canadian-born Janice Poon began a career as a designer, where she worked on movie sets, created storyboards for animation, and worked as a fashion designer. Poon is also a painter and sculptor, and her work has been exhibited in both the United States and Canada. While design work caused her to move frequently—from such Canadian locales as Vancouver, British Columbia, Calgary, Alberta, and Toronto, Ontario, to London, England, and Paris, France—she ultimately returned to Canada and now makes her home in Toronto. Once in Canada, Poon began coauthoring cookbooks, and has also written graphic novels for children.

Poon's first graphic novel, *Claire and the Bakery Thief,* finds Claire unhappy about having to move with her family from the city to Bellevale, a rural town that is the direct opposite of everything the girl has known and loved all her life. Her parents have initiated the move to open an organic bakery, but the stress is causing them to bicker, upsetting Claire further. Applauding the book in a *Kirkus Reviews* article, a critic noted that Poon's story "starts out as a perfectly nice bit of realistic fiction." *Quill & Quire* online contributor Jean Mills was also impressed, writing that, "while the story wavers, the illustrations never falter, depicting the action with clarity and style." Mills also praised the book's protagonist, writing that Claire "certainly has the potential to be an engaging heroine." In *Claire and the Water Wish* the girl returns in a story that *Booklist* critic Kat Kan cited for its "simple and clear black-and-white art, with expressive faces."

## Biographical and Critical Sources

*PERIODICALS*

*Booklist,* April 15, 2009, Kat Kan, review of *Claire and the Water Wish,* p. 44.
*Canadian Book Review* (annual), January 1, 2006, John R. Abbott, review of *The Cocktail Chef: Entertaining in Style,* p. 131.
*Kirkus Reviews,* March 1, 2008, review of *Claire and the Bakery Thief;* March 1, 2009, review of *Claire and the Water Wish.*
*Manitoba Library Association Bulletin,* May, 1987, Leslie McGrath, review of *The Dinah's Cupboard Cookbook: Recipes and Menus for Elegant Home Entertaining.*
*Quill & Quire,* March, 2008, Jean Mills, review of *Claire and the Bakery Thief.*
*School Library Journal,* September, 2009, Sadie Mattox, review of *Claire and the Water Wish,* p. 190.

*ONLINE*

*Cocktail Chef Web site,* http://www.cocktailchef.com (August 2, 2009).
*Cordon d'Or Cuisine Web site,* http://www.cordondor cuisine.com/ (August 2, 2009), "Janice Poon."
*Douglas & McIntyre Web site,* http://www.dmpibooks. com/ (August 2, 2009), "Janice Poon."
*Kids Can Press Web site,* http://www.kidscanpress.com/ (April 15, 2011), "Janice Poon."*

# R

## RACZKA, Bob 1963-

### Personal

Born August 24, 1963, in Chicago, IL; married June 6, 1987; wife's name Amy (a home economist); children: Robert, Carl, Emma. *Education:* University of Illinois, B.F.A. (graphic design), 1985.

### Addresses

*Home and office*—Glen Ellyn, IL. *E-mail*—bob.raczka@ yahoo.com.

### Career

Writer. Bish Creative Display, Northfield, IL, designer, 1985-87; Sears & Roebuck, Chicago, IL, advertising copywriter, 1987; Hoffman, York & Compton, Milwaukee, WI, copywriter, 1987-91; Ogilvy Chicago, creative director and writer, beginning 1991; freelance author and presenter at schools.

### Member

Society of Children's Book Authors and Illustrators.

### Writings

*"ART ADVENTURES" SERIES*

*No One Saw: Ordinary Things through the Eyes of an Artist,* Millbrook Press (Brookfield, CT), 2002.
*More than Meets the Eye: Seeing Art with All Five Senses,* Millbrook Press (Brookfield, CT), 2003.
*Art Is . . .,* Millbrook Press (Brookfield, CT), 2003.
*Unlikely Pairs: Fun with Famous Works of Art,* Millbrook Press (Minneapolis, MN), 2006.
*Here's Looking at Me: How Artists See Themselves,* Millbrook Press (Minneapolis, MN), 2006.
*Where In the World?: Around the Globe in Thirteen Works of Art,* Millbrook Press (Minneapolis, MN), 2007.

*3-D ABC: A Sculptural Alphabet,* Millbrook Press (Minneapolis, MN), 2007.
*Artful Reading,* Millbrook Press (Minneapolis, MN), 2008.
*The Art of Freedom: How Artists See America,* Millbrook Press (Minneapolis, MN), 2008.
*Name That Style: All about Isms in Art,* Millbrook Press (Minneapolis, MN), 2008.
(Editor) *Speaking of Art: Colorful Quotes by Famous Painters,* Millbrook Press (Minneapolis, MN), 2009.
*The Vermeer Interviews: Conversations with Seven Works of Art,* Millbrook Press (Minneapolis, MN), 2009.
*Action Figures: Paintings of Fun, Daring, and Adventure,* Millbrook Press (Minneapolis, MN), 2010.
*Before They Were Famous: How Seven Artists Got Their Start,* Millbrook Press (Minneapolis, MN), 2011.

*PICTURE BOOKS*

*Spring Things,* illustrated by Judy Stead, Albert Whitman (Morton Grove, IL), 2007.
*Who Loves the Fall?,* illustrated by Judy Stead, Albert Whitman (Morton Grove, IL), 2007.
*Snowy, Blowy Winter,* illustrated by Judy Stead, Albert Whitman (Morton Grove, IL), 2008.
*Summer Wonders,* illustrated by Judy Stead, Albert Whitman (Morton Grove, IL), 2009.
*Fall Mixed Up,* illustrated by Chad Cameron, Carolrhoda Books (Minneapolis, MN), 2010.
*Guyku: A Year of Haiku for Boys,* illustrated by Peter Reynolds, Houghton Mifflin Books for Children (Boston, MA), 2010.
*Lemonade, and Other Poems Squeezed from a Single Word,* illustrated by Nancy Doninger, Roaring Brook Press (New York, NY), 2011.
*Joy in Mudville: A Casey Sequel,* Carolrhoda Books (Minneapolis, MN), 2012.

### Sidelights

Having established his career as a copywriter and creative director at a Chicago-based advertising agency, Bob Raczka now shares his enthusiasm for fine art through his "Art Adventures" series of books and talks with younger children. Composed of a range of unique books that include *More than Meets the Eye: Seeing Art with All Five Senses, Unlikely Pairs: Fun with Famous Works of Art, Where in the World?: Around the Globe in Thirteen Works of Art, Name That Style: All about Isms in Art,* and *Action Figures: Paintings of Fun, Daring, and Adventure,* Raczka's series helps readers approach art and the creative life from a variety of enriching perspectives. His edited *Speaking of Art: Colorful Quotes by Famous Painters* pairs quotations from nineteenth-and twentieth-century artists alongside images representative of their work, resulting in "a clever and inspiring" book that "provide[s] insightful glimpses" into the art world, according to *School Library Journal* contributor Lisa Glasscock.

In *More than Meets the Eye* Raczka "stimulates an awareness of the breadth and diversity of art," according to Lynda Ritterman in *School Library Journal.* In the book he encourages children to experience a work of art with all five senses, thereby gaining exposure to the many dimensions of creativity contained in a single work. He also pairs brief biographies of the relevant artist with each work discussed to provide a fuller context for study. Carolyn Phelan, reviewing *More than Meets the Eye* for *Booklist,* commented that while "Raczka's short, rhyming text gives structure to the book," the color reproductions of "well-chosen, vivid paintings steal the show" to produce "a simple concept, beautifully executed."

Raczka's *No One Saw: Ordinary Things through the Eyes of an Artist* also focuses on art, this time explaining what each of a number of individual artists are known for. *Booklist* reviewer Gillian Engberg enjoyed the book, commenting that the author "gets to the heart of what artists do: create unique perspectives of the world." *School Library Journal* reviewer Rosalyn Pierini also found the book unique, writing that in *No One Saw* "the singularity of artistic vision is celebrated in [Raczka's] . . . gentle text."

In *Art Is . . .* Raczka examines twenty-seven diverse works of art, ranging from the Lascaux cave paintings to a Greek vase and a Tiffany lamp. He also discusses the works of French sculptor Auguste Rodin, African-American painter and collagist Romare Bearden, and Bulgarian-born environmental artist Christo. Writing in *School Library Journal,* Laurie Edwards called *Art Is . . .* "an interesting look at the forms art can take."

Raczka offers an unorthodox way to view artworks in *Unlikely Pairs,* then explains the fourteen terms critics and others use to pigeonhole creative approaches in *Name That Style.* In one example from *Unlikely Pairs* the author juxtaposes Rodin's sculpture "The Thinker" and Paul Klee's modernistic painting "Chessboard" to create an unusual and humorous scene. From the naturalism of the Renaissance to twentieth-century Op art and photorealism, the history, main practitioners, and identifying characteristics of each main school of West-

ern art is described and then illustrated with an example in *Name That Style,* which *Booklist* contributor Ian Chipman recommended as "an obvious choice for museum-bound children." In *School Library Journal* Donna Cardon recommended *Unlikely Pairs* to teachers and parents looking for "an amusing way to introduce children to famous works of art."

Self-portraits are the subject of Raczka's *Here's Looking at Me: How Artists See Themselves.* In the work, the author explores the techniques used by an eclectic group of Western artists, including German Renaissance engraver Albrecht Dürer, Spanish painter Francisco de Goya, French post-Impressionist Henri Rousseau, Dutch illustrator M.C. Escher, and U.S. photographer Cindy Sherman. *School Library Journal* critic Wendy Lukehart praised the work, calling it a "top-notch introduction to self-portraiture," and Phelan suggested that *Here's Looking at Me* could serve as "an intriguing starting place for children inspired (or assigned) to create their own self-portraits."

In *Where in the World?* Raczka introduces readers to Japanese artist Hokusai's prints of Mount Fuji, French artist Paul Gaugin's paintings of Tahiti, and landscape photographer Ansel Adams's studies of Mount McKinley. *Booklist* critic Hazel Rochman applauded the "chatty, interesting text offering background on the artist," and Robin L. Gibson observed in *School Li-*

*Bob Raczka's* **Artful Reading** *collects works of art that depict people of all eras in the act of reading.* (Copyright © 2008 Estate of Pablo Picasso/Artist Rights Society (ARS), New York. All rights reserved. Reproduced by permission.)

*Raczka introduces poetry to a traditionally poetry-averse audience in* Guyku: A Year of Haiku for Boys, *featuring artwork by Peter H. Reynolds.*
(Illustration copyright © 2010 by Peter H. Reynolds. Reproduced with permission of Houghton Mifflin Harcourt Publishing Company.)

*brary Journal* that the artworks "evoke a strong sense of place." Raczka looks at such celebrated twentieth-century sculptures as Marcel Duchamp's "Bicycle Wheel" and Constantin Brancusi's "The Kiss" in *3-D ABC: A Sculptural Alphabet.* The author's "strength lies in selecting images high in child appeal and combining them in fresh, provocative ways," Lukehart stated of this book.

*Artful Reading* contains a selection of paintings, among them Antonello da Messina's "St. Jerome in His Study," Jacob Lawrence's "The Library," and other works showing people enjoying the act of reading. "A delightfully delivered message appears on every page of this bright,

appealing" title, asserted a critic in reviewing the work for *Kirkus Reviews,* while Mary Jean Smith wrote in *School Library Journal* that Raczka's book affirms for technology-minded young children that "reading has engrossed humankind for centuries." Samuel Anderson Robb, John Trumbull, Georgia O'Keefe, and Judy Chicago are among the artists featured in *The Art of Freedom: How Artists See America,* a collection of eighteen paintings, photographs, and sculptures that examine the diversity of perspectives that exist in the United States. From Trumbull's "The Declaration of Independence" forward to Thomas Hart Benton's "Cradling Wheat," *The Art of Freedom* "brings history and art together," according to Rochman, and a *Kirkus Reviews* writer asserted that Raczka's "eye-catching format is brilliant" in a book "best shared by older elementary readers."

In *School Library Journal* Laura Lutz dubbed Raczka's *The Vermeer Interviews: Conversations with Seven Works of Art* a "clever art history book . . . that makes Johannes Vermeer's masterpieces accessible." Selecting seven of the Dutch artist's paintings, the author transcribes an imaginary conversation between the painter and "Bob" in which Vermeer discusses his inspiration, technique, and inspiration for each work. The "Art Adventures" series takes a boy-friendly turn in *Action Figures* as Raczka collects eighteen paintings that feature dragon slaying, sports, and other activities. By linking the works of different artists and eras with descriptive captions, the author also creates what *Booklist* critic John Peters described as "smile-worthy juxtaposition[s]" that contribute an air of whimsy to his book. "Eighteen paintings, and not a bowl of fruit in sight," quipped Glasscock in her positive *School Library Journal* appraisal of *Action Figures,* while a *Kirkus Reviews* cited the range of artists—from Paolo Ucello and Pieter Bruegel to Diego Rivera and Roy Lichtensten—in Raczka's assemblage of "movement-rich paintings that each exhibit child appeal."

In addition to his nonfiction titles, Raczka has written a number of picture books that celebrate the seasons. In *Spring Things,* for example, describes changes in the weather and a host of outdoor activities by employing gerunds such as "thunderstorming" and "lemonading." A contributor to *Kirkus Reviews* praised the "catchy rhyming text" and Phelan observed that Raczka's "apt expressions . . . are sometimes childlike or inventive." *Who Loves the Fall?,* another work told in verse, focuses on the pleasures of autumn, including picking apples, building bonfires, and preparing for Thanksgiving, while the other seasons are brought to life in *Summer Wonders* and *Snowy, Blowy Winter.* Reviewing *Summer Wonders* in *Booklist,* Phelan observed that Stead's "expressive paintings . . . sometimes seem to radiate heat," while the author's "staccato rhymes" pair with those paintings to "deliver . . . the sensory experiences of summer with pure joy," according to *School Library Journal* contributor Anne Beier. A *Kirkus Reviews* critic described *Who Loves the Fall?* as an "action-packed, rollicking book of noun-oriented rhyme," while in *Snowy, Blowy Winter* readers are treated to a "simple and bouncy" text that pairs with "cartoon illustrations [that] are bright, clear, and inclusive," according to *School Library Journal* contributor Rachael Vilmar.

Raczka collects two dozen structured short, season-spanning poems in *Guyku: A Year of Haiku for Boys,* while *Lemonade, and Other Poems Squeezed from a Single Word* pairs twenty-eight super-succinct verses with artwork by Nancy Doninger. While admitting that "nonrhyming poetry can be a tough sell for kids," *Booklist* critic Daniel Kraus was quick to add of *Guyku* that "intimidating is one thing this book is not." Praising the illustrations by Peter Reynolds that are paired

with each haiku, Joan Kindig wrote in *School Library Journal* that "artwork and . . . text dovetail beautifully and help set the inquisitive and playful intent of the poems." Also impressed with *Guyku,* a *Publishers Weekly* critic predicted that young readers will "appreciate Raczka's humor" while adults will enjoy the author's "wistful visions" of his own childhood years.

Raczka once told *SATA:* "I have always been a creative person. As a child I loved to draw and make models, and I took numerous art and writing classes in school. I studied art and advertising in college and ended up becoming an advertising writer. However, after ten years in advertising I needed a more personally fulfilling creative outlet, so I decided to try writing children's books, a field that had always impressed me with its literary and artistic talent. It took me five years to sell my first manuscript, but in the process I also found my niche: creating books that help kids to better appreciate art.

"Writing books for children is the most rewarding thing I have ever done, and I hope to build upon the small success I've had so far."

## Biographical and Critical Sources

*PERIODICALS*

*Booklist,* January 1, 2002, Gillian Engberg, review of *No One Saw: Ordinary Things through the Eyes of an Artist,* p. 861; November 1, 2003, Carolyn Phelan, review of *More than Meets the Eye: Seeing Art with All Five Senses,* p. 513; May 1, 2006, Carolyn Phelan, review of *Here's Looking at Me: How Artists See Themselves,* p. 83; November 1, 2006, Gillian Engberg, review of *3-D ABC: A Sculptural Alphabet,* p. 66; February 15, 2007, Carolyn Phelan, review of *Spring Things,* p. 86; June 1, 2007, Hazel Rochman, review of *Where in the World?: Around the Globe in Thirteen Works of Art,* p. 66; February 1, 2008, Hazel Rochman, review of *The Art of Freedom: How Artists See America,* p. 46; November 1, 2008, Ian Chipman, review of *Name That Style: All about Isms in Art,* p. 52; March 15, 2009, Carolyn Phelan, review of *Summer Wonders,* p. 67; November 1, 2009, John Peters, review of *Action Figures: Paintings of Fun, Daring, and Adventure,* p. 57; June 1, 2010, Daniel Kraus, review of *Guyku: A Year of Haiku for Boys,* p. 84.

*Daily Herald* (Arlington Heights, IL), October 3, 2003, Henry Stuttley, "Book Aims to Teach Children about Art" (profile of Raczka).

*Kirkus Reviews,* November 1, 2003, review of *More than Meets the Eye,* p. 1313; January 15, 2007, review of *Spring Things,* p. 80; August 15, 2007, review of *Who Loves the Fall?;* September 15, 2007, review of *Artful Reading;* July 15, 2008, review of *The Art of Freedom;* September 15, 2008, review of *Snowy, Blowy Winter;* October 1, 2009, review of *Action Figures.*

*Publishers Weekly,* September 20, 2010, review of *Guyku,* p. 62.

*School Arts,* February, 2003, Ken Marantz, review of *No One Saw,* p. 58; April, 2006, Rebecca J. Martin, review of *Unlikely Pairs: Fun with Famous Works of Art,* p. 62.

*School Library Journal,* January, 2002, Rosalyn Pierini, review of *No One Saw,* p. 123; October, 2003, Laurie Edwards, review of *Art Is . . .,* p. 156; January, 2004, Lynda Ritterman, review of *More than Meets the Eye,* p. 121; December, 2005, Donna Cardon, review of *Unlikely Pairs,* p. 172; June, 2006, Wendy Lukehart, review of *Here's Looking at Me,* p. 184; November, 2006, Wendy Lukehart, review of *3-D ABC,* p. 123; March, 2007, June Wolfe, review of *Spring Things,* p. 184; August, 2007, Robin L. Gibson, review of *Where in the World?,* p. 138; September, 2007, Barbara Katz, review of *Who Loves the Fall?,* p. 174; October, 2007, Mary Jean Smith, review of *Artful Reading,* p. 139; February, 2008, Heidi Estrin, review of *The Art of Freedom,* p. 108; September, 2008, Paula Willey, review of *Name That Style,* p. 210; December, 2008, Rachael Vilmar, review of *Snowy, Blowy Winter,* p. 100; May, 2009, Laura Lutz, review of *The Vermeer Interviews: Conversations with Seven Works of Art,* p. 127; June, 2009, Anne Beier, review of *Summer Wonders,* p. 98; October, 2009, Lisa Glasscock, review of *Action Figures,* p. 113; May, 2010, Lisa Glasscock, review of *Speaking of Art: Colorful Quotes by Famous Painters,* p. 100; September, 2010, Joan Kindig, review of *Guyku,* p. 139.

ONLINE

*Bob Raczka Home Page,* http://www.bobraczka.com (March 10, 2011).

*Society of Children's Book Authors and Illustrators—Illinois Web site,* http://www.scbwi-illinois.org/ (March 20, 2011), "Bob Raczka."*

\* \* \*

# REIDY, Jean

## Personal

Female; children: four.

## Addresses

*Home*—CO. *Agent*—Erin Murphy Literary Agency, Flagstaff, AZ. *E-mail*—reidy.jean@gmail.com.

## Career

Author of books for children. Freelance writer; presenter at schools.

## Member

Society of Children's Book Writers and Illustrators.

## Writings

*Too Pickley!,* illustrated by Geneviève Leloup, Bloomsbury Children's Books (New York, NY), 2010.

*Too Purpley!,* illustrated by Geneviève Leloup, Bloomsbury (New York, NY), 2010.

*Light up the Night,* illustrated by Margaret Chodos-Irvine, Disney Hyperion (New York, NY), 2011.

*There's a Corner in My House,* illustrated by Robert Neubecker, Disney Hyperion (New York, NY), 2012.

*Too Princessy!,* illustrated by Geneviève Leloup, Bloomsbury (New York, NY), 2012.

*All through the Town,* illustrated by Leo Timmers, Bloomsbury Children's Books (New York, NY), 2012.

Contributor to periodicals, including *Christian Science Monitor, Denver Post, Rocky Mountain News, Twin Cities Sports,* and *Writer.*

## Sidelights

Following her interest in families and children, Jean Reidy has authored articles and essays for dozens of magazines. As the mother of four children, Reidy surprised few people when she also expanded her writing career by becoming a children's author with the companion picture books *Too Pickley!* and *Too Purpley!,* both illustrated by Geneviève Leloup. "I've always loved to read and when my children were young, I loved reading to them," the Colorado-based writer noted on her home page, discussing her beginnings as a children's author. "On a cross country road trip, I was listening to a book on tape with my kids and came up with an idea for my own middle-grade novel. As I rattled off thoughts about characters and plot points, I had my daughter take notes on a map. And when I got home, I started writing."

In Reidy's picture books she introduces two decidedly single-minded children who many adults will recognize. In *Too Purpley!* a budding fashionista sorts through her available outfits, but each one inspires an objection, be it the color, the style, the texture, or for a variety of more imaginative reasons. A picky eater is the focus of *Too Pickley!,* and here color and texture also arouse suspicion, as do smell, stickiness, slurpiness, and the food's effects on one's tummy. "Leloup's bright . . . illustrations keep up with the comic pace of Reidy's bouncy rhymes," wrote Martha Simpson in her *School Library Journal* review of *Too Pickley!,* while *Booklist* critic Randall Enos voted the picture book a "place among the glut of picture books about picky eaters." A "fun book," *Too Purpley!* "has lots of descriptive words that tickle the ear," observed *School Library Journal* critic Elaine Lesh Morgan, and a *Kirkus Reviews* contributor exclaimed of Reidy's story: "Fussy dressers, this one's for you!"

## Biographical and Critical Sources

PERIODICALS

*Booklist,* January 1, 2010, Kay Weisman, review of *Too Purpley!,* p. 100; May 1, 2010, Randall Enos, review of *Too Pickley!,* p. 92.

*Kirkus Reviews,* January 1, 2010, review of *Too Purpley!*
*Publishers Weekly,* January 11, 2010, review of *Too Purpley!,* p. 46.
*School Library Journal,* January, 2010, Elaine Lesh Morgan, review of *Too Purpley!,* p. 81; July, 2010, Martha Simpson, review of *Too Pickley!,* p. 69.

ONLINE

*Jean Reidy Home Page,* http://www.jeanreidy.com (March 20, 2011).
*Jean Reidy Web log,* http://jeanreidy.blogspot.com (March 20, 2011).

\* \* \*

# ROSE, Naomi C.

## Personal

Married Robin Weeks. *Hobbies and other interests:* Painting, nature, reading storytelling, movies.

## Addresses

*Home*—Sedona, AZ. *E-mail*—naomicrose@aol.com.

## Career

Author and illustrator of books for children. Presenter at schools.

## Awards, Honors

Independent Publisher Award honorable mention, and Nautilus Book Award for Best Children's Illustrated Book, both 2005, and *Storytelling World* Honor designation, 2006, all for *Tibetan Tales for Little Buddhas;* Nautilus Book Award Silver designation, and International Book Award finalist for Best Picture Book, both 2010, both for *Tibetan Tales from the Top of the World.*

## Writings

### SELF-ILLUSTRATED

*Tibetan Tales for Little Buddhas,* Tibetan translation by Pasang Tenzin, preface by the Dalai Lama, Clear Light Pub. (Santa Fe, NM), 2004.
*Tibetan Tales from the Top of the World,* Tibetan translation by Pasang Tenzin, preface by the Dalai Lama, foreword by Richard Gere, Clear Light Pub. (Santa Fe, NM), 2009.
*Tashi and the Tibetan Flower Cure,* Lee & Low (New York, NY), 2011.
*Where Snow Leopard Prowls: Wild Animals of Tibet,* Dancing Dakini Press, 2011.

### OTHER

(Adaptor) *Escape to Freedom: The Dangerous Trek of Tibetan Youth* (based on *Child Exodus from Tibet* by Birgit Vandewijer), photographs by Vandewijer, Paljor Publications (New Delhi, India), 2011.

*Naomi C. Rose* (Photograph by Andrew Cameron Baxter. Reproduced by permission.)

Contributor to periodicals.

## Sidelights

Author and illustrator Naomi C. Rose is a strong believer in perseverance. While living on an island near Seattle, Washington, as an adult, Rose decided to enroll in art school, even though she doubted that she had any "natural" talent and was aware that she lacked the years of training of many of her classmates. In another moment of insight, Rose decided to study Tibetan culture and wisdom because she felt that the Tibetan ways of peace and kindness reflected her own spiritual path. She shares the wisdom and insight from such Tibetan traditions in her self-illustrated picture books *Tibetan Tales for Little Buddhas* and *Tibetan Tales from the Top of the World,* Rose further explores the history and culture of the Tibetan people in her stories and art for *Tashi and the Tibetan Flower Cure* and *Where Snow Leopard Prowls: Wild Animals of Tibet.*

The three stories in *Tibetan Tales for Little Buddhas* are adapted from traditional Tibetan wisdom tales, and in the book's preface His Holiness the Dalai Lama predicted that they would enlighten young readers and aid them in discovering happier lives. In "Yeshi's Luck" a young boy goes in search of his lost horse and discovers many surprising truths along the way. A girl discovers a strange sight that makes her afraid until she approaches it with curiosity in "Jomo and the Dakini Queen," while in "Chunda's Wisdom Quest" an injured yeti—the Himalaian version of Bigfoot—teaches a young monk about kindness. "I not only had to translate these tales from Eastern thinking to Western thinking, but into a form children could understand," Rose explained to *Santa Fe New Mexican* interviewer Julia Bell. "Although this is primarily seen as a children's book, I believe wisdom can sink in at any age, from three years old to 103 years old."

*Rose shares her Buddhist faith in self-illustrated picture books that include* Tibetan Tales for Little Buddhas. (Copyright © 2004 by Naomi C. Rose. Reproduced with permission from Clear Light Books.)

Reviewing *Tibetan Tales for Little Buddhas* in *School Library Journal,* Robin L. Gibson wrote that Rose's retellings feature a "unique sense of place" due to "vivid, dynamic paintings" that "capture the appeal of the landscape and the people." While Gillian Engberg characterized the chosen stories as "purposeful," she added in her *Booklist* review that "children will enjoy the exciting fairy-tale elements," as well as touches of the supernatural. Featuring a map of Tibet as well as a glossary, *Tibetan Tales for Little Buddhas* also includes translations into Tibetan by Pasang Tenzin, making the bilingual picture book useful to Tibetan immigrants attempting to learn English. The Tibetan script also adds fascination and interest to the American reader.

Similar to *Tibetan Tales for Little Buddhas, Tibetan Tales from the Top of the World* features three more stories with traditional origins: "Prince Jampa's Surprise," "Sonam and the Stolen Cow," and "Tashi's Gold." Commending Rose's illustrations, with their mix of "periwinkle, teals, reds, golds, pinks, and purples," Mary Jean Smith added in *School Library Journal* that the collected tales "shine a light on the hearts of the Tibetan people." A *Kirkus Reviews* writer also cited the "bright" and "expressive" illustrations in *Tibetan Tales from the Top of the World,* recommending Rose's work as "a good addition to large folklore collections."

"When I was in third grade, I wrote my first book," Rose told *SATA.* "It was a collection of short stories. Each story had a lesson in how to live a good life. I wrote each story in my very best handwriting, put it all together in a little notebook, and put a title on it. Then I gave it to my mother and stepfather for Christmas. They loved it. Little did I know way back in third grade that as an adult I would also be writing stories on how to live a good life!

"I love visiting classrooms and spending time with students. I'm sure I learn at least as much from them as they learn from me."

## Biographical and Critical Sources

*PERIODICALS*

*Booklist,* December 15, 2004, Gillian Engberg, review of *Tibetan Tales for Little Buddhas,* p. 745.

*Kirkus Reviews,* October 15, 2009, review of *Tibetan Tales from the Top of the World.*

*Santa Fe New Mexican,* November 14, 2004, Barbara Harrelson, "Dealing with Life through the Tales of the Tibetans," p. F7; November 15, 2004, Julia Bell, "Down the Street" (profile), p. E1.

*School Library Journal,* March, 2005, Robin L. Gibson, review of *Tibetan Tales for Little Buddhas,* p. 202; February, 2010, Mary Jean Smith, review of *Tibetan Tales from the Top of the World,* p. 102.

ONLINE

*Naomi C. Rose Home Page,* http://www.naomicrose.com (February 20, 2011).

\*     \*     \*

# ROY, Ron 1940-

## Personal

Born April 29, 1940, in Hartford, CT; son of Leo Joseph and Marie Roy. *Education:* University of Connecticut, B.A., 1965; University of Hartford, M.Ed., 1974. *Hobbies and other interests:* Reading, hiking, swimming, cooking for friends, gardening, travel.

## Addresses

*Home*—CT.

## Career

Writer. West Hill School, Rocky Hill, CT, teacher, 1975-79; freelance writer, 1978—. Institute of Children's Literature, instructor, 1982-84. *Military service:* U.S. Navy, 1958-60; served as hospital corpsman.

## Member

Society of Children's Book Writers and Illustrators, Authors Guild.

## Awards, Honors

Children's Choice selection, International Reading Association, 1982, for both *Nightmare Island* and *Frankie Is Staying Back.*

## Writings

*FICTION FOR CHILDREN*

*Old Tiger, New Tiger,* illustrated by Patricia M. Bargielski, Abingdon (Nashville, TN), 1978.
*A Thousand Pails of Water,* illustrated by Vo-Dinh Mai, Knopf (New York, NY), 1978.
*Awful Thursday,* illustrated by Lillian Hoban, Pantheon (New York, NY), 1979.
*Three Ducks Went Wandering,* illustrated by Paul Galdone, Seabury Press (New York, NY), 1979.
*The Shadow in the Pond,* Scholastic (New York, NY), 1979.
*Breakfast with My Father,* illustrated by Troy Howell, Clarion (New York, NY), 1980.
*Nightmare Island,* illustrated by Robert MacLean, Dutton (New York, NY), 1981.
*Frankie Is Staying Back,* illustrated by Walter Kessell, Clarion (New York, NY), 1981.
*The Great Frog Swap,* illustrated by Victoria Chess, Pantheon (New York, NY), 1981.
*Avalanche!,* illustrated by Robert MacLean, Dutton (New York, NY), 1981.
*I Am a Thief,* illustrated by Mel Williges, Dutton (New York, NY), 1982.
*Where's Buddy?,* illustrated by Troy Howell, Clarion (New York, NY), 1982.
*Million Dollar Jeans,* illustrated by Joyce Audy dos Santos, Dutton (New York, NY), 1983.
*The Chimpanzee Kid,* Clarion (New York, NY), 1985.
*Big and Small, Short and Tall,* illustrated by Lynne Cherry, Clarion (New York, NY), 1986.
*Whose Hat Is That?,* illustrated by Rosmarie Hausherr, Clarion (New York, NY), 1987.
*Whose Shoes Are These?,* illustrated by Rosmarie Hausherr, Clarion (New York, NY), 1988.
*Someone Is Following Pip Ramsey,* illustrated by Elizabeth Wolf, Random House (New York, NY), 1996.

*"A TO Z MYSTERIES" SERIES; FOR CHILDREN; ILLUSTRATED BY JOHN STEVEN GURNEY*

*The Absent Author,* Random House (New York, NY), 1997.
*The Bald Bandit,* Random House (New York, NY), 1997.
*The Canary Caper,* illustrated by John Steven Gurney, Random House (New York, NY), 1998.
*The Deadly Dungeon,* illustrated by John Steven Gurney, Random House (New York, NY), 1998.
*The Empty Envelope,,* Random House (New York, NY), 1998.
*The Falcon's Feathers,,* Random House (New York, NY), 1999.
*The Goose's Gold,,* Random House (New York, NY), 1999.
*The Haunted Hotel,,* Random House (New York, NY), 1999.
*The Invisible Island,,* Random House (New York, NY), 1999.
*The Jaguar's Jewel,,* Random House (New York, NY), 2000.
*The Kidnapped King,,* Random House (New York, NY), 2000.
*The Lucky Lottery,,* Random House (New York, NY), 2000.
*The Missing Mummy,,* Random House (New York, NY), 2001.
*The Ninth Nugget,,* Random House (New York, NY), 2001.
*The Orange Outlaw,,* Random House (New York, NY), 2001.
*The Panda Puzzle,,* Random House (New York, NY), 2002.

*The Quicksand Question,*, Random House (New York, NY), 2002.

*The Runaway Racehorse,*, Random House (New York, NY), 2002.

*The School Skeleton,*, Random House (New York, NY), 2003.

*The Talking T. Rex,*, Random House (New York, NY), 2003.

*The Unwilling Umpire,*, Random House (New York, NY), 2004.

*The Vampire's Vacation,*, Random House (New York, NY), 2004.

*The White Wolf,*, Random House (New York, NY), 2004.

*The X'ed-out X-ray,*, Random House (New York, NY), 2005.

*The Yellow Yacht,*, Random House (New York, NY), 2005.

*The Zombie Zone,*, Random House (New York, NY), 2005.

*"A TO Z MYSTERIES" SUPER EDITION SERIES; FOR CHILDREN; ILLUSTRATED BY JOHN STEVEN GURNEY*

*Detective Camp*, Random House (New York, NY), 2006.

*Mayflower Treasure Hunt,*, Random House (New York, NY), 2007.

*White House White-out,*, Random House (New York, NY), 2008.

*Sleepy Hollow Sleepover,*, Random House (New York, NY), 2010.

*"CAPITAL MYSTERIES" SERIES; FOR CHILDREN*

*Who Cloned the President?*, illustrated by Liza Woodruff, Random House (New York, NY), 2001.

*Kidnapped at the Capital*, illustrated by Liza Woodruff, Random House (New York, NY), 2002.

*The Skeleton in the Smithsonian*, illustrated by Timothy Bush, Random House (New York, NY), 2003.

*A Spy in the White House*, illustrated by Timothy Bush, Random House (New York, NY), 2004.

*Who Broke Lincoln's Thumb?*, illustrated by Timothy Bush, Random House (New York, NY), 2005.

*Fireworks at the FBI*, illustrated by Timothy Bush, Random House (New York, NY), 2006.

*Trouble at the Treasury*, illustrated by Timothy Bush, Random House (New York, NY), 2006.

*Mystery at the Washington Monument*, illustrated by Timothy Bush, Random House (New York, NY), 2007.

*A Thief at the National Zoo*, illustrated by Timothy Bush, Random House (New York, NY), 2007.

*The Secret at Jefferson's Mansion*, illustrated by Timothy Bush, Random House (New York, NY), 2009.

*The Ghost at Camp David*, illustrated by Timothy Bush, Random House (New York, NY), 2010.

*Trapped on the D.C. Train!*, illustrated by Timothy Bush, Random House (New York, NY), 2011.

*"CALENDAR MYSTERIES" SERIES; FOR CHILDREN; ILLUSTRATED BY JOHN STEVEN GURNEY*

*January Joker,*, Random House (New York, NY), 2009.

*February Friend,*, Random House (New York, NY), 2009.

*March Mischief,*, Random House (New York, NY), 2010.

*April Adventure,*, Random House (New York, NY), 2010.
*May Magic,*, Random House (New York, NY), 2011.
*June Jam,*, Random House (New York, NY), 2011.

*OTHER*

*What Has Ten Legs and Eats Corn Flakes?: A Pet Book,* illustrated by Lynne Cherry, Clarion (New York, NY), 1982.

*More over, Wheelchairs Coming Through!: Seven Young People in Wheelchairs Talk about Their Lives* (nonfiction), illustrated by Rosmarie Hausherr, Clarion (New York, NY), 1985.

Author's works are included in the deGrummond Collection, University of Southern Mississippi.

## Sidelights

Ron Roy is the author of more than sixty works for young readers, including picture books, beginning readers, and novels. Roy is noted for his sensitivity in depicting the kind of incidents that truly impact young

*Ron Roy's easy-reading elementary-grade mysteries include* **Who Broke Lincoln's Thumb?,** *featuring artwork by Timothy Bush.* (Stepping Stone Books, 2010. Illustration copyright © 2005 by Timothy Bush. Reproduced with permission of Random House Children's Books, a division of Random House, Inc.)

children's imaginations, as well as for creating books
that encourage reluctant male readers through plots focusing on adventure, mystery, and rough-and-tumble
hijinks. He is perhaps best known for the twenty-six
works in his "A to Z" mystery series, featuring a group
of young amateur sleuths. "I feel privileged to be a
writer of children's books," the author stated in an essay on *KidsReads.com.* "This job puts me in contact
with kids, and allows me to travel around the world.
My writing also lets me use my love for words every
day. Best of all, I get to meet the kids who also love to
read. What more could a man want?"

Born in Connecticut in 1940, Roy fell in love with storytelling and literature at a young age. "When I turned
nine," he remarked in an essay on the Random House
Web site, "I received for my birthday a wonderful
gift—a book. It was about King Arthur and his knights.
Even though I vividly remember the shiny blue and red
cover and the smell of the new paper, I don't remember
the author. But I thank her or him every day of my
writing life. That writer stirred up something in me that
has been bubbling ever since: a love for reading, and
the urgent need to put words down on paper." Roy and
his family moved away from the city into a quiet suburb when he was ten. Finding it difficult to make friends
in his new neighborhood, he spent his free time exploring his new neighborhood. "There was a library on the
corner," Roy later recalled to *SATA,* "and one day I
wandered in. I never really wandered out again."

After high school, Roy enrolled at the University of
Connecticut and earned his bachelor's degree in 1965.
After also completing earning his master's degree, he
began teaching elementary school. Although he continued to teach until 1979, Roy began writing in earnest in
1974. "After I received my first rejection letter in the
mail, I was hooked," he remembered. "The fact that I
knew nothing about preparing manuscripts and ap-
proaching editors was all beside the point. I wanted to
write so I wrote. I bought a copy of Jane Yolen's book
*Writing Books for Children* and the writing world suddenly began to make sense." In 1977, his efforts paid
off, and his first book was published as *Old Tiger, New
Tiger.*

In addition to his continuing passion for reading, Roy
has also had a lifelong affection for animals. "As a kid
I spent a lot of time caring for baby animals, which I
would scoop up whenever I happened to come across
one that seemed to need my ministration," he recalled.
"My mother seemed to understand my need for their
company and allowed small creatures to invade her
home regularly. Squirrels, snakes, owls, fish, turtles, it
didn't matter," as he admitted. Many of Roy's books
for children would have "animals lurking somewhere in
the text." In one of his early picture books, *A Thousand
Pails of Water,* the animal lurking in the text is a whale,
which a young Japanese boy attempts to keep alive
when it becomes stranded along a shallow coastline.
Carrying pail after pail of water to the floundering ani-

*Roy's "A to Z Mysteries" novels include* **The Deadly Dungeon,** *featuring cover art by John Steven Gurney.* (Stepping Stone Books, 1998. Illustration
copyright © 1998 by John Steven Gurney. Used by permission of Random House Children's Books, a division of Random House, Inc.)

mal, the boy gradually attracts the attention of his fellow villagers, who summon the compassion to help a
creature that they would otherwise have hunted. Noting
that the story contains a proverbial quality, *Booklist*
critic Betsy Hearne wrote that the lesson "is greatly extended by the understated compassion for both human
and animal life."

Roy's book *Three Ducks Went Wandering* had its beginnings in some brainstorming between the author and his
father on a trip back from visiting Roy's ninety-seven-
year-old grandmother in Boston. "We were together in
the car for two hours," the author recalled, "and I asked
him to help me put together an idea I'd had about three
baby ducks who wander off. At the end of the trip the
story was complete." While they encounter all manner
of would-be predators—snakes, hawks, foxes, and even
an angry bull—the three ducklings return safely to their
mother in a picture book that a *Junior Bookshelf* reviewer praised enthusiastically for its "cunningly contrived" text and the "deliciously unbearable" suspense
that builds up before each page is turned. In concept
books such as *Big and Small, Short and Tall,* basic
ideas about size and shape are expressed through the

use of animals, such as the biggest of the big, the whale shark, and the smallest of the small, the bee hummingbird. In Roy's picture-book debut, *Old Tiger, New Tiger,* a group of monkeys wise up and change their ways when they gradually realize that the old tiger they are busy taunting as being slow and blind will, if allowed to die, be replaced by a young beast with sharper teeth and claws—and a voracious appetite for monkeys!

Roy's stories featuring human protagonists include *Awful Thursday,* in which a lucky mistake saves Jack from what would have been an unlucky accident. *Frankie Is Staying Back* finds best friends Frankie and Jonas about to be separated when Frankie has to re-do the third grade. At first dismayed by Frankie's unwillingness to talk about it, Jonas gradually finds a way to support and help his friend in a story that a *Publishers Weekly* contributor called "tender and funny." A pair of boys also figures in *The Great Frog Swap,* as Wally and Marvin's attempt to orchestrate a trade for the fastest frog in town falls flat when they think they're getting the high-jumping Eater but wind up with the lethargic Lulu instead. In *Million Dollar Jeans* Tommy promises half the earnings from a winning lottery ticket to his best friend Twigg and then discovers that his mom has given away the jeans attached to the pocket where the ticket was stashed. "Thus begins a chase that is funny, fast-paced, and cheerfully improbable," quipped a *Bulletin of the Center for Children's Books* contributor in reviewing *Million Dollar Jeans,* and Brooke Selby Dillon predicted in a *Voice of Youth Advocates* review that, with characters that are "warm, likable, and alive, . . . this is a book that many young readers won't be able to put down."

Several of Roy's stories feature serious themes. *Avalanche!* is a brief adventure that "should keep readers' pulses racing," in the opinion of *School Library Journal* contributor Chris Hatten. In the story, Scott's parents have sent him to Aspen, Colorado, to visit his older brother, Tony, while they work out the details of their divorce. Scott and Tony head to the mountains to ski and share some brief moments of brotherly bonding, but they get caught in an avalanche. The story relates the brothers' struggle to survive in what Hatten termed "a rich, thoroughly absorbing style." *Voice of Youth Advocates* reviewer Brooke Selby Dillon called *Avalanche!* "exciting, believable, [and] realistic, with a likable and resourceful young hero." She also declared that the book is "certain to appeal" to young readers.

*Where's Buddy?* takes place on the Maine coast and finds middle-schooler Mike put in charge of his willful and diabetic younger brother during their parent's day-long absence. When Mike decides to leave home and go to a football game, seven-year-old Buddy sneaks away with his best friend, Pete, and winds up trapped in a cave without the insulin necessary to prevent diabetic shock. The "theme of taking responsibility for one's irresponsible actions develops through one taut,

realistic incident," noted *Horn Book* reviewer Nancy C. Hammond in praise of *Where's Buddy?,* and a *Kirkus Reviews* contributor called the work "tightly knit—and finely shaded."

In *The Chimpanzee Kid* Roy takes a stand against the mistreatment of laboratory animals in recounting the adventures of thirteen-year-old Harold and his friend Todd in their efforts to free a chimp from a local pharmaceutical laboratory. "Roy writes with feeling and warmth," maintained *Booklist* contributor Barbara Elleman in a review of this book, the critic adding that the author captures "Harold's rebellion and determination with equal understanding and aplomb."

Among Roy's most popular books are the "A to Z Mysteries," illustrated with pen and ink by John Steven Gurney. Including such titles as *The Absent Author, The Lucky Lottery,* and *The Zombie Zone,* the series features the adventures of grade-schoolers Josh, Dink, and Ruth Rose as they use their sleuthing abilities to assist friends and family with a host of intriguing problems. In *The Goose's Gold,* for example, the trio comes to the aid of Ruth Rose's grandmother, whose plans to invest in a

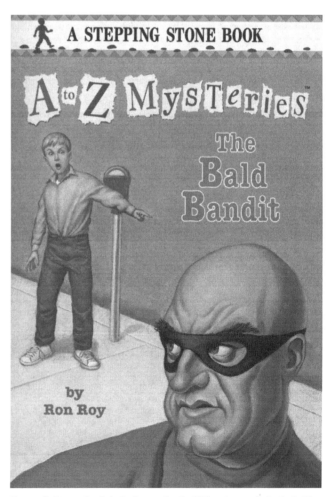

*Roy and Gurney's alphabet's worth of children's novels include* **The Bald Bandit,** *which pits a savvy young sleuth against a sinister character.* (Illustration copyright © 1997 by John Steven Gurney. Reproduced by permission of Random House Children's Books, a division of Random House, Inc.)

shipwreck recovery operation are called into question when the youngsters overhear a suspicious-looking fellow planning a robbery. "Young mystery buffs will enjoy the children's adventures uncovering the fraud," observed *School Library Journal* reviewer Shelley Townsend-Hudson. In *The School Skeleton,* a teacher comes under suspicion when some valuable equipment goes missing from the nurse's office. Reviewing this story, *Booklist* critic Hazel Rochman applauded "the cozy story, which has just a touch of the shivers." Pamela K. Bomboy, writing in *School Library Journal,* stated that Roy's "A to Z Mysteries" comprise "an appealing combination of intrigue, ingenuity, and good fun."

In his "Calendar Mysteries" series Roy introduces four new protagonists, all of whom are related to the "A to Z Mysteries" cast: Bradley and Brian, the younger brothers of Josh; Nate, the sibling of Ruth Rose; and Lucy, cousin to Dink. In *January Joker* the foursome are convinced that aliens have invaded their hometown after viewing eerie lights in the sky, spotting a strange pattern in the snow, and reading an article about extraterrestrials left on Josh's computer. When Josh, Dink, and Ruth Rose go missing, the younger sleuths are convinced that they have been kidnapped by extraterrestrials. "The story is full of clever twists and turns," Beth Cuddy remarked in *School Library Journal,* and a *Kirkus Reviews* contributor described *January Joker* as "a fine first mystery for the ready-for-chapter-book set."

In *Kidnapped at the Capital,* an installment in Roy's "Capital Mysteries" series, K.C. Corcoran and her friend, Marshall Li, frantically search through Washington, DC, when the president of the United States vanishes, along with K.C.'s mother. "This is a fun, accessible mystery for new readers," Kathy Broderick observed in her review of *Kidnapped at the Capital* for *Booklist.*

Roy turns to nonfiction in *Move over, Wheelchairs Coming Through!: Seven Young People in Wheelchairs Talk about Their Lives,* as young people aged nine through nineteen describe what it is like to be confined to a wheelchair. Appraising the work, a *Booklist* contributor concluded that *Move over, Wheelchairs Coming Through!* "should do much to lessen ignorance and fear and help the disabled as well as those who stigmatize them."

Why did Roy decide to devote his life to writing for children? The answer is simple. "I like kids a lot," the author once told *SATA.* "I write for them, to them, about them. I remember how important books were to me when I was young. One of the reasons I write is to try to bring to kids some of the joy I derive from books."

## Biographical and Critical Sources

*PERIODICALS*

*Booklist,* October 1, 1978, Betsy Hearne, review of *A Thousand Pails of Water,* p. 299; June 1, 1985, review

*Roy weaves elements of nineteenth-century American literature in his entertaining story for* **Sleepy Hollow Sleepover.** *(Stepping Stone Book, 2010. Illustration copyright © 2010 by John Steven Gurney. Reproduced with permission of Random House Children's Books, a division of Random House, Inc.)*

of *Move over, Wheelchairs Coming Through!: Seven Young People in Wheelchairs Talk about Their Lives,* p. 1405; February 1, 1986, Barbara Elleman, review of *The Chimpanzee Kid,* p. 812; October 15, 1999, Shelley Townsend-Hudson, review of *The Goose's Gold,* p. 446; September 1, 2002, Kathy Broderick, review of *Kidnapped at the Capital,* p. 126; May 1, 2003, Hazel Rochman, review of *The School Skeleton,* p. 1529.

*Bulletin of the Center for Children's Books,* September, 1983, review of *Million Dollar Jeans,* p. 16.

*Horn Book,* August, 1982, Nancy C. Hammond, review of *Where's Buddy?,* p. 409.

*Junior Bookshelf,* October, 1980, review of *Three Ducks Went Wandering,* p. 234.

*Kirkus Reviews,* April 15, 1982, review of *Where's Buddy?,* p. 491; November 15, 2009, review of *January Joker.*

*Publishers Weekly,* July 10, 1981, review of *Frankie Is Staying Back,* p. 91.

*School Library Journal,* February, 1982, Chris Hatten, review of *Avalanche!,* pp. 79-80; January, 1998, Elaine E. Knight, review of *The Bald Bandit,* p. 92; October, 1998, Pamela K. Bomboy, review of *The Deadly Dungeon,* pp. 112-113; December, 2009, Beth Cuddy, review of *January Joker,* p. 90.

*Voice of Youth Advocates,* February, 1982, Brooke Selby Dillon, review of *Avalanche!,* pp. 37-38; April, 1984, Brooke Selby Dillon, review of *Million Dollar Jeans,* p. 35.

ONLINE

*KidsReads.com,* http://www.kidsreads.com/ (April 25, 2005), Ron Roy, autobiographical essay, and Shannon McKenna, interview with Roy.
*Random House Web site,* http://www.randomhouse.com/ (April 15, 2011), "Ron Roy."
*Ron Roy Home Page,* http://www.ronroy.com (April 15, 2011).*

* * *

# RYCROFT, Nina

## Personal
Born in Australia; married; children: two. *Education:* Randwick College TAFE (Technical and Further Education), B.A. (graphic design), 1992.

## Addresses
*Home*—Auckland, New Zealand. *Agent*—Margaret Connolly, P.O. Box 945, Wahroonga, New South Wales 2076, Australia. *E-mail*—contact@ninarycroft.com.

## Career
Graphic designer and illustrator. Worked as a designer in Sydney, New South Wales, Australia, and London, England, beginning c. 1993; freelance author and illustrator. Literature Live!, cofounder. Presenter at schools. *Exhibitions:* Work exhibited in group shows at International Exhibition of Children's Book Illustration, Hughenden Hotel, Woollahra, New South Wales, Australia, and Customs House Gallery, Warrnambook, Victoria, Australia, and included in permanent collection at National Centre for Picture Book Art.

## Member
Australian Society of Authors, Society of Children's Book Writers and Illustrators, Publish! Blue Mountains.

## Awards, Honors
Children's Book Council of Australia Notable Book designation, 2001, for *Little Platypus* by Nette Hinton; CJ Picture Book Awards International Awards finalist, 2009, for *Ballroom Bonanza.*

## Writings
*My First Animal Alphabet,* Pan Macmillan (Sydney, New South Wales, Australia), 2007.

*Nina Rycroft* (Reproduced by permission.)

(And coauthor) Stephen Harris, *Ballroom Bonanza: A Hidden Pictures ABC Book,* Working Title Press (Kingswood, South Australia, Australia), 2009, Abrams Books for Young Readers (New York, NY), 2010.

ILLUSTRATOR

Sam Bowring, *Sir Joshua and the Unprofessional Dragon,* Koala Books (Mascot, New South Wales, Australia), 1999.
Jackie French, *Charlie's Gold,* Koala Books (Mascot, New South Wales, Australia), 1999.
Nette Hilton, *Little Platypus,* Koala Books (Mascot, New South Wales, Australia), 2000.
Jane Bowring, *Tricky Little Hippo,* Koala Books (Mascot, New South Wales, Australia), 2005.
Sue Whiting, *Elephant Dance,* Koala Books (Mascot, New South Wales, Australia), 2007.
Mike Dumbleton, *Hippopotamouse,* Era Publications (Brooklyn Park, South Australia, Australia), 2007.
Phil Cummings, *Boom Bah!,* Working Title Press (Kingswood, South Australia, Australia), 2008, Kane-Miller (La Jolla, CA), 2010.
Margaret Wild, *No More Kisses,* Little Hare (Surry Hills, New South Wales, Australia), 2009.
Sherryl Clark, *Now I Am Bigger,* Working Title Press (Kingswood, South Australia, Australia), 2010.

## Sidelights
A popular illustrator in her native Australia, Nina Rycroft has contributed her engaging pencil and watercolor artwork to stories by such authors as Margaret Wild, Stephen Harris, Jackie French, Phil Cummings, and Nette Hinton. "Picture books have always captured my imagination; I still treasure a collection of books from when I was a child," Rycroft noted on her home

page. "I love the creative potential of a picture book and the collaboration it requires. I approach my work with fun, laughter, and lots of love."

Together with coauthor Stephen Harris, Rycroft has also created *Ballroom Bonanza: A Hidden Pictures ABC Book,* which pairs her water-color illustrations with a story inspired by the experiences of a family member who spent three decades as band master at a hotel ballroom. In the book's pages the coauthors take readers on a high-energy tour through the alphabet that features a menagerie of dancing animals—from alpacas and bears to zebras—competing for the top prize in a nighttime ballroom dance competition. In addition to the A-to-Z roster of critters which appear in Rycroft's art, *Ballroom Bonanza* also features a list of instruments that readers can search for in its pages, as well as a variety of entertaining dances.

One of Rycroft's most successful illustration projects, *Boom Bah!,* features a text by Cummings that is filled with sounds. Beginning with a gentle "Ting!" as a house mouse taps a cup with silver teaspoon, the noise level rises with each turn of the page as another animal musician joins in. Finally, with a brassy "Boom Bah!," Rycroft's illustrations reveal an entire band of marching animals, each contributing a sound with its homemade instrument. "Cummings's simple, exclamatory rhymes are like blasts from a trumpet," exclaimed a *Publishers Weekly* critic, and that "infectious joy" is captured in the artist's "effervescent" illustrations. Reviewing *Boom Bah!* in *School Library Journal,* Lauralyn Persson noted Rycroft's use of "fluid lines and soft, clear colors" and

recommended the book as "a natural fit for toddler [storytime] programs." "Hide the silverware!," urged a *Kirkus Reviews* critic, citing the inspiring nature of Cummings' story to musically inclined toddlers. In *Horn Book* Kitty Flynn asserted that "Rycroft's large, clean pencil and watercolor illustrations are as exuberant as [the book's] . . . bouncy rhyming text." A testament to its popularity among story-hour fans, *Boom Bah!* was also adapted as a stage performance that toured Australia, Korea, and Singapore, beginning in 2007.

## Biographical and Critical Sources

*PERIODICALS*

*Horn Book,* May-June, 2010, Kitty Flynn, review of *Boom Bah!,* p. 66.
*Kirkus Reviews,* January 15, 2010, review of *Boom Bah!*
*Publishers Weekly,* February 1, 2010, review of *Boom Bah!,* p. 46.
*School Library Journal,* June, 2010, Stacy Dillon, review of *Ballroom Bonanza: A Hidden Pictures ABC Book,* p. 83; May, 2010, Lauralyn Persson, review of *Boom Bah!,* p. 80.

*ONLINE*

*Nina Rycroft Home Page,* http://www.ninarycroft.com (March 20, 2011).
*Lateral Learning Web site,* http://www.laterallearning.com/ (March 20, 2011), "Nina Rycroft."

*Rycroft combines an entertaining story with her fanciful, detailed art in the picture book* **Ballroom Bonanza.** (Illustration copyright © 2009 by Nina Rycroft. Reproduced with permission of Abrams Books for Young Readers, an imprint of Abrams.)

# S

## SAVADIER, Elivia 1950-

### Personal

Born March 26, 1950, in Postmasburg, South Africa; immigrated to United States; daughter of Hayam (a physician) and Sadye Savadier; married Stanley Sagov (a physician), October, 1985; children: Sadye. *Education:* Attended Michaelis School of Art, University of Cape Town; Royal Society of Arts (London, England), teaching diploma; Lesley College (Cambridge, MA), B.A. (human development), M.A. (expressive arts therapy and mental health counseling). *Politics:* "Left of center/humanistic/pacifist, strong anti-apartheid history." *Religion:* "Jewish background, Buddhist leanings."

### Addresses

*Home and office*—45 Walnut Hill Rd., Chestnut Hill, MA 02167. *Agent*—Jane Feder, 305 E. 24th St., New York, NY 10010. *E-mail*—elivia@savadierstudio.com.

### Career

Children's book author and illustrator. Worked variously as middle-school art teacher, English-as-a-second-language instructor in the United States and England, and adult literacy teacher in England, the United States, and South Africa. Freelance illustrator, beginning c. 1990; art therapist for children and adults dealing with abuse, PTSD, adoption, ADHD, and other difficulties. Presenter at schools and workshops.

### Member

Graphic Artists Guild, Society of Children's Book Writers and Illustrators, International Arts Therapy Association, American Art Therapy Association, American Mental Health Counseling Association, American Counseling Association.

### Awards, Honors

Sydney Taylor Award for Best Children's Picture Book, Jewish Association of Libraries, 1993, and *Smithsonian* Notable Book designation, 2000, both for *The Unin-*

*Elivia Savadier* (Reproduced by permission.)

*vited Guest and Other Jewish Holiday Tales* by Nina Jaffe; Children's Choice designation, International Reading Association/Children's Book Council, 1995, for *Hotter than a Hot Dog!* by Stephanie Calmenson; American Booksellers Association Pick of the List designation, 1996, for *A Bedtime Story* by Mem Fox; Sydney Taylor Award, 1997, for *The Mysterious Visitor* by Jaffe, and 2003, for *Jewish Holidays All Year Round* by Ilene Cooper; Nebraska Golden Sower Award nomination, *Americas* Award Commended Book designation, and Top Children's Book for a Global Society selection,

Boise State University—Idaho, all c. 2002, all for *I Love Saturdays y domingos* by Alma Flor Ada; Best Books for Babies designation, Center for Early Literacy, 2002, for *Boo Hoo Boo-Boo* by Marilyn Singer; Jewish Book Council Award finalist, 2002-03, for *Jewish Holidays All Year Round.*

# Writings

*SELF-ILLUSTRATED*

*No Haircut Today,* Roaring Brook Press (New Milford, CT), 2005.
*Time to Get Dressed!,* Roaring Brook Press (New Milford, CT), 2006.
*Will Sheila Share?,* Roaring Brook Press (New Milford, CT), 2008.

*ILLUSTRATOR*

Marjorie Weinman, *The Best Place for Imagining,* Silver Burdett (Upper Saddle River, NJ), 1992.
Juanita Havill, *Treasure Nap,* Houghton (Boston, MA), 1992.
Andrew Clements, *Billy and the Bad Teacher,* Picture Book Studio (Natick, MA), 1993.
Nina Jaffe, *The Uninvited Guest and Other Jewish Holiday Tales,* Scholastic (New York, NY), 1993.
Stephanie Calmenson, *Hotter than a Hot Dog!,* Little, Brown (Boston, MA), 1994.
Nelly Palacio Jaramillo, *Las nanas de abuelita,* Henry Holt (New York, NY), 1994.
Libby Hathorn, *Grandma's Shoes,* Viking (New York, NY), 1994.
Mem Fox, *A Bedtime Story,* Mondo (Australia), 1996.
Diane Hoffmeyer, *Mama Mabena's Magic,* Little Library/Cambridge University Press (South Africa), 1996.
Nina Jaffe, *The Mysterious Visitor: Stories of the Prophet Elijah,* Scholastic (New York, NY), 1997.
Norma Farber, *I Swim an Ocean in My Sleep,* Henry Holt (New York, NY), 1997.
Marilyn Singer, *Boo Hoo Boo-boo,* HarperFestival (New York, NY), 2002.
Alma Flor Ada, *I Love Saturdays y domingos,* Atheneum (New York, NY), 2002.
Ilene Cooper, *Jewish Holidays All Year Round: A Family Treasury,* Harry N. Abrams (New York, NY), 2002.
Joyce Sidman, *When I Am Young and Old,* Millbrook Press (Minneapolis, MN), 2003.
Leslea Newman, *The Eight Nights of Chanukah,* Harry N. Abrams (New York, NY), 2005.
Amy Hest, *When You Meet a Bear on Broadway,* Farrar, Straus & Giroux (New York, NY), 2009.

Also illustrator of juvenile and English-as-a-second-language publications for numerous publishers, including Harcourt, D.C. Heath, Children's Television Workshop, U.S. Kids Magazine, Walker, Oxford University Press, and Cambridge University Press.

# Adaptations

*I Love Saturdays y domingos* was adapted as a video recording, Disney Educational, 2002.

# Sidelights

Born and educated in South Africa, author and illustrator Elivia Savadier pursued her education at London's Royal Society of Arts before relocating to the United States and beginning her career in children's picture books. Her first illustration project, Marjorie Weinman's *The Best Place for Imagining,* encouraged Savadier to continue in the field, and other projects have paired her watercolor art with stories by Andrew Clement, Marilyn Singer, Mem Fox, Leslea Newman, Alma Flor Ida, Ilene Cooper, and Amy Hest. She has also moved into the author's role herself with *No Haircut Today!,* the first of several toddler-friendly stories featuring her colorful art. Reviewing Savadier's artwork for Hest's *When You Meet a Bear on Broadway,* a *Kirkus Reviews* writer noted that her "delicate black-line drawings capture, with just-right accuracy, a busy Upper West Side neighborhood," while Stephanie Zvirin exclaimed upon the illustrator's "freewheeling-art style—at once expressive, mischievous, and joyous" in a *School Library Journal* review of Newman's *The Eight Nights of Chanukah.*

Born and raised in Cape Town, South Africa, Savadier was strongly influenced by the country's "sensuous atmosphere, filled with warmth, color, luminous light and shifting moods," as she once told *SATA.* "This seaport city is on Africa's southernmost tip, where the Indian and Atlantic oceans meet. It is bathed in a Mediterranean climate with aquamarine seas and purple mountains, named Lion's Head, Devil's Peak, and the Twelve Apostles. Cradled by the town, magnificent flat-topped Table Mountain becomes awe-inspiring when a cascading waterfall of clouds tumbles over it, threatening to engulf the city before it evaporates. Even growing up in an apartheid era, different South African languages and dialects filled the air; as did people descended from Africa, Asia, and Europe fill the streets. It remains a life-force that I carry deeply with me."

A "touching and playful story" about young Dominic's first haircut, according to *School Library Journal* reviewer Wanda Meyers-Himes, *No Haircut Today!* addresses the trauma that confronts many young children when confronted with a pair of sharp scissors wielded by a white-smocked stranger in a barber shop. In Savadier's simple tale, Dominic is lucky: his mother is a hairdresser, but he still hopes to postpone the inevitable. The author/illustrator's "graphic black strokes, jabs and squiggles" enhance her "spare" text, which a *Kirkus Reviews* noted combines varied fonts, italics, and other typesetting techniques to "mirror . . . the maniacal mishmash" of the young boy's unruly locks.

Savadier continues her depiction of the adventures of young children in *Time to Get Dressed!* and *Will Sheila Share?,* both of which feature colorfully drawn charac-

*Savadier's use of strong lines and gentle curves is a highlight of her endearing, self-illustrated picture book* No Haircut Today! (Copyright © 2005 by Elivia Savadier. Reproduced by permission of Roaring Brook Press, a division of Henry Holt & Company, LLC. All rights reserved.)

ters set against white backgrounds and paired with a simple text. In the first, Solomon is determined to put on his clothes by himself, but to a toddler a pair of pants with two legs and a shirt with two sleeves are hard to tell apart. *Will Sheila Share?* addresses a problem common to many parents: a toddler's unwillingness to let others play with his or her own toys. Worried Sheila is protective about all her things, but the redhead relaxes when she feels confident that there are enough toys, food, and love for everyone in her family. Calling *Time to Get Dressed!* "a fun day on a fairly common topic," Lauralyn Persson praised Savadier's mix of "rhythmic, lean text and charming" watercolor art, while Jennifer Mattson predicted in *Booklist* that the book's "expressive pictures will elicit grins of recognition" from parents. The author/illustrator "has captured the essence of a child's reluctance to share" in her "deceptively simple ink-and-watercolor" art for *Will Sheila Share?,* according to *School Library Journal* contributor Susan Weitz, while a *Publishers Weekly* critic observed that the book's "pithy text and expressive, economical pictures deliver a reassuring response along with solid comedy."

In her illustrations for books by other authors, Savadier has been praised for creating gentle watercolor art that reassures young picture-book fans. Praising Ada's *I Love Saturdays y domingos,* which was also adapted for video, *School Library Journal* contributor Barbara Auerbach cited the "colorful, homey watercolor illustrations" that bring to life the story, and a *Kirkus Reviews* writer noted that the paintings "highlight the diversity

and similarity" in Ada's multicultural tale. Savadier creates what a *Publishers Weekly* reviewer praised as "joyful pencil-and-watercolor works" for Nina Jaffe's *Stories of the Prophet Elijah,* while Cooper's *Jewish Holidays All Year Round: A Family Treasury* benefits from what *School Library Journal* contributor Martha Link described as "lively pen-and-ink and color sketches of diverse families celebrating." Cooper did not work directly with Savadier on this volume, a project sponsored by the Jewish Museum, but her reaction was also positive. "I didn't see Elivia's contributions until the book was almost finished," the author explained to *Booklist* colleague Zvirin. "I was really pleased. I think her pictures are so joyous. . . . reminding readers that Judaism is a religion whose adherents come from many places."

"Since 2006 I have pursued academic studies in human development and healing," Savadier told *SATA.* "So much recent research on child and adult suffering has pointed to children's early-attachment patterns with primary caretakers. I have a keen interest in using my academic training and artistic skills to create literature for children whose inner experience is of feeling and being different. Children who carry secrets of abuse, or the grief of losing a loved one; children who struggle at school because of learning difficulties; children who struggle with identity issues through adoption; Children who love at or below the poverty line."

## Biographical and Critical Sources

*PERIODICALS*

*Booklist,* August, 2002, Hazel Rochman, review of *Boo Hoo Boo-boo,* p. 1976; October 1, 2002, Stephanie Zvirin, review of *Jewish Holidays All Year Round: A Family Treasury,* p. 345; May 1, 2005, Jennifer Mattson, review of *No Haircut Today!,* p. 1593; October 15, 2005, Stephanie Zvirin, review of *The Eight Nights of Chanukah,* p. 58; April 1, 2006, Jennifer Mattson, review of *Time to Get Dressed!,* p. 49; November 1, 2009, Gillian Engberg, review of *When You Meet a Bear on Broadway,* p. 35.
*Horn Book,* May-June, 2006, Jennifer M. Brabander, review of *Time to Get Dressed!,* p. 302.
*Kirkus Reviews,* December 1, 2001, review of *I Love Saturdays y domingos,* p. 1680; April 15, 2002, review of *Boo Hoo Boo-boo,* p. 579; April 15, 2005, review of *No Haircut Today!,* p. 481; November 1, 2005, review of *The Eight Nights of Chanukah,* p. 1195; March 15, 2006, review of *Time to Get Dressed!,* p. 299; January 15, 2008, review of *Will Sheila Share?;* September 15, 2009, review of *When You Meet a Bear on Broadway.*
*New York Times Book Review,* April 20, 2003, review of *Jewish Holidays All Year Round,* p. 20.
*Publishers Weekly,* August 19, 1996, review of *A Bedtime Story,* p. 67; February 24, 1997, review of *The Mysterious Visitor: Stories of the Prophet Elijah,* p. 83; De-

cember 10, 2001, review of *I Love Saturdays y domingos,* p. 69; September 20, 2002, review of *Jewish Holidays All Year Around,* p. 68; September 26, 2005, review of *The Eight Nights of Chanukah,* p. 84; May 15, 2006, review of *Time to Get Dressed,* p. 70; January 28, 2008, review of *Will Sheila Share?,* p. 67.

*School Library Journal,* December, 1996, Liza Bliss, review of *A Bedtime Story,* p. 92; June, 1997, Susan Pine, review of *The Mysterious Visitor,* p. 108; January, 2002, Ann Welton, review of *I Love Saturdays y domingos,* p. 89; March, 2003, Martha Link, review of *Jewish Holidays All Year Round,* p. 216; June, 2005, Wanda Meyers-Himes, review of *No Haircut Today!,* p. 126; March, 2006, Lauralyn Persson, review of *Time to Get Dressed!,* p. 201; April, 2008, Susan Weitz, review of *Will Sheila Share?,* p. 122; October, 2009, Sara Paulson-Yarovoy, review of *When You Meet a Bear on Broadway,* p. 94.

*ONLINE*

*Elivia Savadier Home Page,* http://www.savadierstudio. com (April 15, 2011).

\*      \*      \*

## SEGAL, Lore 1928-
### (Lore Groszmann Segal)

### Personal

Born March 8, 1928, in Vienna, Austria; immigrated to United States, 1951; daughter of Ignatz (an accountant) and Franzi Groszmann; married David Isaac Segal (an editor), November 3, 1961 (died, 1970); children: Beatrice, Jacob. *Education:* Bedford College, London, B.A. (with honors), 1948. *Religion:* Jewish.

### Addresses

*Home*—New York, NY. *Agent*—Cynthia Cannell, 833 Madison Ave., New York, NY 10021. *E-mail*—lore@ usa.net.

### Career

Author and educator. Teacher in Dominican Republic, 1948-51; Columbia University, New York, NY, professor of creative writing, 1969-78; University of Illinois at Chicago Circle, professor of English, beginning 1978; Ohio State University, Columbus, professor of English until 1996, professor emeritus, 2004—. Visiting professor at Bennington College, 1973; teacher at Princeton University, 1974, Sarah Lawrence College, 1975-76, and 92nd-Street Y, New York, NY. Appeared in films *My Knees Were Jumping: Remembering the Kindertransports,* 1998, and *Into the Arms of Strangers: Stories of the Kindertransport,* Warner Bros., 2000.

### Member

PEN, American Academy of Arts and Science.

*Lore Segal* (Photograph by Ellen Dubin Reproduced by permission.)

### Awards, Honors

Guggenheim fellowship in creative writing, 1965-66; National Council of the Arts and Humanities grant, 1967-68; Creative Artists Public Service Program grant, 1972-73; Children's Spring Book Festival first prize, *Washington Post Book World,* and American Library Association Notable Book designation, both 1970, both for *Tell Me a Mitzie; All the Way Home* and *The Juniper Tree, and Other Tales from Grimm* included in Children's Book Showcase, 1974; Notable Book designation, *New York Times,* 1985, for *The Story of Mrs. Lovewright and Purrless, Her Cat,* and 1987, for *The Book of Adam to Moses;* American Academy of Arts and Letters Award, 1985, for *Her First American;* Pulitzer Prize finalist, 2008, for *Shakespeare's Kitchen;* Dorothy & Lewis B. Cullman Center for Scholars fellowship, 2008-09.

### Writings

*FOR CHILDREN*

*Tell Me a Mitzi,* illustrated by Harriet Pincus, Farrar, Strauss (New York, NY), 1970.

*All the Way Home,* illustrated by James Marshall, Farrar, Strauss (New York, NY), 1973.

*Tell Me a Trudy,* illustrated by Rosemary Wells, Farrar, Strauss & Giroux (New York, NY), 1977.

*The Story of Old Mrs. Brubeck and How She Looked for Trouble and Where She Found Him,* illustrated by Marcia Sewall, Pantheon (New York, NY), 1981.

*The Story of Mrs. Lovewright and Purrless, Her Cat,* illustrated by Paul O. Zelinsky, Knopf (New York, NY), 1985, reprinted, Atheneum Books for Young Readers (New York, NY), 2005.

*The Book of Adam to Moses,* illustrated by Leonard Baskin, Knopf (New York, NY), 1987.

*The Story of King Saul and King David,* illustrations from the Pamplona Bible, Schocken Books (New York, NY), 1991.

*Morris the Artist,* illustrated by Boris Kulikov, Farrar, Strauss & Giroux (New York, NY), 2003.

*Why Mole Shouted, and Other Stories,* illustrated by Sergio Ruzzier, Farrar, Strauss & Giroux (New York, NY), 2004.

*More Mole Stories and Little Gopher, Too,* illustrated by Sergio Ruzzier, Farrar, Strauss & Giroiux (New York, NY), 2005.

*FICTION*

*Other People's Houses* (autobiographical novel; originally serialized in *New Yorker,* 1962-64), Harcourt (New York, NY), 1964, reprinted, New Press (New York, NY), 2004.

*Lucinella,* Farrar, Strauss (New York, NY), 1976, reprinted, Melville House, 2009.

*Her First American,* Knopf (New York, NY), 1985, reprinted, New Press (New York, NY), 2007.

*Shakespeare's Kitchen: Stories,* New Press/W.W. Norton (New York, NY), 2007.

*TRANSLATOR*

(With W.D. Snodgrass) Christian Morgenstern, *Gallows Songs* (poetry), University of Michigan Press (Ann Arbor, MI), 1967.

(With Randall Jarrell) Wilhelm and Jacob Grimm, *The Juniper Tree, and Other Tales from Grimm,* illustrated by Maurice Sendak, Farrar, Strauss & Giroux (New York, NY), 1974, revised edition, 2003.

Wilhelm and Jacob Grimm, *The Bear and the Kingbird,* Farrar, Strauss & Giroux (New York, NY), 1979.

*OTHER*

Short stories anthologized in books, including *Best American Short Stories,* 1989; and *O. Henry Prize Stories,* 1990, 2008. Contributor of stories to periodicals, including *New Yorker, Saturday Evening Post, New Republic, Epoch, Commentary, New American Review,* and *Story.* Contributor of reviews to *New York Times Book Review* and *New Republic.* Contributor of translations of poetry to *Mademoiselle, Atlantic Monthly, Hudson Review, Poetry,* and *Tri-Quarterly.*

## Adaptations

*The Story of Mrs. Lovewright and Purrless, Her Cat* was adapted for audio cassette by Random House/ Miller-Brody Productions, 1986; *Tell Me a Mitzi* was adapted for audio cassette by Scholastic, 1986; *Her First American* was adapted for audio cassette by New Letters, 1990.

## Sidelights

Lore Segal was born in Austria in 1928, and by the time the Jewish girl reached age ten, German chancellor Adolf Hitler was ruler of her European homeland. Fearing that harm would come to their daughter, Ignatz and Franzi Groszmann made the difficult decision facing thousands of other Jewish parents in Austria, Germany, and Czechoslovakia, and sent Lore to England. One among the 10,000 European children whose flight to foster homse became known as the Kindertransport, Segal boarded a train for Great Britainin 1938, leaving her parents behind to endure Hitler's effort to rid the world of all persons of Jewish descent. When her parents also made their escape to England, Segal and her family found themselves impoverished. The girl continued to live as a refugee, boarding with five different English families before reaching age eighteen. Attending Bedford College, London, she earned her B.A. in English with honors in 1948.

In 1951, Segal and her now-widowed mother immigrated to the United States and made a new home in New York City. Her first years in the United States were difficult: she worked as a filing clerk in a shoe factory, as a receptionist, and for a textile design studio. During this period Segal also began writing fiction, and was soon selling stories to such vaunted magazines as *Commentary* and the *New Yorker.* In 1961, at age thirty-three, she married David Segal, with whom she had two children before he passed away, tragically and unexpectedly, nine years later. Trained as a teacher, Segal eventually joined the English department at Columbia University and continued teaching creative writing on the college level until her retirement in 2004.

In 1964 Segal's first novel, *Other People's Houses,* was published. Autobiographical, the book traces the author's own life as it follows its protagonist from Austria to England to the United States. *Other People's Houses* was highly praised by critics, Elizabeth Thalman describing it in a *Library Journal* review as "a story of courage, endurance and humor."

In 1970, with *Tell Me a Mitzi,* Segal began to address a younger readership, inspired by her more upbeat experiences as the mother of young children. *Tell Me a Mitzi* collects several tales about a little girl named Mitzi who gets into trouble with her baby brother Jacob. Each story is written as if it is being told by a parent to a child, and the children beg their parent to "tell me a Mitzi" when they want to hear another tale. The same technique is used in *Tell Me a Trudy,* and Segal has noted that both the tales and the phrase requesting them are based on the bedtime traditions she enjoyed with her own children.

In addition to writing her own books for children, Segal has translated two collections of fairy and folk tales collected by the Brothers Grimm. With its illustrations by noted artist Maurice Sendak, *The Juniper Tree, and Other Tales from Grimm* has become a childhood classic and has remained in print ever since its 1973 publication. Her other books for children, such as *The Story of Old Mrs. Brubeck and How She Looked for Trouble and Where She Found Him,* are written using classic fairy-tale techniques.

Departing from her own experiences, Segal creates what *Horn Book* contributor Deirdre F. Baker described as "an idiosyncratic, comfortable world where affection rules" in her review of *More Mole Stories and Little Gopher, Too.* In the four tales contained in this book, as well those as its prequel, *Why Mole Shouted, and Other Stories,* Segal focuses on the close bond between a preschool-aged child and a grandmother, although in this case the "child" is in fact a mole. Navigating the childhood temptation of a cookie meant to be eaten after chores are done, the difficulty in sharing favorite toys, and the desire for attention, Segal's text was praised by Baker as "perceptive" and "amusing," while a *Kirkus Reviews* contributor referred to the author's "classically droll style." *Why Mole Shouted, and Other Stories* impressed a *Publishers Weekly* reviewer, who remarked that the author "again proves she's in tune with a child's mindset." In *School Library Journal,* Linda M. Kenton wrote of the same book that "Segal captures the caprice and occasionally challenging nature of young children" in a book featuring Italian-born artist Sergio Ruzzier's "dreamy, almost surreal" illustrations.

*Morris the Artist,* which *Booklist* contributor Gillian Engberg described as an "unusual, visually stimulating story," illustrates the complex dynamics at play in children's relationships and "letting creativity loose." In Segal's tale a boy named Morris grudgingly takes time away from his favorite activity—painting—to attend friend Benjamin's birthday party. Finding the perfect gift is easy: paints, of course. However, when it comes time to relinquish the gift, Morris clings to the nice new paint box. Ultimately the boy finds a way to keep the gift and give it to Brian at the same time when he turns the party into a painting frenzy, sparking his friends' creativity and inspiring them with his talent and enthusiasm for art. Praising Segal's text for its "empathy and imagination," a *Publishers Weekly* reviewer also noted Boris Kulikov's "extraordinary paintings," with their "off kilter, funhouse feeling." Within what Engberg described as Kulikov's "odd, fantastical world," Segal's story highlights a childhood situation that the critic dubbed "universal."

In her writing career, Segal has continued to weave adult novels within her list of books for children. Her second novel, *Lucinella,* is a story of the eponymous poet, who navigates a surreal publishing world where Greek gods and older and younger versions of herself can show up at industry cocktail parties. This book was followed almost nine years later by *Her First American,* Segal's third novel and winner of the American Academy of Arts and Letters Award in 1985. The novel's plot features protagonist Ilka Weissnix, a new immigrant from Vienna who speaks very little English; the story takes place just after the end of World War II. After Ilka meets Carter Bayoux, a black journalist who is also an overweight alcoholic, they fall in love and the bulk of the novel portrays their budding relationship, as well as their comedic attempts to grapple with the language barrier between them. As a *Time* critic noted, "the voluble, repetitious Bayoux cannot match [Ilka's] lunatic poignancy, but he can be an apt foil." In a glowing *New York Times Book Review* article, Carolyn Kizer stated that "Segal may have come closer than anyone to writing The Great American Novel" in *Her First American.* Ultimately, Kizer concluded, "Segal, in her mix of history, memory and invention, and the ruthless honesty which has always characterized her work, shows us ourselves."

Ilka returns in *Shakespeare's Kitchen: Stories,* which became a Pulitzer Prize finalist in 2008. In Segal's linked stories, Ilka is now fully assimilated into American culture, and her accent has faded. She begins working at a think tank in Connecticut, and although she is afraid that she will not find friends among her intellectual coworkers, she does. Critics applauded *Shakespeare's Kitchen, Booklist* critic Keir Graff calling it "a perfect" look at "the roles we play and the truths and lies we tell ourselves about ourselves." Commenting on "the intrigue and angst stirred up in [Segal's] self-absorbed characters' internal monologues," a *Publishers Weekly* reviewer concluded that "when stacked together, these vignettes are hilarious and telling."

## Biographical and Critical Sources

*BOOKS*

Lanes, Selma, *Down the Rabbit Hole,* Atheneum (New York, NY), 1971.
Segal, Lore, *Other People's Houses,* Harcourt (New York, NY), 1964.

*PERIODICALS*

*Atlantic Monthly,* September 1, 2007, review of *Shakespeare's Kitchen: Stories,* p. 130.
*Booklist,* August, 2003, Gillian Engberg, review of *Morris the Artist,* p. 1990; May 1, 2004, Hazel Rochman, review of *Why Mole Shouted, and Other Stories,* p. 1564; April 1, 2007, Keir Graff, review of *Shakespeare's Kitchen,* p. 29.

*Commentary,* March, 1965, Cynthia Ozick, review of *Other People's Houses.*

*Contemporary Fiction,* fall, 1993, Philip G. Cavanaugh, "The Present Is a Foreign Country: Lore Segal's Fiction," p. 475.

*Country Living Gardener,* December 22, 2003, "Once upon a Time," p. 16.

*Entertainment Weekly,* April 20, 2007, "Jejune Bugs," p. 66; December 28, 2007, Jennifer Reese, "Fiction of the Year," p. 134.

*Financial Times,* December 5, 2009, Adrian Turpin, review of *Lucinella,* p. 19.

*Horn Book,* March-April, 2005, Deirdre F. Baker, review of *More Mole Stories and Little Gopher, Too,* p. 194.

*Internet Bookwatch,* October 1, 2007, review of *Shakespeare's Kitchen.*

*Kirkus Reviews,* May 1, 2003, review of *Morris the Artist,* p. 683; April 1, 2004, review of *Why Mole Shouted, and Other Stories,* p. 337.

*Library Journal,* November 15, 1964, Elizabeth Thalman, review of *Other People's Houses;* March 15, 2007, Amy Ford, review of *Shakespeare's Kitchen,* p. 66.

*New Republic,* December 12, 1964, Richard Gilman, review of *Other People's Houses;* August 15, 1985, Laura Obolensky, review of *Her First American,* p. 41.

*New Statesman,* March 19, 1965, review of *Other People's Houses.*

*Newsweek,* July 8, 1985, review of *Her First American.*

*New York Times Book Review,* May 17, 1970, review of *Tell Me a Mitzi,* p. 26; October 24, 1976, review of *Lucinella,* p. 20; May 19, 1985, Carolyn Kizer, review of *Her First American,* p. 7; May 6, 2007, Sue Halpern, review of *Shakespeare's Kitchen,* p. 29.

*People Weekly,* July 8, 1985, Campbell Geeslin, review of *Her First American,* p. 12; April 9, 2007, review of *Shakespeare's Kitchen,* p. 47.

*Publishers Weekly,* April 7, 2003, review of *Morris the Artist,* p. 66; March 22, 2004, review of *Why Mole Shouted, and Other Stories,* p. 85; December 31, 2007, review of *Shakespeare's Kitchen,* p. 23.

*Saturday Review,* July 25, 1970, review of *Tell Me a Mitzi;* October 16, 1976, review of *Lucinella.*

*School Library Journal,* April, 2004, Linda M. Kenton, review of *Why Mole Shouted, and Other Stories,* p. 124.

*Time,* July 1, 1985, review of *Her First American,* p. 60.


*ONLINE*


*Lore Segal Home Page,* http://www.loresegal.net (May 1, 2010).

---

*Autobiography Feature*

---

# Lore Segal

I was born in Vienna on March 8, 1928, in a snow-storm that was unusual, if not unheard of in Austria, for a day so close to spring. My mother was twenty-two and surprised the nurse by picking up a little table and carrying it around her hospital room. She was feeling cheerful and happy that I was going to be born.

I lived the first ten comfortable years as my parents' only child, my grandparents' only grandchild, my father's and my mother's brothers' only niece: the center of attention, admiration, and the focus of great expectations.

My parents and I lived in a respectable apartment on one of Vienna's main streets. I can still say the address if I start at the beginning and nobody stops me till I've got to the end: Josephstädter Strasse 81/83 Zweite Stiege Erster Stock Tür 9.

Forty years later, in 1968, when I went back to Vienna, I walked down that cobbled street with its four-story buildings and spider webs of electric cables that power the Vienna tram cars, and recognized Hammerling Park, where my mother used to take me to play, and Studio Steffi Stahl, where she took me for my ballet and gymnastic lessons.

I walked into number 81/83 and up the stairs that circle the central elevator in its wrought-iron cage. I rang the bell of door number nine, leaned my ear toward the door, and listened. I could hear the slurp of slippers coming out of my parents' bedroom on the right. I knew very well that the blond wood double bed, the lace bed-spread, had been gone these thirty-five years, and tried—and failed—to imagine that room without these familiar furnishings. It excited me to know exactly that the front door would open into the foyer right across from the door of the toilet, a separate room from the bathroom. Left was the kitchen with its window look-ing down into the square, gray yard where the beggars had stood and sung. My mother used to wrap a coin into a corner of newspaper. I would throw it down and watch the beggar pick it up and bow and tip his hat.

Beyond the kitchen was the narrow little maid's room. My grandmother had sent us a series of country girls. It was Lina I had loved to sit in the kitchen with. I think it was Lina my mother sent away because she stole my golden chain with the Star of David.

*"Gisella Groszmann, my father's mother, who lived in Pressburg, a Hungarian town that became Czech after World War I; her younger son, 'Mimi' (inset left); and my father, 'Igo'"* (Courtesy of Lore Segal.)

Now the slippers must be passing the place where there used to stand a little cupboard for my coats and dresses. I could tell the slippers were rounding the corner past the living-room door.

The living-room door had a frosted-glass inset. When my mother sent me to go to the toilet before bed, I used to hunker down out of sight outside the door and count the steps I ought to have been walking down the un-lighted foyer. I'd count the seconds it would have taken me to open the door into that toilet full of ghosts and robbers. I would count the seconds it should have taken me to do what I was supposed to do, to open and close the door, to walk back, and *now* I would stand up, and walk back into the living room.

I used to lie in my bed listening to the grown-ups in the dining room—my father and mother, the dinner guests, and whichever one of the two uncles happened to be living with us at the time—sitting around the big table. Sometimes there would be several voices talking at once, then one, then a burst of laughter. Oh, the thrill—the mystery—of that imagined conversation of the grown-ups!

The slippers had reached the door. I could hear the chain being fastened inside. The door cracked open. An old woman's voice said, "*Ja bitte?* Yes, please? What do you want?" and I surprised myself by asking for my father.

She said there was no Ignatz Groszmann living there. I knew that there wasn't: My father had been dead these twenty-five years.

*

My father had been a very tall man. I have inherited his sharp nose. From my fifth year on, my father was often ill. My mother and I would take the electric tram across Vienna to visit him lying flat on his back in a hospital bed. When he was well, he worked in a bank. I remember sitting on his lap asking him what he did there. I meant: What did it look like where he did what he did?

*Segal, with her mother and father, and a friend, "on holiday in the Austrian Alps before Hitler annexed Austria"* (Courtesy of Lore Segal.)

228

This document of identity is issued with the approval of His Majesty's Government in the United Kingdom to young persons to be admitted to the United Kingdom for educational purposes under the care of the Inter-Aid Committee for children.

## THIS DOCUMENT REQUIRES NO VISA.

### PERSONAL PARTICULARS.

Name  GROSSMANN  Lore

Sex  Female     Date of Birth  1928 / 8/3

Place  Vienna

Full Names and Address of Parents

Grossmann  Ignatz
2 Holland Strasse
Vienna 8

*The document that enabled Lore's passage to England, at Harwich; it is stamped "12 DEC 1938" on the reverse side* (Courtesy of Lore Segal.)

Were there curtains in the window? Were there other people and what did they look like? I was asking the kinds of questions to which stories give us the answers. My father answered that he did numbers. He was never any good at telling me the things I needed to know.

The person, in my childhood, who gave me my ideas was my mother's young brother Paul, who lived with us while he studied medicine at the University of Vienna. It was Paul who would tuck me in and sit on the side of my bed and tell me what was going on in the world of politics, science, poetry. He told me stories.

The arbiter of my taste was my mother. She had been a student at the Vienna Academy of Music and played Bach on the piano. Because she said that Bach was best, I said he was best, though in my secret heart I preferred the juicier sounds of Chopin. My later taste has caught up with my childish hypocrisy.

So went the first decade of my life: I went to the *Volksschule*—the public school around the corner. Afternoons I played with my cousin Inge or my friend Ditta. Summers we spent in the Austrian Alps or in Fischamend in my grandparents' house.

My grandparents lived in a great, rambling, thick-walled old house in the village of Fischamend on the river Danube, half an hour's train ride from Vienna and not far from the Czechoslovak border. My grandparents ran a dry-goods store that sold everything: shoelaces, bolts of fabric, aprons sewed by my grandmother, along with buttons, hairbrushes, gum boots, and catgut for violin strings. My grandfather lent me his young shop assistant, Mitzi, to play with. Mitzi and I sat out in the sunlit yard and talked. Or rather I talked. I told Mitzi my life plans: I was going to look blonde and pretty just like her and I was going to go the university just like my uncle Paul.

*

It was in March 1938 (four days after my tenth birthday) that German chancellor Adolf Hitler annexed Austria to Germany. His Nazi troops marched into Vienna and were welcomed by members of the Austrian Nazi party. It was the beginning of the deadly chapter in the history of European Jews.

Early that first morning my parents and I went down to get our money out of the bank, but the bank did not open. All around were young men in strange new uniforms saluting each other with right arms stretched forward. New red flags with the black swastika in a white circle flew in the bright March air. My parents hurried me back home.

By May, our maid, Poldi, had to leave us: non-Jews were no longer allowed to work in Jewish households. Nor were Jews allowed to work in non-Jewish organizations, and my father was fired from the bank. A week later, a uniformed member of the SS—Hitler's special troops—commandeered our flat and everything in it, and we went to live with my grandparents in Fischamend. Uncle Paul, too, soon turned up there with one ear half dangling: he had got into a fight with some Nazis at the University. That was the end of his studies.

Now the Fischamend Nazis—the young men and women with whom my mother and Uncle Paul had gone to school—set out to make our lives impossible for us. They wrote "DON'T BUY FROM THE JEW" in red paint on the walls outside my grandfather's store. My grandfather went outside and patiently scrubbed the walls. The words faded but the blood-red color remained. At night they threw stones through the bedroom windows. One evening they brought ladders and stepped right through the living-room windows and carried away whatever they felt like taking. Next evening the three men—my grandfather, my father, and Uncle Paul—were taken to the police station, beaten up a bit, and told to leave Fischamend within twenty-four hours.

*Father, Ignatz (Igo) Groszmann* (Courtesy of Lore Segal.)

We came back to Vienna with no roof over our heads. The members of the family found aunts and cousins to stay with. I went to live with my friend Ditta and her family. On the way to the school reserved for Jewish children and taught by Jewish teachers, we passed copies of a journal called *Der Stürmer* ("The Storm Maker") posted on the walls. *Der Stürmer* specialized in cruel Jewish stereotypes. And it was a common sight to see a couple of youthful Nazis forcing an old Jewish man or woman to scrub the sidewalks on which someone had painted anti-Jewish slogans with that blood-colored paint.

Then began the nocturnal knocking on the doors. Jewish men were hauled out of their beds—or they might be picked up in the street—and taken to concentration camps.

Now the single subject of conversation among the grown-ups was how to get out of the country, how to find a country that would let Jews in, how to make sure the Nazis would let us out. And what, *if* we got out, would we do in a country whose language we wouldn't know? I remember that my uncle Paul took courses in farming and massage; my mother learned large-quantity cooking; my father tried in vain to learn machine knitting and the making of little leather wallets.

*

On December 10, 1938, my father and mother took me to the station and put me on a train that was to transport 500 Jewish children out of Austria. A hundred children stayed in Holland, where the Nazis overtook them a year later, and the rest of us crossed the channel into England.

We were housed in a summer camp on the east coast in what turned out to be the coldest winter in living memory. The water froze in the faucets. We slept in our coats. We sat in our coats and mittens in a great hall built of glass and steel and waited for English families to come and take us home with them.

I have written a book about these experiences and called it *Other People's Houses.* From the time I arrived in England until I went to the University of London at eighteen years of age, I lived with five different English families.

The first was a Jewish family in Liverpool, in the north of England. Mr. and Mrs. Cohen—Aunt Essie and Uncle Sam, as they wanted me, and as I never could get myself to call them—lived comfortably in a large house with a pleasant little garden in back. They had six grown daughters. The youngest, Ruth, was sixteen, a clever, spirited girl who took an interest in me, and I loved her most gratefully.

I had arrived in England thinking I had learned to speak English in my school in Vienna. I was surprised to find that I couldn't understand what anybody was saying. I kept thinking if I just listened harder, I would understand, and so I listened so hard that very soon I did understand.

One of the things I understood was that these English people had only the dimmest idea of what was going on in Vienna, and that it was my business to tell them. I bought myself an exercise book and filled it cover to cover with my Hitler stories. Ruth found someone to translate it into English, and that, I suppose, is how I turned into a writer.

But there was a piece of writing that I had done sitting in the camp, in my coat and mittens: I had written a letter to my father's cousins, who had already immigrated to London, asking them to save my parents from the Nazis. The cousins sent the letter to a refugee committee which found an English family who needed a cook and butler and they sent my parents a visa to come to England.

On March 8, 1939, on my eleventh birthday, my parents turned up in Liverpool. They were able to stay a couple of nights before travelling south to their first jobs as servants in an English household. While I was visiting my parents for the summer holidays, the Cohens wrote that they could not have me back.

The local refugee committee found me a new home with a family called Gillham, in Tunbridge, a small town within visiting distance from my parents. Mr. Gillham was a fireman on the railroad and a union member—a clever, witty man. Mr. and Mrs. Gillham had two daughters, Joy and Marie. Marie was two years older than I. We became great friends. The Gillhams lived in a narrow brick row house, but it was big enough to accommodate the Jewish refugee child as well as an orphan boy from the local orphanage. He was called Harold. Harold hated me most heartily, and must have felt guilty about it; he alternately threatened me, and bought me games—Monopoly, Snakes & Ladders. Marie and I both won scholarships to the local private school, where the girls played tennis and wore green uniforms. I was happy and accepted, but Marie continued at the town school in her plain black uniform. To go to the "la-di-dah" school, she said, would be a betrayal of her working-class father.

The Gillhams soon found that they could no longer keep me, and I went to live with the family of a munitions worker whose name I don't remember, though I recall that they had one girl and two boys, one a spastic and a little one who set the bathroom on fire. When the munitions worker's family moved to another town they sent me to live with the wife's parents.

Old Mr. Foster was a milkman who delivered the morning bottles with his little pony and cart. These were wonderfully good old people. They lived in an even tinier row house crowded with grown sons and a boy

*Mother, Franziska (Franzi) Groszmann, née Stern* (Courtesy of Lore Segal.)

evacuated from London, where the bombs were falling night after night. I remember that the middle-aged daughter, who worked as a lady's maid across town, slept at the neighbor's so I could have her little bedroom which overlooked the bomb shelter that the sons were digging in the strip of backyard: World War II had been declared in September 1939.

Early in 1940 my father and Uncle Paul and all male German-speakers over age sixteen had been interned on the Isle of Man. Now Kent was designated a "protected area" out of bounds to all "enemy aliens."

For a while my mother and I lived in a very grand country house. It must have been a bitter time for my mother: my father was interned and wrote that he felt unwell; my mother kept asking every English person she met if they could do something to bring my grandparents, whom she had had to leave behind in Hitler's Vienna, to England. It must have been a formidable task to cook the elaborate meals for the lady of the house and feed the staff in the servants' hall. There was a housekeeper, a butler, a houseboy, I think, and all the upper and under house and kitchen maids. The chauffeur and his wife had their own establishment over the old stables. There was, I remember, a small army of gardeners. I cannot find it in my heart to be sorry that I experienced those times: How many people have the opportunity to see the orderly and courteous life of "upstairs" and "downstairs" from the inside?

But the unquietness of so many moves took a toll. I was twelve when my mother and I arrived in the ancient market town of Guildford in Surrey, and I was throwing up. Between bouts, I lay on a bed in a narrow room at the head of a steep stair and my mother read me *David Copperfield* and the concept "writer" burst upon me and I knew that that's what I was going to be. Come to think of it, I had *been* writing since I was ten.

This was also the day when my father suffered his first and minor stroke. The authorities must have taken a look at him and seen that he didn't look like much of a threat to England's war effort, so they sent him "home." My father arrived in Guildford with our temporary address on a piece of paper. The policeman, whom he approached for directions, arrested him for being out after curfew, took him to the police station, and booked him. Then he put my father in a police car and drove him to the house with the steep stairs. All night I kept waking from a nauseous sleep and seeing my parents sitting together on the edge of the other bed, talking. I saw my father cry.

The Guildford refugee committee lady was called Miss Wallace. She found my father a job as a gardener where he gardened until his next stroke. She got my mother a job as a cook with the Macgregors, who lived in a seventeenth-century watermill. They had four daughters and an ancient grandmother, a sickly aunt and a scruffy dog, and every weekend the house was full of visitors come to rest up from the strain and horror of the London blitz. My mother worked hard, but she loved the Macgregors and they loved her and forgot about her being their cook, and she became a member of the family with whom she lived through the bitter war.

Miss Wallace had taken me home to live with her and her older companion, Miss Ellis, in a grand Victorian house with plum trees, and gooseberry bushes and currant bushes, a rockery, and a rose garden.

*The author with her husband, David Segal, daughter, Beatrice, and baby son, Jacob, 1964* (Courtesy of Lore Segal.)

Miss Ellis and Miss Wallace kept me from my twelfth till my eighteenth year. Miss Wallace paid for my piano lessons. Miss Ellis bought me a green silk dress to wear evenings in the elegant drawing room.

In 1939 my uncle Paul and his young wife, Edith, had moved to the Dominican Republic, where the twenty-one-year-old Edith, who was pregnant with their first child, died of blood poisoning. Paul redoubled his efforts and managed to get my grandparents out of Vienna.

My father, meanwhile, became increasingly ill. He had one stroke after the other and was in and out of the hospital. My mother cooked lunch and took the bus to the hospital and took the bus back to cook dinner. My father died in 1945, a few days before the end of the war.

I had done well at my high school and received what strikes me now as a remarkably generous scholarship for a foreigner to go to the University of London. The scholarship paid for my tuition and, at the beginning of each semester, I sent in an itemized list of what I would need for rent, food, clothes, and books, and would receive a check to cover these expenses.

My mother and I moved to London in the summer of 1945. We lived in a good-sized bed-sitter with a sink and a hotplate. I remember that the carpet, curtains, and bedspread were a no-color midway between maroon and khaki. My mother found a job as companion to an old German doctor. I took the underground to Baker Street Station, walked into Regents Park, and crossed the little bridge over a lake full of ducks and swans into Bedford College for Women. I was an indifferent scholar, but the books from *Beowulf* to T.S. Eliot dazzled me; London dazzled me—the streets, the theater, the museums of art, above all, dazzled me. Summers my friends and I youth-hostled into the English Lake Country.

It was at the beginning of my third year in college that my grandfather became ill. My mother packed herself up and went to the Dominican Republic to help look after him. It was our understanding that after my final examination I would follow her.

When the time came I went, but unwillingly. I lived several months in a tiny, dusty inland town of Santiago de los Caballeros in a room in back of my uncle Paul's grocery store. Paul sold European products to the local population in pennyworth quantities. He encouraged me to move to the capital—in those days it was called Ciudad Trujillo—where I supported myself by teaching English at the business school and privately to members of the diplomatic set. I taught the Argentinean ambassador and the daughter of the French consul, and I groused and bemoaned my fate. It is my years in the Dominican Republic that I have learned to regret. I don't mean my being there, but my being there with such ill will that I

*The author's husband, book editor David Isaac Segal: "He died in December 1970, at age forty-two."* (Courtesy of Lore Segal.)

did not look about me, did not see or enjoy what there was to be seen and enjoyed, and managed to not learn Spanish. Let youth be my excuse. In 1938, when Hitler came to Austria, my father had put our names on the "American Quota" and we had started waiting for the number that would allow us to enter the United States. I was twenty one and in love with London. So far as I could tell, I was to spend an infinite number of years in this Latin-American backwater.

My grandfather died the following year, and soon after my grandmother and Uncle Paul received their American numbers and left for the United States. My mother and I followed on May 1, 1951. The four of us lived in a two-bedroom apartment in Manhattan's Upper West Side.

New immigrants are grateful for the most insufficient and unsuitable jobs. My uncle Paul worked cleaning bottles and animal cages in a research lab; after that he worked in a philatelist's office. My mother cooked at Schraffts, sold bread in a bakery, and worked as a baby nurse.

I got a job as a filing clerk in a shoe factory. I went to secretarial school in the evenings, but never managed to master either shorthand or typing. I got fired from my first job as a receptionist and went to work in a textile-design studio, where I freelanced, achieving the goal of my life which I have followed to this day: to earn my living in the afternoons in order to have my mornings free for writing.

\*

Segal contributed the following update to her autobiographical essay in 2010:

I'm grateful that the latter half of my life promises to be less interesting than the beginning. History, having

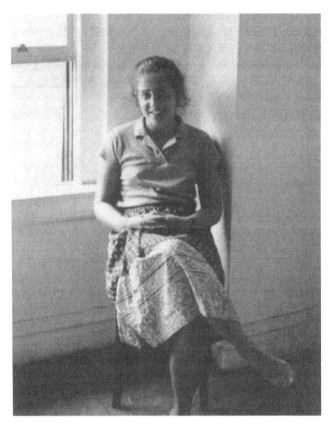

*Daughter Beatrice Segal, age twenty* (Courtesy of Lore Segal.)

cut up my childhood and rearranged my teen years and young womanhood, did, in the main, move its worst business to other parts of the world.

Let me catch up with the several characters in my story.

My grandmother's American life was not happy, but she had never been happy. A handsome, witty woman who tended to paranoia and depression, she never learned to speak English. She quarreled with her last living sister, who had also immigrated to New York. My grandmother spent her days in the apartment cooking beautiful suppers and looking out of the window waiting for us to come home. One day she stopped eating—stopped lifting the fork to her mouth. Her last years, to my mother's very great sorrow, my grandmother lived in an old-age home where she died on her eighty-first birthday.

Uncle Paul: When Paul arrived in New York he looked in the phone book and found the name of his Viennese friend, Dolf Plazcek. Dolf had married the English writer, Jan Struther, the original creator of Mrs. Miniver. Paul, whose first young wife had died in the Dominican Republic, married Dolf's sister, Susan.

Until his death in his mid-nineties, my uncle Paul remained my dear friend and collaborator for a number of translations. They include *The Gallows Songs* by Christian Morgenstern: we turned the German verse into literal and heavily annotated English and my friend, the

late W.D. Snodgrass, turned it into English poetry. Paul helped me with the translation of *The Juniper Tree and Other Tales from Grimm,* which was illustrated by Maurice Sendak, as well as two biblical narratives, *The Book of Adam to Moses* and *The Story of King Saul and King David.*

Paul's sons Peter and John, their wives, and children constitute the essential kinships that replace all the aunts, uncles, and cousins killed in the concentration camps or dispersed throughout the world by that worst of bad histories.

*

I, in the meanwhile, was earning my living as a textile designer. This could be done in the afternoon and night hours, leaving my mornings free to write. The first story I sold was to a magazine long since defunct, called *Husk.* Payment was two free copies. My next story sold to *Audience* and paid $15. The following story was bought by *Commentary* for $138, and the next sold to the *New Yorker,* which sent me a check for $1,500, which I threw down the incinerator. Accidentally, or did my subconscious need to register disbelief? The *New Yorker* gave me a replacement check and invited me to write a series on the subject with which I had filled that first exercise book in Liverpool, and which I have briefly retold in the first part of this essay. That is how I came to write *Other People's Houses* which was serial-

*Son Jacob Segal, age eighteen* (Courtesy of Lore Segal.)

ized in the magazine from 1962 to 1964. Harcourt Brace published it in book form the same year in which I gave birth to my son Jacob. It has been reissued several times, most recently in 2004, by the New Press, together with my novel, *Her First American.* In 2007 the New Press published my collection of related short stories, *Shakespeare's Kitchen,* which became one of the three finalists for that year's Pulitzer Prize.

Was it Freud who said what matters is work and love? In 1961, I had married David Segal who left his job as a salesman in his father's yarn business, which he didn't like and was no good at, to spend the next seven years of the life left to him as an editor, a happy man in the right job doing what he knew how to do. A shelf that stretches from wall to wall across one side of my living room holds the books he published. They include, to mention just a few, the work of Cynthia Ozick, William Gass, and John Gardener, the poetry of W.D. Snodgrass, and Frederick Exley's *A Fan's Notes.*

David died of a heart attack a few weeks before his forty-first birthday when our children were eight and six.

*

Our daughter Beatrice was born on March 2, 1962, a delicious, fat baby with enormous eyes. Mornings after her bath, breakfast, and an hour's play, Beatrice was always so kind as to go back to sleep for a couple of hours and let me do my writing. Red-headed Jacob, born March 3, 1964, never seemed to go to sleep at all.

"What does every working woman need?" asked a joke in the early days of feminism. The answer: A wife. My wonderful mother Franzi had come to live in her own apartment in the same building and took as much care of us as we would allow. She would come upstairs and do what she was good at: grandmothering. I went down to her apartment and did what I was good at: writing. It took me eighteen years to write *Her First American.* One way to describe the novel is to say that it tells the Americanization of a young Jewish-Austrian immigrant through her alliance with an intellectual black American. It was originally published by Farrar Straus & Giroux in 1978. I had taken a couple of years off to write *Lucinella,* a bit of a lark about the New York publishing world. *Lucinella,* was published in 1976 and was reissued by Melville House in 2009.

I have had the opportunity for two waves of children's books. The first lot, written in the 'Sixties, was for my children, Beatrice and Jacob. These include *Tell Me a Mitzi* and *Tell Me a Trudy* where "Mitzi" and "Trudy" are the characters who ask for the stories to be told in which they figure as the protagonists. Each of the girls has a Jacob as her little brother. I had asked Jacob if he wanted to be in the book and he did. I asked the shy

*Lore Segal, 1990* (Courtesy of Lore Segal.)

Beatrice and she said no, she didn't, a decision that, she tells me, she used to regret. These are domestic tales: If you get into a taxi and don't know your grandparents' address, the taxi driver can't take you there. And it was fun to slip so easily from the details of a very daily life into the details of a fantasy: If Jacob yells for the president's motorcade to come back, it stops and makes a U turn. The president even finds that in one of the pockets of the members of his entourage there is a stash of chewing gum for Jacob and for Mitzi and for their father. If there are nightly robbers in Trudy's bathroom, she writes Superman a letter, and he drops by to take care of things. *The Story of Mrs. Lovewright and Purrless, Her Cat* was dedicated to a pet of ours who would not be cozy, or sit on our laps, or purr.

The second wave of picture books came forty years later and was written for my children's children. *Why Mole Shouted, and Other Stories* and its sequel, *More Mole Stories and Little Gopher, Too,* are made up of several small stories about Mole and his grandmother Mole who live in a hole in the forest. Why *does* Mole shout? you are supposed to ask. Same reason you and I shout: We mean "Notice me!" Why can't Mole ever find his glasses? Because, like you and me, he never puts things back where they belong. Why won't Mole finish the ants on his plate before he eats up all the chocolate chip cookies? As if you and I don't know all

*Segal's grandchildren, Benjamin, Isaiah, and Leina, Riverside Park, 2009* (Photograph by Ellen Dubin Reproduced by permission.)

about chocolate chips, about cookies. Mole will never entirely obey his grandmother Mole, and Grandmother Mole will always love him.

I want to mention the blessed fun of having worked with the most talented and witty illustrators: Maurice Sendak, Harriet Pincus, Rosemary Wells, James Marshall, Boris Kullikov, and Paul O. Zelinsky.

\*

It was my mother, in those early years, who made it possible for me to work, no longer in textiles, but as a professor of creative writing, at first on a part-time schedule, at Columbia University's School of the Arts, at Princeton, Bennington, and Sarah Lawrence College. At a point in my fifties, I woke to the fact that my old age was not going to have a pension or health coverage and accepted a full-time appointment at the University of Illinois' Circle Campus. For fourteen years I commuted between my Riverside Drive apartment in New York and Chicago and, for the five years before my retirement in 1997, between New York and Ohio State

University in Columbus. Feeling at home in New York had been too hard to come by. I was not going to emigrate anywhere ever again.

My mother died three months before her 101st birthday. Beatrice, a school counselor and therapist, married another David Segal. Jacob, a political theorist, married Jean Halley. Both are college professors. The three beloved grandchildren are Beatrice's eleven-year-old Benjamin, and Jacob's Isaiah, now ten, and Leina, four.

The ageing writer retires *to* her true job. At eighty-two I still write mornings from eight till one, seven days a week, getting toward the end of a novel provisionally titled *The Seventh Floor.* It's my good fortune to find everything fascinating, everything a possible story. *The Seventh Floor* is the sad comedy of being old.

\*     \*     \*

## SEGAL, Lore Groszmann
### See SEGAL, Lore

\*     \*     \*

## SHANNON, David 1959-

### Personal

Born October 5, 1959, in Washington, DC; son of Roger (a radiologist) and Martha Shannon; married, 1988; wife's name Heidi (a voice-over artist); children: Emma. *Education:* Art Center College of Design, B.F.A., 1983. *Hobbies and other interests:* Fishing, playing guitar, playing baseball.

### Addresses
*Home*—Los Angeles, CA.

### Career
Author and illustrator of children's books.

### Awards, Honors
*New York Times* Best Illustrated Book selection, 1994, for *How Georgie Radbourn Saved Baseball,* and 1998, for *No, David!;* Best Books designation, *School Library Journal,* and Blue Ribbons designation, *Bulletin of the Center for Children's Books,* both 1998, and Caldecott Honor book designation, 1999, all for *No, David!;* Golden Kite Award, Society of Children's Book Writers and Illustrators, 2000, for *The Rain Came Down;* Booksense Best Picture Book selection, 2004, for *How I Became a Pirate* by Melinda Jay; *New York Times* Notable Book designation, 2006, for *Good Boy, Fergus!*

### Writings

*SELF-ILLUSTRATED*

*How Georgie Radbourn Saved Baseball,* Blue Sky Press (New York, NY), 1994.

*The Amazing Christmas Extravaganza,* Blue Sky Press (New York, NY), 1995.

*A Bad Case of Stripes,* Blue Sky Press (New York, NY), 1998.

*The Rain Came Down,* Blue Sky Press (New York, NY), 2000.

*Duck on a Bike,* Blue Sky Press (New York, NY), 2002.

*Alice the Fairy,* Blue Sky Press (New York, NY), 2004.

*Duck and a Book,* Scholastic (New York, NY), 2005.

*Good Boy, Fergus!,* Blue Sky Press (New York, NY), 2006.

*Too Many Toys,* Blue Sky Press (New York, NY), 2008.

*SELF-ILLUSTRATED; "DIAPER DAVID" SERIES*

*No, David!,* Blue Sky Press (New York, NY), 1998.

*David Goes to School,* Blue Sky Press (New York, NY), 1999.

*David Gets in Trouble,* Blue Sky Press (New York, NY), 2002.

*Oops!,* Blue Sky Press (New York, NY), 2005.

*David Smells!,* Blue Sky Press (New York, NY), 2005.

*Oh, David!,* Blue Sky Press (New York, NY), 2005.

*It's Christmas, David!,* Blue Sky Press (New York, NY), 2010.

*ILLUSTRATOR*

Julius Lester, *How Many Spots Does a Leopard Have? And Other Tales,* Scholastic (New York, NY), 1989.

Isaac Asimov, *Robbie,* Creative Education (Mankato, MN), 1989.

Isaac Asimov, *Franchise,* Creative Education (Mankato, MN), 1989.

Isaac Asimov, *All the Troubles of the World,* Creative Education (Mankato, MN), 1989.

Isaac Asimov, *Sally,* Creative Education (Mankato, MN), 1989.

Rafe Martin, *The Rough-Face Girl,* Putnam (New York, NY), 1992.

Jane Yolen, *Encounter,* Harcourt (San Diego, CA), 1992.

Rafe Martin, *The Boy Who Lived with the Seals,* Putnam (New York, NY), 1993.

Mark Shannon, *Gawain and the Green Knight,* Putnam (New York, NY), 1994.

Jane Yolen, *The Ballad of the Pirate Queens,* Harcourt (San Diego, CA), 1995.

Roger Culbertson, *African Folktales,* Running Press (Philadelphia, PA), 1995.

Audrey Wood, *The Bunyans,* Blue Sky Press (New York, NY), 1996.

Jane Yolen, *Sacred Places,* Harcourt (San Diego, CA), 1996.

Robert D. San Souci, *Nicholas Pipe,* Dial (New York, NY), 1997.

Mark Shannon, *The Acrobat and the Angel,* Putnam (New York, NY), 1999.

Rafe Martin, *The Shark God,* Arthur A. Levine (New York, NY), 2001.

Melinda Long, *How I Became a Pirate,* Harcourt (San Diego, CA), 2003.

Melinda Long, *Pirates Don't Change Diapers,* Harcourt (Orlando, FL), 2007.

(With others) Hunter McKown, *Meet Jack Truck!,* Little Simon (New York, NY), 2008.

(With others) Tom Mason and Dan Danko, *Who's That Truck?,* Little Simon (New York, NY), 2008.

Jon Scieszka, *Robot Zot!,* Simon & Schuster Books for Young Readers (New York, NY), 2009.

(With others) Sydney Parker, *Scoop That Snow!,* Little Simon (New York, NY), 2009.

(With others) Jon Scieszka, *Truckery Rhymes,* Simon & Schuster Books for Young Readers (New York, NY), 2009.

(With others) Lara Bergen, *Let's Dig It!,* Little Simon (New York, NY), 2010.

(With others) Jon Scieszka, *The Great Truck Rescue,* Simon & Schuster Books for Young Readers (New York, NY), 2010.

## Adaptations

Shannon's "Diaper David" character has been adapted as a plush toy. *Alice the Fairy* was adapted for CD, Scholastic Audio, 2009.

## Sidelights

Children's author and illustrator David Shannon's work has appeared in some of the most widely read publications in North America, including the *New York Times* and *Time* magazine. However, to his many young fans, Shannon is best known as the author of the humorous "Diaper David" picture books as well as of the self-illustrated picture books *The Rain Came Down, Duck on a Bike,* and *Too Many Toys.* A popular illustrator, Shannon has also brought to life stories by writers such as Audrey Wood, Jane Yolen, Rafe Martin, Isaac Asimov, Robert D. San Souci, Melinda Long, and Jon Scieszka. "I got involved with children's books almost by accident," he once explained to *SATA.* "I was amazed at the quality and variety of children's stories, and more and more found myself drawing things I drew as a boy: baseball players, pirates, knights, and Native Americans. I realized that children's books were what I had been working toward my whole life."

Born in Washington, DC, Shannon grew up in Spokane, Washington, knowing that he wanted to be an artist. During his college studies at the Art Center of Design in Pasadena, California, he realized that he did not want to become a fine-art painter; instead Shannon decided to work in illustration, where his engaging style of drawing was a perfect fit. After graduation he spent some time in New York City and ended up becoming a regular contributor to the *New York Times* Op Ed section, then the *New York Times Book Review.* Finally Shannon's work was noticed by an editor at Scholastic, who asked if he would like to illustrate Julius Lester's *How Many Spots Does a Leopard Have? And Other Tales,* a collection of adaptations of traditional African and Jewish folk tales. "I accepted, thinking it would be

*David Shannon teams up with award-winning writer Jon Scieszka to create the entertaining picture book* **Robot.** (Illustration copyright © 2009 by David Shannon. Reprinted with permission of Simon & Schuster Books for Young Readers, an imprint of Simon & Schuster's Children's Publishing Division.)

a good break, a one-shot," Shannon confessed in an interview for *Publishers Weekly.* "Once that book came out in 1989, other editors started sending me manuscripts." In the book, Shannon's use of "rich, warm, earth tones" creates images that "are particularly evocative," maintained *School Library Journal* contributor Kay McPherson, while a critic for *Publishers Weekly* termed the book's artwork "striking" and "as full of depth as the stories themselves."

Shannon's first self-illustrated picture book, *How Georgie Radbourn Saved Baseball,* tells the story of the villainous Boss Swaggert, a former major-league baseball star who suffered a slump, was booed off the field, and as a result has made it his life's work to eradicate the sport from the planet. Swaggert does this by becoming a rich and powerful media mogul, and he even has the president of the United States arrested for throwing the first pitch of the season opener. With baseball outlawed, spring ceases to arrive, and the world is one long winter where ballparks are now prisons for anyone who utters baseball-related slang. Into this world comes Georgie Radbourn, a precocious boy who can only, inexplicably, speak in such terms like "Batter up!" Georgie becomes a cause celebre and makes the evil Swaggert a deal: if he cannot hit Georgie's three pitches, the sport will be

restored. In her *Booklist* review of *How Georgie Radbourn Saved Baseball,* Stephanie Zvirin remarked on the "echoes of an Orwellian future" and the "strong, bleak vision Shannon conjures up so well in his dramatic illustrations." A *Kirkus Reviews* critic remarked that at the final showdown, the author-illustrator "gives this contest . . . an epic feel—plus a broad streak of comedy."

In *The Amazing Christmas Extravaganza* Mr. Merriweather suffers the taunts of his neighbor when he puts up just a modest string of lights on his house for the holiday season. Soon the two homeowners begin constructing competing, very elaborate displays that draw a nightly traffic-jam of visitors. As a result, adjoining neighbors turn on the Merriweathers, attacking their homes' Christmas display with common household tools and sporting equipment. "Rarely do pictures have so much narrative in them," noted a *Kirkus Reviews* contributor, who called the sum of the visual parts "startling." Zvirin wrote in *Booklist* that, although *The Amazing Christmas Extravaganza* is aimed at primary graders, the book has a definite adult appeal in its setup and comedy and its "brilliant colors, depth, and meticulous details" might lure older children as well. A *School Library Journal* contributor praised the book's "deft phrasing and amazing illustrations," and termed *The Amazing Christmas Extravaganza* "a singular tale" that is likely to "provoke discussion, both with its plot and its remarkable artwork."

Like *The Amazing Christmas Extravaganza, The Rain Came Down* features a group of tense neighbors; no one in Shannon's story seems happy when the rains come. The fighting of the animals who live in one house result in the yelling of the man who lives there, which wakes his baby, beginning a chain reaction that ends up in a traffic jam and lots of shouting. When the rain stops, the sun seems to bring out the best in everyone, helping all to make amends. Shannon's pictures use clothing and settings from early 1960s America, and they are seen from such angles as right in the middle of traffic to a bird's-eye view of the whole town. A reviewer for *Publishers Weekly* noted that "Shannon expertly uses vertiginous angles as he builds suspense," and *Booklist* critic Gillian Engberg called *The Rain Came Down* a "spirited, beautifully illustrated new work." Although most of the characters depicted are adults, Lisa Dennis maintained in her *School Library Journal* review that "kids will just enjoy it as a fun story cheerfully told and amusingly illustrated."

A mischievous duck is the star of *Duck on a Bike.* When Duck discovers a bicycle in the farmyard, he decides he is going to learn to ride it. When he finally does, Shannon shows the reactions of all the other farm animals to Duck's new toy: some are envious, like Mouse, while Cat cannot be bothered and Horse is sure he can run faster. When a group of children leave their bikes riderless Duck's animal friends all do their best to catch a ride. "The exuberant fun really takes off in Shannon's crayon-bright paintings," praised Joanna Rudge Long in her review of *Duck on a Bike* for *Horn Book,* and Marianne Saccardi predicted in *School Library Journal* that readers will be "chiming in on the repeated phrases," as well as the noises of the barnyard animals. In *Booklist* Ilene Cooper concluded that Shannon's "whole bright book is tons of fun."

The West Highland terrier who has starred as a background character in several of Shannon's books is the titular hero in *Good Boy, Fergus!* Unlike the title, Fergus is not always a well-behaved dog: in fact, he rarely responds to his name, loves to chase cats, piddles as he pleases, and enjoys biting the heads off the flowers in his owner's garden. As Shannon reveals in his illustrations, however, the blame for this bad-dog behavior is partially that of Fergus's unseen owner, who sneaks the puppy treats and rewards bad behavior with welcome attention. Based on Shannon's real-life pup, Fergus is "an irrepressibly charming canine," wrote a *Kirkus Reviews* writer, and his goal is always to find "a new way to be pampered by his adoring owner." Calling *Good Boy, Fergus!* "delightful," Patricia T. O'Conner added in her *New York Times Book Review* appraisal that Shannon's "beautifully illustrated" story features doggy antics that "ring true" as "authentic."

Spencer, the young star of *Too Many Toys,* has a bedroom that rivals F.A.O. Schwartz, as Shannon's colorful artwork makes plain. When Spencer's mother grows tired of sorting and shelving and dusting the boy's plethora of playthings, she decides that it is time to downsize, toy-wise. "Snappy dialogue and an absolutely on-target understanding of the psyches of both mother and child make the negotiation scene absolutely priceless," wrote a *Kirkus Reviews* writer, and in *Publishers Weekly* a critic asserted that the boy's "not-so-delicate negotiations give Shannon . . . plenty of opportunity to display his flair for kid-friendly expressionism and domestic satire." *Too Many Toys* "carries an attitude large enough to entertain a big group, while the illustrations are detailed enough to engage even the most inattentive," concluded Thom Barthelmess in *Booklist.*

Shannon addresses a younger audience in his "Diaper David" series, which includes *No, David!, David Gets in Trouble, David Smells!,* and several others. The inspiration for *No, David!* came from a book Shannon had written when he was only five years old. "His mother sent it to him from her archives . . . when he was already a successful children's book author and illustrator," explained an interviewer for *Publishers Weekly.* Shannon used the original book as his inspira-

*David Shannon introduces a rambunctious young character in a series of self-illustrated picture books that include* **No, David!** (Copyright © 1998 by David Shannon. Reproduced by permission of Scholastic, Inc.)

*Shannon captures the landing of Christopher Columbus, a pivotal moment in North American history, in his artwork for Jane Yolen's* Encounter.
(Illustrations copyright © 1992 by David Shannon. Reproduced by permission of Voyager Books, an imprint of Harcourt, Inc.)

tion throughout, then tried to rework it with more realistic illustrations. "When I got to doing the paintings, they weren't working," he admitted. "The pictures were too flat—they just lay there. I wanted a little kid's style." Ultimately, David retained the round head and pointy teeth he had when Shannon first drew him.

With a story fine-tuned for preschoolers, *No, David!* follows a monstrously devious though well-intentioned toddler as he conducts all manner of mischief at his home, including running outside naked. Inside, he draws on walls, plays baseball, puts his fingers up his nose, and breaks things. The title derives from David's mother's incessant admonitions; when his antics push her too far one day, he is punished, but the ending is reassuring. Susan Pine, writing for *School Library Journal,* found that the "stick-figure body" of Shannon's young hero "conveys every nuance of [a child's] anger, exuberance, and defiance." *No, David!* met with popular and critical success and also earned Shannon a Caldecott Honor Book designation.

*David Goes to School* brings David into a setting with many more kids. David means well, but seems to get everything wrong, from chewing gum in class to writing on his desk, pulling a girl's hair, and starting a food fight in the cafeteria. The reactions of the other students show up in Shannon's illustrations, if not in the text, and reveal who David's friends are at the end of the day. A critic for *Booklist* commented on Shannon's "mix of tenderness and hilarity," while a reviewer for *Publishers Weekly* commented that the events would be "eminently recognizable" to young readers.

When David returns in *David Gets in Trouble* he has adopted the word "No," which is useful when denying his badness. *Oops!* finds the young boy tormenting his

exasperated mother with everything from yards of toilet paper to new words that punctuate his exploits. *It's Christmas, David!* finds the feisty free spirit bounding outside in the snow, with new cap, mittens, and books . . . and nothing else. "Shannon's artwork is deceptively simple," wrote Ilene Cooper in her *Booklist* review of *David Gets in Trouble,* and Piper L. Nyman asserted in *School Library Journal* that in *Oops!* the author proves himself to be "a master at capturing the behavior of young children in an endearing and humorous manner."

A reviewer for *Publishers Weekly* pointed out that in his "Diaper David" books "Shannon carefully hews to a child's-eye view of the world," never fully revealing the adults in the story. "What a blessing he lives on the page and not in our lives," joked a *Kirkus Reviews* contributor discussing Shannon's young hero, and GraceAnne A. DeCandido wrote in reviewing *David Goes to School* for *Booklist:* "We know David turned out all right, because he's making these books now."

Careful to avoid singling out girls from the "Diaper David" treatment, Shannon has also introduced a wild little girl in *Alice the Fairy.* Describing the book's young star, who plays out her life like a fairy tale, Robin Smith wrote in *Horn Book* that Alice's "enormous eyes radiate an unmistakably David-like energy" and her bouncing blonde ringlets "cover a very round head."

Shannon's work as a illustrator has continued to supplement his work creating original stories, both standalone picture books and book series such as Scieszka's "Trucktown," which find the artist teaming up with fellow illustrators Loren Long and David Gordon to bring to life what *School Library Journal* contributor Lynn K. Vanca described as "a vibrant locale inhabited by personified vehicles" that is "sure to be a hit with truck lovers." His work with Martin includes *The Rough-Face Girl,* which retells an Algonquin folktale featuring a Cinderella-type title character, and *The Boy Who Lived with the Seals,* which retells a Chinook legend set in the Pacific Northwest. In *School Library Journal* Susan Scheps wrote that Shannon's illustrations "embody the full flavor of the story" in *The Rough-Face Girl,* and *Booklist* critic Carolyn Phelan termed the artwork "striking and often rich in atmosphere." *The Boy Who Lived with the Seals* was praised by another *Booklist* reviewer, Janice Del Negro, who called the work "grippingly illustrated" and praised Shannon for integrating the beauty of Chinook artistic traditions into "striking acrylic paintings [that] impressively conjure the drama and conflict of the story."

Shannon also provided illustrations for acclaimed children's author Yolen's *Encounter,* which depicts the landing of Christopher Columbus on the island of San Salvador, as told through the eyes of a native Taino boy. As the story opens, the boy dreams that the coming ships will bring harm to his people, but his Taino elders ignore his warnings. Shannon's drawings show the youth being captured into slavery by Columbus's men, and the ultimate fulfillment of his foreboding dream. This "visionary style," declared a *Publishers Weekly* critic, "is an ideal complement" for Yolen's prose. The commentator added that Shannon's "atmospheric illustrations are of heroic proportions and full of contrast."

Shannon's work with Yolen resulted in *The Ballad of the Pirate Queens,* which retells the story of Anne Bonney and Mary Reade, as these real-life pirates sailed the seven seas in 1720. When their ship is attacked by a governor's vessel, Bonney and Reade battle the enemy singlehandedly, while their male counterparts continue to carouse below deck. Ultimately captured, the women escape the hangman's noose by claiming to be pregnant. A critic for *Publishers Weekly* termed Shannon's illustrations for Yolen's story "ironic in their stateliness" and with "a sly humor" that helps make the book "offbeat and grimly amusing." Helen Gregory, writing in *School Library Journal,* praised the "depth of [Shannon's] art," which she termed "reminiscent of great classic illustrators working in oil, especially N.C. Wyeth."

Pirates are also the focus of Shannon's art for Long's *How I Became a Pirate,* in which a boy leaves his family at the beach and joins a band of humorous scallywags until it is time to go home for soccer practice. "Shannon plays off the straight text," commented a reviewer for *Publishers Weekly,* and his "gleefully madcap illustrations" exaggerate the fun of Long's tale. In *School Library Journal* Laurie Edwards commented on the artist's use of perspective, writing that his "colorful crew of pop-eyed, snaggly toothed pirates [are] seen from a variety of zany viewpoints (including upside down)." Author and illustrator have also teamed up for a sequel, the humorous *Pirates Don't Change Diapers.*

Shannon has also collaborated with his brother, drawing the images to accompany Mark Shannon's retelling of the age-old tale of an honorable warrior in *Gawain and the Green Knight.* Based on a Celtic myth, the story finds young Gawain impressing the knights of King Arthur's Round Table by taking up a monstrous intruder's challenge to chop his head off. Gawain succeeds, but the Green Knight simply picks up his own head before departing, reminding Gawain that according to the terms of their agreement, they will meet again in a year's time for another duel. Hazel Rochman asserted in *Booklist* that "the glowing, sophisticated paintings . . . express the demonic drama of the story." Another collaboration between the Shannon brothers, *The Acrobat and the Angel,* retells a French folktale about an young orphan who is taken in at a monastery but then asked to give up his adventurous ways.

Other illustration projects include Audrey Wood's *The Bunyans,* which follows an entire family of fictional giants across North America as they carve out canyons and construct the Rocky Mountains with their frolic; a famed hot-water geyser in Wyoming has its origins here as Mrs. Bunyan's hot-water faucet. "Better than the text is the BIG artwork," asserted Cooper in *Booklist,* the critic adding that Shannon's art "is where most of the humor is." In *Nicholas Pipe,* with a text by renowned reteller Robert D. San Souci, a half-man/half-fish lives on land but must touch the sea daily to survive. Nicho-

*Melinda Long provides the entertaining story that results in Shannon's whimsical artwork for* **How I Became a Pirate.** (Illustrations copyright © 2003 by David Shannon. Reproduced by permission of Harcourt, Inc.)

las risks all when he falls in love with Margaret, a fisherman's daughter, and is ultimately carted away from the sea. "Shannon's stunning acrylic paintings are fitting to this powerful story," asserted *School Library Journal* contributor Beth Tegart, while a *Publishers Weekly* critic called *Nicholas Pipe* "a stylish collaboration."

In an interview for the Children's Book Council Web site, Shannon explained that when he illustrates, he focuses on the characters. "One of the first things I do when I'm illustrating a book is draw the character studies," he explained. "I try to picture what a particular character looks like, what he is wearing, and what kind of personality he has. . . . Sometimes it's as if the character stands up off the paper and starts running around my drawing table."

## Biographical and Critical Sources

*PERIODICALS*

*Booklist,* April 15, 1992, Carolyn Phelan, review of *The Rough-Face Girl,* p. 1533; March 15, 1993, Janice Del Negro, review of *The Boy Who Lived with the Seals,* p. 1321; January 15, 1994, Stephanie Zvirin, review of *How Georgie Radbourn Saved Baseball,* p. 939; June 1, 1994, Hazel Rochman, review of *Gawain and the Green Knight,* p. 1832; September 15, 1995, Stephanie Zvirin, review of *The Amazing Christmas Extravaganza,* p. 172; September 15, 1996, Ilene Cooper, review of *the Bunyans,* p. 252; January 1, 1998, Stephanie Zvirin, review of *A Bad Case of Stripes,* p. 825; August, 1999, GraceAnne A. DeCandido, review of *David Goes to School,* p. 2053; October 15, 2000, Gillian Engberg, review of *The Rain Came Down,* p. 447; February 15, 2002, Ilene Cooper, review of *Duck on a Bike,* p. 1013; September 15, 2002, Ilene Cooper, review of *David Gets in Trouble,* p. 233; September 15, 2003, Shelle Rosenfeld, review of *How I Became a Pirate,* p. 238; November 15, 2004, Ilene Cooper, review of *Alice the Fairy,* p. 592; January 1, 2006, Ilene Cooper, review of *Good Boy, Fergus!,* p. 119; November 15, 2007, Hazel Rochman, review of *Smash! Crash!,* p. 51; October 1, 2008, Thom Barthelmess, review of *Too Many Toys,* p. 48; August 1, 2009, Daniel Kraus, review of *Robot Zot!,* p. 81; September 15, 2010, Carolyn Phelan, review of *It's Christmas, David!,* p. 71.

*Horn Book,* July-August, 1993, Mary M. Burns, review of *The Boy Who Lived with the Seals,* p. 472; September, 2000, review of *The Rain Came Down,* p. 556; November-December, 2001, Mary M. Burns, review of *The Shark God,* p. 761; March-April, 2002, Joanna Rudge Long, review of *Duck on a Bike,* p. 203; January-February, 2005, Robin Smith, review of *Alice the Fairy,* p. 87; November-December, 2009, Roger Sutton, review of *Robot Zot!,* p. 660.

*Globe & Mail* (Toronto, Ontario, Canada), April 8, 2006, Susan Perren, review of *Good Boy, Fergus!,* p. D18; December 19, 2009, Susan Perren, review of *Robot Zot!,* p. F. 3.

*Kirkus Reviews,* March 1, 1994, review of *How Georgie Radbourn Saved Baseball,* p. 310; October 15, 1995, review of *The Amazing Christmas Extravaganza,* p. 1502; August 1, 2002, review of *David Gets in Trouble,* p. 1143; September 15, 2003, review of *How I Became a Pirate,* p. 1177; October 1, 2004, review of *Alice the Fairy,* p. 969; March 1, 2006, review of *Good Boy, Fergus!,* p. 239; January 15, 2007, review of *Pirates Don't Change Diapers,* p. 76; August 1, 2008, review of *Too Many Toys;* August 1, 2009, review of *Robot Zot!*

*New York Times Book Review,* May 14, 2006, Patricia T. O'Conner, p. 25; March 11, 2007, Julie Just, review of *Pirates Don't Change Diapers,* p. 17; March 15, 2008, Gregory Cowles, refiew of *Smash! Crash!,* p. 14.

*Publishers Weekly,* October 27, 1989, review of *How Many Spots Does a Leopard Have?, and Other Tales,* p. 68; March 9, 1992, review of *Encounter,* p. 57; April 13, 1992, review of *The Rough-Face Girl,* p. 57; April 17, 1994, review of *The Ballad of the Pirate Queens,* p. 59; May 5, 1997, review of *Nicholas Pipe,* p. 209; January 12, 1998, review of *A Bad Case of Stripes,* p. 59; July 19, 1999, Sonja Bolle, "David Shannon: A Merry Prankster," p. 168; November 1, 1999, review of *David Goes to School,* p. 57; October 16, 2000, review of *The Rain Came Down,* p. 75; October 15, 2001, review of *The Acrobat and the Angel,* p. 74; November 5, 2001, review of *The Shark God,* p. 67; December 17, 2001, review of *Duck on a Bike,* p. 90; June 24, 2002, review of *David Gets in Trouble,* p. 55; July 7, 2003, review of *How I Became a Pirate,* p. 70; October 11, 2004, review of *Alice the Fairy,* p. 78; January 2, 2006, review of *Good Boy, Fergus!,* p. 60; January 1, 2007, review of *Pirates Don't Change Diapers,* p. 48; November 26, 2007, review of *Smash! Crash!,* p. 51; September 1, 2008, review of *Too Many Toys,* p. 53; August 10, 2009, review of *Robot Zot!,* p. 53.

*School Library Journal,* November, 1989, Kay McPherson, review of *How Many Spots Does a Leopard Have?,* p. 99; May, 1992, Susan Scheps, review of *The Rough-Face Girl,* p. 124; June, 1995, Helen Gregory, review of *The Ballad of the Pirate Queens,* p. 126; October, 1995, review of *The Amazing Christmas Extravaganza,* pp. 41-42; May, 1997, Beth Tegart, review of *Nicholas Pipe,* p. 124; March, 1998, Carolyn Noah, review of *A Bad Case of Stripes,* p. 188; August, 1998, Susan Pine, review of *No, David!,* p. 146; September, 1999, Barbara Scotto, review of *David Goes to School,* p. 205; October, 2000, Lisa Dennis, review of *The Rain Came Down,* p. 136; March, 2002, Marianne Saccardi, review of *Duck on a Bike,* p. 201; September, 2002, Adele Greenlee, review of *David Gets in Trouble,* p. 206; September, 2003, Laurie Edwards, review of *How I Became a Pirate,* p. 184; July, 2004, Lisa G. Kropp, review of *A Bad Case of Stripes,* p. 44; November, 2004, Marie Orlando, review of *Alice the Fairy,* p. 118; March, 2005, Piper L. Nyman, review of *Oh, David!,* p. 188; January, 2008, Lynn K. Vanca, review of *Smash! Crash!,* p. 97; August, 2008, Gloria Koster, reviews of *Zoom! Boom! Bully* and *Pete's Party,* both p. 102; January, 2009,

Piper Nyman, review of *Too Many Toys,* p. 84; October, 2009, April Mazza, review of *Alice the Fairy,* p. 60; November, 2009, Stacy Dillon, review of *The Spooky Tire,* p. 88.

*Teacher Librarian,* June, 2000, Shirley Lewis, review of *David Goes to School,* p. 49.

*ONLINE*

*BookPage.com,* http://www.bookpage.com/ (September, 1999), Miriam Drennan, interview with Shannon.

*Harcourt Trade Publishers Web site,* http://www.harcourt books.com/ (April 1, 2004), interview with Shannon and Melinda Long.

*Scholastic Web site,* http://www2.scholastic.com/ (April 1, 2011), "David Shannon."*

\*       \*       \*

# SHIGA, Jason 1976-

## Personal

Born 1976. *Education:* University of California at Berkeley, B.S. (pure mathematics), 1998.

## Addresses

*Home*—Oakland, CA. *E-mail*—jason@shigabooks.com.

## Career

Cartoonist and author. Freelance cartoonist beginning 1996; Oakland Public Library, Oakland, CA, library aide, 1998—, lead graphic designer and Webmaster, 2006—. Presenter at workshops.

## Awards, Honors

Xeric Award, 1999, for "Double Happiness"; Ignatz Award for Outstanding Story, 2004, for "Fleep"; Eisner Award, 2004, for Talent Deserving of Wider Recognition, and nomination for Best Single Issue or One-Shot, for "Fleep"; Ignatz Award nomination for Outstanding Graphic Novel, 2007, for *Bookhunter.*

## Writings

*SELF-ILUSTRATED*

*Bookhunter,* Sparkplug Comics (New York, NY), 2007.
*Meanwhile: Pick a Path. 3,856 Story Possibilities,* Amulet Books (New York, NY), 2010.
*Empire State: A Love Story (or Not),* Abrams ComicArts (New York, NY), 2011.

Creator of comics, including "Doorknob Bob," "Double Happiness," "Fleep," "Mortimer Mouse," "Grave of the Crickets," "Moderntales," and "Meanwhile." Contribu-

*Jason Shiga* (Photograph by Jonathan Cross. Reproduced by permission.)

tor of comic strips to *Nickelodeon* magazine, beginning 2003, and to periodicals including *Asian Week, San Francisco Examiner,* and *Sparkplug Comics.*

## Sidelights

Jason Shiga is an Oakland, California-based comics artist whose awards include an Ignatz award and the 2004 Eisner Award for Talent Deserving of Wider Recognition. Shiga started creating serial stories after graduating from college with a degree in pure math, producing the comics "Doorknob Bob," "Grave of the Crickets," and "Moderntales." A longer project, *Bookhunter,* was inspired by his "real" job working at the Oakland Public Library and recounts the 1973 theft of a valuable book and the efforts of the valiant Bookhunters who have only hours to discover the volume's whereabouts and return it to its place on the library shelf. Although originally published online, several other works by Shiga have gained broader audiences as graphic novels, among them *Meanwhile: Pick a Path. 3,856 Story Possibilities* and *Empire State: A Love Story (or Not).*

Shiga's fascination with abstract, theoretical mathematics inspired *Meanwhile,* which "blows the choose-your-own-adventure concept out of the water," according to *Booklist* reviewer Ian Chipman. The comic had its beginnings in a series of flowcharts Shiga created to map the consequences of a choice between two alternatives. The story arc was designed with the help of computer-run algorithms and took Shiga almost a decade to complete. *Meanwhile* begins as a boy named Jimmy decides whether chocolate or vanilla ice cream is more to his liking. From this A-or-B decision point, readers can follow colored tubes into a maze of options that interweave back and forth through the remaining pages and involve everything from a search for the men's bathroom and a giant squid to a spooky mansion, a time-travel device, and the (fortunately) yet-untested Killitron, which is capable of destroying all life on Earth. Every "read" of the book yields a different result, noted a *Publishers Weekly* critic, and Shiga's "charming" cartoons, "bursting with color and energy, lend a wry counterpoint" to Jimmy's sometimes perilous predicaments. In *School Library Journal* Janet Weber encouraged younger comics fans by noting that Shiga's "text is clearly written." For "seasoned graphic-novel fans," she added, the "action-packed" story in *Meanwhile* will entertain while aiding them in "developing problem-solving skills." Chipman recommended *Meanwhile* as "the perfect kid-friendly initiation to the many-worlds interpretation of quantum mechanics," while a *Kirkus Reviews* contributor cautioned readers that Shiga's "truly ingenious graphic novel" might take them from an innocent choice about ice cream into a story that could be anything "from the utterly bizarre to the devastatingly apocalyptic."

While *Meanwhile* draws on its author's intellectual pursuits, *Empire State* is grounded in the mathematician's mundane reality. The geeky hero of the piece, Jimmy, works at the Oakland Public Library, where his days are punctuated by the slow, solemn rumble of library carts through the stacks. When Sara, Jimmy's best friend, moves to New York City to pursue a career in publishing, he realizes that he misses her. Then he realizes that he must love her. A letter to Sara announces his upcoming visit, as Jimmy braves a coast-to-coast bus journey in order to reveal his true feelings. With his world expanded through his travels, the small-town Seattle-ite arrives in New York, where both surprise and a possible heartbreak await. Reviewing *Empire State* in *Publishers Weekly,* a critic wrote that Shiga's angular "penciling style . . . draws the reader very effectively" into the worldview of the story's naive hero, while his "wicked sense of comic timing" captures the "awkward pauses and slapstick physicality" that enliven his humorous and artful bildungsroman.

## Biographical and Critical Sources

*PERIODICALS*

*Booklist,* January 1, 2010, Ian Chipman, review of *Meanwhile: Pick a Path. 3,856 Story Possibilities,* p. 81.
*Kirkus Reviews,* February 15, 2010, review of *Meanwhile.*
*Publishers Weekly,* February 1, 2010, review of *Meanwhile,* p. 52; May, 2011, review of *Empire State: A Love Story (or Not).*
*School Library Journal,* March, 2010, Janet Weber, review of *Meanwhile,* p. 186.

*ONLINE*

*Jason Shiga Home Page,* http://www.shigabooks.com (March 20, 2011).*

\*     \*     \*

# SMITH, Icy 1966-

## Personal

Born 1966, in Hong Kong; married; children: two daughters. *Hobbies and other interests:* Traveling, hiking.

## Addresses

*Home*—Manhattan Beach, CA. *Office*—East West Discovery Press, P.O. Box 3585, Manhattan Beach, CA 90266. *E-mail*—info@eastwestdiscovery.com.

## Career

Writer and publisher. East West Discovery Press, Manhattan Beach, CA, founder.

## Awards, Honors

Clarion Award, Association for Women in Communications, 2002, for *The Lonely Queue;* Moonbeam Children's Book Award, and Independent Publisher Book Award, both 2008, and Best Children's Book Award, Chinese-American Librarian Association, 2009, all for *Mei Ling in China City;* International Honor Award, Society of School Librarians, Moonbeam Children's

*West Coast illustrator Shiga's sequential-art projects include the original graphic novel* Meanwhile. (Illustration copyright © 2010 by Jason Shiga. Reproduced with permission of Amulet Books, an imprint of Abrams.)

Book Award, 2009, and Benjamin Franklin Award finalist, and *Skipping Stones* Honor Award, both 2010, all for *Half Spoon of Rice.*

## Writings

*The Lonely Queue: The Forgotten History of the Courageous Chinese Americans in Los Angeles,* East West Discovery Press (Manhattan Beach, CA), 2000, revised edition, 2001.

(Editor) *Voices of Healing: Spirit and Unity after 9/11 in the Asian-American and Pacific Islander Community,* East West Discovery Press (Manhattan Beach, CA), 2004.

*Mei Ling in China City,* illustrated by Gayle Garner Roski, East West Discovery Press (Manhattan Beach, CA), 2008.

*Half Spoon of Rice: A Survival Story of the Cambodian Genocide,* illustrated by Sopaul Nhem, East West Discovery Press (Manhattan Beach, CA), 2010.

## Sidelights

Icy Smith, the founder of East West Discovery Press, a publisher and distributor of multicultural books, is also the author of several works for young readers, including *Mei Ling in China City* and *Half Spoon of Rice: A Survival Story of the Cambodian Genocide.* Discussing her business venture with *PaperTigers* online interviewer Marjorie Coughlan, Smith remarked: "It's good to be working in something that is all about doing good for society. We help children enjoy reading while promoting understanding among people of different racial and ethnic backgrounds."

Set in California in 1942 and based on a true story, *Mei Ling in China City* centers on the relationship between a Chinese-American girl and her best friend, a Japanese-American girl who is sent with her family to a relocation camp during World War II. The story, Smith observed in an interview on the Organization of Chinese Americans Web site, "reveals both some of the fascinating history of China City and the dark history of the Japanese American internment. The lives of many Chinese and Japanese Americans during WWII resonate in the friendship of Mei Ling and Yayeko."

In *Half Spoon of Rice* Smith describes a family's experiences during the brutal Khmer Rouge regime that controlled Cambodia during the late 1970s. Based on accounts provided by survivors of the genocide, Smith's story is told through the eyes of Nat, a nine year old who is driven from his urban home, separated from his parents, and forced to work for years under incredibly harsh conditions in a labor camp. "This powerful child's-eye view of war is harsh and realistic—like its subject—though accessible and thought-provoking," Barbara Auerbach noted in her *School Library Journal* review of *Half Spoon of Rice,* while Hazel Rochman, critiquing the work in *Booklist,* called Smith's novel "an important addition to the Holocaust curriculum."

## Biographical and Critical Sources

*PERIODICALS*

*Booklist,* December 15, 2009, Hazel Rochman, review of *Half Spoon of Rice: A Survival Story of the Cambodian Genocide,* p. 38.

*Kirkus Reviews,* December 15, 2009, review of *Half Spoon of Rice.*

*Publishers Weekly,* December 21, 2009, review of *Half Spoon of Rice,* p. 60.

*School Library Journal,* May, 2008, Mary Elam, review of *Mei Ling in China City,* p. 109; December, 2009, Barbara Auerbach, review of *Half Spoon of Rice,* p. 132.

*ONLINE*

*Organization of Chinese Americans Web site,* http://www. ocanational.org/ (April 1, 2011), "OCA Weekly Author Feature: Icy Smith."

*PaperTigers.org,* http://www.papertigers.org/ (May, 2008), Marjorie Coughlan, interview with Smith.*

\* \* \*

## SNELL, Gordon 1933(?)-

## Personal

Born c. 1933, in England; married Maeve Binchy (a writer), 1977.

## Addresses

*Home*—Dalkey, Ireland.

## Career

Author and journalist. British Broadcasting Corporation, London, England, broadcast journalist, c. 1970s; freelance writer and author of librettos.

## Writings

*FOR CHILDREN*

*The King of Quizzical Island,* illustrated by David McKee, A. & C. Black (London, England), 1978, Candlewick Press (Cambridge, MA), 2009.

*The Cool Mac Cool: Heroic Deeds of Finn Mac Cool, Legendary Celtic Hero,* illustrated by Wendy Shea, O'Brien Press (Dublin, Ireland), 1988.

*Tom's Amazing Machine Takes a Trip,* Hutchinson (London, England), 1990.

*Hysterically Historical: Madcap Rhymes of Olden Times,* illustrated by Wendy Shea, Hutchinson Children's (London, England), 1990.

*Cruncher Sparrow, High Flier,* illustrated by Michael O'Clery, Poolbeg for Children (Dublin, Ireland), 1990.

*Cruncher Sparrow's Flying School,* illustrated by Michael O'Clery, Poolbeg Press (Dublin, Ireland), 1991.

*The Red Spectacles Gang,* Hutchinson Children's (London, England), 1991.

*Tex and Sheelagh,* illustrated by Mary Murphy, Poolbeg Press (Dublin, Ireland), 1992.

*The Joke Thief,* illustrated by Mary Murphy, Poolbeg Press (Dublin, Ireland), 1993.

*Dangerous Treasure,* Poolbeg for Children (Dublin, Ireland), 1994.

*Lottie's Letters,* illustrated by Peter Bailey, Orion (London, England), 1996.

*Amy's Wonderful Nest,* illustrated by Fergus Lyons, O'Brien Press (Dublin, Ireland), 1997.

*The Phantom Horseman,* Poolbeg Press (Dublin, Ireland), 1997.

*The Wonderful Thursday Club: Animal Poems,* illustrated by Anthony Flintoft, Dolphin (London, England), 2001.

*Fear at the Festival,* Poolbeg for Children (Dublin, Ireland), 2001.

*Twelve Days: A Christmas Countdown,* illustrated by Kevin O'Malley, HarperCollins (New York, NY), 2002.

*'Twas the Day after Christmas,* illustrated by Sean Delonas, HarperCollins (New York, NY), 2003.

*Tina and the Tooth Fairy,* illustrated by Peter Blodau, O'Brien Press (Dublin, Ireland), 2005.

*The Deadly Camera,* Poolbeg Press (Dublin, Ireland), 2005.

*The Ballygandon Giants,* Poolbeg Press (Dublin, Ireland), 2005.

*The Supermarket Ghost,* illustrated by Bob Byrne, O'Brien Press (Dublin, Ireland), 2007.

Contributor to books, including *Freaky Stories,* Red Fox (London, England), 1999.

*ANTHOLOGIES*

(Compiler) *The Book of Theatre Quotes: Notes, Quotes, and Anecdotes of the Stage,* Angus & Robertson (London, England), 1982.

(Selector with Joan Ryan) *Land of Tales: Stories of Ireland for Children,* Glendale (Sandycove, Ireland), 1982, Dufour Editions (Chester Springs, PA), 1983.

(Selector with Joan Ryan) *Sea Tales of Ireland for Children,* Glendale Press (Dublin, Ireland), 1983.

(Selector with Joan Ryan) *The Haunted Hills: Ghost Tales of Ireland for Children,* Glendale Press (Dublin, Ireland), 1984.

(Selector with Joan Ryan) *The Furry Glens: A Treasury of Animal Tales from Ireland,* Glendale Press (Sandycove, Ireland), 1990.

(Editor) *Thicker than Water: Coming-of-Age Stories by Irish and Irish-American Writers,* Delacorte Press (New York, NY), 2001.

*OTHER*

*The Rhyming Irish Cookbook,* illustrated by Cathy Henderson, O'Brien Press (Dublin, Ireland), 1992.

*Oh, Canadians!: Hysterically Historical Rhymes,* illustrated by Aislin (pseudonym of Terry Mosher), McArthur (Toronto, Ontario, Canada), 1997.

*Oh, No! More Canadians!: Hysterically Historical Rhymes,* illustrated by Aislin (pseudonym of Terry Mosher), McArthur (Toronto, Ontario, Canada), 1997.

*Yes! Even More Canadians!: Hysterically Historical Rhymes,* illustrated by Aislin (pseudonym of Terry Mosher), McArthur (Toronto, Ontario, Canada), 2000.

*The Oh, Canadians! Omnibus,* illustrated by Aislin (pseudonym of Terry Mosher), McArthur (Toronto, Ontario, Canada), 2001.

*More Marvelous Canadians!: Hysterically Historical Rhymes,* illustrated by Aislin (pseudonym of Terry Mosher), McArthur (Toronto, Ontario, Canada), 2002.

*Further Fabulous Canadians!: Hysterically Historical Rhymes,* illustrated by Aislin (pseudonym of Terry Mosher), McArthur (Toronto, Ontario, Canada), 2004.

*The Best of Oh, Canadians!: Hysterically Historical Rhymes,* illustrated by Aislin (pseudonym of Terry Mosher), McArthur (Toronto, Ontario, Canada), 2006.

## Sidelights

A former writer and journalist for England's British Broadcasting Corporation, Gordon Snell has written librettos and song lyrics as well as editing and authoring numerous books for both children and adults. The husband of noted novelist Maeve Binchy, he now lives in Binchy's home town of Dalkey, near Dublin, Ireland, where the two authors have resided since the late 1970s. Snell's anthologies include several collaborations with Joan Ryan, such as *Land of Tales: Stories of Ireland for Children,* as well as his own *Thicker than Water: Coming-of-Age Stories by Irish and Irish-American Writers,* which includes twelve tales about adolescence by writers such as Binchy, Shane Connaughton, Chris Lynch, Emma Donoghue, and Vincent Banville. He also takes aim at the northernmost North Americans in *Oh, Canadians!: Hysterically Historical Rhymes* and its sequels, a series of books featuring caricatures by cartoonist Aislin (the pseudonym of Terry Mosher) and that focus on political foibles and satirize historical events.

Incorporating what a *Kirkus Reviews* writer recommended as a "modern" approach "that may be more accessible to today's children," Snell's picture book *Twelve Days: A Christmas Countdown* pairs the author's updated lyrics to a beloved holiday song with Kevin O'Malley's gentle illustrations. In the story, a little girl receives a small pine tree on the twelfth day before Christmas that replaces the partridge and pear tree of the traditional song. Subsequent gifts seem innocent enough: two candy canes, then three mice, followed the next day by four teddy bears. Soon the sequential offer-

*Gordon Snell's story* The King of Quizzical Island, *with illustrations by David McKee, has been a perennial favorite since its first publication in the 1970s.* (Illustration copyright © 1978, 2009 by David McKee. Reproduced with permission of Candlewick Press on behalf of Walker Books, London.)

ings become more numerous and more cumbersome. When the pine topiary proves too small to shelter the ever-increasing number of gifts, Dad sets to work to make it larger, resulting in "increasing madness" and a ride in Santa's sleigh, according to *School Library Journal* critic Mara Alpert. In a similar work, *'Twas the Day after Christmas,* Snell sets another well-known holiday song slightly forward in time and follows a tiny house mouse as it explores the tangle of wrapping paper and ribbons left under the Christmas tree. Praising the "photographic clarity" of the paintings by Sean Delonas that accompany Snell's lyrical rhyming text, *Booklist* critic Ilene Cooper dubbed *'Twas the Day after Christmas* "good holiday fun."

Snell also entertains young children in his humorous picture book *The King of Quizzical Island,* where his rhyming text is captured in cartoon art by David McKee. In the story, the king of Quizzical Island is unique among his citizenry in that he has curiosity. When the royal wizard cannot answer royal questions about what lies beyond the boundary of the royal kingdom, the monarch determines to sail to the edge of the world and find out. With a ship made from lumber from a Tea-Bag Tree, rigging crafted of spider's webbing, and other fanciful supplies, the king sets out, making his way past Jigsaw Land and Vertical Land and into the Sea of Dreadful Dreams. When he returns with the conclusion that the Earth is round, doubters still challenge him, prompting the resourceful king to begin yet another whimsical journey. "McKee's lively black-and-white drawings," in which the king is the only element

tinted with color, "match the mood of [Snell's] . . . fanciful tale," concluded Barbara Elleman in her *School Library Journal* review of *The King of Quizzical Island.* In *School Librarian* Prue Goodwin remarked on the amusing details and quirky perspective, predicting that the story "will inspire curiosity, exploration and research in any group of young learners—especially those still at the stage of asking 'Why?' all the time." In a *Kirkus Reviews* appraisal of the book, a critic wrote that Snell "delights the readers with some lovely, sophisticated words and phrases," dubbing *The King of Quizzical Island* "marvelous fun."

## Biographical and Critical Sources

*PERIODICALS*

*Booklist,* January 1, 2001, John Peters, review of *Thicker than Water: Coming-of-Age Stories by Irish and Irish-American Writers,* p. 941; September 1, 2003, Ilene Cooper, review of *'Twas the Day after Christmas,* p. 136.

*Horn Book,* March, 2001, review of *Thicker than Water,* p. 213.

*Kirkus Reviews,* November 1, 2002, review of *Twelve Days: A Christmas Countdown,* p. 1626; October 15, 2009, review of *The King of Quizzical Island.*

*New York Times,* April 29, 2009, Liza Foreman, "Irish Cottage Becomes Author's Home."

*Publishers Weekly,* February 26, 2001, review of *Thicker than Water,* p. 88.

*School Librarian,* spring, 2010, Prue Goodwin, review of *The King of Quizzical Island,* p. 32.

*School Library Journal,* May, 2001, Karen Hoth, review of *Thicker than Water,* p. 160; October, 2002, Mara Alpert, review of *Twelve Days,* p. 64; October, 2003, Susan Patron, review of *'Twas the Day after Christmas,* p. 68; November, 2009, Barbara Elleman, review of *The King of Quizzical Island,* p. 88.*

\*    \*    \*

## SPEARING, Craig J.

### Personal

Son of Dar Spearing (a geologist); married; children: two. *Education:* Rhode Island School of Design, B.F.A. (illustration), 1992.

### Addresses

*Home*—Portland, OR. *E-mail*—cjspearing@gmail.com.

### Career

Illustrator.

## Illustrator

Jo and Josephine Harper, *Prairie Dog Pioneers,* Turtle Books (Emeryville, CA), 1998.

Lisa Simone, *Liberty!,* Macmillan (New York, NY), 2000.

Judith Stamper, *California or Bust!,* Scholastic (New York, NY), 2002.

Linda B. Ross, *A Man in Motion: Galileo Galilei,* Macmillan (New York, NY), 2002.

Joseph Slate, *The Great Big Wagon That Rang: How the Liberty Bell Was Saved,* Marshall Cavendish (New York, NY), 2002.

Jackie Mims Hopkins, *Our Texas,* Charlesbridge (Watertown, MA), 2010.

Contributor to periodicals, including *Dungeon* and *Dragon.*

## Sidelights

Oregon-based artist Craig J. Spearing started working as an illustrator in 1995, shortly after completing his B.F.A. at the prestigious Rhode Island School of Design. His first book-illustration project, creating the artwork for Jo and Josephine Harper's *Prairie Dog Pioneers,* marked the first of several picture books to feature his art. Created using sepia-toned linoleum-block prints tinted with watercolor and colored pencil, Spearing's illustrations for the Harpers' story echo the prairie setting "and give the book an elegant feel befitting the poignant text," according to *Booklist* contributor Kay Weisman.

*Craig J. Spearing's illustration projects include creating the art for* Our Texas, *Jacky Mims Hopkin's picture-book ode to the Lone Star State.* (Illustration copyright © 2010 by Craig J. Spearing. Reproduced with permission of Charlesbridge Publishing, Inc.)

Other illustration project by Spearing include bringing to life texts by authors Lisa Simone, Judith Stamper, Linda B. Ross, Joseph Slate, and Jackie Mims Hopkins, the last whose *Our Texas* features colorful, dark-lined paintings that capture the many sights, sounds, and critters that can be found in the Lone Star State. In his artwork for Slate's rhyming picture-book history *The Great Big Wagon That Rang: How the Liberty Bell Was Saved,* Spearing again evokes a block-print effect, and the "warm hues" in his "attractive illustrations" create "a look consistent with the [story's] early American setting," according to *Booklist* contributor Carolyn Phelan. This "linear, printlike quality" injects the images with "a[n] historical feel, while their bright colors and dramatic perspectives appeal to the eye," maintained Robin L. Gibson in her *School Library Journal* review of *The Great Big Wagon That Rang.* Further praise came from a *Kirkus Reviews* writer, who commended Spearing for achieving the goal of an accomplished illustrator. "He sticks to authentic details and keeps his pages uncluttered," the critic observed, "effectively focusing the reader's attention."

While Spearing initialy employed traditional artist's media in his book-illustration work, the discovery of digital media has combined with a growing interest in role-playing games to prompt a change of focus. Beginning in 2008, he began to concentrate on science-fiction and fantasy illustration, including the settings and characters in the Pathfinder, Forgotten Realms, and Dungeons & Dragons role-playing games. Discussing his new focus, Spearing quipped on his Web log: "seriously, painting tentacle-faced bad guys never gets old."

## Biographical and Critical Sources

*PERIODICALS*

*Booklist,* September 15, 1998, Kay Weisman, review of *Prairie Dog Pioneers,* p. 237; November 1, 2002, Carolyn Phelan, review of *The Great Big Wagon That Rang: How the Liberty Bell Was Saved,* p. 509.

*Kirkus Reviews,* August 15, 2002, review of *The Great Big Wagon That Rang,* p. 1237.

*Publishers Weekly,* September 21, 1998, review of *Prairie Dog Pioneers,* p. 85.

*School Library Journal,* October, 1998, Steven Engelfried, review of *Prairie Dog Pioneers,* p. 100; November, 2002, Robin L. Gibson, review of *The Great Big Wagon That Rang,* p. 138.

*ONLINE*

*Craig J. Spearing Home Page,* http://www.craigspearing. com/ (March 20, 2011).

*Craig J. Spearing Web log,* http://cjspearing.blogspot.com (March 20, 2011).

# STANLEY, George Edward 1942-2011

(M.T. Coffin, Franklin W. Dixon, a house pseudonym, Laura Lee Hope, a house pseudonym, Carolyn Keene, a house pseudonym, Adam Mills, Stuart Symons)

## Personal

Born July 15, 1942, in Memphis, TX; died of a ruptured aneurysm, February 7, 2011, in Oklahoma City, OK; son of Joseph (a farmer) and Cellie (a nurse) Stanley; married Gwen Meshew (a Slavic specialist), June 29, 1974; children: James Edward, Charles Albert Andrew. *Education:* Texas Tech University, B.A., 1965, M.S., 1967; University of Port Elizabeth, South Africa, D.Litt., 1974. *Politics:* Democrat. *Religion:* Baptist.

## Career

Writer and educator. East Texas State University, Commerce, instructor in English as a foreign language, 1967-69; University of Kansas, Lawrence, instructor in English as a foreign language, 1969-70; Cameron University, Lawton, OK, instructor, 1970-73, assistant professor, 1973-76, associate professor, 1976-79, professor of African and Middle-Eastern languages, 1979-2011, chairman of department of English, Foreign Languages, and Journalism, 1984-2000. Fulbright lecturer at University of Chad, 1973; member of faculty, Institute of Children's Literature, Redding Ridge, CT, 1986-92, and Writer's Digest School, Cincinnati, OH, 1992-99. Director, annual Cameron University/Society of Children's Book Writers Writers of Children's Literature conference.

## Member

African Language Teachers Association, American Association of Teachers of Arabic, American Association of Teachers of Slavic and East European Languages, American Association of Teachers of Persian, American Association of Teachers of Turkic Languages, American Institute for Yemeni Studies, National Council of Less-commonly-taught Languages, Society of Children's Book Writers and Illustrators, Syrian Studies Association.

## Awards, Honors

Distinguished Faculty Award, Phi Kappa Phi, 1974; Member of the Year Award, Society of Children's Book Writers, 1979; inducted into Oklahoma Writers Hall of Fame, 1994; Best Books for the Teen Age citation, New York Public Library, 1994, for *Rats in the Attic;* Cameron University Faculty Hall of Fame Award, 2005, Hackler Award for Teaching Excellence, and inducted into Cameron Alumni Association Faculty Hall of Fame; Oklahoma Center for the Book Award, 2010, for *Night Fires.*

## Writings

*FICTION; FOR CHILDREN*

*Mini-Mysteries,* Saturday Evening Post Company (Indianapolis, IN), 1979.

*The Crime Lab,* illustrated by Andrew Glass, Avon (New York, NY), 1980.

*The Case of the Clever Marathon Cheat,* Meadowbrook (Minnetonka, MN), 1985.

*The Ukrainian Egg Mystery,* Avon (New York, NY), 1986.

*The Codebreaker Kids!,* Avon (New York, NY), 1987.

*The Italian Spaghetti Mystery,* Avon (New York, NY), 1987.

(Under house pseudonym Laura Lee Hope) *The New Bobbsey Twins: The Case of the Runaway Money,* Simon & Schuster (New York, NY), 1987.

*The Mexican Tamale Mystery,* Avon (New York, NY), 1988.

(Under house pseudonym Laura Lee Hope) *The Bobbsey Twins: The Mystery on the Mississippi,* Simon & Schuster (New York, NY), 1988.

*The Codebreaker Kids Return,* Avon (New York, NY), 1989.

*Hershell Cobwell and the Miraculous Tattoo,* Avon (New York, NY), 1991.

*Rats in the Attic; and Other Stories to Make Your Skin Crawl,* Avon (New York, NY), 1994.

*Happy Deathday to You; and Other Stories to Give You Nightmares,* Avon (New York, NY), 1995.

*Snake Camp* ("Road to Reading" series), Golden Books (New York, NY), 2000.

*Ghost Horse* ("Road to Reading" series), Golden Books (New York, NY), 2000.

*Night Fires,* Aladdin (New York, NY), 2009.

*"SCAREDY CATS" SERIES*

*The Day the Ants Got Really Mad,* Simon & Schuster (New York, NY), 1996.

*There's a Shark in the Swimming Pool!,* Simon & Schuster (New York, NY), 1996.

*Mrs. O'Dell's Third-Grade Class Is Shrinking,* Simon & Schuster (New York, NY), 1996.

*Bugs for Breakfast,* Simon & Schuster (New York, NY), 1996.

*Who Invited Aliens to My Slumber Party?,* Simon & Schuster (New York, NY), 1997.

*The New Kid in School Is a Vampire Bat,* Simon & Schuster (New York, NY), 1997.

*A Werewolf Followed Me Home,* Simon & Schuster (New York, NY), 1997.

*The Vampire Kittens of Count Dracula,* Simon & Schuster (New York, NY), 1997.

*"SPINETINGLERS" SERIES; UNDER PSEUDONYM M.T. COFFIN*

*Billy Baker's Dog Won't Stay Buried!,* Avon (New York, NY), 1995.

*Where Have All the Parents Gone?*, Avon (New York, NY), 1995.

*Check It out and Die!*, Avon (New York, NY), 1995.

*Don't Go to the Principal's Office*, Avon (New York, NY), 1996.

*The Dead Kid Did It!*, Avon (New York, NY), 1996.

*Pet Store*, Avon (New York, NY), 1996.

*Escape from the Haunted Museum*, Avon (New York, NY), 1996.

*The Curse of the Cheerleaders*, Avon (New York, NY), 1997.

*Circus F.R.E.A.K.S*, Avon (New York, NY), 1997.


*"THIRD-GRADE DETECTIVES" CHAPTER-BOOK SERIES*

*The Clue of the Left-handed Glove*, illustrated by Salvatore Murdocca, Aladdin (New York, NY), 1998, published as *The Clue of the Left-handed Envelope*, 2000.

*The Puzzle of the Pretty Pink Handkerchief*, illustrated by Salvatore Murdocca, Aladdin (New York, NY), 1998.

*The Mystery of the Hairy Tomatoes*, illustrated by Salvatore Murdocca, Aladdin (New York, NY), 2001.

*The Cobweb Confession*, illustrated by Salvatore Murdocca, Aladdin (New York, NY), 2001.

*The Secret of the Green Skin*, illustrated by Salvatore Murdocca, Aladdin (New York, NY), 2003.

*The Case of the Dirty Clue*, Aladdin (New York, NY), 2003.

*The Mystery of the Wooden Witness*, Aladdin (New York, NY), 2004.

*The Case of the Sweaty Bank Robber*, Aladdin (New York, NY), 2004.

*The Mystery of the Stolen Statue*, Aladdin (New York, NY), 2004.


*"KATIE LYNN COOKIE COMPANY" CHAPTER-BOOK SERIES*

*The Secret Ingredient*, illustrated by Linda Dockey Graves, Random House (New York, NY), 1999.

*Frogs' Legs for Dinner*, illustrated by Linda Dockey Graves, Random House (New York, NY), 2000.

*The Battle of the Bakers*, illustrated by Linda Dockey Graves, Random House (New York, NY), 2000.

*Bottled Up!*, illustrated by Linda Dockey Graves, Random House (New York, NY), 2001.

*Wedding Cookies*, illustrated by Linda Dockey Graves, Random House (New York, NY), 2001.


*"HARDY BOYS" NOVEL SERIES; UNDER HOUSE PSEUDONYM FRANKLIN W. DIXON*

*The Case of the Psychic's Vision*, Simon & Schuster (New York, NY), 2003.

*The Mystery of the Black Rhino*, Simon & Schuster (New York, NY), 2003.

*The Secret of the Soldier's Gold*, Simon & Schuster (New York, NY), 2003.

*One False Step*, Simon & Schuster (New York, NY), 2005.


*"NANCY DREW" NOVEL SERIES; UNDER HOUSE PSEUDONYM CAROLYN KEENE*

*The Mystery in Tornado Alley*, Simon & Schuster (New York, NY), 2000.

*Danger on the Great Lakes*, Simon & Schuster (New York, NY), 2003.

*Stop the Clock*, Simon & Schuster (New York, NY), 2005.

*Framed*, Simon & Schuster (New York, NY), 2006.


*"NANCY DREW AND THE CLUE CREW" SERIES; UNDER HOUSE PSEUDONYM CAROLYN KEENE*

*The Circus Scare*, Simon & Schuster (New York, NY), 2007.

*Thanksgiving Thief*, Simon & Schuster (New York, NY), 2008.

*Camp Creepy*, Simon & Schuster (New York, NY), 2009.

*Designed for Disaster*, Simon & Schuster (New York, NY), 2010.


*"ADAM SHARP" SERIES*

*Adam Sharp, the Spy Who Barked*, illustrated by Guy Francis, Golden Books (New York, NY), 2002, published as *The Spy Who Barked*, Random House (New York, NY) 2003.

*Adam Sharp, London Calling*, illustrated by Guy Francis, Golden Books (New York, NY), 2002, published as *London Calling*, Random House (New York, NY), 2003.

*Swimming with Sharks*, illustrated by Guy Francis, Random House (New York, NY), 2003.

*Operation Spy School*, illustrated by Guy Francis, Random House (New York, NY), 2003.

*The Riddle of the Stolen Sand*, illustrated by Salvatore Murdocca, Aladdin (New York, NY), 2003.

*Moose Master*, illustrated by Guy Francis, Random House (New York, NY), 2004.

*Code Word Kangaroo*, illustrated by Guy Francis, Random House (New York, NY), 2004.


*"TWIN CONNECTION" NOVEL SERIES; UNDER PSEUDONYM ADAM MILLS*

*Hot Pursuit*, Ballantine (New York, NY), 1989.

*On the Run*, Ballantine (New York, NY), 1989.

*Right on Target*, Ballantine (New York, NY), 1989.

*Secret Ballot*, Ballantine (New York, NY), 1989.

*Dangerous Play*, Ballantine (New York, NY), 1989.

*Skyjack!*, Ballantine (New York, NY), 1989.

*High-Tech Heist*, Ballantine (New York, NY), 1989.

*Cold Chills*, Ballantine (New York, NY), 1989.


*NONFICTION; FOR CHILDREN*

*Wild Horses*, illustrated by Michael Langham Rowe, Random House (New York, NY), 2001.

*Geronimo: Young Warrior*, illustrated by Meryl Henderson, Aladdin (New York, NY), 2001.

*Andrew Jackson, Young Patriot,* Aladdin (New York, NY), 2003.

*Mr. Rogers: Young Friend and Neighbor,* Aladdin (New York, NY), 2004.

*Harry S Truman,* Aladdin (New York, NY), 2004.

*Crazy Horse: Young War Chief,* illustrated by Meryl Henderson, Aladdin (New York, NY), 2005.

*Leonardo Da Vinci: Young Artist, Writer, and Inventor,* Aladdin (New York, NY), 2005.

*Pope John Paul II: Young Man of the Church,* Aladdin (New York, NY), 2005.

*Dwight D. Eisenhower: Young Military Leader,* Aladdin (New York, NY), 2006.

*George S. Patton: War Hero,* illustrated by Meryl Henderson, Aladdin (New York, NY), 2007.

*Coretta Scott King: First Lady of Civil Rights,* Aladdin (New York, NY), 2008.

*Davy Crockett: Frontier Legend,* Sterling Publishing (New York, NY), 2008.

*Medical Marvels,* illustrated by Josh Cochran, Sterling Publishing (New York, NY), 2009.

*Sitting Bull: Great Sioux Hero,* Sterling Publishing (New York, NY), 2010.

*"PRIMARY SOURCE HISTORY OF THE UNITED STATES" SERIES*

*The European Settlement of North America: 1492-1754,* World Almanac Library (Milwaukee, WI), 2005.

*The New Republic: 1763-1815,* World Almanac Library (Milwaukee, WI), 2005.

*The Crisis of the Union: 1815-1865,* World Almanac Library (Milwaukee, WI), 2005.

*The Era of Reconstruction and Expansion: 1865-1900,* World Almanac Library (Milwaukee, WI), 2005.

*An Emerging World Power: 1900-1929,* World Almanac Library (Milwaukee, WI), 2005.

*The Great Depression and World War II: 1929-1949,* World Almanac Library (Milwaukee, WI), 2005.

*America and the Cold War: 1949-1969,* World Almanac Library (Milwaukee, WI), 2005.

*America in Today's World: 1969-2004,* World Almanac Library (Milwaukee, WI), 2005.

*RADIO PLAYS*

*The Reclassified Child,* British Broadcasting Corporation (London, England), 1974.

*Another Football Season,* British Broadcasting Corporation (London, England), 1974.

*Better English,* British Broadcasting Corporation (London, England), 1975.

*OTHER*

*Writing Short Stories for Young People,* Writer's Digest (Cincinnati, OH), 1987.

Also author of "Mini-Mystery Series," a monthly short story in *Child Life Mystery and Science Fiction,* beginning 1977. Contributor of short stories, under pseud-

onym Stuart Symons, to *Espionage;* contributor of articles, stories, and reviews to periodicals, including *Bulletin of the Society of Children's Book Writers, Children's Playmate, Darling, English Studies in Africa, Health Explorer, Jack and Jill, Junior Medical Detective, Linguistics, Texas Outlook,* and *Women's Choice.*

## Sidelights

George Edward Stanley wrote over one hundred books for children and young adults during his decades-long career, among them the critically acclaimed *Rats in the Attic; and Other Stories to Make Your Skin Crawl* and *Night Fires.* Stanley, who taught for more than forty years at Cameron University in Lawton, Oklahoma, drew many of the plots for his books from his diverse experiences and his natural curiosity. In addition to penning numerous works under his own name, he also published using several pseudonyms, including the well-known house pseudonyms Carolyn Keene and Franklin W. Dixon when contributing to the perennially popular "Nancy Drew" and "Hardy Boys" novels, respectively.

"When I was growing up in the small town of Memphis, Texas, in the late 1940s and early 1950s, I discov-

*George Edward Stanley's story in* **Geronimo: Young Warrior** *comes to life in Meryl Henderson's detailed art.* (Aladdin Paperbacks, 2001. Illustration copyright © 2001 by Meryl Henderson. Reproduced with permission of Meryl Henderson.)

ered that I had two passions: mysteries and movies," Stanley once recalled to *SATA*. "I read all the mysteries in the public library and went to all the Saturday afternoon matinees, mainly to see the serials. There were two movie houses in Memphis and I would walk to town several times a week just to see the new movie posters. Since I was allowed to go to the movies only on Saturday afternoons, I missed a lot of the great films of those years, but . . . can now watch them anytime I want to! (I also collect movie posters!). Two of my favorite movies from that period are *The Bat* and *Home Sweet Homicide,* because they both have mystery writers as the main characters.

"As I grew older, my interests broadened, of course, and I began studying foreign languages. (Actually, I have always liked anything 'foreign.') In college, I majored in French and Portuguese and minored in German, and I went the route of the typical college professor as far as writing is concerned: I began writing very esoteric articles about linguistics that I doubt many people read.

"When it came time to work on my doctorate, I decided to follow another one of my dreams: going to Africa. I went to South Africa, to the University of Port Elizabeth, to research the problems the Xhosa have learning English and Afrikaans. Following my work in South Africa, I accepted a Fulbright professorship to the University of N'Djamena in Chad, central Africa. It was there that I began writing fiction (something else I had always wanted to do) and I sold my first radio play to the British Broadcasting Corporation's World Service in London.

"I grew up reading mysteries and wanting to write mysteries. I never got over Nancy Drew, the Dana Girls, or the Hardy Boys. If Nancy Drew had been a forensic scientist, I might be in a different occupation today. But she wasn't and that's why I created Dr. Constance Daniels, head of the Forensic Science laboratory of the Bay City Police Department. Dr. Daniels first appeared in *Child Life* magazine. Later, I introduced a new, younger character in the series, Marie-Claire Verlaine, and moved the locale to Paris, but the forensic science solutions remained. If I had known someone like Dr. Daniels, or Marie-Claire, when I was studying biology, chemistry, and physics, I might have excelled in science."

Inspired, in part, by his diverse life experiences, Stanley continued to focus his writing on books for younger readers until his death in 2011. In *The Codebreaker Kids* he introduced audiences to three enterprising kids who start a business encoding and decoding messages for would-be spies. In what *School Library Journal* reviewer Elaine Knight called an "off-the-wall but very funny spy mystery," the three friends become enmeshed in both sides of tricky situations. A *Publishers Weekly* critic found the book's humor to be somewhat far-

fetched, but the inclusion of real codes propels the story into a "fast-paced caper" in which "Dinky's careful instructions for using them" become a fine embellishment.

Reviewers have often commented upon Stanley's skill in writing books that are not only engaging, but are also very easy for young readers to complete by themselves, and his "Third Grade Detectives" series is a good example. Mr. Merlin was once a spy, but now he teaches third grade and leads his class in solving simple mysteries. Readers can follow the clues through each short, illustrated chapter book and try to solve the mystery before the characters do. Each book in the series contains simple codes and riddles for readers to decipher as well. The types of mysteries that the children solve vary widely and include several actual crimes. The puzzle of the series' first book, *The Clue of the Left-handed Envelope,* is not so serious, however, as this time out the task is to figure out who sent classmate Amber Lee a secret admirer letter. The class succeeds, with the assistance of Mr. Merlin's helpful friend, Dr. Smiley, a forensic scientist working in a police lab.

The "Third Grade Detectives" series continues in *The Puzzle of the Pretty Pink Handkerchief,* as the children try to discover who trespassed in Todd's treehouse and left behind the titular pink handkerchief. Todd is also the victim in *The Cobweb Confession,* when his baseball card collection disappears. Todd's friend Noelle is at the center of other volumes, including *The Mystery of the Hairy Tomatoes,* in which her dog is wrongly accused of digging in Mrs. Ruston's vegetable garden. The two work together on solving serious, adult crimes in the volumes *The Case of the Sweaty Bank Robber* and *The Mystery of the Stolen Statue.*

In *The Case of the Dirty Clue* Mr. Merlin's students want to know who ran over Misty's brand new bicycle. The broken bike is covered with their best clue: an unusual red soil, left there by the vehicle that crumpled it. With Mr. Merlin's help, the third graders discover that this type of soil comes from Arizona, leading them to the offending car and its driver. In *School Library Journal* Andrea Tarr cited *The Case of the Dirty Clue* for its "believable characters and . . . fast-paced plot," while *Booklist* critic Hazel Rochman predicted that "readers will enjoy the puzzles and the forensics."

Also part of the "Third Grade Detectives" series, *The Cobweb Confession* shares a feature common to many of Stanley's books: children overcoming their fears, particularly of creepy-crawly animals. This theme reappears in the stand-alone story *Snake Camp*. Stevie's parents send him to "Viper" camp, thinking that Viper is a computer program. Much to his surprise, the camp features real snakes—and Stevie *hates* snakes. By the end of the book, though, one of the reptiles has stolen Stevie's heart and become his pet. "The plot is decidedly contrived," Rochman commented in her *Booklist* review of *Snake Camp,* "but the hissing, slimy, scaly stuff is fun."

Stanley combines adventure and a dose of humor in his "Scaredy Cat" series, which includes *The Day the Ants Got Really Mad.* Intended for beginning readers, the book tells how young Michael copes with the discovery that his family's home is built on top of the world's largest anthill. Maura Bresnahan, in her review for *School Library Journal,* wrote that Stanley's informative story about ants "combines humor and a semi-scary situation" in a way "children will find immensely entertaining." A more frightening work, *Rats in the Attic,* is meant to be read aloud. Reviewer Larry Prater predicted in *Kliatt* that "middle schoolers will . . . revel in the soft-core gore and mayhem" of these stories, which involve kids who flirt with danger and the supernatural and pay dearly.

In his award-winning novel *Night Fires,* a work of historical fiction set in 1928, Stanley explores the effects of racial prejudice. After the untimely death of his father, thirteen-year-old Woodrow Harper moves with his mother from Washington, DC, to Lawton, Oklahoma, where his father was raised. There Woodrow is befriended by a neighbor, Senator George Crawford. Crawford is a member of the Oklahoma legislature who lost his son in World War I, and he and Woodrow quickly become inseparable. The boy soon discovers an ugly secret about the senator, however: Crawford is one of the leaders of the local chapter of the Ku Klux Klan. Torn between his conscience and his loyalty to Crawford, who has served as his surrogate father, Woodrow makes a fateful decision when he is pressured to deliver a whipping to a black man. Noting the imbalance of power in the relationship between Woodrow and the senator, Stanley told Bowllan: "Unfortunately, . . . *Night Fires* could happen today—and I think it does. I don't necessarily think it happens to young people on the same social level . . . as Woodrow, but it certainly happens to young people who (wanting to blame everyone else for their ills, whatever those ills are) will listen to adults spewing hatred and become followers." "Stanley's highly charged, emotional story tells of a very dark period in this country's history," Sharon Morrison remarked in her *School Library Journal* review of *Night Fires.*

Stanley's highly regarded, eight-volume "Primary Source History of the United States" series follows the country's path in books such as *The New Republic: 1763-1815, The Era of Reconstruction and Expansion: 1865-1900,* and *America and the Cold War: 1949-1969.* According to *School Library Journal* critic Rebecca Sheridan, "Stanley explains and connects events utilizing clear language," offering readers "an overall understanding of the major trends of each period examined." "What a project," the author once remarked to *School Library Journal* interviewer Amy Bowllan. "It took an enormous amount of research . . .—and I think it's a fascinating look at the United States from around 1492 until 2004—through all kinds of documents."

"Writing for young people carries with it a great responsibility," Stanley once told *SATA.* "Some young person is actually going to read what you've written and be influenced by it. Keeping this in mind can be helpful because it makes you want to put your best foot forward and produce not only something that you'll be proud of, but something that the young reader will never forget, whether it carries a lesson for life or simply recounts an exciting adventure. . . .

"One of the great things about writing for young people is that they're interested in learning about everything. This can't help but inspire the writer to reach greater heights. You want to teach them, to entertain them, to make them read what you've written. It's quite mind-boggling, frankly, when they come up to you and tell you that they really enjoy reading your stories. . . .

"I think most children are looking for something that will excite them and carry them off to other worlds. They can see enough realism on the nightly news to last them a lifetime. Give them something they can

*A snake-hating boy signs up for a summer at Camp Viper thinking that its all about his favorite computer game in Stanley's amusing* **Snake Camp,** *featuring artwork by Jared Lee.* (Illustration copyright © 2000 by Jared D. Lee Studio, Inc. Used by permission of Golden Books, an imprint of Random House Children's Books, a division of Random House, Inc.)

look forward to, something that will stir their sense of adventure and make them want to become the best in whatever they finally end up doing. But don't forget to make them laugh!"

A world traveler who taught more than thirty languages, including Arabic, Indonesian, Kurdish, Swahili, and Zulu, Stanley believed that literature could be used to bridge social and cultural differences. As he remarked to Bowllan, "Fiction is often a better 'textbook' than non-fiction because fiction allows readers to 'live' what's happening on the pages. That's why I think novels that promote tolerance and understanding of EVERYONE in our society should be required reading."

## Biographical and Critical Sources

*PERIODICALS*

*Booklist,* March 15, 1991, review of *Hershell Cobwell and the Miraculous Tattoo;* December, 2000, Hazel Rochman, review of *Snake Camp,* p. 727; August, 2001, Carolyn Phelan, review of *Wild Horses,* p. 2112; May 1, 2003, Stephanie Zvirin, review of *The Secret of the Green Skin,* pp. 1529-1530; February 1, 2004, Hazel Rochman, review of *The Case of the Dirty Clue,* p. 977.

*Kirkus Reviews,* May 15, 2009, review of *Night Fires*; December 15, 2009, review of *Medical Marvels.*

*Kliatt,* May, 1995, Larry W. Prater, review of *Rats in the Attic; and Other Stories to Make Your Skin Crawl,* pp. 18-19.

*Publishers Weekly,* January 16, 1987, review of *The Italian Spaghetti Mystery,* p. 74; May 8, 1987, review of *The Codebreaker Kids,* p. 71.

*School Library Journal,* August, 1986, Maura Bresnahan, review of *The Day the Ants Got Really Mad,* p. 130; June-July, 1987, Blair Christolon, review of *The Italian Spaghetti Mystery,* p. 101; September, 1987, Elaine E. Knight, review of *The Codebreaker Kids,* p. 183; March, 2001, Maura Bresnahan, review of *Ghost Horse,* p. 205; March, 2003, John Sigwald, review of *The Riddle of the Stolen Sand,* pp. 207-208; August, 2003, Pat Leach, review of *The Secret of the Green Skin,* p. 144; January, 2004, Andrea Tarr, review of *The Case of the Dirty Clue,* p. 107; July, 2005, Rebecca Sheridan, reviews of *The European Settlement of North America: 1492-1763, The New Republic: 1763-1815, An Emerging World Power: 1900-1929,* and *America in Today's World: 1969-2004,* all p. 122; September, 2009, Sharon Morrison, review of *Night Fires,* p. 174; November, 2010, S. McClendon, review of *Sitting Bull: Great Sioux Hero,* p. 142.

*ONLINE*

*George Edward Stanley Home Page,* http://www.cameron. edu/~georges (April 15, 2011).

*School Library Journal Online,* http://blog.schoollibrary journal.com/bowllansblog/ (February 11, 2011), Amy Bowllan, "21st Century Storytelling: Remembering George E. Stanley"; (February 20, 2011) "Writers against Racism: George E. Stanley's W.A.R. Biography."

## Obituaries

*ONLINE*

*Lawton Constitution,* http://www.swoknews.com/ (February 9, 2011).

*Publishers Weekly Online,* http://www.publishersweekly. com/ (February 8, 2011).

*School Library Journal Online,* http://www.schoollibrary journal.com/ (February 10, 2011).*

*       *       *

## STEAD, Rebecca 1968-

### Personal

Born January 16, 1968, in New York, NY; married Sean O'Brien (an attorney); children: two sons. *Education:* Vassar College, bachelor's degree, 1989.

### Addresses

*E-mail*—rebecca@firstlightbook.com.

### Career

Children's author. Formerly worked as an attorney and public defender.

### Awards, Honors

John Newbery Medal, American Library Association, 2010, for *When You Reach Me.*

### Writings

*First Light,* Wendy Lamb Books (New York, NY), 2007.
*When You Reach Me,* Wendy Lamb Books (New York, NY), 2009.

### Sidelights

Rebecca Stead, a former public defender, revisited her interest in writing while raising her daughter and produced the middle-grade novel *First Light.* In addition to tapping current concerns about global climate change, the novel also engages preteens' love of fantasy and adventure and "rests on an intriguing premise" about a secret world, according to a *Publishers Weekly* contributor.

*First Light* focuses on twelve-year-old Peter, the son of a glaciologist whose focus of study is global warming. When he accompanies his parents to Greenland, where his father is studying the Arctic ice shield, Peter is excited about the potential for cold-weather adventures in an exotic location. He is also increasingly plagued with the unusual headaches that trouble his genetic scientist mom. Then Peter meets Thea, a fourteen year old who descended from the Englishwoman who established the secret commune called Gracehope, which is located deep under the Arctic glaciers. As Grace's last direct female descendent, Thea realizes that the time has come for her community to rejoin the rest of mankind. She meets Peter as she reaches Earth's surface and sees the sun for the first time. As Stead's story unfolds, Peter and Thea discover a surprising bond as they grapple with the secrets of past generations.

The *Publishers Weekly* critic called *First Light* "a testament to [Stead's] . . . storytelling" that the alternate world and adventurous young protagonists in "are both credible and absorbing." "Gracehope itself is sketched with sure strokes, its icy setting and its matriarchal social structure fresh and believable," wrote Vicky Smith in her *Horn Book* review of Stead's novel, and *School Library Journal* contributor Connie Tyrrell Burns deemed the book "an exciting, engaging mix of science fiction, mystery, and adventure." While Jennifer Hubert noted several "gaps in Gracehope's invented mythology" in her *Booklist* review, she nonetheless dubbed *First Light* a "solid, well-meaning fantasy," and a *Kirkus Reviews* critic described the novel as a "compelling contemporary ice-age mystery."

Published in 2009, *When You Reach Me* is set in the late 1970s in New York City's Upper West Side. The narrator of this complex story is twelve-year-old Miranda, a latchkey kid whose single mother has dropped out of law school. Events are set in motion when Miranda starts receiving enigmatic notes suggesting that someone is watching her and knows what is going to happen to her in the future. Over the course of her sixth-grade year, Miranda details three separate plots—her mother's upcoming appearance on television's *The 20,000 Dollar Pyramid,* the sudden and inexplicable ending of her lifelong friendship with her neighbor Sal after he is beat up at school, and the appearance of a crazed vagrant dubbed "the laughing man." Eventually these plots come together.

*When You Reach Me* took Stead about a year and a half to complete, and in 2010 it received a Newbery Medal for the most distinguished contribution to children's literature. Reviewers were particularly impressed by Stead's ability to bring her three plots together. "The beauty of Stead's writing is found in the way she weaves subplots and settings together seamlessly," noted Augusta Scattergood in a review of *When You Reach Me* for the *Christian Science Monitor.* "Although it may take more than a first pass to get your bearings, this book has tremendous appeal." "In this taut novel, every word, every sentence, has meaning and substance," asserted *New York Times* reviewer Monica Edinger."A hybrid of genres, it is a complex mystery, a work of his-

torical fiction, a school story and one of friendship, with a leitmotif of time travel running through it." In her *Booklist* reviewer, Ilene Cooper remarked that "the mental gymnastics required of readers are invigorating, while Caitlin Augusta wrote in *School Library Journal* that Stead's "unusual, thought-provoking mystery will appeal to several types of reader."

## Biographical and Critical Sources

*PERIODICALS*

*Booklist,* April 15, 2007, Jennifer Hubert, review of *First Light,* p. 45; June 1, 2009, Ilene Cooper, review of *When You Reach Me,* p. 66.
*Bulletin of the Center for Children's Books,* September, 2007, April Spisak, review of *First Light,* p. 56.
*Christian Science Monitor,* July 28, 2009, Augusta Scattergood, review of *When You Reach Me,* p. 25.
*Horn Book,* July-August, 2007, Vicky Smith, review of *First Light,* p. 405; July 1, 2009, Roger Sutton, review of *When You Reach Me.*
*Kirkus Reviews,* June 1, 2007, review of *First Light.*
*New York Daily News,* January 19, 2010, Leo Standora, "Native New Yorker Rebecca Stead Wins John Newbery Medal for Contribution to Children's Literature."
*New York Times,* August 16, 2009, Monica Edinger, review of *When You Reach Me,* p. 15; January 19, 2010, Motoko Rich, "A Very New York Novel Wins Newbery Medal."
*Publishers Weekly,* June 18, 2007, review of *First Light,* p. 54; June 22, 2009, review of *When You Reach Me,* p. 45.
*School Library Journal,* August, 2007, Connie Tyrrell Burns, review of *First Light,* p. 126; July 1, 2009, Rick Margolis, interview with Stead, and Caitlin Augusta, review of *When You Reach Me.*
*Voice of Youth Advocates,* June, 2007, Ruth Cox Clark, review of *First Light,* p. 168.

*ONLINE*

*American Library Association Web site,* http://www.ala.org/ (January 18, 2010), "Rebecca Stead and Jerry Pinkney Win Newbery, Caldecott Medals."
*Class of 2k7 Web site,* http://classof2k7.com/ (March 18, 2008), "Rebecca Stead."
*First Light Web site,* http://www.firstlightbook.com/ (March 18, 2008).
*Random House Web site,* http://www.randomhouse.com/ (March 28, 2008), "Rebecca Stead."
*Rebecca Stead Home Page,* http://www.rebeccasteadbooks.com (April 15, 2011).*

\* \* \*

## SYMONS, Stuart
## See STANLEY, George Edward

# T

## TELGEMEIER, Raina 1977-

### Personal

Born May 26, 1977, in San Francisco, CA; married Dave Roman (a cartoonist). *Education:* School of Visual Arts (New York, NY), B.F.A. (illustration), 2002.

### Addresses

*Home*—Queens, NY. *Agent*—Judy Hansen, Hansen Literary Agency, New York, NY, hansenliterary@msn.com. *E-mail*—goraina@yahoo.com.

### Career

Author and illustrator of comics. Worked as an editorial assistant for a New York City publisher. Presenter at schools; panelist at workshops, festivals, and conferences.

### Awards, Honors

Ignatz Award nominations for Promising New Talent and Outstanding Mini-comic, both 2003; Eisner Award nomination for Talent Deserving of Wider Recognition, 2005; two Web Cartoonists' Choice Award nominations for Outstanding Slice-of-Life Webcomic, for "Smile (A Dental Drama)"; Great Graphic Novels for Teens listee, YALSA/American Library Association, and *Booklist* Top-Ten Graphic Novels for Youth selection, both 2007, both for *Kristy's Great Idea; Booklist* Top-Ten Graphic Novels for Youth selection, *Boston Globe/Horn Book* Award Honor designation, and Editor's Choice selection, *New York Times Book Review,* all 2010, all for *Smile.*

### Writings

*GRAPHIC NOVELS; SELF-ILLUSTRATED*

(Adaptor) Ann M. Martin, *Kristy's Great Idea* ("Baby-sitters Club" series), Graphix (New York, NY), 2006.

(Adaptor) Ann M. Martin, *The Truth about Stacey* ("Baby-sitters Club" series), Graphix (New York, NY), 2006.

*Cover of Raina Telgemeier's graphic-novel adaptation of Anne M. Martin's* **Mary Anne Saves the Day,** *the novel that spawned the "Baby-Sitter's Club."* (Illustration copyright © 2007 by Raina Telgemeier. Reproduced by permission of Scholastic. Inc.)

(Adaptor) Ann M. Martin, *Mary Anne Saves the Day*
   ("Baby-sitters Club" series), Graphix (New York, NY),
   2007.
(Adaptor) Ann M. Martin, *Claudia and Mean Janine*
   ("Baby-sitters Club" series), Graphix (New York, NY),
   2008.
(With husband Dave Roman and Anzu) *Misfits* ("X-Men
   1" manga series), Del Rey (New York, NY), 2009.
*Smile (A Dental Drama)* (originally serialized on girlamat-
   ic.com), Graphix (New York, NY), 2010.

*OTHER*

Author of mini-comics; Contributor to anthologies, including *Broad Appeal*, Friends of Lulu; *Bizarro's World*,
DC Comics; *Flight*, Volume 4; and *Agnes Quill: An Anthology of Mystery*, SLG Publishing (San Jose, CA),
2007.

## Sidelights

A graduate of New York City's prestigious School of
Visual Arts, award-winning comics artist Raina Telgemeier is credited with introducing Ann M. Martin's
popular "Baby-sitters Club" books to a new generation
of readers through her adaptation of four of the series
many installments into graphic novels. Telgemeier's
manga-influenced art also pairs with her personal story
of teen strife in the autobiographical graphic novel *Smile
(A Dental Drama)*, and is highlighted in *Misfits*, a collaboration with comics artist/husband Dave Roman that
features characters from DC Comics' popular "X-Men"
series. "Drawing in a deceptively simple style, Telgemeier has a knack for synthesizing the preadolescent
experience in a visual medium," noted Elizabeth Bird,
reviewing *Smile* for the *New York Times Book Review.*

Telgemeier became a fan of comic strips such as
"Calvin and Hobbes" while growing up and she soon
discovered that she too had an affinity for pairing pictures and brief texts to tell stories. She was busy creating and self-publishing short mini-comics when her
short story "Beginnings" came to the attention of a
Scholastic Publishing editor. Although the young artist
had no desire to move from the short-to long-form
comic, Scholastic handed her a project that she could
not turn down: creating illustrated adaptations of the
"Baby-sitters Club" books she had loved while growing
up. "I was just out of college and working as an editorial assistant at a book publisher, and was happy to give
that a try," Telgemeier recalled to Christopher Irving for
the *Graphic NYC* Web site. "I did a twenty-page treatment and some character designs, and they decided
within a few weeks, it all happened really fast. They
signed me up for two books and, before I was done
with the first book, they signed me up for two more."
Scholastic's choice for the four novels: *Kristy's Great
Idea, The Truth about Stacey, Mary Anne Saves the
Day*, and *Claudia and Mean Janine.*

Popular with girls who became readers during the
1980s, Martin's "Baby-sitter's Club" books number in
the hundreds and have been credited with spawning the

*Telgemeier's art for Martin's "Baby-sitter's Club" adaptation of* Claudia and Mean Janine *adds updated elements to the popular story.* (Illustration copyright © 2008 by Raina Teigemeier. Reproduced with permission of Scholastic,
Inc.)

craze for elementary-grade series fiction. In adapting
the four prose stories into illustrated serials, Telgemeier
replaces references to outdated technology, adds up-to-
date teen expressions, and salts each story with a visual
helping of current pop culture. *Kristy's Great Idea*, the
introductory "Baby-sitters Club" story, introduces the
four central middle-school characters and follows tom-
boyish Kristy as she starts her baby-sitting service.
Praising the work as a "spirited graphic-novel adaptation," a *Publishers Weekly* critic added that Telgemeier
"adds abundant energy" and "ably captures each character's personality." Stephanie Zvirin remarked in her
*Booklist* review on the "clean-lined, black-and-white
art" in *Kristy's Great Idea*, noting that its "stark black
details nicely differentiate" the four likeable preteens,
while in *School Library Journal* Ronnie Gordon observed that the book's text "is simple enough for slow
or reluctant readers." In *The Truth about Stacey* Telgemeier's cartoons reveal the artist's "keen eye for fash-
ionable details," according to *Kliatt* critic Jennifer
Feigelman, and in a review of *Claudia and Mean Janine Booklist* critic Kat Kan asserted that the story's "expressive . . . art plays a key role" in communicating
the relationships between characters.

Because each "Baby-sitters Club" adaptation required
over 190 drawings, they provided Telgemeier with a
perfect introduction the longer-format story arc she
would employ to such good effect in *Smile*. During
sixth grade Telgemeier fell on concrete and severely
damaged two of her front teeth. The resulting dental
and orthodontic surgery took several years to complete,
and its evidence was hard to hide. Teasing was a conse-
quence, but vicious taunting by the classmates she had

looked upon as friends was a surprise to the future cartoonist, who responded by drawing more and searching out new friends once she entered high school. This adolescent experience resonated so acutely that Telgemeier eventually started chronicling it in a weekly comic posted on girlamatic.com. Eventually collected and published in book form as *Smile,* her chronicle was the first graphic novel ever nominated for the prestigious *Boston Globe/Horn Book* award.

"Telgemeier's storytelling and full-color cartoony images form a story that will cheer and inspire any middle-schooler dealing with orthodontia," predicted Francisca Goldsmith in a review of *Smile* for *Booklist.* Dubbing the work "a charming addition to the body of young-adult literature that focuses on the trials and tribulations of the slightly nerdy girl," a *Publishers Weekly* contributor added that the author/illustrator is "deft at illustrating her characters' emotions in a dynamic, playful style." In *School Library Journal* Douglas P. Davey deemed *Smile* "straightforward and entertaining," while a *Kirkus Reviews* writer compared Telgemeier's story to works by Judy Blume, deeming it "irresistible, funny and touching—a must read for all teenage girls, whether en-braced or not."

*In Telgemeier's comic-strip-turned graphic novel* Smile *she recounts a personal teen trauma.* (Copyright © 2010 by Raina Telgemeier. Reproduced with permission of Scholastic, Inc.)

Telgemeier's schedule as a working cartoonist has found a new balance as increasing opportunities have arrived. For nine months out of each year she draws full-time, and then uses the next three months to plan and sketch out new projects. "I like writing for a younger audience," she explained to Irving. "I don't really think in graphic violence or adult situations when I'm writing. It's easier to be a successful writer if you stick with an audience, because that audience will always stay with you. Ten years from now, a ten-year old girl might say 'I just read this book *Smile,* and hey, there are six other books from the same person for me to read.'"

## Biographical and Critical Sources

*PERIODICALS*

*Booklist,* March 15, 2006, Stephanie Zvirin, review of *Kristy's Great Idea,* p. 56; November 1, 2007, Stephanie Zvirin, review of *Mary Anne Saves the Day,* p. 38; March 1, 2009, Kat Kan, review of *Claudia and Mean Janine,* p. 61; December 15, 2009, Francisca Goldsmith, review of *Smile (A Dental Drama),* p. 37.

*Kirkus Reviews,* January 1, 2010, review of *Smile.*

*Kliatt,* January, 2007, Jennifer Feigelman, review of *The Truth about Stacey,* p. 32.

*New York Times Book Review,* May 16, 2010, Elizabeth Bird, review of *Smile,* p. 21.

*Publishers Weekly,* April 24, 2006, review of *Kristy's Great Idea,* p. 61; September 25, 2006, review of *Agnes Quill: An Anthology of Mystery,* p. 52; July 27, 2009, review of *Misfits,* p. 50; December 7, 2009, review of *Smile,* p. 51.

*School Library Journal,* July, 2006, Ronnie Gordon, review of *Kristy's Great Idea,* p. 128; March, 2009, Beth Gallego, review of *Claudia and Mean Janine,* p. 173; March, 2010, Douglas P. Davey, review of *Smile,* p. 186.

*Record* (Bergen County, NJ), April 24, 2006, Solvej Schou, "Book Series Fans Draws on Her Talents," p. F8.

*ONLINE*

*Raina Telgemeier Home Page,* http://goraina.com (February 20, 2011).

*Graphic NYC Web site,* http://www.nycgraphicnovelists.com/ (February, 2010), Christopher Irving, interview with Telgemeier.*

\*    \*    \*

# TEPPER, Yona 1941-

## Personal

Born 1941, in Kibbutz Dafna, Israel. *Education:* Degree in education and creative drama.

## Addresses

*Home*—Israel.

## Career

Educator and author. Teacher, then school principal. Hakibbutz Hameuchad Publishing House, Tel Aviv, Israel, curently editor for children and youth.

## Awards, Honors

Ze'ev Prize, 1995, 2005; Prime Minister's Prize, 2001; International Board on Books Honor Book citation, 2007; Israel Ministry of Science and Culture Award, 2008.

## Writings

*Rega she Kashe Lishkoah,* Hakibbutz Hameuchad (Tel Aviv, Israel), 1982.

*Hatzavim al Niyar,* Hakibbutz Hameuchad (Tel Aviv, Israel), 1985.

*Bakbuk ha-Bosem Shel Ima,* Hakibbutz Hameuchad (Tel Aviv, Israel), 1986.

*Shupuli le-yom Huledet,* Hakibbutz Hameuchad (Tel Aviv, Israel), 1987.

*Avital Ve-Nahash ha-Mayim,* Sifriyat po'alim (Tel Aviv, Israel), 1988.

*Liftan Tzimukim ha-Ketanah,* Zmora Bitan (Israel), 1988.

*Tammy ha-Ketanah ve ha-Mabul ha-Gadol,* Ma'ariv (Israel), 1990.

*Matai atah hozer?,* Schocken Books(Tel Aviv, Israel), 1990.

*David Hetzi-Hetzi* Hakibbutz Hameuchad (Tel Aviv, Israel), 1990.

*Yonatan u-magen ha-Yono'inim,* Hakibbutz Hameuchad (Tel Aviv, Israel), 1992.

*Ha-Ofano'an mi-Shevil-he-halav,* Massada (Israel), 1993.

*Pele Zera-etz,* Hakibbutz Hameuchad (Tel Aviv, Israel), 1993.

*Ha-Masah el ha-Emek ha-Nistar,* Hakibbutz Hameuchad (Tel Aviv, Israel), 1993.

*La 'azov Bayit,* Hakibbutz Hameuchad (Tel Aviv, Israel), 1994.

*Ve-rak me-Ahavah,* Hakibbutz Hameuchad (Tel Aviv, Israel), 1995.

*No'am, Dori va-hatsi ha-te'omim,* Hakibbutz Hameuchad (Tel Aviv, Israel), 1995.

*Timoret Yeladim,* Hakibbutz Hameuchad (Tel Aviv, Israel), 1995.

(With Mirik Snir) *Ani veha-mishpahah sheli,* [Israel], 1995.

*Ha-Nesichah 'Yeocholah ha-Col Be-Atzmi',* Hakibbutz Hameuchad (Tel Aviv, Israel), 1996.

*Meruti,* Hakibbutz Hameuchad (Tel Aviv, Israel), 1996.

*Michal Mehapeset et ha-Aviv,* Am Oved (Tel Aviv, Israel), 1996.

*Matai Kvar Yihiye li Kelev?,* Matar (Israel), 1997.

*Va-Alai lo Ichpat Lach,* Hakibbutz Hameuchad (Tel Aviv, Israel), 1998.

*Be-Ikvot ha-Zar Im ha-Matzlemah,* Keter (Tel Aviv, Israel), 1998.

*Mat'im lakh kakhah she-at tsoheket,* Hakibbutz Hameuchad (Tel Aviv, Israel), 1999.

*Sus ha-Shamaim Shel Saari,* Hakibbutz Hameuchad (Tel Aviv, Israel), 2000.

*Shava Avney ha-Nesicha,* Hakibbutz Hameuchad (Tel Aviv, Israel), 2002.

*Yael Metzitza la-Rchov,* illustrated by Gil-ly Alon Curiel, Hakibbutz Hameuchad (Tel Aviv, Israel), 2004, translated by Deborah Guthman as *Passing By,* Kane Miller (Tulsa, OK), 2010.

*Kemo dekkirat sakin,* Sifriyat po'alim (Tel Aviv, Israel), 2005.

*Sod im Knafaim,* Hakibbutz Hameuchad (Tel Aviv, Israel), 2006.

*Avanim Ktanot Shel Ahava,* Hakibbutz Hameuchad (Tel Aviv, Israel), 2007.

*Eize Min Shem Ze,* Hakibbutz Hameuchad (Tel Aviv, Israel), 2008.

*Mi Hachi Gavoha?,* Hakibbutz Hameuchad (Tel Aviv, Israel), 2009.

*Dubilbul,* Hakibbutz Hameuchad (Tel Aviv, Israel), 2009.

Author's work has been translated into Arabic, German, and Korean.

## Biographical and Critical Sources

*PERIODICALS*

*Kirkus Reviews,* February 15, 2010, review of *Passing By.*

*Publishers Weekly,* January 25, 2010, review of *Passing By,* p. 116.

*School Library Journal,* May, 2010, Martha Simpson, review of *Passing By,* p. 92.

*ONLINE*

*Institute for the Translation of Hebrew Literature Web site,* http://www.ithl.org/ (March 15, 2010), "Yona Tepper."*

\*        \*        \*

## TOCHER, Timothy 1946-

## Personal

Born August 18, 1946; married; wife's name Judy.

## Addresses

*Home*—Suffern, NY.

## Career

Writer and retired teacher. Visiting writer at elementary schools; guest lecturer.

## Awards, Honors

Merit Plaque, Society of Children's Book Writers and Illustrators, 2002, for "Sgt. Monday and the Enchanted Kingdom Police"; Best Book for Young Adults designation, American Library Association, 2005, for *Chief Sunrise, John McGraw, and Me.*

## Writings

*Long Shot* (middle-grade novel), Meadowbrook Press (Minnetonka, MN), 2001.
*Playing for Pride* (middle-grade novel), Meadowbrook Press (New York, NY), 2002.
*Chief Sunrise, John McGraw, and Me* (young-adult novel), illustrated by Greg Copeland, Cricket Books (Chicago, IL), 2004.
*Bill Pennant, Babe Ruth, and Me* (sequel to *Chief Sunrise, John McGraw, and Me*), Cricket Books (Chicago, IL), 2009.

Contributor of short stories to books, including *Newfangled Fairy Tales,* and to periodicals, including *Cricket.* Contributor of poems to collections, including *Kids Pick the Funniest Poems, Rolling in the Aisles,* and *No More Homework! No More Tests!*

## Sidelights

A former teacher, Timothy Tocher now writes humorous verse for young readers. Tocher has also written juvenile novels with sports themes, including *Long Shot* and *Playing for Pride,* both featuring a young basketball star named Laurie. In *Long Shot,* fifth-grader Laurie must adjust to a new school and a new team when her father, a basketball coach, takes a job in a new town. *Playing for Pride* focuses on Laurie's experiences on the softball team, where her skills are not as great as they are on the basketball court.

In the young-adult novel *Chief Sunrise, John McGraw, and Me* Tocher tells a fast-moving story set in 1919. The protagonist is Hank Cobb, a fifteen year old who roams the country with his abusive father, a baseball player. When presented with an opportunity to escape his cruel father, Hank seizes it. He falls in with another baseball player who is four years older than himself. A Seminole who goes by the name of Chief Sunrise, Hank's new companion is a gifted player who is set upon locating New York Giants manager John McGraw in order to win a spot on the team. Along the way the duo has numerous misadventures, including running a con game at a carnival, unloading trucks, and doing janitorial work at stadiums. Cobb eventually discovers the reason for Chief Sunrise's secrecy: he is actually an African American passing as a Seminole because he would not be allowed to play in the major leagues if his real background were known.

"Tocher creates two intriguingly ambiguous characters . . . and masterfully positions them in a post-World War I America," noted Elizabeth Bush in her review of *Chief Sunrise, John McGraw, and Me* for the *Bulletin of the Center for Children's Books.* While some parts of the story are humorous, "there's nothing laughable . . . about the racism that forces Chief to hide his identity in order to bring his prodigious ability into a proper arena," noted Bush. Reviewing Tocher's novel for *School Library Journal,* Marilyn Taniguchi called it "a deft blend of baseball lore and fiction," and concluded that the author's "treatment of issues of prejudice is sensitive yet the tone remains upbeat." A *Kirkus Reviews* writer praised Tocher for his accurate, well-researched portrayal of the era and recommended *Chief Sunrise, John McGraw, and Me* as "engaging and engrossing."

*Bill Pennant, Babe Ruth, and Me* is set in 1920, and like its prequel it mixes fact and fiction. Hank Cobb is now sixteen, and John McGraw's Giants are sharing the Polo Grounds with the Yankees and their newest player, Babe Ruth. McGraw has acquired a wildcat mascot and named it Bill Pennant, and he charges Hank with taming and training the creature. Hank and the big cat stay in New York when the team travels. Yankee manager Miller Huggins watches Hank work with Bill Pennant and thinks he might have a calming effect on the volatile Babe. By the time McGraw and the team return, Hank has enjoyed several adventures with Ruth and the great newspaperman and writer Damon Runyon, and he and the Babe are now good friends. *School Library Journal* reviewer Kim Dare wrote that Tocher's retelling of an era in baseball history "is a must-read for fans of Chief Sunrise, but it easily stands alone." A *Kirkus Reviews* contributor deemed Hank "a sympathetic, fully developed character whose thoughts and choices are completely in sync with his time and place."

"I grew up less than a block from a public library," Tocher once commented."There were no highways to cross or buses to ride. I just ran down from the hilltop where I lived and had access to all the books I wanted for free. Inside every avid reader, the germ of a writer is growing.

"As an elementary-school teacher, I read my students the best children's books I could find. Roald Dahl, Farley Mowatt, E.B. White, Richard Peck, and Louis Sachar are among the writers I learned to admire by sharing their work with my third and fourth graders.

"Whenever I rewrite, I read my work out loud. This is especially useful for editing dialogue. Each character has to have a distinctive voice if the reader is to accept him/her as a real person. Hard work is more important than inspiration. A great idea may arrive in a split second, but it takes hours of work to bring it to life on paper.

"Of my books, *Chief Sunrise, John McGraw, and Me* is my favorite. I am a lifelong baseball fan who grew up rooting for the Brooklyn Dodgers. Writing this novel gave me the opportunity to research the 'deadball era,' a period in which strategy and intelligent play were more important than brawn. I hope to share some of the pleasure that baseball has given me with my readers."

## Biographical and Critical Sources

*PERIODICALS*

*Booklist,* May 15, 2004, Shelle Rosenfeld, review of *Chief Sunrise, John McGraw, and Me,* p. 1630.
*Bulletin of the Center for Children's Books,* July-August, 2004, Elizabeth Bush, review of *Chief Sunrise, John McGraw, and Me,* p. 451.
*Kirkus Reviews,* April 15, 2004, review of *Chief Sunrise, John McGraw, and Me,* p. 402; January 15, 2009, review of *Bill Pennant, Babe Ruth, and Me.*
*School Library Journal,* September, 2004, Marilyn Tanigu-chi, review of *Chief Sunrise, John McGraw, and Me,* p. 219; June 1, 2009, Kim Dare, review of *Bill Pennant, Babe Ruth, and Me,* p. 139.

*ONLINE*

*Author Illustrator Source,* http://www.autor-illustrator-source.com/ (March 7, 2010), "Timothy Tocher."
*Authors in Schools Web site,* http://www.authorsinschools.com/ (March 7, 2010), "Timothy Tocher."*

\*    \*    \*

# TOWLE, Ben 1970-

## Personal

Born 1970; married; children: one daughter. *Education:* Davidson College, B.A. (philosophy); Savannah College of Art and Design, degree (sequential art), M.F.A. Teacher at North Carolina Governor's School and Sawtooth Center for Visual Art. Cofounder, National Association of Comics Art Educators (nonprofit).

## Addresses

*Home*—Winston-Salem, NC. *E-mail*—ben@trainedchimp.com.

## Career

Cartoonist and illustrator. Freelance graphic artist and illustrator. Former musician with rock band Come on Thunderchild; Savannah College of Art and Design, Savannah, GA, former instructor.

## Awards, Honors

Multiple Eisner Award nominations.

## Writings

*SELF-ILLUSTRATED GRAPHIC NOVELS*

*Farewell, Georgia,* Slave Labor Graphics (San Jose, CA), 2003.

**Ben Towle** (Photograph by James Sack. Reproduced by permission.)

*Midnight Sun* (originally published in five volumes in comic-book format), Slave Labor Graphics (San Jose, CA), 2007.

Author of online comic "OysterWar." Contributor of comics to periodicals and to anthologies, including *24-Hour Comics Day Highlights,* About Comics, 2004.

*ILLUSTRATOR*

Sarah Stewart Taylor, *Amelia Earhart: This Broad Ocean,* Disney/Hyperion Books (New York, NY), 2010.

## Sidelights

Ben Towle turned to a career in comics after the novelty of playing in a local rock band wore off and he needed to make a living. Towle's longtime love of comic books and his talent as an artist and storyteller have combined to earn him success in an increasingly competitive field but expanding field. In addition to producing the original graphic novels *Farewell, Georgia* and *Midnight Sun,* as well as his ongoing Web comic "Oyster War," Towle has also created the artwork for Sarah Stewart Taylor's *Amelia Earhart: This Broad Ocean,* an illustrated biography that follows the future aviator on her first flight across the Atlantic Ocean as a passenger.

When Towle decided to become a cartoonist, he realized that his B.A. in philosophy from Davidson College would need to be supplemented by more-relevant training. He found that training at the Savannah College of Art and Design, where he completed his M.F.A. in sequential art. While spending time in Georgia, Towle collected the four stories that he retells in *Farewell,*

*Georgia.* Drawn in black and white, these illustrated retellings capture the story's southern roots and introduce tall-tale characters that include a monkey that hunts raccoons and taciturn baseball legend Ty Cobb.

First published as a five-volume comic-book series, *Midnight Sun* again features Towle's black-and-white drawings, but this time he takes as his subject an actual event that took place in May of 1928. An Italian aircraft landed near the North Pole and deposited a flag and a crucifix blessed by the Pope. When its attempt to retake the skies resulted in a crash, nine crew members remained alive, stranded on the ice. Several major newspapers funded a search for the missing aircraft, fueling the drama with their colorful reportage, and weeks later all but one of the crew were rescued by a Russian ship. Towle follows the adventure from the viewpoint of a fictional reporter who hopes to rescue a career destroyed by alcoholism with a headline-grabbing front-page story. Praising *Midnight Sun* as "vividly imagined," a *Publishers Weekly* contributor added that Towle's "high-quality graphic historical fiction" ranges inventively into "alternative history" while adhering to the basic facts.

Set a month after *Midnight Sun, Amelia Earhart* focuses on the famous pilot's first flight from Newfoundland to Europe. Joining pilots William S. Stultz and Lew Cordon in their hydroplane, Earhart flew from the Canadian town of Trepassey to Northern Ireland almost fifteen hours later, becoming the first woman to fly across the Atlantic in the process. In Taylor's story Earhart captures the admiration of a preteen named Grace, who manages to speak to the aviatrix and receive encouragement to follow her own dreams of becoming a journalist. In *Amelia Earhart* "Taylor and Towle have combined their talents for research, narrative, and image to offer a fresh view" of their well-known subject, asserted Francisca Goldsmith in *Booklist,* the critic going on to praise the "excellent" quality of Towle's sequential black-and-white drawings, with their subtle cyan blue shadings. Noting that both text and art are "emotionally restrained," a *Publishers Weekly* critic added that Towle's renderings of "the bleak landscape . . . emphasize the courage of people willing to take ultimate risks." The "mono-color illustrations have a classic feel that enlivens the tale with casual grace," asserted Douglas P. Davey in his *School Library Journal* review of *Amelia Earhart,* while a *Kirkus Reviews* contributor wrote that "Towle's detailed art truly makes this stellar book a visual feast."

Despite its small scale and stylized approach, sequential art is very labor-intensive to produce. By Towle's own estimates, it takes approximately ten hours to map out a page in pencil, then another six or more hours to ink the lines and add blocks of contrast. Scanning each page and adding dimensions through shading takes another four hours of work. In a book such as *Midnight Sun,* that adds up to over 2,500 hours of work—a year spent on a single project—on top of the time needed to plan, research, and write the story. Fortunately, as an independent artist Towle can work at his own pace: in addition to his comics projects and teaching art at several schools near his home in Winston-Salem, North Carolina, he also finds time to work on behalf of the National Association of Comics Art Educators, a nonprofit he helped found that promotes the use of comic books as educational resources.

## Biographical and Critical Sources

*PERIODICALS*

*Booklist,* March 15, 2010, Francisca Goldsmith, review of *Amelia Earhart: This Broad Ocean,* p. 58.
*Horn Book,* May-June, 2010, Susan Dove Lempke, review of *Amelia Earhart,* p. 92.
*Kirkus Reviews,* January 15, 2010, review of *Amelia Earhart.*
*New York Times Book Review,* March 14, 2010, Tanya Lee Stone, review of *Amelia Earhart,* p. 15.
*Publishers Weekly,* December 24, 2007, review of *Midnight Sun,* p. 35; November 2, 2009, review of *Amelia Earhart,* p. 55.
*School Library Journal,* May, 2010, Douglas P. Davey, review of *Amelia Earhart,* p. 142.
*Teacher Librarian,* June, 2010, Joe Sutliff Sanders, review of *Amelia Earhart,* p. 27.
*Winston-Salem Journal,* July 20, 2006, Tim Clodfelter, "Ben Towle Teaches Others to Be Sequential Artists" (profile), p. 5.

*ONLINE*

*Ben Towle Home Page,* http://www.benzilla.com (March 20, 2011).
*Oyster War Web site,* http://oysterwar.tumblr.com/ (March 20, 2011), site of "Oyster War" comic.

\*    \*    \*

## TRUMBAUER, Lisa 1963-
## (Jake Maddox, a house pseudonym, Lisa Trutkoff Trumbauer)

### Personal

Born February 15, 1963, in New York, NY; daughter of Fred and Sigrid Trutkoff; married David Trumbauer. *Education:* University of Maryland, B.S., 1985.

### Addresses

*Home*—Hillsborough, NJ. *E-mail*—ltrumbauer@aol.com.

### Career

Author and editor of books for children. Editor for educational publishers in New York, NY, 1988-94; freelance writer.

## Member

Society of Children's Book Writers and Illustrators.


## Writings

*The Runaway Valentines,* illustrated by Pamela Cote, Troll (Mahwah, NJ), 1994.

(As Lisa Trutkoff Trumbauer) *Has Anyone Seen My Green Dinosaur?,* illustrated by Frank Daniel, Longmeadow Press (Stamford, CT), 1995.

(As Lisa Trutkoff Trumbauer) *I Swear I Saw a Witch in Washington Square,* illustrated by Frank Daniel, Longmeadow Press (Stamford, CT), 1995.

*About One Hundred Years Ago,* Yellow Umbrella Books (Mankato, MN), 2000.

*Everyone Is a Scientist,* Yellow Umbrella Books (Mankato, MN), 2000.

*Food for Thought,* Yellow Umbrella Books (Mankato, MN), 2000.

*Teamwork,* Yellow Umbrella Books (Mankato, MN), 2000.

*Families,* Yellow Umbrella Books (Mankato, MN), 2000.

*Who Is a Friend?,* Yellow Umbrella Books (Mankato, MN), 2001.

*Communities,* Yellow Umbrella Books (Mankato, MN), 2001.

*Animal Ears,* Yellow Umbrella Books (Mankato, MN), 2001.

*At School,* Yellow Umbrella Books (Mankato, MN), 2001.

*On the Go,* Yellow Umbrella Books (Mankato, MN), 2001.

*Our Favorite Things to Do,* Yellow Umbrella Books (Mankato, MN), 2001.

*Palmistry,* illustrated by Dan Regan, Troll (Mahwah, NJ), 2001.

*Seasons,* Yellow Umbrella Books (Mankato, MN), 2001.

*Graph It!,* Yellow Umbrella Books (Mankato, MN), 2002.

*How to Talk So Boys Will Listen and Listen So Boys Will Talk,* Troll (Mahwah, NJ), 2002.

*Exploring Animal Rights and Animal Welfare,* four volumes, Greenwood Press (Westport, CT), 2002.

*Take Away,* Yellow Umbrella Books (Mankato, MN), 2003.

*What Is a Thermometer?,* Children's Press (New York, NY), 2003.

*What Is Electricity?,* Children's Press (New York, NY), 2003.

*What Is Friction?,* Children's Press (New York, NY), 2003.

*What Is Gravity?,* Children's Press (New York, NY), 2003.

*Who Needs Plants?,* Yellow Umbrella Books (Mankato, MN), 2003.

*Why We Measure,* Yellow Umbrella Books (Mankato, MN), 2003.

*You Can Use a Compass,* Children's Press (New York, NY), 2003.

*Montana,* Children's Press (New York, NY), 2003.

*Wisconsin,* Children's Press (New York, NY), 2003.

*The Body in Motion,* Chelsea Clubhouse Books (Philadelphia, PA), 2003.

*Eating Well,* Red Brick Learning (Bloomington, MN), 2003.

*Trees Are Terrific!,* Yellow Umbrella Books (Bloomington, MN), 2003.

*Fun-to-Solve Map Mysteries,* Scholastic (New York, NY), 2003.

*Fifty Ways to Love Your Pet,* Troll (Mahwah, NJ), 2003.

*Let's Graph,* Yellow Umbrella Books (Bloomington, MN), 2004.

*Let's Meet Frederick Douglass,* Chelsea Clubhouse Books (Philadelphia, PA), 2004.

*Let's Meet Sojourner Truth,* Chelsea Clubhouse Books (Philadelphia, PA), 2004.

*A Tooth Is Loose,* illustrated by Steve Gray, Children's Press (New York, NY), 2004.

*What Are Atoms?,* Children's Press (New York, NY), 2004.

*Russian Immigrants,* Facts on File (New York, NY), 2005.

*Tiny Life in Your Home* ("Rookie Read-about Science" series), Children's Press (New York, NY), 2005.

*What Does a Mail Carrier Do?,* Enslow Publisher (Berkeley Heights, NJ), 2005.

*Floods,* Franklin Watts (New York, NY), 2005.

*Forest Fires,* Franklin Watts (New York, NY), 2005.

*German Immigrants,* Facts on File (New York, NY), 2005.

*Grand Canyon* ("Rookie Read-about Geography" series), Children's Press (New York, NY), 2005.

*The Hidden Dragon,* illustrated by Emily Fiegenshuh, MirrorStone (Renton, WA), 2005.

*Hopes Fulfilled: The Irish Immigrants in Boston,* Zaner-Bloser (Columbus, OH), 2005.

*King Ludwig's Castle: Germany's Neuschwanstein,* Bearport (New York, NY), 2005.

*Living in a City,* Capstone Press (Mankato, MN), 2005.

*Living in a Rural Area,* Capstone Press (Mankato, MN), 2005.

*Living in a Small Town,* Capstone Press (Mankato, MN), 2005.

*Living in a Suburb,* Capstone Press (Mankato, MN), 2005.

*Marian Anderson: A Life of Song,* Zaner-Bloser (Columbus, OH), 2005.

*Mystery at Canyon Creek,* Great Source Education Group (Wilmington, MA), 2005.

(With Karin Wulf) *Pennsylvania, 1643-1776,* National Geographic Society (Washington, DC), 2005.

*What Does a Truck Driver Do?,* Enslow Elementary (Berkeley Heights, NJ), 2006.

*What Is an Insect?,* Yellow Umbrella Books (Mankato, MN), 2006.

*What Is Volume?,* Children's Press (New York, NY), 2006.

*What Makes Ten?,* Yellow Umbrella Books (Mankato, MN), 2006.

*A Year in the Desert,* Red Brick Learning (Bloomington, MN), 2006.

*Animal Giants,* Red Brick Learning (Bloomington, MN), 2006.

*Corn,* Red Brick Learning (Bloomington, MN), 2006.

*Dachshunds,* Capstone Press (Mankato, MN), 2006.

*Discover the Rain Forest,* Red Brick Learning (Bloomington, MN), 2006.

*Double the Animals,* Red Brick Learning (Bloomington, MN), 2006.

*Golden Retrievers,* Capstone Press (Mankato, MN), 2006.

*Poodles,* Capstone Press (Mankato, MN), 2006.

*A Practical Guide to Dragons,* Wizards of the Coast (Renton, WA), 2006.

*Set in Stone,* Yellow Umbrella Books (Bloomington, MN), 2006.

*The Story of Orange Juice,* Red Brick Learning (Bloomington, MN), 2006.

*Water,* Yellow Umbrella Books (Bloomington, MN), 2006.

*What Does a Nurse Do?,* Enslow Elementary (Berkeley Heights, NJ), 2006.

*Body Warriors: The Immune System,* Raintree (Chicago, IL), 2007.

*The First Americans,* Heinemann (Chicago, IL), 2007.

*Lighthouses of North America!: Exploring Their History, Lore, and Science,* Williamson Books (Nashville, TN), 2007.

*Mountain Manor Mystery,* illustrated by Kevin Hawkes, Mondo (New York, NY), 2007.

*To the Core: Earth's Structure,* Raintree (Chicago, IL), 2007.

*Lost!,* Raintree (Chicago, IL), 2007.

*Fighter Jet,* Raintree (Chicago, IL), 2008.

*The Haunted Ghoul Bus,* illustrated by Jannie Ho, Sterling (New York, NY), 2008.

*A Practical Guide to Dragon Riding,* illustrated by Daren Bader, Wizards of the Coast (Renton, WA), 2008.

*Poly Pocket Pocket Lodge Snowed In!,* Meredith Books (Des Moines, IA), 2008.

*A Practical Guide to Vampires,* compiled by Treval Vorgard, Wizards of the Coast (Renton, WA), 2009.

*The Great Reindeer Rebellion,* illustrated by Jannie Ho, Sterling (New York, NY), 2009.

*Standoff: Remembering the Alamo,* illustrated by Brent Schoonover, Stone Arch Books (Mankato, MN), 2009.

(Reteller) *The Three Little Pigs* (graphic novel), illustrated by Aaron Blecha, Stone Arch Books (Minneapolis, MN), 2009.

Author's work has been translated into Spanish.

### "COOL SITES" SERIES

*Free Stuff for Kids on the Net,* Millbrook Press (Brookfield, CT), 1999.

*Hot Stars for Kids on the Net,* Millbrook Press (Brookfield, CT), 1999.

*Super Sports for Kids on the Net,* Millbrook Press (Brookfield, CT), 1999.

*Homework Help for Kids on the Net,* Millbrook Press (Brookfield, CT), 2000.

### "CLICK IT!: COMPUTER FUN" SERIES

*Christmas,* Millbrook Press (Brookfield, CT), 1999.

*Geography,* illustrated by Sydney Wright, Millbrook Press (Brookfield, CT), 1999.

*Halloween,* Millbrook Press (Brookfield, CT), 1999.

*Math,* Millbrook Press (Brookfield, CT), 1999.

*Science,* Millbrook Press (Brookfield, CT), 1999.

*Reading,* illustrated by Sydney Wright, Millbrook Press (Brookfield, CT), 1999.

*Social Studies,* Millbrook Press (Brookfield, CT), 2000.

*Writing,* Millbrook Press (Brookfield, CT), 2000.

### "WHAT ARE . . ." SERIES

*What Are Deserts?,* Pebble Books (Mankato, MN), 2002.

*What Are Forests?,* Pebble Books (Mankato, MN), 2002.

*What Are Mountains?,* Pebble Books (Mankato, MN), 2002.

*What Are Oceans?,* Pebble Books (Mankato, MN), 2002.

### "LIFE CYCLES" SERIES

*The Life Cycle of a Chicken,* Pebble Books (Mankato, MN), 2002.

*The Life Cycle of a Cat,* Pebble Books (Mankato, MN), 2002.

*The Life Cycle of a Dog,* Pebble Books (Mankato, MN), 2002.

*The Life Cycle of a Frog,* Pebble Books (Mankato, MN), 2002.

*The Life Cycle of a Butterfly,* Pebble Books (Mankato, MN), 2002.

*The Life Cycle of a Whale,* Pebble Books (Mankato, MN), 2003.

*The Life Cycle of a Cow,* Pebble Books (Mankato, MN), 2003.

*The Life Cycle of a Bee,* Pebble Books (Mankato, MN), 2003.

*The Life Cycle of a Kangaroo,* Pebble Books (Mankato, MN), 2003.

*The Life Cycle of a Salmon,* Pebble Books (Mankato, MN), 2003.

*The Life Cycle of a Grasshopper,* Pebble Books (Mankato, MN), 2004.

*The Life Cycle of a Penguin,* Pebble Books (Mankato, MN), 2004.

*The Life Cycle of a Rabbit,* Pebble Books (Mankato, MN), 2004.

*The Life Cycle of a Turtle,* Pebble Books (Mankato, MN), 2004.

### "HELPERS IN OUR COMMUNITY" SERIES

*We Need Child Care Workers,* Pebble Books (Mankato, MN), 2003.

*We Need Construction Workers,* Pebble Books (Mankato, MN), 2003.

*We Need Garbage Collectors,* Pebble Books (Mankato, MN), 2003.

*We Need Zoo Keepers,* Pebble Books (Mankato, MN), 2003.

### "ROOKIE READ-ABOUT SCIENCE" SERIES

*All about Heat,* Children's Press (New York, NY), 2003.

*All about Light,* Children's Press (New York, NY), 2003.

*All about Sound,* Children's Press (New York, NY), 2003.

### "FIRST BIOGRAPHIES" SERIES

*Sam Houston,* Pebble Books (Mankato, MN), 2003.

*Paul Revere,* Pebble Books (Mankato, MN), 2004.

*Sitting Bull,* Pebble Books (Mankato, MN), 2004.

*Eleanor Roosevelt,* Pebble Books (Mankato, MN), 2005.

*"LIFE IN THE TIMES OF . . ." SERIES*

*Abraham Lincoln and the Civil War,* Heinemann (Chicago, IL), 2008.
*George Washington and the Revolutionary War,* Heinemann (Chicago, IL), 2008.
*Pocahontas and the Early Colonies,* Heinemann (Chicago, IL), 2008.

*"JAKE MADDOX SPORTS STORY" READER SERIES; UNDER HOUSE PSEUDONYM JAKE MADDOX*

*Kart Crash,* illustrated by Sean Tiffany, Stone Arch Books (Minneapolis, MN), 2008.
*Storm Surfer,* illustrated by Sean Tiffany, Stone Arch Books (Minneapolis, MN), 2008.
*Skater's Secret,* illustrated by Tuesday Mourning, Stone Arch Books (Minneapolis, MN), 2009.
*Pit Crew Crunch,* illustrated by Sean Tiffany, Stone Arch Books (Minneapolis, MN), 2009.

## Sidelights

A prolific author of children's books, Lisa Trumbauer got her start in publishing as an editor for educational publishers. While much of Trumbauer's work is series nonfiction and covers a wide spectrum of topics, she has also created picture books, chapter books, and other imaginative works, such as her whimsical how-to books *A Practical Guide to Dragons* and *A Practical Guide to Vampires,* her humorous holiday story *The Great Reindeer Rebellion,* and her text for the graphic-novel version of *The Three Little Pigs.* Illustrated by Jannie He, *The Great Reindeer Rebellion* inspired *Booklist* contributor Hazel Rochman to note that He's colorful, tactile art pairs well with Trumbauer's "wry, rhyming story." In *School Library Journal* Joy Fleishhaker recommended *A Practical Guide to Dragons* as a "well-imagined manual" "filled with interesting and quirky details" that should appeal to fans of the "Dragonlance" and other fantasy series.

Reviewing *Homework Help for Kids on the Net,* one of Trumbauer's contributions to the "Cool Sites" computer-themed series, *School Library Journal* critic Yapha Nussbaum Mason praised the book as an "accessible" resource that readers would be wise to "keep . . . handy" when doing Web searches for school reports. *All about Light* and *All about Sound,* two of Trumbauer's contributions to the "Rookie Read-about Science" series published by Children's Press, were cited by *Booklist* critic Gillian Engberg for their ability to "admirably explain fundamental concepts for the very young." Another nonfiction project, the author's four-volume *Exploring Animal Rights and Animal Welfare,* is "equally suited for assignment use or for personal explorations of a tough and touchy subject," according to *School Library Journal* contributor John Peters.

Under the house pseudonym Jake Maddox, Trumbauer has also contributed books such as *Kart Crash, Storm Surfer* and *Pit Crew Crunch* to the "Jake Maddox Sports Story" readers series, which weaves themes of sportsmanship and teamwork into fast-paced tales about young athletes. Reviewing *Kart Crash,* which focuses on a boy whose go-cart racing eventually yields him some new friends, Ian Chipman wrote in *Booklist* that, true to the series' focus, Trumbauer's use of "heavy repetition and emphasis on action will help draw struggling readers along."

Trumbauer once told *SATA:* "I was quite the goofball as a kid. My friends and I had a clubhouse, and we wrote tons of secret codes, always hoping for adventures that never really happened. Thank goodness for books! I became a huge bookworm, and I filled countless notebooks with diaries, stories, and poems. One of those poems was published in *Seventeen* magazine when I was in high school.

"At the University of Maryland, I studied education and journalism. I also wrote for the school newspaper, *The Diamondback.* After college, I combined my education and journalism experiences to work as an editor for educational publishers. Soon I began writing as well as editing. Now I write all the time, both fiction and nonfiction books for kids. In between projects, I love to travel and go to baseball games to see the Baltimore Orioles. I live in New Jersey with my husband, Dave, and our 'dysfunctional pet family': a dog named Blue and two cats named Cosmo and Cleo."

## Biographical and Critical Sources

*PERIODICALS*

*Booklist,* September 1, 2003, Carolyn Phelan, reviews of *We Need Child Care Workers* and *We Need Construction Workers,* both p. 126; September 1, 2004, Gillian Engberg, reviews of *All about Light* and *All about Sound,* both p. 138; November 15, 2008, Ian Chipman, review of *Kart Crash,* p. 40; November 15, 2009, Hazel Rochman, review of *The Great Reindeer Rebellion,* p. 42.
*Kirkus Reviews,* September 15, 2009, review of *The Great Reindeer Rebellion.*
*School Library Journal,* December, 1999, Kristina Aaronson, review of *Math,* p. 129; February, 2000, Yapha Nussbaum Mason, review of *Halloween,* p. 115; July, 2000, Yapha Nussbaum Mason, review of *Homework Help for Kids on the Net,* p. 123; July, 2002, Eldon Younce, review of *The Life Cycle of a Chicken,* p. 112; June, 2003, John Peters, review of *Exploring Animal Rights and Animal Welfare,* p. 92; September, 2004, Donna Cardon, review of *Sam Houston,* p. 186; February, 2005, Karen Stuppi, review of *Let's Graph,* p. 114; April, 2005, Linda Greengrass, review of *German Immigrants,* p. 81; July, 2005, Be Astengo, re-

view of *Grand Canyon,* p. 90; April, 2006, Kathleen Meulen, review of *What Does a Truck Driver Do?,* p. 123, and Jean Lowery, review of *Tiny Life in Your Home,* p. 124; January, 2007, Joy Fleishhacker, review of *A Practical Guide to Dragons,* p. 140; January, 2008, Carol S. Surges, review of *Abraham and the Civil War,* p. 104; November, 2008, Martha Simpson, review of *The Haunted Ghoul Bus,* p. 102; September, 2009, Carrie Rogers-Whitehead, review of *The Three Little Pigs,* p. 190; October, 2009, Maria Alpert, review of *The Great Reindeer Rebellion,* p. 84; November, 2009, Donna Rosenblum, review of *A Practical Guide to Vampires,* p. 123.

*Science & Children,* January, 2008, Maria Mesires, review of *Body Warriors: The Immune System,* p. 68.

*ONLINE*

*Kidsreads.com,* http://www.kidsreads.com/ (October 16, 2003), "Lisa Trumbauer."*

\*    \*    \*

**TRUMBAUER, Lisa Trutkoff**
**See TRUMBAUER, Lisa**

# V

## Van DUSEN, Chris 1960-

### Personal
Born 1960, in Portland, ME; married 1989; wife's name Lori; children: Ethan, Tucker. *Education:* University of Massachusetts at Dartmouth, B.F.A., 1982. *Hobbies and other interests:* Collecting toys; biking and hiking with family.

### Addresses
*Home*—Camden, ME.

### Career
Author and illustrator. Worked previously as an art director and cartoon editor for a teen magazine. Presenter at schools and libraries.

### Awards, Honors
Read with Me/Maine Reads selection, 2005, for *Down to the Sea with Mr. Magee;* E.B. White Read-aloud Award, Association of Booksellers for Children, 2006, for *If I Built a Car.*

### Writings

*SELF-ILLUSTRATED*

*Down to the Sea with Mr. Magee,* Chronicle Books (San Francisco, CA), 2000.
*A Camping Spree with Mr. Magee,* Chronicle Books (San Francisco, CA), 2003.
*If I Built a Car,* Dutton Children's Books (New York, NY), 2005.
*The Grey's Anatomy Guide to Healing with Love; With Dr. Sydney Heron,* Hyperion (New York, NY), 2008.
*The Circus Ship,* Candlewick Press (Somerville, MA), 2009.

*Learning to Ski with Mr. Magee,* Chronicle Books (San Francisco, CA), 2010.

*ILLUSTRATOR*

Karen Trella Mather, *Silas, the Bookstore Cat,* Down East Books (Camden, ME), 1994.

*ILLUSTRATOR; "MERCY WATSON" SERIES BY KATE DICAMILLO*

*Mercy Watson to the Rescue,* Candlewick Press (Cambridge, MA), 2005.
*Mercy Watson Goes for a Ride,* Candlewick Press (Cambridge, MA), 2006.
*Mercy Watson Fights Crime,* Candlewick Press (Cambridge, MA), 2006.
*Mercy Watson: Princess in Disguise,* Candlewick Press (Cambridge, MA), 2007.
*Mercy Watson Thinks like a Pig,* Candlewick Press (Cambridge, MA), 2008.
*Mercy Watson: Something Wonky This Way Comes,* Candlewick Press (Somerville, MA), 2009.

Series books have been translated into French.

### Sidelights
Author and illustrator Chris Van Dusen often uses rhyming couplets in his self-illustrated children's books, engaging young readers with lively words and boisterous illustrations in works such as *Down to the Sea with Mr. Magee* and *If I Built a Car.* As a child, Van Dusen was influenced by the works of Dr. Seuss and author/ illustrator Robert McCloskey. Besides writing and illustrating his own children's books, he has also contributed artwork to children's-book texts by other writers, such as the popular "Mercy Watson" series by award-winning author Kate DiCamillo. Reviewing *Mercy Watson Goes for a Ride,* part of DiCamillo's series of easy readers about a naughty young piglet and her adventures, Stephanie Zvirin wrote in *Booklist* that "Van Dus-

en's larger-than-life characters and retro sensibility extend the dry humor" of the story's text, while *School Library Journal* critic Joy Fleishhacker noted that Mercy's "facial expressions are laugh-out-loud funny, and the idealized 1950s setting strikes just the right tone of innocence."

Van Dusen's first self-illustrated picture book, *Down to the Sea with Mr. Magee,* was cited as a "strong debut" by *School Library Journal* critic Hennie Vaandrager. The amusing book centers on the boating adventure of Van Dusen's titular hero and Magee's dog Dee. While at sea the duo encounters a playful whale that accidentally shipwrecks their boat against a spruce tree. "The momentum of the story is fast, and the rhyming text is sure to delight children," noted *School Library Journal* critic Hennie Vaandrager, and Michael Cart wrote in *Booklist* that Van Dusen creates a "sing-song, rhyming story" while the accompanying "cheerful, candy-colored cartoon illustrations provide equal fun for the eye." A contributor to *Publishers Weekly* noted of *Down to the Sea with Mr. Magee* that "Van Dusen's exacting verse and kitschy, perfectionistic gouaches make this one

whale of a tale." Mr. Magee's exploits are further chronicled in both *A Camping Spree with Mr. Magee,* and *Learning to Ski with Mr. Magee.*

In his self-illustrated *If I Built a Car* Van Dusen utilizes rhyming couplets to portray an imaginative young lad who describes his dream car: one that is chauffeured by a robot and even includes a swimming pool and a fire place! The text of *If I Built a Car* is highlighted by double-page paintings embellished with vibrant, compelling colors. "The brightly colored, crisp, cartoon-style illustrations, reminiscent of the Jetsons, are likely to keep viewers' attention," noted *School Library Journal* reviewer Amy Lilien-Harper. Equally enthusiastic about the book, a *Publishers Weekly* critic wrote of *If I Built a Car* that Van Dusen's "energetic verse and jubilant, action-packed artwork make this tale of a young inventor's fantastic daydream a joy ride."

Based on an actual incident that occurred in the early 1800s, *The Circus Ship* tells an adventurous tale about fifteen circus animals that are being transported by boat down the East Coast to Boston when a shipwreck occurs. Freed from the wreck, the creatures—from alligators to tigers to zebras—make their way to a small is-

*Chris Van Dusen tells a rousing adventure tale in his self-illustrated picture book* **The Circus Ship.** (Copyright © 2009 by Chris Van Dusen. Reproduced with permission of Candlewick Press.)

land off the coast of Maine, where they live among the somewhat surprised but accepting local residents. When Mr. Paine, the cruel circus owner, arrives with the intent of retrieving his animals, the creatures are kept hidden by their new island friends. Within his brightly colored images of island life, Van Dusen hides these circus creatures, allowing the attentive reader to discover them while Mr. Paine does not. According to Randall Enos, reviewing *The Circus Ship* for *Booklist,* Van Dusen's "vividly colored, meticulously drawn, cartoon-style illustrations articulate the story so well that they could practically stand on their own." Joined by the author/illustrator's "rollicking" rhyming text, the images in *The Circus Ship* "burst with color and energy and utilize perspective and texture to add drama and humor," according to *School Library Journal* contributor Gay Lynn Van Vleck, while a *Kirkus Reviews* writer wrote that the artist's use of bright gouache tones and "dizzying perspective perfectly suit this picaresque tale." "With the cadence and excitement of the story-poems of Longfellow and the tongue-twisters of [Margaret] Mahy," *The Circus Ship* "begs to be read aloud," concluded *Horn Book* contributor Robin L. Smith.

Discussing where he gets his story ideas on his home page, Van Dusen wrote: "Story ideas come from all different places. Sometimes I think of a picture first and then write a story around it. That's how *Down to the Sea with Mr. Magee* happened. Sometimes I recall something from my childhood, like a game I used to play. That's how *If I Built a Car* developed. An article in a magazine can also spark a story idea. That's how I came up with *The Circus Ship.* I even had a dream once that I thought would make a good story, so you never know where an idea is going to come from." And why do his picture books have a mid-mod flair? "This is the stuff I grew up with! I love the way things looked in the '50s and '60s. The colors, shapes and patterns were so bold and bright and it's fun to paint them in my illustrations."

## Biographical and Critical Sources

*PERIODICALS*

*Booklist,* February 1, 1995, Mary Harris Veeder, review of *Silas, the Bookstore Cat,* p. 1010; June 1, 2000, Michael Cart, review of *Down to the Sea with Mr. Magee,* p. 1911; May 15, 2005, Todd Morning, review of *If I Built a Car,* p. 1667; August, 2005, Ilene Cooper, review of *Mercy Watson to the Rescue,* p. 2022; May 1, 2006, Stephanie Zvirin, review of *Mercy Watson Goes for a Ride,* p. 82; October 15, 2006, Ilene Cooper, review of *Mercy Watson Fights Crime,* p. 44; July 1, 2007, Ilene Cooper, review of *Mercy Watson: Princess in Disguise,* p. 58; June 1, 2008, Ilene Cooper, review of *Mercy Watson Thinks like a Pig,* p. 90; August 1, 2009, Randall Enos, review of *The Circus Ship,* p. 77.

*Bulletin of the Center for Children's Books,* July-August, 2005, review of *If I Built a Car,* p. 513.
*Horn Book,* November-December, 2009, Robin L. Smith, review of *The Circus Ship,* p. 661.
*Kirkus Reviews,* May 1, 2005, review of *If I Built a Car,* p. 584; September 1, 2005, review of *Mercy Watson to the Rescue,* p. 971; May 15, 2006, review of *Mercy Watson Goes for a Ride,* p. 516; August 1, 2006, review of *Mercy Watson Fights Crime,* p. 784; July 1, 2007, review of *Mercy Watson: Princess in Disguise;* June 1, 2008, review of *Mercy Watson Thinks like a Pig;* August 15, 2009, review of *The Circus Ship.*
*Publishers Weekly,* December 5, 1994, review of *Silas, the Bookstore Cat,* p. 77; March 6, 2000, review of *Down to the Sea with Mr. Magee,* p. 110; June 20, 2005, reviews of *If I Built a Car,* p. 75, and *Mercy Watson to the Rescue,* both p. 77; May 14, 2007, review of *If I Built a Car,* p. 57; September 24, 2007, review of *Mercy Watson: Princess in Disguise,* p. 75.
*School Library Journal,* May, 2000, Hennie Vaandrager, review of *Down to the Sea with Mr. Magee,* p. 156; July 25, 2005, Amy Lilien-Harper, review of *If I Built a Car,* p. 84; October, 2005, Lee Bock, review of *Mercy Watson to the Rescue,* p. 112; June, 2006, Joy Fleishhacker, review of *Mercy Watson Goes for a Ride,* p. 110; November, 2006, Elaine Lesh Morgan, review of *Mercy Watson Fights Crime,* p. 90; August, 2007, Mary Elam, review of *Mercy Watson: Princess in Disguise,* p. 78; August, 2008, Farida S. Dowler, review of *Mercy Watson Thinks like a Pig,* p. 86; August, 2009, Mary Jean Smith, review of *Mercy Watson: Something Wonky This Way Comes,* p. 73; September, 2009, Gay Lynn Van Vleck, review of *The Circus Ship,* p. 136.

*ONLINE*

*Chris Van Dusen Home Page,* http://www.chrisvandusen.com (April 15, 2011).
*Chronicle Books Web site,* http://www.chroniclebooks.com/ (September 11, 2006), "Chris Van Dusen."*

\* \* \*

# VELASQUEZ, Crystal

## Personal

Female. *Education:* Pennsylvania State University, B.A. (creative writing); New York University Summer Publishing Institute, graduate. *Hobbies and other interests:* Travel, reading.

## Addresses

*Home*—Queens, NY. *E-mail*—crystal.velasquez@rocketmail.com.

## Career

Author and editor. Freelance proofreader.

## Writings

*"MAYA AND MIGUEL" CHAPTER-BOOK SERIES*

*My Twin Sister/My Twin Brother,* illustrated by Jeff Albrecht, Scholastic, Inc. (New York, NY), 2005.
*Neighborhood Friends,* Scholastic, Inc. (New York, NY), 2005.
*Paint the Town,* illustrated by Jay Johnson, Scholastic, Inc. (New York, NY), 2006.
*The Valentine Machine,* Scholastic, Inc. (New York, NY), 2006.

*"YOUR LIFE, BUT . . ." TEEN NOVEL SERIES*

*Your Life, but Better!,* Delacorte Press (New York, NY), 2010.
*Your Life, but Cooler!,* Delacorte Press (New York, NY), 2010.
*Your Life, but Sweeter!,* Delacorte Press (New York, NY), 2010.

## Biographical and Critical Sources

*PERIODICALS*

*Kirkus Reviews,* December 15, 2009, review of *Your Life, but Better!*
*School Library Journal,* February, 2010, Emily Chornomaz, review of *Your Life, but Better!,* p. 125.

*ONLINE*

*Crystal Velasquez Home Page,* http://www.crystalvelasquez.com (February 20, 2011).
*Crystal Velasquez Web log,* http://yourlifebutbetter.blogspot.com (April 1, 2011).

\*    \*    \*

# VOLPONI, Paul

## Personal

Male. *Education:* Baruch College, City University of New York, B.A. (English); City College of New York, M.A. (American literature).

## Addresses

*Home*—New York, NY. *Agent*—Rosemary Stimola, Stimola Literary Agency, New York, NY. *E-mail*—pavolpo@cs.com.

## Career

Writer, journalist, and educator. Teacher of reading and writing at Rikers Island, NY, 1992-98, and day drug treatment centers in New York, NY, 1998-2004. *The Blood Horse,* former New York correspondent.

## Awards, Honors

Black Heron Press Award for Social Fiction, 2002, for *Rikers;* American Library Association (ALA) Best Book for Young Adults nomination, International Reading Association Young-Adult Novel of the Year designation, and ALA Quick Pick for Reluctant Readers selection, all 2005, New York Public Library Books for the Teen Age selection, and *Booklist* Top Ten Sports Books for Young Adults designation, both 2006, and Texas Library Association selection, 2006-07, all for *Black and White;* ALA Best Book for Young Adults and Quick Pick for Reluctant Readers selections, and New York Public Library Books for the Teen Age selection, all 2006, all for *Rooftop;* ALA Quick Pick for Reluctant Readers selection, 2007, for *Rucker Park Setup,* 2009, for *Response,* 2010, for *Rikers High.*

## Writings

*Rikers* (for adults; also see below), Black Heron Press (Seattle, WA), 2002.
*Black and White,* Viking (New York, NY), 2005.
*Rooftop,* Viking (New York, NY), 2006.
*Rucker Park Setup,* Viking (New York, NY), 2007.
*Hurricane Song: A Novel of New Orleans,* Viking (New York, NY), 2008.
*The Hand You're Dealt,* Atheneum Books for Young Readers (New York, NY), 2008.
*Homestretch,* Atheneum Books for Young Readers (New York, NY), 2009.
*Response,* Viking (New York, NY), 2009.
*Rikers High* (middle-grade fiction; based on *Rikers*), Viking (New York, NY), 2010.
*Crossing Lines,* Viking (New York, NY), 2011.

Contributor to Associated Press, and to periodicals, including *New York Post.*

## Adaptations

*Hurricane Song* was adapted for audiobook, read by Jacob C. Norman, Brilliance Audio, 2008.

## Sidelights

During the 1990s Paul Volponi worked at Rikers Island Educational Facility, a school for incarcerated teens that was established on Rikers Island in 1959. "The job was incredibly rewarding, and eye opening," the author recalled on his home page. "Unfortunately, one of the most striking elements on Rikers Island is race." The treatment of African Americans, as opposed to whites, within the U.S. justice system struck Volponi as unequal, and he addresses issues of race, justice, and equality in young-adult novels that include *Rikers High, Black and White, Hurricane Song: A Novel of New Orleans, Homestretch,* and *Response.*

Winner of the Black Heron Press Award for Social Awareness, Volponi's first novel, *Rikers,* is set on Rikers Island and tells the story of seventeen-year-old inmate Martin Stokes. Known as Forty, which is the number of the bed to which he is assigned, Martin faces violence from other inmates on a daily basis. Eventually, his face is slashed by a fellow prisoner. Given the opportunity for revenge, Martin must decide how this decision will affect the rest of his life. In *Rikers High* Volponi retells Martin's story for a young-adult readership, focusing on the teen's final weeks on the island after spending five months learning to survive prison life. "Rare is the reader who won't find his [Martin's] narrative sobering," predicted John Peters in his *Booklist* review of *Rikers High,* while in *Publishers Weekly* a critic noted that Volponi "writes with an authenticity that will make readers feel Martin's fear."

Marcus Brown and Eddie Russo, best friends despite their racial differences, are the protagonists of *Black and White.* Both rising stars in basketball, the two teens have earned scholarships to play ball in college. Unfortunately, they decide to risk it all in order to gain some extra spending money by holding people up. When Eddie accidentally shoots an African-American man, Marcus takes the fall for both of them, landing in prison while Eddie goes off to college. "Social conflicts, basketball fervor, and tough personal choices make this title a gripping story," wrote Gerry Larson in *School Library Journal.* As a *Publishers Weekly* critic noted, the novel's "fast-paced action, vivid on-court scenes and gritty, natural dialogue make this a page-turner of a tale." While a *Kirkus Reviews* contributor called *Black and White* "hugely discussable," Gillian Engberg wrote in *Booklist* that the characters' "authentic voices . . . will draw in both strong and reluctant readers."

Basketball also provides the backdrop for *Rucker Park Setup,* in which Volponi captures Harlem's park basketball culture. In the novel Mackey (a.k.a. Hold the Mustard) is playing in the championship game of the famed Rucker Park Basketball Tournament in Harlem. His best friend, J.R., was killed on the same court in front of Mackey just a few weeks before. However, Mackey, who is betting against his own team, has yet to come forward and identify the teacher. J.R.'s father is refereeing the game, and the killer is watching the action, too, believing that Mackey does not have the guts to expose him. Reviewing *Rucker Park Setup* in *Kliatt,* Paula Rohrlick noted that Volponi's "brief but powerful basketball story . . . has much to say about loyalty and betrayal," and *School Library Journal* contributor Marilyn Taniguchi deemed it an "intense sports novel" that pulls readers along through its "driving sports action and nuanced characterizations."

In *Rooftop* Clay is sent to a drug treatment center after he is caught with a bag of marijuana. At the rehabilitation center, the African-American teen is reunited with his cousin Addison, a young addict who has no intentions of cleaning up or ending his drug-dealing career. Despite his own decision to stop doing drugs, Clay admires his cousin, and when Addison is killed during a rooftop chase by a White officer, Clay has to make a

decision: either tell the truth about his cousin's death or side with activists attempting to paint the shooting as an example of racially motivated police brutality. While finding *Rooftop* "less cynical" than *Black and White,* a *Kirkus Reviews* contributor added that Volponi's novel "follows closely in the steps of the first." Holly Koelling called the novel a "thoughtfully crafted, deceptively simple story" in her *Booklist* review, and Rohrlick, writing in *Kliatt,* deemed it "gritty and believable."

New Orleans is the setting of *Hurricane Song,* which finds sixteen-year-old football fanatic Miles living in the Louisiana city with his jazz musician dad now that his mom has remarried. Although father and son have such dissimilar interests that their relationship is strained, when Hurricane Katrina bears down on the city they band together, along with Miles' Uncle Roy. Unable to evacuate, they ultimately wind up with hundreds of other city residents at the Superdome, where they witness local gangs taking advantage of the chaos, desperation, and power outages to declare their turf within the sports complex. Father and son witness more senseless violence when they return to their neighbor-

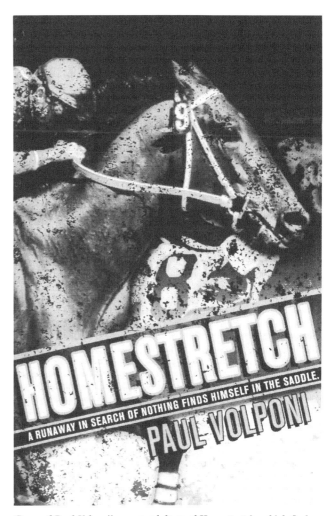

*Cover of Paul Volponi's young-adult novel* Homestretch, *which finds a teen working in a racing stable and finding a new community that accepts him.* (Atheneum Books for Young Readers, 2009. Jacket photograph by Jupiter Images. Reproduced with permission of Simon & Schuster, Inc.)

hood and attempt to stop the looting of a local jazz club. "A sprinkling of common vulgarities realistically punctuates the fast-paced story" in *Hurricane Song,* wrote Joel Shoemaker in his review of the novel for *School Library Journal,* while Rohrlick praised Volponi's "powerful tale of the evolution of the relationship between a boy and his father" as a "quick but indelible read." The author's "passionate outrage is palpable," asserted *Booklist* critic Michael Cart, "and his infectious indignation will surely invite much reflection and discussion." In *Kirkus Reviews* a critic recommended *Hurricane Song* as "a riveting and readable exploration of the effects of race in today's world."

For Huck Porter, the teen protagonist in *The Hand You're Dealt,* the game of poker is the only thing that makes him feel connected to his late father, who recently died following a stroke. Now Mr. Abbott, Huck's math teacher and a cocky and self-important poker player, has acquired the silver trophy wristwatch that Mr. Porter had won each year in the local tournament and worn proudly. When Huck decides to honor his father by winning the next tournament and reclaiming the watch, poker quickly becomes the center of his life as he lies, bluffs, and attempts to outplay other more-practiced players. Dubbed "an angsty teen drama" by *Booklist* contributor Ian Chipman, *The Hand You're Dealt* will appeal to reluctant readers with its "lightly message-oriented" story and "high-interest hook." "In true Volponi style, this book grabs hold and won't let go," exclaimed *School Library Journal* critic Leah Krippner, while a *Kirkus Reviews* writer cited *The Hand You're Dealt* for its "riveting opening" and fairy-tale elements.

The death of a parent also motivates the hero in *Homestretch,* which is set near the U.S.-Mexico border. After Gaston Giamanco's mother is killed during a police chase involving illegal immigrants, his alcoholic father lashes out in anger at everyone around him. Fleeing the abuse, the seventeen year old leaves home and winds up in Arkansas, where he finds a job at a horse-racing track. Living and working with the Mexicans who staff the stable and groom the horses, Gaston loses the bigotry he inherited from his parents and gains valuable support in making decisions about the rest of his life. Because Volponi's work as a journalist included reporting on horse-racing events, *Homestretch* is rich with "an insider's precise knowledge of the behind-the-scenes world of the track" according to *Booklist* critic Engberg. "From the first page, Volponi is off and running, delivering a fast-paced book that will sustain the interest of reluctant readers," maintained Debbie Rothfield in her *School Library Journal* review of the novel, and a *Kirkus Reviews* contributor recommended *Homestretch* as "an intense novel that treats controversy with commendable honesty."

Racial hatred is the focus of *Response,* which focuses on Noah Jackson and his run-in with three Italian-American teens. Noah is seventeen, African American, and the father of his girlfriend's infant child. When he joins some friends in a plan to steal a car from a nearby Italian neighborhood and sell it for parts, things go horribly wrong and Noah is severely beaten instead. Rather than look at the teen's intent, Noah's lawyer spins the incident as a hate crime, turning Noah into a celebrity while two of his three attackers are sent to jail. As the trial begins to fragment the community along racial lines, the students at Noah's school also chose sides. Volponi explores the incident from the point of view of both Noah and his main attacker, Charlie Scaturro, who *School Library Journal* critic Johanna Lewis characterized as an "unrepentant bat wielder." Although Lewis enjoyed the "suspenseful mood" of *Response,* she questioned the realism of depicting all of Charlie's "friends and family [as] . . . unabashedly racist." A *Kirkus Reviews* critic posited that the novel's unbalance stems from the fact that "Noah's first-person [account] carries the narrative," while Charlie's perspective is provided through transcripts of "script-like dialogues" and "newspaper stories." For *Booklist* critic Daniel Kraus, *Response* is about more than just the altercation that unites its two central characters. "Writing in an authentic voice, Volponi balances sensitivity and rage," noted Kraus, "but his most subtle achievement is the multi-generational family drama."

In *Crossing Lines,* football is the sport of choice for Adonis, and his high-school career revolves around his recognition as a top star on the school team. Adonis travels in different social circles than Alan, a new student in school who is taunted for his effeminate behaviors, but the two finally meet when Alan becomes a good friend of Adonis's mom, sister, and even his girlfriend. When Alan decides to flaunt school dress codes and arrive for class in a dress, Adonis is faced with a dilemma: whether to defend a classmate he has come to know as a person or stand by his buddies and a tradition that seeks to abolish anything out of the 'norm.' Reviewing *Crossing Lines* in the *Voice of Youth Advocates,* Lynn Evarts praised Volponi's novel as "an effective book on a very timely topic" that presents gay-bashing and intolerance from the perspective of the perpetrator rather than the victim.

Volponi's own experiences on Rikers Island, as well as his time living in New York City, continue to influence his decision to focus on racial inequality and criminal justice in his fiction. "I'm satisfied that I can channel what I've experienced and what I feel into books for young adults," he asserted on his home page. Discussing his writing process with *ALAN Review* interviewer Shelbie White, the novelist noted: "I like to write every day, several times a day, with lots of breaks in between—getting my daughter off to school, walking the dogs, family dinner, shooting baskets, jogging and hitting a heavy bag. A lot of the scenes I'm most proud of occurred more or less unplanned, while I was writing, so I'm intrigued by this thought: If I don't sit down to write today, will what I come up with tomorrow be the same? That keeps me going when I'm tired or not in the mood to write. I don't want to miss out on what may have been coming my way only today."

## Biographical and Critical Sources

*PERIODICALS*

*ALAN Review,* winter, 2007, Shelbie White, interview with Volponi.
*Booklinks,* May, 2006, Laurie Miller Hornik, review of *Black and White,* p. 28.
*Booklist,* September 1, 2005, Gillian Engberg, review of *Black and White,* p. 116; April 15, 2006, Holly Koelling, review of *Rooftop,* p. 46; May 1, 2008, Michael Cart, review of *Hurricane Song: A Novel of New Orleans,* p. 79; August 1, 2008, Ian Chipman, review of *The Hand You're Dealt,* p. 59; September, 2008, Leah Krippner, review of *The Hand You're Dealt,* p. 194; November 15, 2008, Daniel Kraus, review of *Response,* p. 39; September 15, 2009, Gillian Engberg, review of *Homestretch,* p. 49; December 1, 2009, John Peters, review of *Rikers High,* p. 38.
*Journal of Adolescent & Adult Literacy,* October, 2009, David M. Pegram, review of *Hurricane Song,* p. 184.
*Kirkus Reviews,* April 15, 2005, review of *Black and White,* p. 484; June 1, 2006, review of *Rooftop,* p. 582; April 1, 2007, review of *Rucker Park Setup;* May 1, 2008, review of *Hurricane Song;* August 15, 2008, review of *The Hand You're Dealt;* January 15, 2009, review of *Response;* August 1, 2009, review of *Homestretch;* January 1, 2010, review of *Rikers High.*
*Kliatt,* May, 2006, Paula Rohrlick, review of *Rooftop,* p. 16; May, 2007, Paula Rohrlick, review of *Rucker Park Setup,* p. 21; July, 2008, Paula Rohrlick, review of *Hurricane Song,* p. 21.
*New York Times Book Review,* May 16, 2010, Jessica Bruder, review of *Riker's High,* p. 22.
*Publishers Weekly,* June 20, 2005, review of *Black and White,* p. 78; September 21, 2009, review of *Homestretch,* p. 60; January 18, 2010, Jessica Bruder, review of *Rikers High,* p. 50.
*School Library Journal,* June, 2005, Gerry Larson, review of *Black and White,* p. 170; November, 2007, Marilyn Taniguchi, review of *Rucker Park Setup,* p. 139; August, 2008, Joel Shoemaker, review of *Hurricane Song,* p. 136; September, 2008, Leah Krippner, review of *The Hand You're Dealt,* p. 194; March, 2009, Johanna Lewis, review of *Response,* p. 157; December, 2009, Debbie Rothfield, review of *Homestretch,* p. 135; January, 2010, Megan Honig, review of *Rickers High,* p. 115.
*Voice of Youth Advocates,* June, 2009, interview with Volponi; April, 2010, Marla K. Unruh and Colby Smith, review of *Rikers High,* p. 64; April, 2011, Lynn Evarts, review of *Crossing Lines,* p. 71.

*ONLINE*

*Paul Volponi Home Page,* http://www.paulvolponibooks.com (March 10, 2011).

*Penguin Group Web Site,* http://us.penguingroup.com/ (November 30, 2006), "Paul Volponi."

\*    \*    \*

# VYNER, Tim 1963-

## Personal

Born 1963, in England; married; wife's name Florence (a teacher); children: two. *Education:* Camberwell College of Arts, B.A. (with honours); Royal College of Art, graduate degree, 1988.

## Addresses

*Home*—Bath, England. *E-mail*—tim@timvyner.com.

## Career

Reportage artist and illustrator. Bath School of Art and Design, Bath, England, senior lecturer in graphic communications. *Exhibitions:* Work included in numerous exhibitions, including at Curwen Gallery, London, England, New Academy Gallery, London, and Bankside Gallery, London. Paintings included in permanent collection of Professional Footballer's Association, Manchester, England.

## Member

Royal Watercolour Society (associate member).

## Awards, Honors

Named Official World Cup Artist of Britain's Professional Footballers' Association, 2002; Royal Watercolor Society Open Competition Award, 2000; numerous other art awards.

## Writings

*SELF-ILLUSTRATED*

*The Tree in the Forest,* Collins (London, England), 1994, Barron's Educational Series (Hauppauge, NY), 1995.
*Dragon Mountain,* Collins (London, England), 1996.
*World Team,* Roaring Brook Press (Brookfield, CT), 2002.

Author's work has been translated into several languages, including Danish, Greek, Italian, Japanese, Korean, and Swedish.

*ILLUSTRATOR*

Sue Vyner, *The Stolen Egg,* Gollancz (London, England), 1991, Viking (New York, NY), 1992.
Sue Vyner, *Arctic Spring,* Gollancz (London, England), 1992, Viking (New York, NY), 1993.

Sue Vyner, *Swim for Cover!: Adventure on the Coral Reef,* Crown (New York, NY), 1995, published as *The Coral Trail,* Victor Gollancz (London, England), 1995.

Marcial Bóo, *The Butterfly Kiss,* Harcourt Brace (San Diego, CA), 1995.

Caroline Heaton, *Yi-min and the Elephant: A Tale of Ancient China,* Frances Lincoln (London, England), 2002.

Paul Stewart, *In the Dark of the Night,* Frances Lincoln (London, England), 2008.

*OTHER*

Contributor to periodicals, including London *Independent.*

## Sidelights

In addition to teaching illustration on the college level, Tim Vyner has found a way to combine his twin passions—world-class athletics and painting—in a rewarding career as a reportage artist specializing in one of the most followed sporting events in the world. Focusing on World Cup soccer (or football to the British Vyner) as well as on the Olympic games, he travels throughout the world, capturing the excitement of athletic competition both on the playing field and in the streets. From the stadium complexes of Japan and Portugal to the open-air soccer fields in Ghana, Vyner captures the unique settings of each competition, armed only with a camera, an ink pen, and a sketchbook. Interestingly, his work in sports has developed alongside his work as a children's book author and illustrator:

Vyner's original self-illustrated picture book *World Team* resulted in his appointment as Official World Cup artist of Britain's Professional Footballers' Association in 2002.

Vyner earned degrees at both the Camberwell College of Arts and the Royal College of Art, and in the late 1980s he began his career in picture books creating artwork for texts written by his mother, author Sue Vyner. Together, the couple released three books: *Arctic Spring, Swim for Cover!: Adventure on the Coral Reef,* and *The Stolen Egg,* the last in which "the close perspective of brisk earth-tone illustrations heightens the drama," according to a *Publishers Weekly* contributor. Other illustration projects have included Caroline Heaton's *Yi-min and the Elephant: A Tale of Ancient China* and *In the Dark of the Night,* a story by noted fantasy novelist Paul Stewart that captures the first journey of a wolf cub into the wider world. In a *School Library Journal* review, Linda L. Walkins praised *In the Dark of the Night* as a "lovely" story in which Vyner's evocative water colors follow the action from the "dark and shadowy" forest setting to "later images bathed in soft moonlight."

With its theme of soccer as a sport that the world shares, Vyner's *World Team* was his second original self-illustrated picture book to be published. As readers turn the book's pages, they are carried on a tour of the globe, meeting children from Asia, Europe, Africa, and the Americas who all love and play soccer. In addition to reflecting the passion many young athletes feel for the game in its combination of art and minimal text, Vyner's

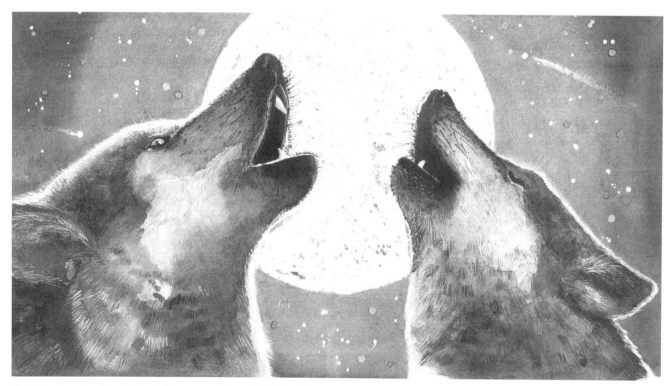

*Tim Vyner's nature-themed illustrations capture the magic of the wild in Paul Stewart's* **In the Dark of the Night.** (Illustration copyright © 2008 by Tim Vyner. Reproduced with permission of Frances Lincoln Children's Books.)

story also "provides an incidental geography lesson," according to London *Sunday Times* writer Nicolette Jones. For Blair Christolon, writing in *School Library Journal*, the value of *World Team* is its illustration of the abstract notion of "time zones" as the author/illustrator's "intriguing watercolors" capture young people practicing their sport in different parts of the world at varied hours of the day. Noting the "nice mix of urban and rural scenes" captured in "Vyner's realistic-but-gritty-edged paintings," a *Kirkus Reviews* writer recommended *World Team* for readers who share the author's "love of the sport."

## Biographical and Critical Sources

*PERIODICALS*

*Booklist,* August, 1995, Mary Harris Veeder, review of *Swim for Cover!: Adventure on the Coral Reef,* p. 1957.

*Kirkus Reviews,* April 15, 2002, review of *World Team,* p. 581; October 15, 2009, review of *In the Dark of the Night.*

*Publishers Weekly,* June 1, 1992, review of *The Stolen Egg,* p. 60.

*School Library Journal,* June, 2002, Blair Christolon, review of *World Team,* p. 112; December, 2009, Linda L. Walkins, review of *In the Dark of the Night,* p. 92.

*Times* (London, England), May 19, 2002, Nicolette Jones, review of *World Team,* p. 46.

*ONLINE*

*Tim Vyner Home Page,* http://www.timvyner.com/ (March 20, 2011).

*Tim Vyner Web log,* http://www.timvyner.blogspot.com (March 20, 2011).

# W-Z

## WALKER, Kristin

### Personal
Born in PA; married; children: three sons. *Education:* Pennsylvania State University, B.A. (theatre arts).

### Addresses
*Home*—Metro Chicago, IL. *E-mail*—kristin@kristin-walker.com.

### Career
Author. Worked variously as an actor, nanny, ballroom dance instructor, and library aide. Presenter at schools and workshops.

### Member
Society of Children's Book Writers and Illustrators.

### Writings

*A Match Made in High School,* Razorbill (New York, NY), 2010.
*Seven Clues to Winning You,* Razorbill (New York, NY), 2012.

Contributor to periodicals, including *Ladybug* and *Wee Ones,* and to books in the "Chicken Soup for the Soul" series.

### Sidelights
Kristin Walker grew up in Pennsylvania and earned a theatre-arts degree from Penn State. She began writing while raising her three children, producing stacks of children's-book manuscripts while honing her writer's voice. With an ability to vividly recall her own teen

years, Walker found a natural fit within the young-adult genre, and her first novel, *A Match Made in High School*, brings all the ups and downs of adolescence

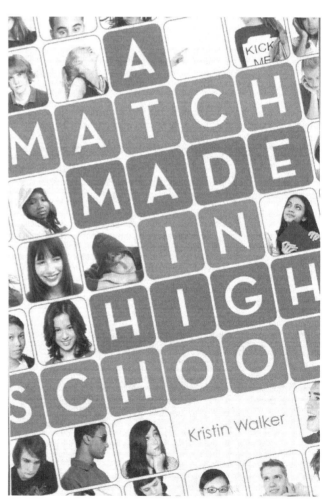

*Cover of Kristin Walker's teen romance* **A Match Made in High School,** *a story about a teen who finds love in a surprising place.* (Razorbill, 2009. Cover Photos © Shutterstock, cover design by Natalie C. Sousa. Reproduced with permission of Penguin Young Readers Group.)

vividly to life. Reviewing the novel in *Publishers Weekly,* a critic maintained that "Walker breathes fresh life into a familiar theme" in her fiction debut and crafts "an entertaining journey for a sassy heroine with heart."

The "sassy heroine" Walker introduces in *A Match Made in High School* is Fiona, a senior and social wallflower at East Columbus High who has definite opinions that rarely waver. Fiona's opinion regarding male cheerleaders is hardly flattering to that species, so when she is "wed" to a male cheerleader named Todd as part of a year-long marriage education class called "Tying the Knot" she prepares for the worst. More disappointments follow however: Gabe, who Fiona has secretly loved since elementary school, is matched with the evil Amanda, and Fiona's best friend, Marcie, has been paired up with Johnny, who seems to hang around all the time, now. In a story that pays homage to Jane Austen's *Pride and Prejudice,* the growing friendship between Todd and Fiona is fueled by a sequence of humorous incidents, resulting in a novel that is both "laugh-out-loud funny" and provocative when addressing "priorities, relationships, and making the most of trying situations," according to *School Library Journal* critic Emily Garrett Cassady. With its "lovable, flawed" heroine, *A Match Made in High School* serves up "an excellent balance of happily-ever-after romance, solid friendships and treatment of marriage as a serious commitment between two partners," concluded a *Kirkus Reviews* writer.

On her home page, Walker gives useful advice to budding writers. "Write as much as you can whenever, wherever, and about whatever you feel like," she counseled. "Write about the large and small things in your life. Oh, man, do not skip the small things. They're crucial. In 10 or 20 years when you can't even remember what you ate for dinner the night before, you'll cherish those details. And details are what make writing come alive."

## Biographical and Critical Sources

*PERIODICALS*

*Kirkus Reviews,* January 1, 2010, review of *A Match Made in High School.*
*Publishers Weekly,* January 25, 2010, review of *A Match Made in High School,* p. 120.
*School Library Journal,* July, 2009, Emily Garrett Cassady, review of *A Match Made in High School,* p. 94.

*ONLINE*

*Kristin Walker Home Page,* http://kristin-walker.com (March 20, 2011).
*Kristin Walker Web log,* http://walkwrite.livejournal.com (March 20, 2011).

# WELTEVREDE, Pieter 1957-

## Personal

Born 1957, in the Netherlands; married; children: three. *Education:* Advanced degree (social sciences); studied yantra painting, beginning 1977.

## Addresses

*Home*—Netherlands.

## Career

Illustrator and teacher. Teacher of iconographic painting; presenter at painting retreats. *Exhibitions:* Works exhibited throughout Europe and in United States.

## Awards, Honors

Recognized as Master Artist by Dutch government, c. 2001.

## Writings

*FOR CHILDREN*

Harish Johari, *The Monkeys and the Mango Tree,* revised and expanded, Healing Arts Press, 1998.
Harish Johari, *The Birth of the Ganga,* revised edition, Inner Traditions India, 1998.
(With Suresh Johari) Harish Johari and Sapna Johari, *Little Krishna,* Bear Cub Books (Rochester, VT), 2002.
Harish Johari and Vatsala Sperling, *How Ganesh Got His Elephant Head,* Bear Cub Books (Rochester, VT), 2003.
Harish Johari and Vatsala Sperling, *How Parvati Won the Heart of Shiva,* Bear Cub Books (Rochester, VT), 2004.
Vatsala Sperling, *Ram the Demon Slayer,* Bear Cub Books (Rochester, VT), 2005.
(With Harish Johari) Vatsala Sperling, *Ganga: The River That Flows from Heaven to Earth,* Bear Cub Books (Rochester, VT), 2008.
Vatsala Sperling, *The Magical Adventures of Krishna: How a Mischief Maker Saved the World,* Bear Cub Books (Rochester, VT), 2009.

*OTHER*

Harish Johari, *Ayurvedic Massage: Traditional Indian Techniques for Balancing the Body and Mind,* Healing Arts Press, 1996.
Harish Johari, *Chakras: Energy Centers of Transformation,* Destiny Books, 2000.

## Biographical and Critical Sources

*PERIODICALS*

*Booklist,* December 1, 2003, Linda Perkins, review of *How Ganesh Got His Elephant Head,* p. 682.

*Children's Bookwatch,* January, 2009, review of *The River That Flows from Heaven to Earth;* February, 2010, review of *The Magical Adventures of Krishna: How a Mischief Maker Saved the World.*

*Kirkus Reviews,* October 15, 2009, review of *The Magical Adventures of Krishna.*

*School Library Journal,* January, 2004, Sue Morgan, review of *How Ganesh Got His Elephant Head,* p. 149.

ONLINE

*Sanatan Society Web site,* http://www.sanatansociety.com/ (April 1, 2011), "Pieter Weltevrede."*

\*      \*      \*

# WHITE, Amy Brecount

## Personal

Married; children: three. *Education:* University of Notre Dame, B.A. (great books); University of Virginia, M.A. (English). *Hobbies and other interests:* Gardening.

## Addresses

*Home*—Arlington, VA. *Agent*—Steven Chudney, The Chudney Agency, 72 N. State Rd., Ste. 501, Briarcliff Manor, NY 10510.

## Career

Educator and author. Teacher of middle-school and high-school English literature.

## Writings

*Forget-Her-Nots,* Greenwillow Books (New York, NY), 2010.

Contributor to periodicals, including the *Washington Post.*

## Sidelights

Although she viewed writing as a hobby for many years, Amy Brecount White eventually found time within her busy life as an English teacher and mom to write what became her first published novel, *Forget-Her-Nots.* While keeping her authorial skills honed by writing occasional articles for the *Washington Post,* White was inspired to consider novel-length fiction while making a "tussie mussie"—a Victorian-era bouquet considered a token of affection—for a good friend suffering from cancer. "I planted and played in my own gardens and grew gradually more and more entranced with blooms," White explained on her home page. "I've found that flowers and fragrance—like songs you know—can awaken precious bits of memory and sway your mood. It was a pretty easy leap of imagination to magic flowers from there."

In *Forget-Her-Nots* readers meet Laurel, a fourteen year old who is grieving the loss of her mom to cancer and not happy about living away from her family at the Avondale School. While presenting a report on the Victorian language of flowers to her English class, Laurel feels almost physically overwhelmed by her quasi-mystical subject. When she gives one of her props, a homemade tussie-mussie, to her unmarried teacher Ms. Spencer, the woman finds a boyfriend almost immediately. The power of her bouquets becomes known around Avondale when their ability to draw both luck and love benefits several of Laurel's friends. Fortunately, the teen's science teacher, Ms. Suarez, recognizes that Laurel's talent as a "Flowerspeaker" is one she inherited from her mother's family, also an Avondale student. Although the teen now knows her power, she does not heed Ms. Suarez's warnings and soon her magic bouquets have circulated into hands where they do not belong—just in time for the school prom. "Laurel is an admirable heroine, always supportive of her friends but never a pushover," according to a *Kirkus Reviews* writer in appraising *Forget-Her-Nots.* In telling the teen's story, "White aptly renders big and small dramas" and injects "a delicate sense of magical possibility" into a "memorable" tale, according to a *Publishers Weekly* critic. In *School Library Journal* Ginny Gustin recommended *Forget-Her-Nots* for "fans of boarding-school stories and gentle teen romances," and Krista Hurley predicted in *Booklist* that White's "diverting read will be popular with girls expecting magic and romance."

## Biographical and Critical Sources

PERIODICALS

*Booklist,* January 1, 2010, Krista Hurley, review of *Forget-Her-Nots,* p. 67.

*Kirkus Reviews,* February 15, 2010, review of *Forget-Her-Nots.*

*Publishers Weekly,* February 8, 2010, review of *Forget-Her-Nots,* p. 52.

*School Library Journal,* March, 2010, Ginny Gustin, review of *Forget-Her-Nots,* p. 169.

*Voice of Youth Advocates,* June, 2010, Marla K. Unruh, review of *Forget-Her-Nots,* p. 172.

ONLINE

*Amy Brecount White Home Page,* http://www.amybrecountwhite.com (February 20, 2011).

# WILLEMS, Mo 1968-

## Personal

Born February 11, 1968; married Cheryl Camp, 1997; children: Trixie. *Education:* New York University, B.F.A. (cum laude).

## Addresses

*Home*—Northampton, MA. *Agent*—Marcia Wernick, Wernick & Pratt Agency, info@wernickpratt.com.

## Career

Animator and illustrator. Children's Television Workshop, New York, NY, researcher, then script writer and animator for *Sesame Street* television series, 1994-2002; Nickelodeon, creator and director of animated series *The Off-Beats,* 1995-98; Cartoon Network, creator and director of animated series *Sheep in the Big City,* 2000-02, head writer of animated series *Codename: Kids Next Door,* 2002-03. Short films have appeared on MTV, HBO, IFC, Tournee of Animation, and Spike and Mike's Festival of Animation. Radio commentator for British Broadcasting Corporation, 1994-97; occasional "Radio cartoonist" for National Public Radio program *All Things Considered.* Former member of Monkeysuit (comix collective), New York, NY. *Exhibitions:* Illustrations and other works exhibited at galleries and museums, including New York University, New York, NY; R. Michelson Gallery, Northampton, MA; Charles M. Schulz Museum, Santa Rosa, CA; and Michelson Museum of Art, Marshall, TX.

## Awards, Honors

ASIFA-East Awards for animation; six Emmy awards for work on *Sesame Street* television series; National Parenting Publications Award, 2003, for *Time to Pee!;* Caldecott Honor Book citation, American Library Association, 2004, for *Don't Let the Pigeon Drive the Bus!,* and 2005, for *Knuffle Bunny: A Cautionary Tale;* Book Sense Book of the Year Children's Illustrated Honor Book designation, American Booksellers Association, 2006, for *Leonardo, the Terrible Monster;* Caldecott Honor Book citation, 2008, for *Knuffle Bunny Too;* Theodor Seuss Geisel Award for Outstanding Books for Beginning Readers, 2008, for *There Is a Bird on Your Head!,* 2009, for *Are You Ready to Play Outside;* (with Paul R. Gagne) Andrew Carnegie Medal for Excellence in Children's Video, 2007, for *Knuffle Bunny,* 2010, for *Don't Let the Pigeon Drive the Bus;* Children's Book of the Year selection, New England Independent Booksellers Association Award, 2010, for *City Dog, Country Frog* illustrated by Jon J. Muth; Christopher Award, and Theodore Seuss Geisel Award Honor Book designation, both 2011, both for *Knuffle Bunny Free.*

## Writings

*SELF-ILLUSTRATED*

*Time to Pee!,* Hyperion (New York, NY), 2003.
*Time to Say "Please"!,* Hyperion (New York, NY), 2005.

*Mo Willems* (Photograph by Richard Bowditch. Reproduced by permission.)

*Leonardo, the Terrible Monster,* Hyperion (New York, NY), 2005.
*You Can Never Find a Rickshaw When It Monsoons: The World on One Cartoon a Day,* foreword by Dave Barry, Hyperion (New York, NY), 2006.
*Edwina, the Dinosaur Who Didn't Know She Was Extinct,* Hyperion (New York, NY), 2006.
*Naked Mole Rat Gets Dressed,* Hyperion Books for Children (New York, NY), 2009.
*Happy Pig Day!,* Hyperion Books for Children (New York, NY), 2011.
*Hooray for Amanda and Her Alligator!,* Balzer + Bray (New York, NY), 2011.

Contributor to books, including *Monkeysuit,* Monkeysuit Press; *Cartoon Cartoons,* DC Comics; and *9-11: The World's Finest Comic Book Writers and Artists Tell Stories to Remember,* DC Comics, 2002.

Author's work has been translated into Spanish.

*SELF-ILLUSTRATED; "PIGEON" SERIES*

*Don't Let the Pigeon Drive the Bus!,* Hyperion (New York, NY), 2003.
*The Pigeon Finds a Hot Dog!,* Hyperion (New York, NY), 2004.

*The Pigeon Has Feelings, Too!*, Hyperion (New York, NY), 2005.

*The Pigeon Loves Things That Go!*, Hyperion (New York, NY), 2005.

*Don't Let the Pigeon Stay up Late!*, Hyperion (New York, NY), 2006.

*The Pigeon Wants a Puppy!*, Hyperion Books for Children (New York, NY), 2008.

*SELF-ILLUSTRATED; "KNUFFLE BUNNY" SERIES*

*Knuffle Bunny: A Cautionary Tale* (also see below), Hyperion (New York, NY), 2004.

*Knuffle Bunny Too: A Case of Mistaken Identity*, Hyperion Books for Children (New York, NY), 2007.

*Knuffle Bunny Free: An Unexpected Diversion*, Balzer + Bray (New York, NY), 2010.

*SELF-ILLUSTRATED; "ELEPHANT AND PIGGIE" SERIES*

*Today I Will Fly!*, Hyperion (New York, NY), 2007.

*My Friend Is Sad*, Hyperion (New York, NY), 2007.

*I Am Invited to a Party!*, Hyperion Books for Children (New York, NY), 2007.

*There Is a Bird on Your Head!*, Hyperion (New York, NY), 2007.

*Are You Ready to Play Outside?*, Hyperion Books for Children (New York, NY), 2008.

*I Love My New Toy!*, Hyperion Books for Children (New York, NY), 2008.

*I Will Surprise My Friend!*, Hyperion Books for Children (New York, NY), 2008.

*Watch Me Throw the Ball!*, Hyperion Books for Children (New York, NY), 2009.

*Elephants Cannot Dance!*, Hyperion Books for Children (New York, NY), 2009.

*Can I Play, Too?*, Hyperion Books for Children (New York, NY), 2010.

*We Are in a Book!*, Hyperion Books for Children (New York, NY), 2010.

*I Am Going!*, Hyperion Books for Children (New York, NY), 2010.

*Pigs Make Me Sneeze*, Hyperion Books for Children (New York, NY), 2010.

*I Broke My Trunk!*, Hyperion Books for Children (New York, NY), 2011.

*Should I Share My Ice Cream?*, Hyperion Books for Children (New York, NY), 2011.

*SELF-ILLUSTRATED; "CAT THE CAT" SERIES*

*Let's Say Hi to Friends Who Fly!*, Balzer + Bray (New York, NY), 2010.

*Cat the Cat, Who Is That?*, Balzer + Bray (New York, NY), 2010.

*Time to Sleep, Sheep the Sheep!*, Balzer + Bray (New York, NY), 2010.

*What's Your Sound, Hound the Hound?*, Balzer + Bray (New York, NY), 2010.

*OTHER*

*City Dog, Country Frog*, illustrated by Jon J. Muth, Hyperion (New York, NY), 2010.

Author of book and lyrics for musical adaptation *Knuffle Bunny: A Cautionary Musical*, produced for the Kennedy Center, 2010.

## Adaptations

*Don't Let the Pigeon Drive the Bus!* was adapted for the stage by Adam Bampton-Smith and produced by Big Wooden Horse Productions, 2005, and was adapted as a short film, 2010. *Knuffle Bunny* was adapted as a short film, 2007.

## Sidelights

Mo Willems, an award-winning television writer and animator, has also gained new fans through his work as an award-winning children's book author. Beginning his animation career on the popular *Sesame Street* television program, Willems has also created dozens of short films, many of which have appeared on MTV, HBO, the Tournee of Animation, and Spike and Mike's Festival of Animation. The creator of the animated television series *Sheep in the Big City* and *The Off-Beats*, he also served as head writer for the Cartoon Network's *Codename: Kids Next Door* series. Since semi-retiring from television in 2003, Willems has channeled his creativity and quirky humor into picture books such as *Don't Let the Pigeon Drive the Bus!*, *Knuffle Bunny: A Cautionary Tale*, and *Today I Will Fly!*, each of which introduces engaging cartoon characters that reappear in

*For Willems,* **Don't Let the Pigeon Drive the Bus!** *was the book that started it all.* (Copyright © 2003 by Mo Willems. Reprinted by permission of Disney/Hyperion, an imprint of Disney Book Group LLC. All rights reserved.)

several other stories. While these characters sometimes make missteps, they ultimately join readers in a good-hearted laugh at their own foibles. As the author/illustrator told Susan Spencer Cramer in an interview for *Publishers Weekly,* "Failure is pervasive in children's lives, but I don't know when it stopped being funny. It needs to be explored and enjoyed and laughed at and understood."

Willems' interest in cartooning began as a child. "I've been drawing funny cartoons my whole life," he noted on his home page. "I started out by drawing Snoopy and Charlie Brown and then started to make up my own characters. Luckily, no one has made me stop yet!" Willems decided on a career in animation during the 1980s, while a student at New York University. "My desire as a kid was to find a way to be funny and draw," he recalled to Martin Goodman in an interview for *Animation World.* "Animation turned out to be the best way for me to do that."

Willems made his first film, *The Man Who Yelled,* while completing his degree at New York University, and this was followed by the acclaimed short film *Iddy Biddy Beat Boy.* His job in the research department at the Children's Television Workshop eventually led to work as an animator for *Sesame Street.* As Willems told Goodman, this opportunity was a "great fit because the kind of films I wanted to make were very close to the kind of films they wanted to air. I really felt that I was making personal work, even though I was teaching the 'letter of the day' or something like that." During Willems' time with *Sesame Street,* he garnered six Emmy awards for his animation work.

In 1995 Willems began producing *The Off-Beats,* a series of animated shorts airing on Nickelodeon that focus on Betty-Anne Bongo and her unusual friends. The success of this series led to *Sheep in the Big City,* which debuted on the Cartoon Network in 2000. *Variety* reviewer Stuart Levine described *Sheep in the Big City* as "an amusing tale of a shy but determined woolly creature on the lam . . . after government bad guys try to kidnap and use him as a critical component of a high-powered weapon." After the series was canceled in 2002, Willems began writing for *Codename: Kids Next Door,* which follows five ten year olds as they battle the forces of adulthood. In 2003, although *Codename: Kids Next Door* ranked as the highest-rated show on the Cartoon Network, Willems made the decision to leave television and become a stay-at-home father for his daughter, Trixie. He also embarked on his picture-book career.

Published in 2003, *Don't Let the Pigeon Drive the Bus!* jump-started Willems' authorial career and also began his series of picture books featuring his wily, cantankerous pigeon character. "The premise of this cheeky debut is charmingly absurd," wrote a contributor to *Publishers Weekly.* A bus driver steps out of his vehicle for a short break, asking that the reader keep an eye on things while he is gone. Before he leaves, the driver makes one special request: "Don't let the pigeon drive the bus." A big-eyed pigeon soon appears and tries to negotiate a spot behind the wheel, making promises, wheedling, and even threatening the reader. With the pigeon in the midst of a temper tantrum, the driver returns, thanks the reader, and pulls away. The pigeon's disappointment is only temporary, though, as it spots a tractor-trailer coming up the road. "Willems hooks his audience quickly with the pigeon-to-reader approach and minimalist cartoons," noted the *Publishers Weekly* critic, while Gillian Engberg remarked in *Booklist* that "each page has the feel of a perfectly frozen frame of cartoon footage—action, remarkable expression, and wild humor captured with just a few lines."

Willems' wingéd hero makes a return appearance in *The Pigeon Finds a Hot Dog!, The Pigeon Has Feelings, Too!, The Pigeon Loves Things That Go!, Don't Let the Pigeon Stay up Late!,* and *The Pigeon Wants a Puppy!* In *The Pigeon Finds a Hot Dog!* Willems' plucky fowl spies a discarded hot dog and swoops in for a meal. Just as it is about to devour the treat, a tiny duckling scoots in and makes a number of seemingly innocent but calculated inquiries about the hot dog. According to Kitty Flynn in *Horn Book,* "the hot-headed pigeon humorously wrestles with a minor moral dilemma (to share or not to share) that will immediately resonate" with young readers. Willems' "deceptively simple cartoon drawings convincingly portray his protagonist's emotional dilemma," Robin L. Gibson observed in *School Library Journal,* while a *Publishers Weekly* reviewer stated that the cartoonist's use of "voice bubbles, body language, and expressive sizes and shapes of type . . . crafts a comical give-and-take between the characters."

In *The Pigeon Has Feelings, Too!* the bus driver from *Don't Let the Pigeon Drive the Bus!* returns, this time to help cheer up the cantankerous bird. *The Pigeon Loves Things That Go!* finds the pigeon exploring various modes of transportation, although a less-enthusiastic mood strikes it in *Don't Let the Pigeon Stay up Late!,* as bed time approaches. Another outbreak of toddler-type petulance erupts in *The Pigeon Wants a Puppy!,* as the bird is convinced that it needs a pet . . . until a dog actually appears on the scene and prompts second thoughts. As a *Kirkus Reviews* critic noted, *Don't Let the Pigeon Stay up Late* showcases Willems' "whole-hearted sense of fun." Featuring what *Booklist* critic Engberg dubbed a "stubborn preschool impersonator," *The Pigeon Wants a Puppy!* continues Willems' successful meld of cartoon art and childlike antics, and a *Kirkus Reviews* critic assured fans of the series that the book serves up "exactly what they've come to expect: lots of giggles."

A toddler loses her prized possession in *Knuffle Bunny,* a story Flynn predicted "will immediately register with even pre-verbal listeners." In Willems' quaint tale, little Trixie and her dad take a trip to the local Laundromat, but on the way home the girl realizes that her beloved stuffed bunny has been left behind. When the toddler's frantic attempts to communicate are misinterpreted by her clueless father, Trixie adopts a new strategy: she cries. Only after the pair arrive home and Trixie's mom notes the absence of the beloved toy does Dad realize his mistake. In a review of *Knuffle Bunny* a *Kirkus Reviews* contributor dubbed Willems "a master of body language," and Flynn praised the book's "playful illustrations," which feature cartoon characters "rendered in Willems's expressive retro style" and set against sepia-toned photographs of Brooklyn neighborhoods. The author/illustrator's "economical storytelling and deft skill with line lend the book its distinctive charm," wrote a contributor in *Publishers Weekly*.

*Knuffle Bunny* returns in *Knuffle Bunny Too: A Case of Mistaken Identity* and *Knuffle Bunny Free: An Unexpected Diversion*. Trixie is now a toddler in *Knuffle Bunny Too*, and her pale-green stuffed bunny is still her favorite toy. When she spies a shockingly similar rabbit dangling from the hand of a preschool classmate, confusions and misunderstandings ensue but are sorted out in time for both girls to sleep with their beloved

*Willems teams up with illustrator Jon J. Muth to create an upbeat new version of time-honored story in* **City Dog, Country Frog.** (Illustration copyright ©
2010 by Jon J. Muth. Reproduced with permission of Disney/Hyperion, an imprint of Disney Book Group LLC. All rights reserved.)

bunnies. In *Knuffle Bunny Free* a-still-older Trixie and her favorite toy board a plane for the Netherlands, intending to visit her grandparents, but Knuffle Bunny winds up taking a much longer trip, where his adventures can only be imagined. Praising the author/illustrator for his mix of photographic images of Brooklyn and "vivid, hand-drawn characters," Kate McClelland added in her *School Library Journal* review of *Knuffle Bunny Too:* "as readers have come to expect of Willems, his understated text is brief and the visual storytelling is hilariously eloquent." For a *Kirkus Reviews* writer, the artist's "mastery of pacing is evident in every panel" of the second "Knuffle Bunny" story, "and his use of the conventions of cartooning add to the hilarity." In *Booklist*, Daniel Kraus hailed *Knuffle Bunny Free* as a "droll, observant, and seriously heartbreaking ode to growing up," while a *Publishers Weekly* contributor noted that the author's "affectionate sage comes to a reassuring end" in Trixie's dreams of globe-spanning rabbit adventure.

Willems introduces several other engaging characters in his "Elephant and Piggie" books, an easy-reader series that has received several Theodor Seuss Geisel awards. Here young readers meet not only the title characters but also friends such as Squirrel and Snake as they share games, adventures, and both good times and bad. In *My Friend Is Sad*, lighthearted Piggie hopes to chase away the blues keeping Elephant's spirits low, while in *Today I Will Fly* the pig's overly ambitious goal is brought down to earth through Elephant's realistic observations. The friendship holds despite an accident in *I Love My New Toy!*, and a simple game presents greater and greater challenges for Elephant, Piggie, and Squirrel in *I Will Surprise My Friend!* While citing their value to beginning readers building a vocabulary of "useful words," Ilene Cooper added in her *Booklist* reviewer that *I Love My New Toy* and its companion volumes gain their "charm [from] . . . the way Willems captures the emotions of young children" in both his simple dialogue and his "artfully drawn line" art. "Accessible, appealing, and full of authentic emotions about what makes friendships tick," according to *Booklist* contributor Jennifer Mattson, the "Elephant and Piggie" books "will put a contemporary shine on easy-reader collections and give Willems' many fans . . . two more characters to love."

In *Let's Say Hi to Friends Who Fly* and *Cat the Cat, Who Is That?* Willems introduces a new collection of likeable animal characters—among them Cat the Cat, Duck the Duck, Mouse the Mouse, and Fish the Fish—as they visit each other and ask simple questions. Other volumes in the "Cat the Cat" series include *Time to Sleep, Sheep the Sheep!*, which follows the characters through their nighttime routines, and *What's Your Sound, Hound the Hound?*, in which each animal makes the sound that makes it unique. "The real magic" in *Time to Sleep, Sheep the Sheep!* can be found in the art, according to *School Library Journal* contributor Stacy Dillon, the critic noting that each page is full of "details

that children will relish." Instead of a descriptive text, "Willems relies on facial expressions and body posturing to convey humor with minimal detail," explained Mary Hazelton in her *School Library Journal* review of *What's Your Sound, Hound the Hound?* Praising *Cat the Cat, Who Is That?* in *Booklist*, Engberg predicted that the author/illustrator's "exuberant, clean-lined, animation-ready" stories in this series will "widen his already vast fan base," while a *Kirkus Reviews* writer dubbed *Let's Say Hi to Friends Who Fly* "another triumph" for its creator.

In addition to his series books, Willems has also written several standalone books for young readers, among them *Time to Pee!*, *Leonardo, the Terrible Monster*, and *Edwina, the Dinosaur Who Didn't Know She Was Extinct*. "More pep rally than how-to," *Time to Pee!* "is perfectly attuned to preschoolers' sensibilities and funny bones," in the opinion of *Horn Book* contributor Kitty Flynn. Featuring a band of cheerful mice who give advice and encouragement to youngsters undergoing potty training, the book showcases Willems' "genius for spare but expressive lines and an almost uncanny rapport with the preschool audience," according to *Booklist* reviewer Jennifer Matson. The mouse clan returns in *Time to Say "Please!"*, a primer of basic manners that a *Kirkus Reviews* contributor praised as "an entirely kid-centered lesson" that will earn repeated readings at storytime. Calling the book "a painless introduction to good manners," Wendy Lukehart added that *Time to Say "Please!"* should be influential because Willems' "examples speak directly to a young child's experience."

Keying in to children's love of dinosaurs, *Edwina, the Dinosaur Who Didn't Know She Was Extinct* introduces a friendly neighborhood resident who just happens to be a dinosaur. Edwina is kind to everyone, even baking cookies for the local children, until know-it-all neighbor Reginald informs the oversized reptile that she is, in fact, extinct. Describing the sweet-tempered Edwina as "a masterful creation," a *Kirkus Reviews* writer praised *Edwina, the Dinosaur Who Didn't Know She Was Extinct* as "a tribute to the child's rock-solid faith in how the world should be."

Like dinosaurs, monsters also have perennial child appeal, and in *Leonardo, the Terrible Monster* Willems casts a decidedly non-scary member of the Monster clan in what a *Kirkus Reviews* writer called "a sweetly original morality play" about friendship and differences. Calling the tale a "perfectly paced story," *School Library Journal* contributor Marianne Saccardi noted that it perfectly pairs with Willems' pastel-toned cartoon art, and in a *Booklist* review Ilene Cooper praised the book's "smart, striking design."

Other standalone books by Willems include *Naked Mole Rat Gets Dressed*, *Happy Pig Day!*, and *Hooray for Amanda and Her Alligator!*, all of which pair his animation-style cartoons with stories that capture quint-

*A kindly throwback ignores a pesky realist in Willems' self-illustrated picture book* Edwina, the Dinosaur Who Didn't Know She Was Extinct. (Copyright © 2006 by Mo Willems. Reprinted by permission of Disney/Hyperion, an imprint of Disney Book Group, LLC. All rights reserved.)

essential toddler perspectives. Demonstrating his range as a writer, he has also collaborated with illustrator Jon J. Muth on *City Dog, Country Frog,* a story about rural life that he attempted to illustrate for several years before realizing that his characteristic line-and-wash cartoons did not do it justice. Willems' work as author prompted *Booklist* critic Ilene Cooper to observe: "It's hard to imagine a picture book that more consistently (and touchingly) hits all the right notes."

In Willems' picture-book career, he has reproduced many of the successes of his work in television. After only a few years, he earned some of the field's top awards, including two prestigious Caldecott Honor Book citations in recognition of his illustrations. In reviewing his books, critics often make note of the author/ illustrator's minimalist graphic style, a fact that pleases the former animator. As Willems told Goodman, "while I enjoy all forms of drawing, a single line, simply done, is more beautiful than a hundred little lines sort of approximating the same thing. I like my characters to be two-dimensional. Just because you can so something in 3-D doesn't make it better. I want my line to be focused, so the emotions of a character are clear."

## Biographical and Critical Sources

*PERIODICALS*

*Animation World,* September, 1997, Arlene Sherman and Abby Terkuhle, interview with Willems; June 25, 2001, Martin Goodman, "Talking in His Sheep: A Conversation with Mo Willems."

*Booklist,* September 1, 2003, Gillian Engberg, review of *Don't Let the Pigeon Drive the Bus!,* p. 123; November 1, 2003, Jennifer Matson, review of *Time to Pee!,* p. 499; January 1, 2004, review of *Don't Let the Pigeon Drive the Bus!,* p 782; February 15, 2004, Gillian Engberg, review of *The Pigeon Finds a Hot Dog!,* p. 1064; September 15, 2004, Jennifer Matson, review of *Knuffle Bunny: A Cautionary Tale,* p. 241; June 1, 2005, Gillian Engberg, review of *Knuffle Bunny,* p. 1819; July, 2005, Ilene Cooper, review of *Leonardo, the Terrible Monster,* p. 1931; February 15, 2006, Ilene Cooper, review of *Don't Let the Pigeon Stay up Late!,* p. 106; July 1, 2006, Jesse Karp, review of *You Can Never Find a Rickshaw When It Monsoons: The World on One Cartoon a Day,* p. 47; September 1, 2006, Randall Enos, review of *Edwina, the Dinosaur Who Didn't Know She Was Extinct,* p. 142; April 1,

2007, Jennifer Mattson, reviews of *My Friend Is Sad* and *Today I Will Fly!*, both p. 49; May 1, 2008, Gillian Engberg. review of *The Pigeon Wants a Puppy*, p. 94; July 1, 2008, Ilene Cooper, reviews of *I Love My New Toy!* and *I Will Surprise My Friend!*, both p. 64; December 1, 2009, Randall Enos, review of *Pigs Make Me Sneeze!*, p. 52; December 15, 2009, Daniel Kraus, review of *I Am Going*, p. 44; March 15, 2010, Gillian Engberg, review of *Cat the Cat, Who Is That?*, p. 46, and Ilene Cooper, review of *City Dog, Country Frog*, p. 48; May 1, 2010, Ian Chipman, review of *Time to Sleep, Sheep the Sheep!*, p. 94; July 1, 2010, Daniel Kraus, review of *Knuffle Bunny Free: An Unexpected Diversion*, p. 62; September 15, 2010, Daniel Kraus, review of *We Are in a Book!*, p. 71.

*Bookseller,* April 16, 2004, Sonia Benster, review of *Don't Let the Pigeon Drive the Bus!*, p. 31; April 7, 2006, Katie Hawthorne, review of *The Pigeon Finds a Hot Dog!*, p. 13.

*Bulletin of the Center for Children's Books,* October, 2004, review of *Knuffle Bunny*, p. 103; November, 2005, Karen Coats, review of *Leonardo, the Terrible Monster*, p. 127; May, 2006, Karen Coats, review of *Don't Let the Pigeon Stay up Late!*, p. 429; October, 2006, Karen Coats, review of *Edwina, the Dinosaur Who Didn't Know She Was Extinct*, p. 101.

*CBC Magazine,* May, 2005, Mo Willems, "How to Become Rich and Famous in One Easy Step (and Other Stuff That Has Nothing to Do with Making Kids' Books)."

*Charlotte Observer,* April 4, 2006, "Four Questions for Mo Willems."

*Christian Science Monitor,* May 22, 2007, Steven Ellis "He Writes, He Draws, and He's Very Funny!" (profile), p. 19.

*Daily News* (Los Angeles, CA), June 18, 2005, Sherry Joe Crosby, "Author Mo Willems Lets His Imagination Take Wing," p. U7.

*Entertainment Weekly,* October 3, 2003, review of *Time to Pee!*, p. 74.

*Globe & Mail* (Toronto, Ontario, Canada), June 14, 2003, Susan Perren, review of *Don't Let the Pigeon Drive the Bus!*, p. D15; July 17, 2004, Susan Perren, review of *The Pigeon Finds a Hot Dog!*, p. D11; October 23, 2004, Susan Perren, review of *Knuffle Bunny*, p. D22; June 18, 2005, Susan Perren, review of *Time to Say "Please"!*, p. D11; December 31, 2005, Susan Perren, review of *Leonardo, the Terrible Monster*, p. D13.

*Horn Book,* July-August, 2003, Kitty Flynn, review of *Don't Let the Pigeon Drive the Bus!*, p. 449; January-February, 2004, Kitty Flynn, review of *Time to Pee!*, p. 75; May-June, 2004, Kitty Flynn, review of *The Pigeon Finds a Hot Dog!*, p. 323; September-October, 2004, Kitty Flynn, review of *Knuffle Bunny*, pp. 576-577; July-August, 2005, Kitty Flynn, review of *Time to Say "Please"!*, p. 462; September-October, 2005, Kitty Flynn, review of *Leonardo, the Terrible Monster*, p. 569; May-June, 2006, Susan Dove Lempke, review of *Don't Let the Pigeon Stay up Late!*, p. 308; September-October, 2006, Danielle J. Ford, review of *Edwina, the Dinosaur Who Didn't Know She Was Extinct*, p. 572; November-December, 2007, Kitty Flynn,

review of *Knuffle Bunny Too*, p. 671; January-February, 2008, Kitty Flynn, reviews of *I Am Invited to a Party!* and *There Is a Bird on Your Head!*, both p. 97; July-August, 2008, Kitty Flynn, reviews of *The Pigeon Wants a Puppy*, p. 436, and *I Love My New Toy!* and *I Will Surprise My Friends!*, both p. 460; January-February, 2009, Robin L. Smith, review of *Are You Ready to Play Outside?*, p. 104; July-August, 2009, Robin L. Smith, review of *Elephants Cannot Dance!*, p. 433; January-February, 2010, Betty Carter, review of *Pigs Make Me Sneeze!*, p. 96; March-April, 2010, Betty Carter, review of *I Am Going!*, p. 75; May-June, 2010, Robin L. Smith, reviews of *Let's Say Hi to Friends Who Fly!* and *Cat the Cat, Who Is That?*, both p. 95; July-August, 2010, Roger Sutton, review of *City Dog, Country Frog*, p. 97, and Kitty Flynn, review of *Time to Sleep, Sheep the Sheep!*, p. 126; September-October, 2010, Roger Sutton, review of *Knuffle Bunny Free*, p. 68.

*Houston Chronicle,* February 15, 2010, Maggie Galehouse, "Catching up with Children's Author Mo Willems," p. 1.

*Instructor,* April, 2004, Judy Freeman, review of *Don't Let the Pigeon Drive the Bus!*, p. 65.

*Kirkus Reviews,* April 1, 2003, review of *Don't Let the Pigeon Drive the Bus!*, p. 542; October 1, 2003, review of *Time to Pee!*, p. 1233; April 1, 2004, review of *The Pigeon Finds a Hot Dog!*, p. 339; August 1, 2004, review of *Knuffle Bunny*, p. 750; May 15, 2005, review of *Time to Say "Please"!*, p. 597; July 15, 2005, review of *Leonardo, the Terrible Monster*, p. 797; March 1, 2006, review of *Don't Let the Pigeon Stay Up Late!*, p. 242; August 1, 2006, review of *Edwina, the Dinosaur Who Didn't Know She Was Extinct*, p. 799; March 1, 2007, review of *My Friend Is Sad*, p. 234; July 1, 2007, review of *Knuffle Bunny Too*; August 15, 2007, review of *I Am Invited to a Party!*; April 15, 2008, review of *The Pigeon Wants a Puppy!*; December 15, 2009, review of *I Am Going!*; March 1, 2010, reviews of *Lets Say Hi to Friends Who Fly!* and *Cat the Cat, Who Is That?*; April 15, 2010, review of *What's Your Sound, Hound the Hound?*; May 15, 2010, review of *Can I Play Too?*

*News-Leader* (Springfield, MO), July 27, 2005, Samantha Critchell, "Author Quits Day Job to Write Kids' Books."

*New York Times,* April 16, 2000, Peter Marks, "Now Mom and Dad Are Going Cartoon-Crazy, Too."

*New York Times Book Review,* May 16, 2004, Claire Dederer, review of *The Pigeon Finds a Hot Dog!*; November 8, 2009, Sherie Posesorski, review of *Big Frog Can't Fit In*, p. 23; July 18, 2010, Jim Mcmullan, review of *City Dog, Country Frog*, p. L14.

*Publishers Weekly,* February 10, 2003, review of *Don't Let the Pigeon Drive the Bus!*, p. 184; December 15, 2003, review of *Time to Pee!*, p. 71; April 5, 2004, review of *The Pigeon Finds a Hot Dog!*, p. 60; June 10, 2004, Nathalie op de Beeck, interview with Willems; August 16, 2004, review of *Knuffle Bunny*, p. 62; February 21, 2005, Susan Spencer Cramer, interview with Willems, p. 153; May 9, 2005, review of *Time to Say "Please"!*, p. 68; June 27, 2005, review of *Leonardo, the Terrible Monster*, p. 61; February 20, 2006, review of *Don't Let the Pigeon Stay up Late!*, p. 154; July 17, 2006, review of *Edwina, the Dinosaur Who Didn't Know She Was Extinct*, p. 156; February 26, 2007, reviews of *Today I Will Fly!* and *My Friend Is Sad*, both p. 89; July 16, 2007, review of *Knuffle Bunny Too*, p. 163; January 18, 2010, review of *Cat the Cat, Who Is That?*, p. 45; August, 2010, Laura Scott, review of *Can I Play Too?*, p. 88; September 13, 2010, review of *Knuffle Bunny Free*, p. 41.

*School Library Journal*, May, 2003, Dona Ratterree, review of *Don't Let the Pigeon Drive the Bus!*, p. 132; December, 2003, Bina Williams, review of *Time to Pee!*, p. 140; May, 2004, Robin L. Gibson, review of *The Pigeon Finds a Hot Dog!*, pp. 126-127; October, 2004, Martha Topol, review of *Knuffle Bunny*, p. 136; August, 2005, Marianne Saccardi, review of *Leonardo, the Terrible Monster*, p. 108, Julie Roach, reviews of *The Pigeon Has Feelings, Too!* and *The Pigeon Loves Things That Go!*, p. 108, and Wendy Lukehart, review of *Time to Say "Please"!*, p. 108; September, 2005, Barbara Auerbach, review of *Knuffle Bunny*, p. 60; April, 2006, Joy Fleishhacker, review of *Don't Let the Pigeon Stay up Late!*, p. 122; September, 2006, Kate McClelland, review of *Edwina, the Dinosaur Who Didn't Know She Was Extinct*, p. 187; May, 2007, Marilyn Taniguchi, reviews of *Today I Will Fly!* and *My Friend Is Sad*, both p. 112; August, 2007, Kate McClelland, review of *Knuffle Bunny Too*, p. 95; August, 2008, Kelly Roth, reviews of *I Love My New Toy!* and *I Will Surprise My Friend!*, both p. 105; December, 2008, Mary Hazelton, review of *Pigs Make Me Sneeze!*, p. 94; February, 2010, Kristine M. Casper, review of *Cat the Cat, Who Is That?*, p. 97; April, 2010, Mary Hazelton, review of *What's Your Sound, Hound the Hound?*, p. 142; May, 2010, Joy Fleishhacker, review of *City Dog, Country Frog*, p. 94; June, 2010, Gloria Koster, review of *I Am Going!*, p. 86; July, 2010, Stacy Dillon, review of *Time to Sleep, Sheep the Sheep!*, p. 72; August, 2010, Laura Scott, review of *Can I Play Too?*, p. 88; October, 2010, Carolyn Janssen, review of *Knuffle Bunny Free*, p. 96.

*Time*, December 5, 2005, Christopher Porterfield, review of *Leonardo, the Terrible Monster*, p. W1.

*Variety*, November 13, 2000, Stuart Levine, review of *Sheep in the Big City*, p. 39.

*ONLINE*

*CartoonNetwork.com*, http://www.cartoonnetwork.com.au/ (April 7, 2006).

*Cartoon Network's Friday's Fan site*, http://fridays.toonzone.net/ (September 28, 2003), "Behind the Scenes Interviews: Tom Warburton and Mo Willems."

*Mo Willems Home Page*, http://www.mowillems.com (April 15, 2011).

*Mo Willems Web log*, http://mowillemsdoodles.blogspot.com (April 15, 2011).

*Walker Books Web site*, http://www.walkerbooks.co.uk/ (April 15, 2011), "Mo Willems."*

# WITTENSTEIN, Vicki Oransky 1954-

## Personal

Born 1954, in NJ; married; children. *Education:* University of Pennsylvania, B.A. (American civilization and urban studies); Cornell University, J.D.; Vermont College of Fine Arts, M.F.A. (writing for children and young adults). *Hobbies and other interests:* Reading, nature, science.

## Addresses

*Home*—Brooklyn, NY. *E-mail*—vicki@vickiwittenstein.com.

## Career

Author and attorney. Office of New York State Attorney's General, New York, NY, assistant district attorney. Presenter at schools and workshops.

## Member

Authors Guild.

## Awards, Honors

Society of Children's Book Writers and Illustrators Magazine Merit Honor Certificate, 1999; Association of Educational Publishers Distinguished Achievement Award finalist, and named *Highlights for Children* Science Feature of the Year, both 2004, for article "Dr. Geoffrey W. Marcy: Planet Hunter"; Honor Book designation, Society of School Librarians International, 2020, for *Planet Hunter*.

## Writings

*Planet Hunter: Geoff Marcy and the Search for Other Earths*, Boyds Mills Press (Honesdale, PA), 2010.

Contributor to periodicals, including *Faces*, *Highlights for Children*, and *Odyssey*.

## Sidelights

Vicki Oransky Wittenstein turned to writing for young people after spending years working as a criminal prosecutor in Manhattan. Inspired by her long-held interest in science, her book *Planet Hunter: Geoff Marcy and the Search for Other Earths* was the outgrowth of her early efforts writing for children's magazines. Based on an award-winning article Wittenstein published in *Highlights for Children*, *Planet Hunter* required several years of research as well as a trip to visit her scientist subject at his workplace: Hawai'i's W.M. Keck Observatory, which is located 14,000 above sea level, atop the dormant volcano Mauna Kea.

Curious and interested in nature as a child, Wittenstein opted for a career in law but continued to pursue her interest in the advances made in the realm of sciences. As a way to both channel her own curiosity and also share her enthusiasm for science, she decided to make the switch to writing when the opportunity presented itself, and eventually earned an M.F.A. in writing for children at Vermont College of Fine Arts. When she read about astronomer Geoff Marcy and his work exploring other solar systems in search of planets that might be similar to Earth, Wittenstein saw the possibility of a fascinating story. After interviewing Marcy and publishing her article, she still had unanswered questions. If she was left with questions, her readers had questions too. Clearly, a longer work was in order.

In addition to spending several days at the Keck Observatory, Wittenstein researched planet hunting, interviewed several other scientists working in the field, and corresponded with astronomy experts. "My greatest challenge in writing a middle-grade astronomy book was to find a way to hook kids on the science behind planet hunting," the author explained in an online interview with Cynthia Leitich Smith for *Cynsations*. Fortunately, her scientist subject has an interesting life story that many preteens can relate to: he had difficulty in school and only found his vocation after much struggle. "Marcy's life and personal struggles added human interest to the book," explained Wittenstein, "and gave the science a context that readers can latch onto."

In *Planet Hunter* readers learn about the advances in planet hunting that have been made possible due to advancing technology and increased scientific understanding. For Marcy, who searches for relatively small planets orbiting distant suns, high-powered optical telescopes and light-filtering spectrometers have opened windows to solar systems were previously invisible. In fact, since 1995, when the first such "extra-solar" planet was discovered, over 400 new planets have been sighted, and Marcy's team can take credit for half of those sightings. Wittenstein "captures the essence of a research community" by profiling Marcy and his team of astronomers, and "gives attention to competing methodological approaches to detecting planets," according to *Horn Book* contributor Danielle J. Ford. In *Kirkus Reviews* a critic noted that the subject matter of *Planet Hunter* is relatively advanced; despite that, the author's "explanations are clear, well organized and interestingly written with plenty of quotations from the scientists." In addition, Wittenstein supplements her text with glossaries, a bibliography and list of relevant Web sites, and explanatory sidebars. "The profound thrill of searching for . . . planets . . . is deftly captured" in *Planet Hunter*, asserted *School Library Journal* critic John Peters, and Carolyn Phelan concluded in *Booklist* that "readers motivated to learn about the search for distant planets will enjoy [Wittenstein's] . . . attractive book."

"My hope is that another generation of young people will become fascinated with space," Wittenstein admitted to Smith, in discussing the motivation behind *Planet Hunter*. "Perhaps they, like Marcy, will one day search for life beyond the stars."

## Biographical and Critical Sources

*PERIODICALS*

*Booklist,* May 15, 2010, Carolyn Phelan, review of *Planet Hunter: Geoff Marcy and the Search for Other Earths,* p. 33.

*Horn Book,* May-June, 2010, Danielle J. Ford, review of *Planet Hunter,* p. 114.

*Kirkus Reviews,* January 15, 2010, review of *Planet Hunter.*

*School Library Journal,* March, 2010, John Peters, review of *Planet Hunter,* p. 182.

*ONLINE*

*Cynsations Web log,* http://cynthialeitichsmith.blogspot.com/ (May 26, 2010), Cynthia Leitich Smith, interview with Wittenstein.

*Vicki Wittenstein Home Page,* http://www.vickiowittenstein.com (March 20, 2011).*

* * *

*Vicki Oransky Wittenstein's* Planet Hunter *focuses on astronomer Geoff Marcy and his search for other habitable planets.* (Boyds Mills Press, 2001. Illustration copyright © by Lynette Cook. Reproduced with permission of Boyds Mills Press.)

# ZAHLER, Diane

## Personal

Born in NY; married Phil Sicker; children: one son. *Education:* College degree. *Hobbies and other interests:* Travel, history.

## Addresses

*Home*—NY.

## Career

Author. Formerly worked in children's book publishing.

## Writings

*MIDDLE-GRADE NOVELS*

*The Thirteenth Princess,* Harper (New York, NY), 2010.
*A True Princess,* HarperCollins (New York, NY), 2011.

*OTHER*

(With sister, Kathy A. Zahler) *Test Your Cultural Literacy,* Prentice Hall (New York, NY), 1988, updated as *Test-Prep Your IQ with the Essentials of Cultural Literacy,* Thomson/Arco (Lawrenceville, NJ), 2003, published as *Test Your Cultural Literacy IQ,* Pocket Books (New York, NY), 2003.

(With Kathy A. Zahler) *Test Your Countercultural Literacy,* Prentice Hall (New York, NY), 1989.

(Compiler) *Twenty-first Century Guide to Improving Your Writing,* Dell (New York, NY), 1995.

*The Black Death* ("Pivotal Moments in History" series), Twenty-first Century Books (Minneapolis, MN), 2009.

*Than Shwe's Burma* ("Dictatorship" series), Twenty-first Century Books (Minneapolis, MN), 2010.

## Sidelights

Diane Zahler collaborated with sister Kathy A. Zahler on several books before breaking out on her own as a writer for younger readers: the Zahlers' first book, *Test Your Cultural Literacy,* actually went through several editions and remains a popular SAT primer more than two decades after its original 1988 publication. Turning to series' nonfiction, Zahler's *The Black Death* and *Than Shwe's Burma* present well-researched resources for secondary-school students and also draw on the author's long-time interest in history. Reviewing *The Black Death* in *School Library Journal,* Rebecca Donnelly praised Zahler's "well-written and well-researched" text, and in *Than Shwe's Burma* the author "ably depicts life" within the shuttered country now known as Myanmar, according to the critic. In more recent years the author has returned to her first love—fiction—by creating the middle-grade fantasy novels *The Thirteenth Princess* and *A True Princess.*

Zahler grew up in Ithaca, New York, where she discovered the classic "colored" fairy-tale collections of nineteenth-century Scottish folklorist Andrew Lang: *The Red Fairy Book, The Green Fairy Book, The Yellow Fairy Book,* and so forth. From there she moved on to fantasy stories by E. Nesbit and Edward Eager, the "Narnia" stories of C.S. Lewis, and books by Roald Dahl, Norton Juster, Ursula K. Leguin, and E.L. Konigsburg. Zahler kept pace with newer trends in children's literature through her work in local libraries as a high-school and college student, and she finally found herself working in that field after a move to New York City and a job for children's book publishers. "When writing both *The Thirteenth Princess* and *A True Princess,* I reacquainted myself with the girl I had been when I first discovered fairy tales," Zahler explained to an interviewer for the Mother Daughter Book Club online. "That girl craved magic in her own life and found it in the books she read. I realized that the longing for magic has never really left me. Now, though, I can find magic not only in the books I read but in the books I write."

Based on the Grimm Brothers' fairy story "The Twelve Dancing Princesses," *The Thirteenth Princess* introduces Zita, a twelve year old whose mother died while giving birth to her. Angry that he would have no sons, her father, the king, ordered that Zita be raised by the palace servants, apart from her twelve older sisters.

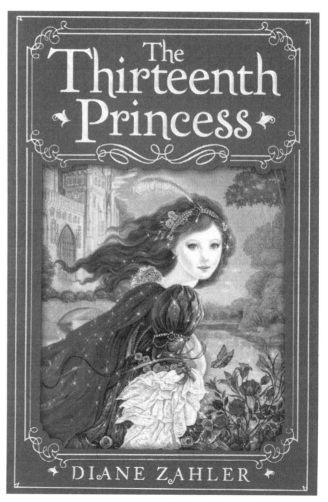

*Cover of Diane Zahler's engaging middle-grade fairy story* **The Thirteenth Princess,** *featuring cover art by Laurel Long.* (Harper, 2010. Jacket art © by Laurel Long. Reproduced with permission of HarperCollins Children's Books, a division of HarperCollins Publishers.)

When the twelve princesses suddenly begin to suffer from a strange malady, Zita realizes that their shoes are becoming as worn and tattered as their spirits. With the help of Breckin the stable boy and a witch named Babette, Zita finds out where the twelve princesses go each night and then seeks a cure for whatever has seemingly bewitched them. In *Booklist* Kathleen Isaacs praised *The Thirteenth Princess* as a "lively reworking" of a well-known story, and a *Publishers Weekly* critic maintained that Zahler "deftly and thoughtfully embellishes the tale's classic elements" in a story that treats preteens to "a graceful and cohesive romantic drama." A "sweetly written reimagining," according to a *Kirkus Reviews* writer, *The Thirteenth Princess* is brought to life through "delicious descriptions of gowns and (worn-out) slippers, teas and sweetmeats."

Zahler turns to another classic fairy tale, Hans Christian Andersen's "The Princess and the Pea," as well as to a fanciful poem by German author Johann Wolfgang Goethe, in crafting the story for *A True Princess*. Lilia has been raised by a kindly shepherd, but when she learns that she will be farmed out as a servant girl she determines to run away and search for her real parents. Joined by step-siblings Kai and Karina, Lilia journeys north into a dark forest that is ruled by the Elf-king. Through a misadventure the travelers arrive at the king's court, where Kai becomes bewitched by the Elf-king's daughter. As Lilia and Karina work to find a way to break their brother's enchantment, their actions determine their future and also help Lilia discover the truth about her past. In a review of *A True Princess*, *School Library Journal* contributor Terri Dorio predicted that "readers who enjoyed Gail Carson Levine's *Ella Enchanted* . . . will also relish this tale."

## Biographical and Critical Sources

*PERIODICALS*

*Booklist*, October 15, 2009, Gillian Engberg, review of *Than Shwe's Burma*, p. 48; December 15, 2009, Kathleen Isaacs, review of *The Thirteenth Princess*, p. 41.
*Bulletin of the Center for Children's Books*, March, 2010), Kate Quealy-Gainer, review of *The Thirteenth Princess*, p. 311.
*Kirkus Reviews*, January 1, 2010, review of *The Thirteenth Princess*.
*Publishers Weekly*, January 18, 2010, review of *The Thirteenth Princess*, p. 49.
*School Library Journal*, May, 2009, Rebecca Donnelly, review of *The Black Death*, p. 129; October, 2009, Rebecca Donnelly, review of *Than Shwe's Burma*, p. 155; March, 2010, Miriam Lang Budin, review of *The Thirteenth Princess*, p. 170; March, 2011, Terrie Dorio, review of *A True Princess*, p. 176.

*ONLINE*

*Diane Zahler Home Page*, http://www.dianezahler.com (February 20, 2011).

*Mother Daughter Book Club Web site*, http://mother daughterbookclub.com/ (February 9, 2011), interview with Zahler.*

*     *     *

# ZUCKER, Jonny

## Personal

Born in England; married; children: three. *Education:* Manchester University, degree; Lancashire Polytechnic (now University of Central Lancashire), studied radio production.

## Addresses

*Home*—London, England. *E-mail*—jonny.zucker@ blueyonder.co.uk.

## Career

Author of books for children and author of television scripts. Primary-school teacher and soccer coach in London, England, early 1990s-2002; full-time writer, beginning 2002. Formerly worked as a stand-up comedian. Presenter at schools.

## Writings

(With David Parker) *A Class Act*, Sapphire Publishers (London, England), 1999.
(With Fiona Zucker) *The Dream Decoder*, Aurum (London, England), 2000.
(With Fiona Starr) *Dream Themes: A Guide to Understanding Your Dreams*, Barnes & Noble (New York, NY), 2001.
(With Ivor Baddiel) *Mystica Magic*, illustrated by Mike Phillips, Hippo (London, England) 2003.
*How to Sparkle at Reading Comprehension*, illustrated by Van Edgar, Brilliant Publications (Dunstable, England), 2003.
*One Girl, Two Decks, Three Degrees of Love*, Piccadilly (London, England), 2004.
(With Ivor Baddiel) *David Feckham: My Backside*, Orion (London, England), 2004.
*James King of England*, illustrated by Barrie Appleby, Meadowside Children's (London, England), 2006.
*Cornflake Coin*, illustrated by Martin Remphry, Oxford University Press (Oxford, England), 2006.
*Basketball War*, illustrated by Paul Savage, Stone Arch Books (Mankato, MN), 2006.
*Skateboard Power*, illustrated by Paul Savage, Stone Arch Books (Mankato, MN), 2006.
*Steel Eyes*, illustrated by Paul Savage, Stone Arch Books (Mankato, MN), 2006.
(With Ivor Baddiel) *Not the Highway Code: The Unofficial Rules of the Road*, Weidenfeld & Nicholson (London, England), 2007.

*The Bombed House,* illustrated by Paul Savage, Stone Arch Books (Mankato, MN), 2007.

*Alien Abduction,* illustrated by Paul Savage, Stone Arch Books (Mankato, MN), 2007.

*Summer Trouble,* illustrated by Paul Savage, Stone Arch Books (Mankato, MN), 2007.

*Inside the Game,* illustrated by Pete Smith, Stone Arch Books (Mankato, MN), 2007.

*Spin Off,* illustrated by Enzo Troiano, Stone Arch Books (Mankato, MN), 2007.

*Soccer Showdown,* illustrated by Enzo Troiano, Stone Arch Books (Mankato, MN), 2007.

*Speed Star,* illustrated by Enzo Troiano, Stone Arch Books (Mankato, MN), 2007.

*Creature Chase,* illustrated by Enzo Troiano, Stone Arch Books (Mankato, MN), 2007.

*Cut-Throat Pirates,* illustrated by Pete Smith, Stone Arch Books (Mankato, MN), 2007.

*Alien Attack* illustrated by Pete Smith, Stone Arch Books (Mankato, MN), 2007.

*Safecrackers,* illustrated by Enzo Troiano, Stone Arch Books (Mankato, MN), 2007.

(Adaptor) *Secrets and Spies* (based on the television series *MI High*), Puffin (London, England) 2008.

*Dan and the Mudman,* illustrated by Hannah Web, Frances Lincoln (London, England), 2008.

*The Phantom Striker,* illustrated by Victor Tavares, Stone Arch Books (Mankato, MN), 2008.

*A Deck of Monsters,* illustrated by Anthony Williams, Stone Arch Books (Mankato, MN), 2008.

*MP3 Mind Control,* illustrated by Lee Wildish, Stone Arch Books (Mankato, MN), 2008.

*Striker Boy,* Frances Lincoln (London, England), 2010.

*Speed Machine,* Scholastic (London, England), 2011.

*Monster Swap,* illustrated by Tony Ross, Hodder Children's (London, England), 2011.

Contributor to periodicals, including *Times Educational Supplement.*

"FESTIVAL TIME!" SERIES

*Apples and Honey: A Rosh Hashanah Story,* illustrated by Jan Barger Cohen, Barron's Educational (Hauppauge, NY), 2002.

*Eight Candles to Light: A Chanukah Story,* illustrated by Jan Barger Cohen, Barron's Educational (Hauppauge, NY), 2002.

*It's Party Time!: A Purim Story,* illustrated by Jan Barger Cohen, Barron's Educational (Hauppauge, NY), 2003.

*Four Special Questions: A Passover Story,* illustrated by Jan Barger Cohen, Barron's Educational (Hauppauge, NY), 2003.

*Hope and New Life!: An Easter Story,* illustrated by Jan Barger Cohen, Barron's Educational (Hauppauge, NY), 2004.

*Fasting and Dates: A Ramadan and Eid-ul-fitr Story,* illustrated by Jan Barger Cohen, Barron's Educational (Hauppauge, NY), 2004.

*Lanterns and Firecrackers: A Chinese New Year Story,* illustrated by Jan Barger Cohen, Barron's Educational (Hauppauge, NY), 2004.

*Light a Lamp: A Diwali Story,* illustrated by Jan Barger Cohen, Barron's Educational (Hauppauge, NY), 2004.

"VENUS SPRING" SERIES

*Venus Spring, Stunt Girl,* Piccadilly (London, England), 2005.

*Body Double,* Piccadilly (London, England), 2006.

*Star Turn,* Piccadilly (London, England), 2007.

*Face Off,* Piccadilly (London, England), 2008.

"MAX FLASH" SERIES

*Game On,* illustrated by Ned Woodman, Stripes (London, England), 2007.

*Supersonic,* illustrated by Ned Woodman, Stripes (London, England), 2007.

*In Deep,* illustrated by Ned Woodman, Stripes (London, England), 2008.

*Grave Danger,* illustrated by Ned Woodman, Stripes (London, England), 2008.

*Sub Zero,* illustrated by Ned Woodman, Stripes (London, England), 2009.

*Short Circuit,* illustrated by Ned Woodman, Stripes (London, England), 2009.

"FULL FLIGHT" SERIES

*Football Killers,* illustrated by Pete Smith, Badger (Stevenage, England), 2007.

*Evil Brain Chips,* illustrated by Ivan Tovey, Badger (Stevenage, England), 2007.

## Sidelights

A prolific writer, Jonny Zucker is best known as the author of engaging tales for the reluctant-reader crowd, such as *The Bombed House, Alien Attack, Dan and the Mudman, Monster Swap,* and *Striker Boy.* While growing up in England, Zucker loved reading stories about soccer, and as a writer he now writes the same type of fast-moving, entertaining tales he enjoyed as a child. In fact, his boyhood dream was to be a professional soccer player, and as he admitted to Graham Marks in a *Rightaway.org* interview, "I often write about boys who discover something about their football skills or get a lucky break and in a way it's my wish-fulfillment."

After completing college, Zucker worked as a primary-school teacher and also coached soccer (or "football" as it is known in the United Kingdom). During his twenties he also found an outlet for his humor in stand-up comedy, performing at various clubs until he and his wife started raising a family. Zucker's talent for writing began to reveal itself in articles he wrote for the *Times Educational Supplement.* On the strength of those articles, he was contacted by Badger Publishing, an educational press, and offered the chance to write. After cutting his teaching down to part time, Zucker eventually left education altogether and in 2002 began to write full time.

Johnny Zucker's many boy-friendly novels for young readers include **Dan and the Mudman,** *featuring artwork by Hannah Web.* (Copyright © 2008 by Frances Lincoln Ltd. Reproduced with permission of the publisher.)

Much of Zucker's work has involved creating multi-volume series, and such was the case with his first professional project: working with illustrator Jan Barger Cohen to create the nonfiction "Festival Time" books for publisher Frances Lincoln. In reviewing one book in this series, *Apples and Honey: A Rosh Hashanah Story,* Susan Pine deemed the book a "pleasant offering" in her *School Library Journal* review while colleague Eva Mitnick cited the winning combination of a "simple text" and "warm watercolor illustrations" in *Eight Candles to Light: A Chanukah Story.* Other series work, includes his "Venus Spring" novels, which focuses on a talented young stunt artist as she balances typical teen school and social activities with risky assignments that invariably lead to adventure. According to London *Daily Telegraph* critic Sinclair McKay, Zucker's "Venus Spring" series will appeal to "girls who feel that the boys get an unfair number of slam-bang adventures to enjoy."

Other series work, such as his "Max Flash" books, allows Zucker to harness his imagination, as does creating standalone novels such as *Striker Boy,* which finds preteen soccer prodigy Nat Cartwright joining a pro team while keeping his true age a secret. In *The Bombed House* Zucker uses short, high-action chapters to relate the story of two brothers who discover a Nazi soldier hiding out in London during the Blitz. Preteen boys in particular will be attracted by the book's prose, which "is fast paced and flows naturally," according to *School Library Journal* contributor Bobbee Pennington. Zucker also deals with serious themes—anti-Semitism and bullying—in *Dan and the Mudman,* which focuses on a Jewish teen whose class assignment to research the history of the legendary Golem provides him with the means to deal with a modern-day schoolyard thug. With its mix of history, school story, and coming-of-age drama, *Dan and the Mudman* also treats middle-grade readers to "excitement and supernatural touches aplenty," according to a *Kirkus Reviews* writer.

Although Zucker is adamant that a book must have a strong plot to pull reluctant readers along, he admitted to Marks that he is "almost plot-phobic." "I find it very difficult," he added. "I really enjoy the actual writing, but plotting is something else and my brain doesn't work like that. I have to sit down and put all the scenes on postcards and move them round till they fit together and the plot is as watertight as possible. I'm very linear, I can't be doing stories told from multiple viewpoints and with timeshifts; I have to see how the whole thing works or I end up going down so many dead ends it becomes very frustrating." As far as a career goes, Zucker also has practical thoughts on that. "With writing you've got to have a modicum of talent," he noted. "But you've also got to be very pushy and you've got to hustle and have some lucky breaks."

## Biographical and Critical Sources

*PERIODICALS*

*Daily Mail* (London, England), Sally Morris, review of *Striker Boy,* p. 60.
*Daily Telegraph* (London, England), July 12, 2008, Sinclair McKay, review of *Face Off,* p. 27.
*Kirkus Reviews,* October 15, 2009, review of *Dan and the Mudman.*
*School Library Journal,* October, 2002, Eva Mitnick, review of *Eight Candles to Light: A Chanukah Story,* p. 65; November, 2002, Susan Pine, review of *Apples and Honey: A Rosh Hashana Story,* p. 142; January, 2007, Bobbee Pennington, review of *The Bombed House,* p. 136; October, 2007, Elizabeth H. Willoughby, review of *Spin Off,* p. 168.

*ONLINE*

*Jonny Zucker Home Page,* http://jonnyzucker.com (February 20, 2011).
*Write Away Web site,* http://writeaway.org.uk/ (June 11, 2010), Graham Marks, review with Zucker.*

**DATE DUE**

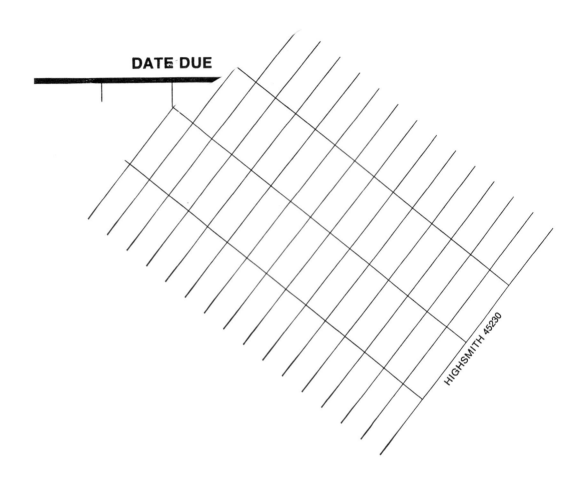

HIGHSMITH 45230